Verilog Styles
for Synthesis of
Digital Systems

WITHDRAWN
LIBRARIES

D0888836

RENEWALS 458-4574

WITHDRAWN
TSA LIBRARIES

Verilog Styles for Synthesis of Digital Systems

David R. Smith
Department of Computer Science,
State University of New York at Stony Brook

with four chapters contributed by

Paul D. Franzon
Department of Electrical and
Computer Engineering,
North Carolina State University

Prentice Hall, Upper Saddle River, New Jersey 07458

Library of Congress Cataloging-in-Publication Data

Smith, David Richard.
    Verilog styles for synthesis of digital systems/David R. Smith, Paul D. Franzon.
      p. cm.
    Includes bibliographical references and index.
    ISBN 0-201-61860-5
    1. Field programmable gate arrays—Computer-aided design. 2. Verilog (Computer
hardware description language) I. Franzon, Paul D. II. Title.

TK7895.G36 S65 2001
621.39′2—dc21
                                                        00-025783

Vice president and editorial director: *Marcia Horton*
Acquisitions editor: *Eric Frank*
Editorial assistant: *Jennifer DiBlasi*
Senior marketing manager: *Danny Hoyt*
Production editor: *Aaron Ramsey, Interactive Composition Corporation*
Executive managing editor: *Vince O'Brien*
Managing editor: *David A. George*
Art director: *Jayne Conte*
Cover designer: *Bruce Kenselaar*
Manufacturing manager: *Trudy Pisciotti*
Manufacturing buyer: *Dawn Murrin*
Vice president and director of production and manufacturing: *David W. Riccardi*

©2000 by Prentice Hall, Inc.
Upper Saddle River, New Jersey 07458

Verilog is a registered trademark of Cadence Design Systems Inc. Synopsys, Design Compiler, DesignWare, HDL compiler, RTL analyzer, VCS, characterize, dont_touch are registered trademarks and used courtesy of Synopsys, Inc. Altera, Byteblaster, Flex 10k, EPF10k20 are registered trademarks of Altera Inc. XC4000XL, LogiBlox are registered trademarks of Xilinx Inc. Advanced Micro-electronics is a division of the Institute for Technology Development, Jackson, Miss.

The authors thank Synopsys, Inc., for the use of their synthesis and simulation tools in their courses and in the preparation of this text.

All rights reserved. No part of this book may be reproduced, in any form or by any means, without permission in writing from the publisher.
Printed in the United States of America

10 9 8 7 6 5 4 3 2

ISBN 0-201-61860-5

Prentice-Hall International (UK) Limited, *London*
Prentice-Hall of Australia Pty. Limited, *Sydney*
Prentice-Hall Canada Inc., *Toronto*
Prentice-Hall Hispanoamericana, S. A., *Mexico*
Prentice-Hall of India Private Limited, *New Delhi*
Prentice-Hall of Japan, Inc., *Tokyo*
Pearson Education Asia Pte. Ltd., *Singapore*
Editora Prentice-Hall do Brasil, Ltda., *Rio de Janeiro*

Library
University of Texas
at San Antonio

Preface

In the last few years, the way that digital hardware is designed has undergone a reinvention. On one hand, manual design with schematic entry tools has been replaced by synthesis from high level specifications. On the other hand, custom integrated circuits are being supplanted by field programmable gate arrays (FPGA) for many applications. This text seeks to help students take their place in this new environment by making it more accessible.

Currently hardware synthesis is complex and not at all like the software compilation to which it is superficially analogous. It might take a competant hardware designer a year or more to become fluent in this technology. The subsets of the two broad-based hardware description languages in current use, Verilog and VHDL, permit myriad different specifications of even the simplest module, with structural and behavioral constructs intermixed at will. Each different description may give a different result and presents different synthesis problems. What is needed is another standardization and simplification like that of Mead and Conway, which availed an earlier VLSI technology to a wider group of users. This book tries to do this by selecting the simpler language, Verilog, and standardizing the methodology to the point where seniors and first-year graduates can see medium to complex designs through to gate-level simulation in a single semester. The text is neither a complete description of the Verilog language, nor simulation, nor synthesizers, nor FPGA chip fitting tools. For these, the reader should consult the large numbers of corresponding manuals. However, using this text, together with the example tools, students can and do get interesting projects working in a single semester course. This could be a semester well spent since the demand from industry for people with this knowledge seems to exceed even that for systems software expertise. After this, with the confidence of having navigated a complete pass through the process, readers can graduate to more esoteric designs and consult the many available manuals at their leisure.

There are several other good books in this general area. Of recent ones, we mention a few:

First [Smith97] (no relation) is an outstanding encyclopedic reference on all matters to do with ASICS. Here the emphasis is on schematic design, layout, and device physics supplemented by specifications in VHDL or Verilog. Then there are books such as

[Palnitkar96], [Arnold99], and [Ciletti99] concentrating specifically on the Verilog language itself. In all of the above, the pedagogical approach has really been to go first through all the language constructs in Verilog available to simulation, and then present the limitations of synthesis afterwards. This is to be contrasted with our treatment in which synthesis issues are introduced from the outset, incorporated into the material throughout, and designed to get students working with synthesis early.

Next there are some works aimed at an audience already familiar with high-level design methodology and more oriented to specialized reference. [Karup97] is really a compendium of tips and case studies in VHDL/Verilog and Synopsys with the corresponding solutions; [Keating98] contains tool usage and style recommendations, specifically for modules intended for reuse in the intellectual property market, but without working examples. So these are more suitable as supplements to some other basic text.

We should also mention the series of books on synthesis by Gajski and Micheli. These are a different kind of book, more oriented to research in the area, and to the few who will design the synthesizers, rather than to the many who will use them to create practical designs and get a job.

Yet there is still no book that covers style recommendations specifically oriented to synthesis, that is illustrated with practical working examples, and that is accessible to the reader who wants to get a start in this field. This is a void that needs to be filled and we are hopeful that this book may do so. All the worked examples and the problems at the end of each chapter have been synthesized and successfully verified by simulation at gate level. The material has been tested in classes over three years aimed at seniors and first-year graduate students having a prerequisite of an introductory course in computer organization and a working knowledge of Unix and X windows. At the moment most industrial designers still prefer this environment, although the tools are now becoming available in the NT and Linux environments.

Synthesis and fitting tools are usually available to universities at nominal maintenance fees under vendors' "university programs." Sometimes a simulator is packaged with a tool suite, sometimes not. In what follows, the exercises have been worked out using the VCS compiled simulator, the FPGA Compiler and Behavioral Compiler available from Synopsys, and the FPGA tool suites from Altera and Xilinx. Of course this is somewhat specific and the reader's location may be committed to alternative tools. We would have really liked to have compared synthesizers available from other vendors. There is really no good solution to this, since even at university pricing, any one site (including ours) cannot afford all the alternatives, nor commit the time and resources involved. All we can do is try to choose some of the best tools currently available and trust that many of the issues faced by users in other environments will be similar. For example even though Verilog and VHDL are rather different, the subsets used for synthesis by the major vendors are quite similar at the moment, which is why automatic translators are available. A complete list of vendors offering tools in the separate areas relevant to this book, such as simulation, synthesis, and FPGA, are listed at regular intervals in trade magazines including *Integrated System Design* (www.isdmag.com). Here the interested reader can gain ready access to the vendor representatives or Web pages to discover the relative advantages of the tools and what is available in the various university programs.

The material of this book is suitable for seniors or first-year graduate students who have had an introduction to Boolean algebra and computer organization. A working knowledge of Unix and X-windows is necessary for the exercises. Some knowledge of a programming language such as 'C' or Java is desirable but not necessary. We usually find that students from a computer science background come to the course with more intuition of the software while students from an electrical engineering background bring more of a intuition on gate networks. So the two arrive at the course with about the same potential to start in on this material.

We should give some explanation of the ordering of the chapters, which might seem a little peculiar at first. This is one of those subjects in which students learn by doing. Accordingly, our approach has been to introduce the use of the simulator and then the synthesizers at the earliest practical point. In this way the students should be able to ramp up on the tool learning curve and follow a trial run of a small design all the way through high-level simulation, the design compiler, FPGA, fitting, and gate-level simulation by about the middle of the semester. With this under their belts, they will be better psychologically prepared to move onto a larger independent project, the behavioral compiler, or download to and test real hardware in the time remaining to them. Thus the ordering we have chosen may be at the cost of breaking the continuity of the treatment of the design language and the examples of specification. If the user of this book disagrees with this philosophy, there is always the option of reordering the chapters accordingly, say by delaying the introduction of simulation of Chapter 4 until the Chapter 7 on validation, or bringing the chapters on specification (3, 5 through 9) together, or by bringing together the sections on testing and debugging from Chapters 4, 7, and 15), or by bringing the materials on the design compiler and the behavioral compiler (Chapters 12, 13, and 16) together before proceding to the FPGA targeting.

For readers who want to try the examples, refer to the home page prepared for the Prentice Hall site at the url http://www.prenhall.com/smith/franzon.

References

[Arnold99] Arnold, Mark, G., *Verilog Digital Computer Design*, Prentice Hall, 1999

[Ciletti99] Ciletti, Michael D., *Modelling, Synthesis, and Rapid Prototyping with the Verilog HDL*, 1999

[Karup97] Karup, Pran, and Taker Abbasi, *Logic Synthesis using Synopsys* (2nd ed.), Kluwer, 1997

[Keating98] Keating, Michael, and Pierre Bricaud, *Re-Use Methodology Manual*, Kluwer, 1998

[Palnitkar96] Palnitkar, Samir, *Verilog HDL: A Guide to Digital Design and Synthesis*, Sunsoft Press, 1996

[Smith97] Smith, Michael J. S., *Application Specific Integrated Circuits*, Addison-Wesley, 1997

Table of Contents

Chapter One

Introduction

With current chip complexities at 50 million active devices and growing, it is no longer possible to design hardware using schematic based methods. Inevitably design must now come almost exclusively from high-level specifications and synthesis. It is an area where the methodologies are not well-established, yet the tools are evolving rapidly to keep up with the headlong expansion of chip complexities.

To place this evolution in perspective, it is pertinent to review how design methods evolved in response to earlier changes in device technology. In the large scale integration (LSI) era, prior to 1980, chip engineers were known to crawl around on their hands and knees, cutting and pasting huge enlargements of the chip layout. Perhaps this is why the overall layout scheme for a chip became known as a *floorplan*. With the advent of "very large scale integration" (VLSI—chips defined as those exceeding 100,000 transistors), this became impractical, and with the introduction of such computer-aided design tools as schematic entry, layout editors, extractors, and simulation tools, design engineers were able to adopt a more dignified position. About this time, this technology was made accessible to students in universities by way of an abstraction and simplification of the layout rules [M&C80]. Device fabrication has continued its evolution into the era of "deep submicron" line widths with chips having 100 million active devices or more and clock speeds to 1 GHz. It has become impossible to comprehend the corresponding circuits at the layout or gate level. Thus schematic entry has been replaced by high-level textual specification and synthesis and chip complexities are now defined by the unit of area used in the reports from these tools.[1] In the dominant dynamic CMOS technology each such gate corresponds to about five active devices (transistors) and so current chip complexities are in the 200,000 to 10 million gate range. In this book the example designs will be somewhat more modest.

This evolution is parallel to that taken by software engineering a generation ago. Few people want to look at the assembly code produced by software compilers, and

---

[1]Unfortunately not always simply related to the gate count—see Chapter 12.

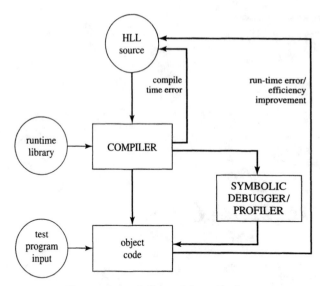

Figure 1.1   *Software Compilation.*

debugging is preferentially done at source code level. In the same way, when the description of something as simple as an alarm clock specification is expanded by the synthesizer from less than two pages of high-level source code into more than 40 sheets of gate schematics, then we would prefer to debug it from the former rather than the latter.

Yet at the present stage of the art, hardware compilation is not at all like that of software. The two are compared in Figures 1.1 and 1.2.

In software processing, syntax and type errors may be caught at compile time and some design errors usually remain at run time, necessitating a return to the source code for the necessary corrections. Optionally a symbolic debugger may be employed to relate run time errors to the corresponding section of the source code, and a profiler may be used to find the most heavily used sections of code where efficiency improvements would be most effective.

In hardware synthesis there are more stages to the process, in each of which further errors may be uncovered. The first stage is the simulation of the high-level source specification to determine if the overall design is sound (Chapter 4). When the design passes muster at this stage the source code is presented to the analysis and elaboration stages of the synthesizer where further errors in the source may be detected (Chapter 12). The synthesizable language constructs are supposed to be a subset of the complete HDL language definition accepted by the simulator. At the current state of the art it is very possible for source accepted by the simulator to be rejected by the synthesizer and occasionally vice-versa. Optionally a profiler tool might be employed to get an idea of the sections of the design which will incur most of the area or time delay. Next, the design is presented to the compile phase of the synthesizer (Chapter 12). Only after this, and when the design has been fitted onto a chip (Chapters 13 and 14), will the true delays in the circuits and connections be known. At this point the design must be submitted again to simulation and possibly a formal verification tool (Chapter 7). By the time the design is actually downloaded to be fabricated into silicon ("tape-out"), it is fervently hoped that no design errors remain. However, unlike software in which the copies are to all intents and purposes

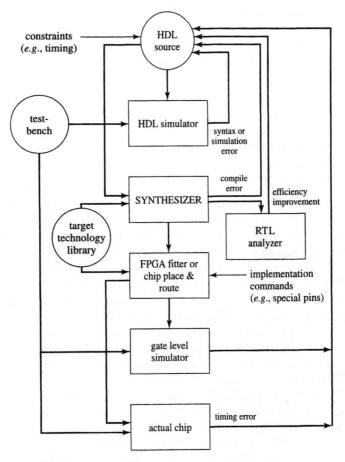

Figure 1.2   *Hardware Synthesis.*

perfect, hardware replication errors may still occur in the fabrication process, necessitating another layer of testing by on- or off-chip facilities (Chapter 15). As shown in Figure 1.2, it is possible to use the same testbench program for all of the testing stages providing this stimulates and senses only the circuit nodes available at the external pins.

Errors may occur at all of these processing stages which necessitate a return to the original source specification for modifications. Throughout this process the high-level source is the single reference point for understanding and correcting the design. The style of this specification therefore has much to do with the quality of the final synthesized result.

In addition to the increased number of steps involved, the hardware synthesizer may have a large number of compiler directives and switches (not all of which may appear in the documentation). It might take a competent hardware designer a year or more to become fluent in this technology. Furthermore, the broad based hardware design languages in current use permit myriad different specifications ranging from pure behavioral to pure structural or any gradation in between. Different ways of specifying the same thing are what we refer to as *writing styles*. We discuss writing styles throughout the book starting in

Chapter 3. Usually the primitive modules at the bottom of a design hierarchy are written in a behavioral style while the upper levels are written as a mixture of structure and behavior. For a given single design, each different style of specification may produce a different result, and presents different synthesis problems.

So what is synthesis exactly?

- Is it an automated collection of the combinational and sequential machine minimization algorithms from what used to be called switching theory?
- Is it a translation between a behavioral specification into a purely structural representation (the netlist)?
- Is it a transformation between a course-grained (high level) representation into a fine-grained (low level) one?

It is all of these, but these views are simplistic because of the optimizations and choices involved in the synthesis process.

Of the two hardware specification languages in general use today, it seems that VHDL is prefered by a majority in U.S. government and contract work, academia, and in Europe, while Verilog is prefered by a majority of commercial designers in this country and Japan. The popularity of Verilog may be due to the fact that many commercial users feel more at home with the Verilog syntax, derived as it is from the 'C' language with which they are already familiar, whereas the VHDL syntax is a derivative of the ADA language. But it may also be due to the fact that Verilog is a smaller and simpler language. While this sometimes places restrictions on what can be specified, there is also some evidence that it can speed a design to a working prototype [Cooley95]. Since our objective was to simplify this process still further, we chose Verilog for our treatment.

In either Verilog or VHDL there are a large number of ways to specify even the simplest hardware module. In fact if nothing else is gained from this text, this is one point that will surely be driven home thoroughly. Conventional styles are covered, up through the implicit style in Chapter 8. In Chapter 9, we introduce a stereotyped form of specification which we have called the *control point* style, a sort of beginners introduction to design reuse and socket design. It shares the advantage of conventional styles in being directly accessible to both industry simulators and synthesizers while at the same time being simple and economical, principally because it uses hierarchy and library components heavily and relies on the synthesizer to infer the controller state machines. In this last respect it is similar to the Synopsys *Behavioral Compiler* styles (Chapter 16), although the examples of Chapters 5 through 15 have been processed only through the more generally available Synopsys *Design Compiler and FPGA compiler*. We have found that this can result in a specification that can be up to an order of magnitude shorter than alternative specifications of the same hardware on designs to which it is suited, without significant penalties in speed or area. The reader does not have to follow this style and is certainly at liberty to use the other economical styles discussed. But by choosing and following a consistent style throughout all the examples, the reader will find it definitely reduces the time needed to get each one to a working state. In general we believe that a shorter specification leads to a faster working prototype.

Finally it is important to note that the Verilog and VHDL languages were both originally designed for simulation not synthesis. This means that unlike the software compilation scenario of Figure 1.1, the synthesizers accept only subsets of the language accepted by the simulators. The usual pedagogical approach has been to go through all the constructs available to simulation first and then present the limitations of synthesis as a postscript. By contrast, in the following treatment synthesis issues are interspersed throughout. It is intended that the reader will eventually have recourse for supplementation to the many vendor manuals available. Meanwhile however, class experience has shown that it is possible from this material alone for students to negotiate a first complete pass through the process for designs of modest size.

References

[Cooley95] Cooley, J., "E.D.A consumer advocate diary," *Integrated System Design*, 7(63):56–60, July 1995

[M&C80] Meade, C., and Conway, L., *Introduction to VLSI Systems*, Addison-Wesley, 1980

Chapter Two

Basic Language Constructs

The following material on the Verilog basic language constructs more or less follows the order of that in the reference manual of the IEEE 1364 standard otherwise known as the *LRM* [IEEE95]. This alone runs to more than 550 pages, so space considerations will not allow us to go much beyond a framework for synthesis. Further details of the language are available in standard references, such as that of Thomas and Moorby (the inventors of Verilog) [Thomas96], or vendor's manuals, like the Synopsys HDL manual. Throughout the rest of this book we follow the convention of using *italics* for emphasis and highlighting *reserved words* in **bold**. We believe that this makes the Verilog specifications easier to read.

2.1 Preliminaries

The syntax of Verilog is very similar to that of the 'C' or Java languages although the semantics are quite different. Verilog has many mechanisms for concurrency as appropriate for hardware modeling. As a result, 'C' or Java programmers who follow their intuition on syntax matters will be right much of the time, although not all of the time.

2.1.1 *Identifiers*

In Verilog identifiers are the names given to hardware objects in a design which may be wires (busses), registers, memories, or modules. These names are made up from the numeric and alphabetic characters including the underline '_' and dollar '$' and are case sensitive. The first character should not be a numeric or the $, which has a special significance to the Verilog programming language interface and the simulators (see Chapter 4). The same strictures apply as in software engineering as to choosing identifiers well for purposes of readability and understanding. This can make code self-documenting to a great extent, although comments are certainly recommended as well if it is desired to remember later what the design is doing and how. The judicious use of the underline and upper case is also useful in this regard. As usual some names are reserved words so one had better not reuse them. For comments there is the double forward slash '//' which is a comment to the end of line, in addition to the usual delineated multiline comment '/* */' as used in 'C' and other languages.

2.1.2   *Operators*

These are again generally the same as in other current languages such as 'C' or Java. There will be a full list later in Section 3.5. For now it is sufficient to note the three different kinds in the following examples of assignments to *scalar carriers*, by which is meant a wire or a flipflop capable of supporting a single bit value:

```
/* unary,   eg: */ out = ~ in; // operator is prefixed, inverter inferred.
/* binary,  eg: */ out = in1 && in2; // infix operator, AND gate inferred.
/* ternary, eg: */ out = select? in1 : in0; // usually multiplexer inferred.
```

Note that as in 'C', all Verilog assignments and most statements end with the semicolon.

2.1.3   *Values*

Verilog has a *value set* [0 1 x z] for the possible signal values which can be supported on a scalar carrier, and a *strength set* depending on how serious the hardware environment is in pulling the signal up to that value. This all has to do with electrical phenomena in circuits considered at quite a low level (called the *switch* level by integrated circuit engineers). Since we are trying to discipline ourselves to think in high-level terms and we have a synthesizer that will conjure up somehow this low level detail, we will not worry about the strength set. But the x and the z will still need to be considered.

Electrically, the z corresponds to a wire node that is isolated from other regions of the circuit by open switches. Textually it can happen when a **wire** is declared and then not initialized, or not driven from the output from some other module or from the power supply directly. In either case a simulator may assign the value z, representing high impedance.

An x value has a distinct significance. It means that the simulator thinks it doesn't have enough information to decide whether the node is driven high or low. Sometimes the simulator may have a tendency to breed x's even in situations where it might be expected to try a little harder, as, for example, in the multiplexer expression used here:

$$out = select? \; in1 \; : \; in0;$$

This construct is also modelled on a similar one in the 'C' language. It means that the Boolean *select* is first tested and depending on the outcome either *in1* is routed to *out* (if *select* is high) else *in0* is routed to *out*. If *select* were x and even though the inputs are both *1*, still some simulators assign x to the output. The only way to avoid this would be to rewrite the multiplexer as a Verilog *user defined primitive* (Chapter 3). The beginner may be horrified to see the simulator initially assigning x's to almost everything in her whole design! Still, don't blame it on the simulator. As in the example above, unknown inputs could represent a possible problem in the design and generally should be hunted down.

Before leaving the subject of unknowns, it should be noted that as far as real hardware and the synthesizer is concerned, there is no such thing. When the power comes on, the flipflops in a circuit very rapidly choose one value or another even if they are not initialized, and unconnected inputs will drift high in most technologies. The synthesizer looks upon *x* values as an opportunity to minimize hardware and will eventually produce a circuit that assigns them one way or the other.

2.1.4 *Expressions*

As in the 'C' language, expressions are made up of identifiers, operators, and constants.

2.2 Datatypes

Datatypes available in Verilog are the **net, reg, integer, real, time, parameter**, and *event*. (Here as later, bold font is employed for reserved words). These are introduced in this section.

2.2.1 *Nets*

For synthesis purposes the only important one is the **wire**. Like its physical counterpart, a wire can have a value on it only if it is continuously driven by something, and the key word in this is "continuously." Otherwise it gets a *z* value by default. The synthesizer will give a warning if it is not so driven, but doesn't care enough to do anything about it.

2.2.2 *Registers*

Represented by the reserved word **reg**. It corresponds to the concept of static storage in VLSI circuits. A **reg** is not necessarily a clocked register though in response to a **reg** declaration the synthesizer will usually end up inserting some register type of its choosing, unless it finds a way of optimizing it away. In the case of a **reg**, if you forget to initialize it, the simulator will assign *x* and have yet another excuse to spawn *x*'s down the line.

2.2.3 *Integer*

Of course the synthesizer does not know how to make hardware to implement an integer as such except that it be used to load registers or as a dimension, such as controlling **for** loops in testbenches or **for** loops which generate parallel structures (see examples later).

Integers are specified most generally in the form:

```
size´base number
```

The closing quote is like a vertical slash in some printed outputs, and is produced by the key just to the left of the *enter* key on PC keyboards, or on workstations, the second to the left (but note the qualification under the preprocessor subsection below). The base may be decimal, octal, hexadecimal, or binary (as in *4'd, 6'o, 8'h, 1'b* respectively), but irrespective of the base, the size will always be in bits. For example, where *v* has been declared as a four bit carrier, the following will be equivalent:

$$v = 4´b1111, \quad v = 4´hf, \quad v = 15$$

The absence of the base invokes decimal as a default. Often there will be no ambiguity and the assignment to a boolean *a = 0*; or *a = 1*; will do the right thing and result in code easier to read to boot. This is because Verilog always truncates to the left when the receiving value is of smaller dimension. Verilog also extends the most significant bit if it is *0, x*, or *z*.

So $y = 32'bx$; or even $y = x$; is OK. A unary negative sign is permitted and results in a two's complement quantity subject to the declared carrier size. For example $v = -1$; will be a quick way of initializing the above declared carrier to all binary ones.

2.2.4   Real

The proposed analog extensions of VHDL and Verilog are now being standardized, and synthesizers for these extensions will be starting to appear. Discussion of this datatype is therefore postponed until Chapter 17.

2.2.5   Time

This is a special datatype used by the simulator to store the current time. The units of time used are specified in a 'timescale statement.

`timescale 100 ns / 100 ps

The first number indicates the units used (in this case 100 nanoseconds where a nanosecond $= 10^{-9}$ second), and the second number indicates the least significant digit to be printed out (in this case 100 picoseconds, where a picosecond $= 10^{-12}$ second). Since the scale may be set quite small (even femtoseconds $= 10^{-15}$ second), large numbers may sometimes be required. So the present implementation uses a 64-bit carrier for this datatype. It may be referenced by the "$time" routine in many simulators (see Chapter 4). The timescale specification will be mandatory for simulation at gate level after synthesis.

2.2.6   Events

This classification covers three mechanisms to specify when something happens in the time dimension:

Integral delay: such as #*n*, inserted to delay activation of subsequent actions by an integral number *n* units of the timescale above. This is ignored by current synthesizers but will still be necessary in test-bench modules.

Sensitivity event: such as *@(signal)* or *@(posedge signal)* or *@(negedge signal)*. Waits for a change in the named signal before activating subsequent actions. This is the mechanism used in Verilog to communicate timing to the synthesizer in Chapter 5 and onward.

There is also a *wait(signal)* as in VHDL but the Verilog equivalent is not recognized by current synthesizers and can be achieved by the previous mechanism anyway.

2.2.7   Bitvector

The **wire** and **reg** types are scalar by default but may be declared in multibit versions by adding a range before the identifier. The range is declared in the form:

[expression1 : expression2]

where the expressions are non-negative, constant value, meaning they contain constants, operators, and parameters only. It is important to note that, regardless of whether *expression1* evaluates to a smaller integer than *expression2* or not, Verilog always considers the left value to be the most significant bit and the right value as the least significant bit. In other words Verilog has a strong sense of left and right besides a sense of right and wrong, and it behooves us to construct any modules utilizing rippling accordingly. The invocations must also respect the selected range in the declaration. For example, after the declaration, **wire** [3:1] tribit; the following invocation assignments have significance as follows:

```
onebit = tribit[2];  selects the middle bit
twobit = tribit[1:0] illegal attempt to select subfield-index out of range
 wobit = tribit[1:2] illegal attempt to select subfield-reversed direction
            of indices
```

2.2.8 *Concatenation and Replication*

A bitvector may be created by the concatenation or replication operators.

The concatenation operation is signified by curly brackets enclosing a list. For example: {c_out, sum}. Had *sum* been previously declared as an 8-bit vector and *c_out* is a scalar, then the result would be a 9-bit vector.

The replication operator uses curly brackets with a preceding integer or variable representing an integer. For example 4{2'b01} creates an 8-bit vector 01010101.

2.2.9 *Arrays*

Although they use the same syntax as the range of indices of a bitvector, arrays are to be clearly distinguished from vectors. We may think of vector elements as "running horizontally" whereas array elements are "running vertically." For synthesis purposes arrays will be used only on the **reg** datatype and usually a **reg** with a vector range. Such an array is equivalent to a memory. For example:

$$\text{reg [15:0] ram [0:255]}$$

declares a memory consisting of 256 words each of 16 bits. The invocation: w = ram[27]; will fetch the twenty-eighth word, so in effect a decoder is inferred in addition to the array of storage elements. If the memory is indeed implemented as an array of latches or flip-flops more economical synthesis may result if the user specifies the decoder explicitly and separately, but this won't usually matter for memories fetched from macro libraries (see Sections 5.5 and 14.2). As in the real world, subfield extraction from a regular RAM requires two successive invocation steps:

$$\text{tmp = ram[27];}\quad\text{y = tmp[3:0];}$$

2.2.10 *Parameters*

This is used to define constants in modules. For example:

```
parameter word_size = 16, pulse_width = 20, capacity = 256;
```

After this for example a bus might be declared as:

```
wire [word_size-1:0] bus;
```

Then if it is desired to change the dimensions later it is only necessary to modify a single line. This is to be prefered over fixed-sized declarations in situations where it is desired to parameterize modules to size later in particular instantiations (see Section 9.2).

2.2.11   *Preprocessor Directives*

Verilog has a preprocessor similar to that of 'C', except that the opening quote is used instead of the sharp sign because Verilog has already used that for other purposes. The opening quote (like a slash sloping like a grave accent in some printed outputs) is the top leftmost key in PC keyboards; on workstations, it is the key just to the left of the *enter* key. The reason for harping on this is that some word processors will change an opening quote to a closing quote and vice versa depending on the perceived context. The result has been that these quotes have printed incorrectly in some Verilog texts.

Continuing with a preprocessing example, if the source is preceded by:

```
`define word_size 16
```

Then everywhere '*word_size* appears in subsequent text it will be replaced by 16. How is this to be distinguished from the previous parameter mechanism? Well that would be preferable if we wanted to use it to parameterize instantiations of a particular module to size since there is a instantiation mechanism which goes along with it. The preprocess method would be suitable for more global purposes:

```
`define opcode instruction[15:12]
   `define BEQ 4'b0100 // opcode for instruction branch if equal to zero
```

The '**include** preprocessor directive is also available. We might use it to include frequently used routines as 'C' does in header files, except in the case of Verilog they might instead be the source files of frequently used submodules, such as:

```
`include  submodule.v
```

2.3   Modules

Hardware systems, like other kinds of systems, naturally partition into modules. To one way of thinking chips set into a board are modules, although chips these days are so complex that we would want to follow the subdivision of function much further down than this. In Verilog a module is expressed in the following format:

```
module modulename(port list);
  parameters
  port declarations
  wire declarations
  reg declarations
  submodule instantiations
    ..text body..
endmodule
```

Of these only the first and last are really mandatory, although it would be a somewhat useless module that had none of the internals. A simple example of a module is the full adder:

```
module fulladder(a, b, c_in, sum, c_out) ; // adds single bit operands
  input a, b, c_in;
  output sum, c_out;
    assign {c_out, sum} = a + b + c_in ; // body to be discussed later
endmodule
```

It is not necessary to declare wires separately if either (a) they are scalar, or (b) they are already declared as input or outputs. Verilog allows ports to be characterized as **inout**. Physically an **inout** port has an electrical circuit which disables the amplifier driving the output during those times when the input mode is being employed; in other words, the output drive is represented by the value z at those times, and the input signal is able to override it.

The next example is a four-bit *ripple adder* which instantiates four copies of the *fulladder* module above. The organization of it is illustrated in Figure 2.1. It is called a ripple adder because of the connection of the carries that imply that each fulladder stage cannot commence its computation until the previous one has completed. Since Verilog thinks of the most significant bit as being on the left, care has been taken to organize this adder so that the ripple direction is leftwards. The specification is shown below.

The instantiations of the fulladder need different identifiers, such as FA0, FA1, and so on, so that we can distinguish them (in synthesis we would say *"uniquify"* them). The wires C0, C1, and C2 serve to indicate how these submodules are interconnected as shown in the figure. Verilog does not make it mandatory to declare them here because they are scalar, although some may prefer the style of including all declarations. Finally, note that the submodules are concurrently active so it doesn't matter in which order they are written. Verilog has many mechanisms for concurrency as will become apparent.

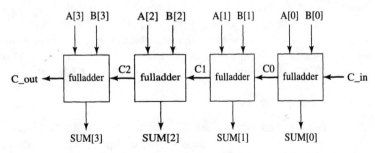

Figure 2.1   *Four-Bit Ripple Adder, Add_4_r.*

```
module add_4_r (A, B, C_in, SUM, C_out);
  input [3:0] A,B;
  input C_in;
  output [3:0] SUM;
  output C_out;
  wire [3:0] A, B, C_in, SUM, C_out;
  fulladder FA3(A[3], B[3], C2,  SUM[3], C_out);
  fulladder FA2(A[2], B[2], C1,  SUM[2], C2);
  fulladder FA1(A[1], B[1], C0,  SUM[1], C1);
  fulladder FA0(A[0], B[0], C_in,SUM[0], C0);
endmodule
```

Specification #1: 4-bit adder (structural).

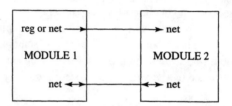

Figure 2.2   *Port Connection Rules.*

2.3.1   *Port Connection Rules*

A port should properly be thought of as a communication path from one module to another (or to others). An (exclusive) output may be driven from either a **net** (coming from a **wire** output of a gate) or a **reg** (coming from the output side of a flipflop[s]). Otherwise, and certainly at the receiving end, the ports must be nets. The situation is illustrated in Figure 2.2, in which the top connection comes from such an exclusive output and corresponds to a unidirectional pathway. The remaining possibility, and the lower connection in the figure, comes from ports of type **inout** and corresponds to a bidirectional pathway. In this case the ends cannot come directly from the output of a **reg** and must be **net**s.

Another way of expressing this rule is that although you can connect several inputs together, it is generally a bad idea to connect outputs together. You cannot force a logic value up the business end of an amplifier or a flipflop. The exception to this rule is when all outputs except one are disabled (high impedance). In many situations it is customary to *register* the outputs of all modules as a matter of course (for example, see discussion of tasks below, and the behavioral compiler styles in Chapter 10).

2.3.2   *Port Lists*

Verilog has two methods for expressing the port argument list in the module instantiations. The first is a simple ordered list as has been used in the example above. This method is economical and suitable for modules of small to medium pin complexity. However it has the disadvantage that the port identifiers of the instantiations FA3, FA2, etc., must appear in exactly the same order as in the header of the original specification of the fulladder and could lead to an error in the event that changes are made. The second method uses a list of paired correspondences. In each pair, the first element (with a dot) is the port identifier from the lower hierarchy level and the second element (enclosed in parentheses) is the port to which it is connected in the upper hierarchical level. For example, the last instantiation in the *add_4_r* module would become:

```
FA0(.a(A[0]), .b(B[0]), .c_out(CO), .sum(SUM[0]), .c_in(C_in));
```

This method is more suitable for modules having many ports because by using it the order in which the paired arguments appear is not critical.

For the small- to medium-sized example modules used in this book the first method is used for the sake of simplicity—it uses up less ink on the page and therefore makes the examples easier to read. We generally list arguments as follows:

```
clock, control inputs, data inputs, control outputs, data outputs
```

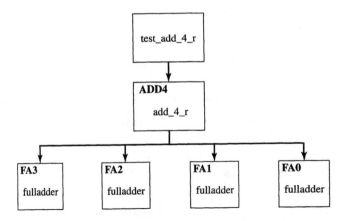

Figure 2.3   *Module Hierarchy.*

This corresponds more or less with the Altera FPGA fitter which puts out the connection lists with the pairs ordered lexically within direction groups and with the input group appearing first. However, note that other vendors may follow a different convention, such as Xilinx, for which the arguments are unified into a single lexically ordered group. So in general, Verilog's second port listing method will cause less heartache. In other words, do as we say, not as we do.

2.3.3 *Hierarchical Names*

The modules used in a design can be thought of as being ordered by hierarchical levels. For example, if a testbench specification is used to stimulate the *add_4_r* module above, then the hierarchy would comprise of three levels and could be illustrated as shown in Figure 2.3.

Inside the top-level testbench a hierarchical dot notation can be used to let Verilog communicate with the various objects in the modules at different levels. For the current adder example the identification of the carry input at the different levels might be characterized as follows (this assumes that the test input for the carry input had been declared in the testbench as C_IN):

```
level 3 (top):                 C_IN
level 2 (top for synthesis): ADD4.C_in
level 1 (bottom):             ADD4.FA0.c_in
```

2.4 Conclusion

Of course this chapter has not covered all the constructs of the Verilog language available to simulation or even synthesis. Some of those pertaining to combinational Boolean functions (those without memory) are considered in the next chapter. But in order to give students an early start on using the simulator, those for sequential machines, including the major control constructs, are delayed until Chapter 5. For a complete description of the features of the Verilog language the IEEE standard Verilog LRM is the ultimate authority, or (probably better if the intention is to synthesize), the Verilog HDL manual of your favorite synthesis vendor.

Exercises

2.1. Tag any of the following statements you believe are invalid in Verilog and why:

```
//declarations:
    parameter n = 3;
    reg [2:0] ptr;
    reg vert [7:0];
    reg [7:0] horiz;
    ...
//invocations:
    u_fixed = horiz[n];
    v_fixed = vert[n];
    u_var = horiz[ptr];
    v_var = vert[ptr];
```

2.2. Rewrite the 4-bit adder structural specification of Section 2.3 using the paired correspondence method of listing the ports in the submodule invocations.

2.3. Describe in Verilog a new module called add_8_r that specifies an 8-bit ripple carry adder. Specify the adder structurally using two of the 4-bit adders modeled in this chapter.

2.4. A design has two clocked modules *A* and *B*. *A* supplies an output which is an input to *B* and vice versa. As we will learn in Chapter 5, common clocked flipflops with a data and clock input are characterized by a *set-up* time, *Tsu*, a minimum time for which the *D* input must be stable before the rising clock edge, and a *hold-time*, *Tho*, the minimum time for which the *D* value must be held stable after the clock edge. Bearing in mind the port connection rules, give a minimum for the necessary clock period.

2.5. A module under test (mut.v) has unidirectional ports for: *operation* (such as: remove, insert), *data_in*, *data_out*, and *status* return (such as: empty, full)
State whether the connection of each of these inside the corresponding stimulating test-module, (test_mut.v), should be to a **reg** or a **wire**, and whether the choice is mandatory, and if so mandated by what.

2.6. Suppose the test module of Figure 2.2 stimulates the 4-bit adder with the two 4-bit operands *op1* and *op2* having bit range 3:0. What identifier strings would you give to the simulator for it to print the leading bit of *op1* at the level of:
a. the testbench?
b. the top level of the adder?
c. the bottom hierarchical level of the adder ?

References

[IEEE95] *IEEE Standard Verilog HDL Language Reference Manual*, IEEE standards department, 1995

[Thomas96] Thomas, D. E., and Moorby, P. R. *The Verilog Hardware Description Language* (3rd ed.), Kluwer, 1996

Chapter Three

Structural and Behavioral Specification

3.1 Introduction

A *structural* specification lists only primitive components and how they are connected together. This is to be contrasted with a purely *behavioral* specification which shows only the functional steps by which the outputs are computed in terms of the inputs. Behavior can be described using assignments and logical expressions. It is possible to write specifications and design languages so that structure and behavior are kept strictly separate. The primitive modules at the base of any design hierarchy have to be described behaviorally of course, but at all levels above a module can be described as either pure structural or pure behavioral [Gopal85], [Awad91]. From the point of view of verification this might have been preferable, but for the hardware design languages Verilog and VHDL now used, an arbitrary mixture is permitted and this mixture runs through every chapter to follow.

The simplest kind of modules with which to introduce this duality are those that implement purely combinational functions, or those with no memory. This chapter starts with common combinational modules specified purely structurally. The back half of the chapter continues with what are sometimes called "dataflow" type specifications, which are a simple type of behavioral description. In between, in order to place the ongoing development of the material in perspective, we digress to introduce the subject of modelling levels and writing styles. This is inserted at this point because it depends on an elementary understanding of gates.

Although the kinds of specifications in this chapter may be a good vehicle for a first introduction to the simulator, they are not recommended as an appropriate use of modern synthesis tools. Better writing styles for this purpose are the procedural type of specifications which start in Chapter 5. For those who need to review, this chapter can also serve as an introduction to the basic logical gates and common combinational Boolean functions.

3.2 Basic Gates

One way of modeling in Verilog is to specify a netlist directly—simply list how each component is connected to every other and to the overall inputs and outputs of the design. If each component is primitive, then this modeling is purely *structural*. A set of primitive modules already defined in Verilog are the basic logic gates. Figure 3.1 shows a selection of these, each with its Verilog name, the usual schematic symbol, and the truth table.

The first one, which is the **not** gate, is an example of a unary operation, while the second, the **and** gate, is an example of a binary operation. The **and, or, xor** (*exclusive or*) gates associate, and so binary gates could be combined in cascade or tree form to obtain the truth table of gates of the same kind with larger numbers of inputs. In most circuit technologies it is easier to build gates with a **not** function incorporated into the output. An example is the ***nand*** (meaning *not-and*) gate illustrated in the figure. Its truth table can be obtained by composing the truth tables of the **and** and **not** constituent functions. The **notif1** gate shown is an example of a transmission type of gate. Such a gate transmits the input through to the output (in this case inverted) when the gate is "opened." In some circuit technologies the outputs of the last two columns of the truth table might be indeterminate, as indicated in the figure by question marks. In such circumstances it is safest to see to it that the corresponding input state combinations do not occur.

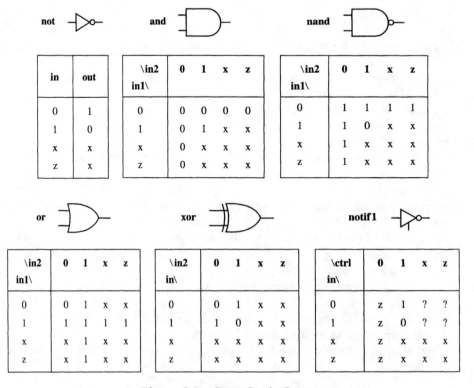

Figure 3.1   *Some Basic Gates.*

3.2.1   *Structural Modules Using Basic Gates*

Verilog already knows about all these gates and their corresponding inverted forms and permits short cuts from the usual rules regarding instantiation of structured modules to be discussed in Section 9.2. For example, it is not necessary to indicate them in any header file or give them identifying names. An example of using such gates to build a simple second-level module is that of the 4-input multiplexer shown in Figure 3.2 and the specification #1 of mux4 below.

    Notice here that Verilog always expects the (single) output to be listed first in the gate port lists, the opposite way from the convention adopted for module arguments in Section 2.3 and in the rest of this book. This discrepancy won't matter much since we will rarely use gates after this and the gate level specification put out by the FPGA fitter will have its ports rearranged anyway. The scalar wires *nslct1*, *nslct0*, *a3*, *a2*, *a1*, and *a0* represent the internal interconnections. Declarations for these are mandatory only if they are vectors, although their inclusion might make the code more readable.

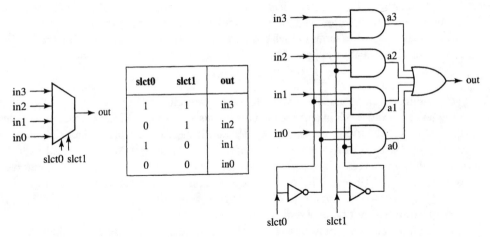

Figure 3.2   *4-Input Multiplexer.*

```
module mux4(slct1, slct0, in3, in2, in1, in0, out);
 input slct1, slct0;
 input in3, in2, in1, in0;
 output out;
  not(nslct1,slct1); not(nslct0,slct0);
  and(a3,in3, slct1 slct0);
  and(a2, in2, slct1 nslct0);
  and(a1, in1, nslct1 slct0);
  and(a0, in0, nslct1 nslct0);
  or(out, a3, a2, a1, a0);
endmodule
```

Specification #1 mux4.

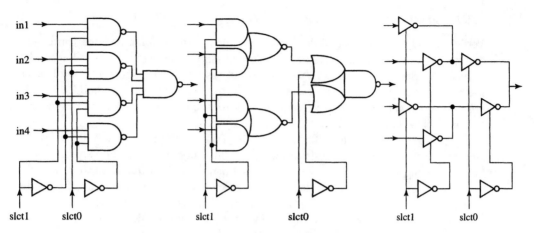

Figure 3.3   *Some Alternative Multiplexer Schematics.*

As mentioned in Chapter 2, it is usually easier in most technologies to build the forms of the gates with inverted outputs. The circuit on the previous page for the multiplexer could be redesigned in terms of such gates as shown in the first variation of Figure 3.3. We can see this by repeatedly applying either form of DeMorgan's rule of Boolean algebra:

$$\sim(a|b) = \sim a \, \& \, \sim b \qquad \sim(a \, \& \, b) = \sim a|\sim b$$

Actually there are many ways to build this circuit. Two further alternatives are shown in the Figure 3.3 in terms of the basic gates seen so far. In most circuit technologies the last two realizations are usually smaller and faster (for example, twenty-eight transistors as opposed to thirty-eight in the *static cmos* technology). When provided with the appropriate resources of library cells, synthesizers are pretty good at sniffing out such optimizations. So it would be to no purpose to restrict the synthesizer's options by over-specifying the structure at this low level. This is why, after the first exercise, this form of specification will not be used further.[1]

Before leaving the subject of gates, we note that the reverse of a multiplexer is a *demultiplexer* which is illustrated in Figure 3.4 along with possible realization in terms of two input nand gates. This circuit could be iterated in tree form to implement demultiplexers with larger numbers of outputs and as shown will always restore the outputs to asserted form. The variation of a demultiplexer in which the input is always high is the *decoder.* This is a very commonly occuring component in hardware designs although most of the time when it occurs later in conjunction with memories it will be implicit.

3.2.2   *User Defined Primitives*

In addition to the built-in gate primitives of Chapter 2, Verilog permits *user-defined-primitives*, otherwise generally abbreviated as UDPs. In these the user can specify either a combinational function or a sequential function by means of a table. The discussion of

---

[1]Caveat: for more complex functions, and ones with wide operands, the synthesizer might spend an inordinate amount of time trying to optimize *unless* it is given some structure; see the examples of shifter, comparator, and adder in Sections 3.5 and 3.8.

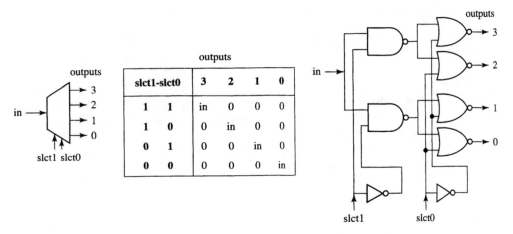

Figure 3.4   *4-Output Demultiplexer.*

sequential functions (those having memory) starts in **Chapter 5**. So this section is restricted to combinational functions.

The form for a primitive definition for a combinational function is illustrated below for the case of a 2-input multiplexer. It follows closely that for a module except that the body is a table instead of a series of assignments. All primitive definitions in Verilog are restricted to a single output. The *?* symbols on the inputs here indicate that the corresponding signal may be *0, 1,* or *x.*

```
primitive prim_mux2(out, in1, n0, slct);
   output out;
   input in1, in0, slct;
   table
      // in1 in0 slct : out
            0   0   ?  :  0;
            1   1   ?  :  1;
            0   ?   1  :  0;
            1   ?   1  :  1;
            ?   0   0  :  0;
            ?   1   0  :  1;
   endtable
```

Notice in this example the table has been set up to obtain a defined output wherever possible. In this respect the behavior of this multiplexer observed through a simulator differs from those obtained for the other multiplexer specifications discussed earlier. But this would not necessarily be a good idea since it would mask possible problems in the environment delivering the multiplexer inputs.

The Verilog user-defined-primitive construct is not used for synthesis but could be duplicated using the **casex** construct of Section 5.4. It also has a counterpart in the tables used in field programmable gate array chips and the corresponding libraries made available by the FPGA vendors (see Chapter 14).

3.3   Modeling Levels

Verilog is flexible enough to model at quite different levels of detail of which the gate
level discussed in the previous section is only one. Figure 3.5 shows the various modeling
levels at which Verilog can be used. In this figure the modeling levels are illustrated with
examples of design fragments involving the gating of signals from a register onto a bus.

Starting at the bottom, the *switch* level models circuits in terms of transistors and
even the equivalents of resistors and capacitors. The example circuit shown is an implementation of the *notif1* transmission gate in terms of transistors in the CMOS technology. For synthesis purposes it is not necessary to understand the functioning at this level
of detail. Next above this is the level of basic gates (and flipflops) as discussed in the

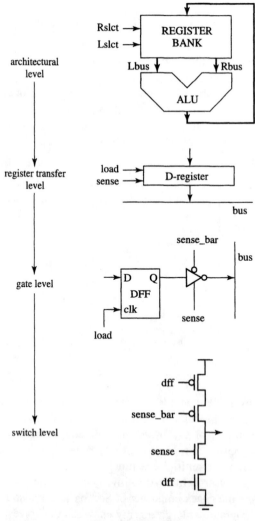

Figure 3.5   *Hierarchy of Modelling Levels.*

previous section. Usually flipflops are included at this level although the discussion of these is delayed until Chapter 5.

Above this in turn is "RTL." This is a commonly used abbreviation for "register-transfer level." Roughly speaking it consists of a sequence of *transfers* between registers and other blocks of similar size, represented as a series of assignments to registers. The right-hand sides of these assignments can include expressions of the type described in the rest of this chapter. In the diagram a register with bus sense is shown which is a vectorization of the flipflop and transmission gate shown at the level underneath. Such details as whether a register is synchronously or asynchronously loaded and whether it is sensed through a gate to a bus will be reported by the synthesizer (see Chapter 12).

Finally the top, or architectural level, uses larger blocks for modelling such as memory units and small subsystems, although again the demarcation is not precisely defined. These will usually be specified as modules composed from RTL statements.

For many years, vendors' cell libraries concentrated on basic gates up to the complexity of 4- or 8-bit slices of extendable modules such as registers and adders. Design at the switch level was already done, and CAD tools were used mainly from the gate schematic level on up. With the introduction of synthesis, designers can move up one level, and practice at the RTL level and up. Since design complexity is always increasing, it is generally recommended to write the specifications at as high a level as possible that will still permit synthesis. The source code is checked for correct operation using an HDL simulator. After synthesis, a further check for correct operation is done at gate level. Since Verilog can be used to describe operations at both levels it is possible to use the same simulator.

Some judgement is required to appropriately select the granularity of module partitions. If it is selected too small then the synthesizer is deprived of the opportunity to optimize, as demonstrated by the multiplexer examples above. This is counterproductive since the synthesizers are very good at Boolean minimization and gate optimization. On the other hand synthesizers can spend inordinate amounts of time attempting to optimize large modules. Clearly they cannot be expected to substitute for the judgement of a human designer at the high architectural level: Should this processor have unified cache? Or at the medium architectural level—a first-in first-out (FIFO) buffer has many judgement calls as we shall see in Chapters 8 and 9. But even at the RTL level the synthesizer will have difficulty with wide modules, for example, such items as comparators, encoders and decoders, parity checkers, and shifters. These either have to be broken up into pieces in an organized way or selected from the tailored library of some target vendor.

3.4   Writing Styles

In addition to the question of modelling levels there is the other dimension mentioned at the outset, namely that between structural and behavioral. The gate level specification of the multiplexer in Section 3.2 is an example of a purely structural style. The identical functionality can be expressed in pure behavioral style as in the conditional statement seen in Chapter 2:

```
assign out = select? in1 : in0;
```

For a module of any complexity at all there will usually be a variety of mixtures between these two extremes. Both Verilog and VHDL, as well as the synthesis tools, permit fairly arbitrary mixtures of structural and behavioral statements. A specification may be structural at one level of Figure 3.5 and behavioral at another. Both the ease of debugging and the quality of the synthesized result may depend quite heavily on the specification writing style which is chosen. Here are some examples of writing styles:

RTL style: As defined in the previous section in connection with modelling levels. This term is also used to denote a writing style. Normally this style is mostly structural and explicit, although as practiced the distinctions are somewhat blurred and the term RTL covers a variety of degrees of detail.

Implicit style: This is introduced in Chapter 8. It lets the synthesizer do most of the work building the controllers (finite state machines).

Behavioral compiler styles: As in the Synopsys *Behavioral Compiler* [Knapp95] and discussed in Chapter 16. These are really dialects of the implicit style. It is sometimes advertised as speeding up the design cycle by an order of magnitude. In fact the plain *Design Compiler* will also support many implicit styles as will be seen in Chapters 8 and 9.

Control-Point style: This is an extension of the implicit style used in Chapters 9, 10, and 15. It also lets the synthesizer do most of the work building the controllers and uses predesigned submodules separated into behavioral and structural regions at each hierarchical level.

Self-timed style: Although synthesis policy supports some asynchronous statements, present synthesizers work best with a synchronous clock. It is possible to synthesize *self-timed* operation without any influence from a clock but this requires some stretching of the tools (see Chapter 16).

Objective styles: Modelled after the object-oriented languages of software engineering. These are again part behavioral and part structural in which the control is implicit. Examples are *OO = VHDL* [Swamy95] and the *encapsulated* style also considered in Chapter 16. So far these are not directly synthesizable by industry tools, but a future HDL might be of this type.

This chapter now continues with simple behavioral specifications in the RTL style.

3.5   Synthesizable Operations

Table 3.1 shows the Verilog combinational operations which may appear in a behavioral specification and which are capable of being synthesized by *operator inference*. By this it is meant that the synthesizer will automatically select a suitable functional module from its library; the alternative is explicit instantiation of a module by the user, to be discussed in Section 9.2. Generally the symbols used follow those of the 'C' language. The table has listed the operations in decreasing order of precedence (highest at the top). Operations included within the same box are considered to have the same precedence. The table is given for general guidance. The relative precedence of unary and binary operators as well as bitwise and reduction operators given here is what seems reasonable to the authors and seems to correspond with current tools. A consortium of industrial representatives called

Table 3.1   *Synthesizable Operations.*

Type	Arguments	Symbols	Remarks Regarding Synthesis
bitwise	unary	~	invert/ones complement
logical	unary	!	**not** gate
arithmetic	unary	+ −	2's complement—with respect to declared length
arithmetic	binary	* / % + −	multiplier, divider, modulus, if modules available adder or incrementer, subtractor or decrementer
shift	binary	<< >>	combinational (barrel) shifter
relational	binary	< <= > >=	various comparators
equality	binary	== !=	equality (non-equality) comparator
bitwise	binary	& ~&[1] ^ ^~ | ~|	array of separate **and(nand)** gates array of separate **xor(xnor)** gates array of separate **or(nor)** gate
reduction	unary	& ~& ^ ^~ | ~|	tree of gates realizing overall **and(nand)** function tree of gates realizing overall **xor(xnor)** function tree of gates realizing overall **or(nor)** function
logical	binary	&& ||	**and** gate **or** gate
conditional	ternary	? :	(usually) two input multiplexer

[1]Either ordering is permitted, i.e., ~& or &~; ~^ or ^~; etc.

the Silicon Integration Initiative Inc (www.si2.org) has been reviewing this matter for standardization among vendor tools. It is recommended as a matter of good style that the users generally not rely on the ordering in this table and establish precedence in their specifications with the use of parentheses.

Proceding generally upwards from the bottom of this table, the logical operations are distinguished from the bitwise operations only by the operands, being single bit or multibit respectively. These operations are *infix*, or between the operands. In contrast the same logical operator preceding a bitvector implies a reduction, which means iterating the operation over the bitvector elements. The implementation comments on the right side of the table may help to clarify this for the reader.

Some judgement is called for when using operators from this table. The synthesizer habitually infers all the basic combinational operators by choosing implementations from available libraries. However to infer the more complex operations, such as multiply (*), divide (/), or modulus (%), would require a license to an advanced library such as the DW02 volume of the Synopsys DesignWare, and the resulting modules would be major hardware by themselves. A common student error is to blythely specify such a complex operator when often a shift or a parity (exclusive OR) would be perfectly satisfactory. Even the exclusive OR and shift operations need to be given some structure if they are large. For example, the combinational right shift:

```
assign out = {15´b0,in} >> amount;
```

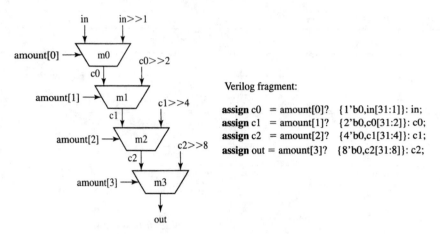

Figure 3.6   *A Structure for a Shifter.*

would do better in synthesis with the equivalent structured version above (Figure 3.6). This uses four two-input multiplexers, each of which operates on a 16-bit vector.

3.6   Continuous Assignments

The simplest behavioral construct which uses the operators of Table 3.1 is the continuous assignment. It is called continuous because the simulator continually examines the right-hand side for any value changes and if so reevaluates for any resulting changes in the left hand side. The syntax is:

$$\text{assign } net = expression;$$

For example: `assign out = dff && mask;`

As a short cut, Verilog allows this to be combined with the declaration of the assigned net:

```
wire out = dff && mask;
```

In either case the syntax models a hardware situation in which a circuit (in this example an **AND** gate) continuously drives the net. The left-hand side of the assignment may also be a vector form, either declared as such or created using the *concatenation* operator of Chapter 2:

```
assign {C_out, SUM} = A + B + C_in;
```

Without the *C_out*, assuming *SUM*, *A*, *B*, had been declared as equal dimension, *SUM* would have been truncated. On the other hand, if in the expression above, *A* and *SUM* had been declared as 16-bit vectors, while *B* was an 8-bit vector, then the shorter one would be extended with zeros. If in doubt, (or if *B* is negative) we could use the replication operator from Chapter 2:

```
assign {C_out, SUM} = A + {8{B[7]},B} + C_in;
```

In the following examples of the use of operators, the continuous assignment construct is used where it sometimes might appear that other constructs like **if ... elseif, case**

```
module mux4(select, Din0, Din1, Din2, Din3, Dout);
    parameter n = 16;
    input   [1:0] select;
    input   [n-1:0] Din0, Din1, Din2, Din3;
    output  [n-1:0] Dout;
    assign Dout = select[1]?
            (select[0]? Din3 : Din2) :
            (select[0]? Din1 : Din0) ;
endmodule
```

Specification #2: 4-input multiplexer.

(described in the next chapter) are more intuitive. This will certainly guarantee that these modules would be synthesized as purely combinational rather than sequential circuits, although sometimes at the cost of invoking tristate outputs with high impedance states. (Recall from basic switching theory that sequential circuits have internal feedback such as to be able to retain information about activation history, whereas combinational circuits have no time characteristics beyond the limited propagation delay through the gates themselves.) Verilog requires all looping and conditional constructs (other than the (? :) operation listed in Table 3.1) to be enclosed in procedural blocks and have the result assigned to a register. However, the synthesizer will often optimize this register away if it determines that it is not really necessary. Thus the specification methods of the next chapter are usually prefered, even for combinational functions.

For the next example consider an alternative to the specification of the 4-input multiplexer earlier in this chapter. Besides being behavioral rather than structural, there is a further distinction in Specification #2. Usually the applications require not so much a single multiplexer but a whole bank of multiplexers, which reroute whole busses. In behavioral specifications this parameterization comes as a low-cost bonus. In this specification the equivalent functionality of the 4-input multiplexer has been obtained by nesting the conditional operator of Table 3.1. Although the parameter n is set to 16 bits, this can be overidden in the instantiations and so this module can be reused for any bus width (see Section 9.2).

The next equivalent specification (#3) utilizes instead the fact that the high impedance value can be overdriven when multiple outputs are connected together. The user must ensure that the specification does not permit more than one output to drive low impedance at a time.

This third construction is more long winded and inferior for synthesis in that it would result in a bidirectional ("tristate") port.

3.6.1 *Operator Inference: Ripple versus Carry Look-Ahead*

In general when a synthesizer encounters combinational operators from Table 3.1 it substitutes gate implementations from cell libraries if they are available. In this section we seek to give some feeling for the kinds of choices which may be available. Table 3.2 shows some theoretical alternatives for the + operator with two input operands having n bits and one carry input.

```
module mux4(select, Din0, Din1, Din2, Din3, Dout);
    parameter n = 16;
    input  [1:0] select;
    input [n-1:0] Din0, Din1, Din2, Din3;
    output [n-1:0] Dout;
    assign  Dout = (select==3) ? Din3 : {n{1'bz}},
            Dout = (select==2) ? Din2 : {n{1'bz}},
            Dout = (select==1) ? Din1 : {n{1'bz}};
            Dout = (select==0) ? Din0 : {n{1'bz}};
endmodule
```

Specification #3: 4-input multiplexer.

Table 3.2   *Adder Characteristics.*

Adder Type	Delay	Area
ripple	$2n$	$9n$
Shannon/Lupanov	2	$2^{2n+1}/(2n+1)$
carry-with-less-delay	$2 + 2\log_2 n$	$9n + 22\log_2 n$

The synthesizer works to time and area constraints, so the table shows time in units of gate propagation delays and areas in units of 2-input gate equivalents. The first entry in the table corresponds to the simple ripple adder of Figure 2.1. Each fulladder stage has a logical depth of at least two gates assuming that gates with three inputs are available, as well as two-rail inputs (both asserted and nonasserted).

This is compared in the second row of the table with the basic Shannon theorem of switching theory. This states that any combinational function, including our $(2n + 1)$ inputs adder, could be realized in principle as a *disjunctive normal form* (DNF) with a logical depth of only two. The snag is that the DNF requires up to the order of 2^{2n+1} of $(2n + 1)$-input gates in the first level and a 2^{2n+1} input gate in the second level. If this were translated to an equivalent number of 2-input gates (the synthesizer's usual way of measuring area[2] with the GTECH library), the area complexity becomes exponential. The bound developed by [Lupanov58] essentially gives the "area" in units equivalent to this but requires more levels than two.

In the language of synthesis, the replacement of the multilevel circuit (or its corresponding Boolean algebra description) of the first table entry into the two-level form of the disjunctive normal form is called *flattening*. The opposite process is called *structuring*. Although the synthesizer can be called upon to flatten a function or a netlist in this way, it will often fail for the same reason as noted in the previous paragraph—the necessary large input gates are not available.

The well known carry-lookahead or *cla* class of circuits (which might better be called *carry-with-less-delay*) described next represent a compromise between the first two. Using area counts that are not much more than the ripple circuit, they achieve

---

[2]In general, the units of area depend on the cell library available.

logarithmic propagation delay times, essentially by replacing the purely linear structure with a tree. The method is widely available in standard texts, for example, [Mano97], and is reviewed briefly here. The conditions for generation of a carry within the *i*th stage *g*, and the propagation of a carry through *i*th stage *p*, are illustrated in Figure 3.7.

The equations for the generate and propagate through the *i*th stage are:

$$g[i] = a[i] \ \& \ b[i]; \quad p[i] = a[i] \ \hat{} \ b[i];$$

from which the *i*th sum bit can be computed as:

$$sum[i] = p[i] \hat{} c[i-1];$$

These *g* and *p* functions are computed by modified stage circuits and fed to a *cld* module which then computes the necessary carries concurrently, as shown for a four-stage adder in Figure 3.8.

The Boolean equations for each carry derive directly from the condition that a carry-out at any internal point could be caused by either a carry generation inside the current stage, or, a generation in the previous stage together with a propagation through the

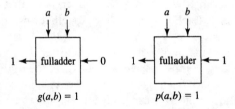

Figure 3.7 *Conditions for Generate and Propagate.*

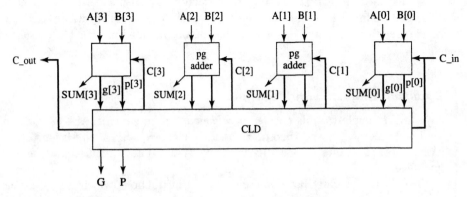

Figure 3.8 *Single-Level Carry-With-Less-Delay.*

current stage. The equations are shown below using (v) for disjunction and (.) for conjunction to try to make the appearance of the equations less confusing:

C[1] = g[0] v p[0].C_in;

C[2] = g[1] v p[1].(g[0] v p[0].C_in);

C[3] = g[2] v p[2].(g[1] v p[1].(g[0] v p[0].C_in));

C[4] = G v P.C_in;

Where the conditions for carry generation and carry propagation through a whole 4-bit nibble may be written:

```
G = g[3]  v p[3].(g[2]  v p[2].(g[1]  v p[1].g[0]));
P = p[3].p[2].p[1].p[0]
```

The process can then be iterated using a further identical CLD module which leads to a network in the form of a tree. The corresponding equivalent delay and gate counts are given in the last line of the table.

The same principle can be applied to any function which can be formulated as a cascade configuration with chained carries going from stage to stage. Figure 3.9 shows some of them. The ones shown are the incrementer (Figure 3.9a minus gates labelled with an *a*), the various flavors of comparator, and the prioritizer. Note that in the last two, the carries flow from MSB to LSB. Each circuit is shown together with the corresponding generate and propagate functions.

The point being made here is that for functions with large numbers of inputs, as in the word sizes of current computers, we cannot expect the optimization algorithms of the synthesizer to be this smart. So target vendors may typically supply libraries with several types of adder and the synthesizer can choose among them according to the overall time and area constraints which the user has set. In the synopsys designware library the fastest alternative is the *bk* (Bent-Kung) implementation. This is a parallel tree architecture normally selected for bitvectors of size 16 or more and is the very fastest one from an available selection which includes also the *rpl* ripple connection), *cla* (carry look-ahead), and *clf* (fast carry look-ahead). The synthesizer's selection may also depend on which libraries are licensed. If the user wishes to predispose a particular implementation, this may be done via pseudo comments. The vendor's on-line documentation should be consulted for details.

Example: Arithmetic and logic unit

As a final example for this chapter an *arithmetic and logic unit* (ALU) as might be used in a processor is specified in the dataflow style (Specification #4: for ALU). It has a whole repertoire of operations selected by the state combination of the input *func* field.

Such ALUs typically have one set of signed instructions which use 2's complement quantities, and another set of instructions which are unsigned. In the latter case, the carry-out indicates overflow directly; but in the former, the overflow condition is more complex. Although other methods of determining the overflow are possible, in the specification here the following method is used: Addition overflow cannot occur

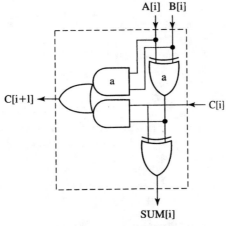

(a) adder (or **incrementer** B[i]=0)

Corresponding propagate and generate functions:
$$p[i]=A[i]\wedge B[i]$$
$$g[i]=A[i]\&B[i]$$

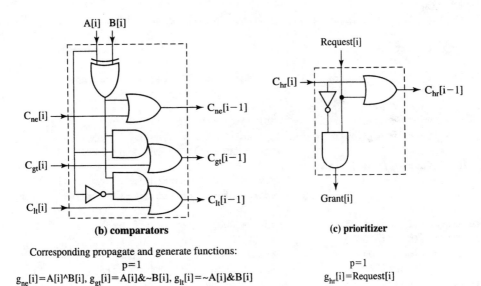

(b) comparators

(c) prioritizer

Corresponding propagate and generate functions:

$$p=1$$
$$g_{ne}[i]=A[i]\wedge B[i],\ g_{gt}[i]=A[i]\&\sim B[i],\ g_{lt}[i]=\sim A[i]\&B[i]$$

$$p=1$$
$$g_{hr}[i]=Request[i]$$

Figure 3.9 *Some Ripple Examples.*

when the two operands are of opposite sign. When they are of the same sign, check to see if the sign of the result is different from the sign of the operands. For subtraction, a similar argument is used except some of the signs are reversed. The signed and unsigned *set-if-less-than* instructions are similar to their corresponding *subtract* counterparts, except that a Boolean flag is used for the result instead of the actual difference. The purpose of these instructions is to set up the information for conditional branch instructions.

```
// repetoire of operations for ALU, selected by func
`define ADD  4`b0111  // 2`s compl add
`define ADDU 4`b0001  // unsigned add
`define SUB  4`b0010  // 2`s compl subtract
`define SUBU 4`b0011  // unsigned subtract
`define AND  4`b0100  // bitwise OR
`define OR   4`b0101  // bitwise AND
`define XOR  4`b0110  // bitwise XOR
`define SLT  4`b1010  // set result=1 if less than 2`s compl
`define SLTU 4`b1011  // set result=1 if less than unsigned
`define NOP  4`b0000  // do nothing

module alu(func, operand0, operand1, result, ovfl);
 parameter n = 16;
 input [3:0] func;
 input [n-1:0] operand0, operand1;
 output [n-1:0] result;
 output ovfl;
 wire carry_out, ovfl;
 wire [n-1:0] operand0, operand1, tmp, result;
assign
{carry_out, tmp} = ((func==`ADDU) || (func==`ADD))? operand1+operand0 :
                                                        {n{1`bz}},
{carry_out, tmp} = ((func==`SUBU) || (func==`SUB))? operand1 - operand0 :
                                                        {n{1`bz}},
{carry_out, tmp} = ((func==`SLTU) || (func==`SLT))? operand1 -operand0 :
                                                        {n{1`bz}};
assign // overflow computation
  ovfl=((func==`ADDU) || (func==`SUBU) || (func==`SLTU))? carry_out:1`bz,
  ovfl=(func==`ADD)? operand0[n-1]&operand1[n-1]&~tmp[n-1]
                         |~operand0[n-1]&~operand1[n-1]&tmp[n-1]  : 1`bz,
  ovfl=((func==`SUB) || (func==`SLT))?
                         operand0[n-1]&~operand1[n-1]&tmp[n-1]  |
                         ~operand0[n-1]&operand1[n-1]&~tmp[n-1]  :1`bz;
assign
 result = ((func==`ADDU)      || (func==`ADD))? tmp : {n{1`bz}},
 result = ((func==`SUBU)      || (func==`SUB))? tmp : {n{1`bz}},
 result = (func==`OR)   ?       operand0 | operand1 : {n{1`bz}},
 result = (func==`AND)  ?       operand0 & operand1 : {n{1`bz}},
 result = (func==`XOR)  ?     operand0 ^ operand1 : {n{1`bz}},
 result = (func==`NOP)  ?                operand0 : {n{1`bz}},
 result = (func==`SLTU) ?               carry_out : {n{1`bz}},
 result = (func==`SLT)  ?         tmp[n-1]^ovfl : {n{1`bz}};
endmodule
```

Specification #4: ALU.

Although this specification uses purely combinational language constructs, it again results in tristate outputs. Using the procedural constructs of the next chapter, a simpler specification will be used that can still result in a combinational circuit after synthesis. Most likely in practice a vendor-supplied synthetic module would be used for this.

Exercises

3.1. For this and the next two questions assume the availability of double-rail inputs (in other words, inputs available in both asserted and non-asserted form). For combinational functions, the synthesizer first tries to do the best it can using standard 2-input **and** and **or** gates where propagation time (logical depth) is its highest priority. Then it tries to modify and optimize to the target library using the user given constraints. Duplicate this process by hand using the fulladder carry function:

$$Z = A\&B \mid A\&C \mid B\&C$$

    a. if the user constraints are depth <= 2, **nand** gates available with two or three inputs.

    b. if the user constraints are depth <= 4, and 2-input **nand** gates only.

3.2. Provide a schematic using 2-input gates for a stage of a ripple incrementer. Assume two-rail (inverted) inputs available except for carry. Count any extra inverter as an extra gate, then compute the "area" in terms of the number of 2-input gates, and the propagation delay in terms of the logical depth of the network of 2-input gates.

3.3. As an alternative to 3.1, write each output of a 4-bit incrementer directly as a Boolean expression in disjunctive normal form (Karnaugh maps are one way to derive these). Then do as the synthesizer would do, factorize the expression, search for common terms, and realize as a multi-output network of 2-input gates. Compare the area and delay to the above.

3.4. Redesign the 4-input multiplexer of Figure 3.3 using only two-input NOR gates and write a structural specification.

3.5. An encoder is the opposite of a decoder—it has a one-hot input vector of width 2^r (one and only one input can be high), and a coded output vector of width r onto which is driven a state combination (binary number) corresponding to the index of the input which is high. For $r = 3$ sketch a network of 2 input NOR and NAND gates that would realize this module. Hint: First make a network of OR gates and transform. Try to minimize the depth and area. Do you think the synthesizer could do any better than you in this case?

3.6. What would be the best circuit for the 4-input parity function in terms of 2-input gate primitives: (i) to optimize delay not area (ii) optimizing area not delay.

3.7. A so-called one-hot bitvector has one and only one bit non-zero at any time. As we shall see in Chapter 8, the set of such vectors is a popular state assignment choice for controller state machines because the need for decoding of the outputs is minimized. A simple example is the ring counter. However a problem with this arrangement is that if, by some error, the bitvector ever becomes *not* one-hot the machine cannot thereafter recover, unless some kind of error correcting circuit is incorporated into the design so as to automatically reset the machine back to a good state. Using only standard gates with two inputs or less, devise a circuit that would give a low output if the ring counter state should become not one-hot. The principle of your circuit should work for any n, and use no more than $3n$ gates and have a logical depth of no more than $n + log\ n$ gate delays. Would your circuit be amenable to further speedup by applying the carry-with-less-delay principle?

3.8. The need for carry-lookahead type of circuits is made less pressing by the availability of fast carry and cascade chains (serial connection) built into FPGAs. As the number of input variables increases what Boolean functions (or what Boolean properties) lend themselves to the cascade treatment? If the synthesizer doesn't know that this feature is available what circuit topology would it select for say the reduction AND or OR operator over a large vector, if it was:
a. Area constrained
b. Time constrained
c. Has only 2-input NAND and NOR gates available? Assume the availability of double-rail inputs.

3.9. The carry-with-less-delay principle can be equally well applied to the prioritizer, using only 2-input OR gates, draw a schematic of a carry-lookahead module for the prioritizer of Figure 3.9(c). This module should have inputs for four request lines, r[3], . . . , r[0], together with a carry input, c_in, plus outputs for three carries, c[2], c[1], c[0], and a group generate, G.

3.10. Draw a logic schematic showing what the following Verilog fragment represents. It should consist of gates and wires but no higher-level blocks (no 'shifter' block).

```
wire [3:0] w, M, stemme;
wire [5:0]z;
wire sel, p, q;
assign stemme = {&M, sel? p:q, z}
assign z[3:0] = w << 2;
```

3.11. Write Verilog that describes the following hardware. Try to give a 1-line solution.

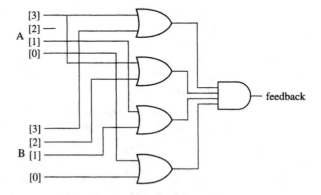

3.12. Draw a schematic showing what the following Verilog code is describing.

```
reg [7:0] D, mix, Rum;
reg [2:0] CB;
reg      A,C,D,E;
assign D = A? {{4{C}}, mix[3:1],D^E} : {8{Rum[CB]}};
```

3.13. Write Verilog that describes the following hardware. Again try to give a 1-line solution. Declare all variables you assign. (These don't count against your "line".)

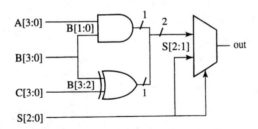

3.14. Write a Verilog code fragment that correctly describes a piece of combinational logic that given a four-bit wide variable data[3:0], sends a signal "flag" high if any adjacent bits in data are both 1's. For example if data = 1100, flag will go high, while if data = 1010, flag will go low.

3.15. a. Using only 2-input OR gates, draw a schematic for a carry-with-less-delay module appropriate for the prioritizer of Figure 3.9(c). This module should have inputs for four request lines, r[3], r[2], r[1], r[0], together with a carry-in, c_in, plus outputs for three carries, c[2], c[1], c[0], and a group generate, G.
b. Modify your schematic so as to use only NAND and NOR gates having not more than two inputs.
c. Using either of the above, write a structural Verilog specification for your carry-with-less-delay module.
d. Using five such modules, write a Verilog structural specification for a "carry-lookahead" prioritizer with sixteen request inputs R[15], . . . , R[1], R[0], together with a carry-in, C-in, plus sixteen outputs, grant[15], . . . , grant[0], together with a group generate output GG. Compare the worst path with that of the simple ripple prioritizer of Figure 3.9(c) in terms of gate delays.
e. Write a testbench for your prioritizer using thirty-two judiciously chosen test vectors generated by FOR constructs.

3.16. A similar digital equivalent to the "winner take all" circuit of the analog domain would be a kind of comparator which has m input binary numbers each of n bits, $xk[i]$, where $n-1>=i>=0$, and gives m outputs such that the kth output is logical 1 if there are no other input binary numbers which are greater.
a. Devise a ripple structure along the lines of Figure 3.9(b) and illustrate with a diagram of logic gates for the ith stage of the case $k = 3$.
b. If this is adapted to the carry-with-less-delay scheme, write expressions for the propagate and generate functions in the general case.

3.17. In the result normalization stage of the floating-point subtraction, the mantissa (binary fraction) must be shifted left until the first non-zero bit overflows the binary point. Devise a circuit which will detect the number of necessary shift positions and implement the required combinational shift. Hint: Cascade two modules already discussed. Estimate the total logical depth of the combined circuit, assuming a target technology with only 2-input gates.

References

[Awad91] Awad, N., Lin, J. C., Sathianathan, R., and Smith, D. R., "Timing validation of hardware descriptions," *Proc. Intl. Workshop on Formal Methods in VLSI*, January 1991, Miami, Fla.

[Gopal85] Gopalkrishnan, G., Smith, D. R., and Srivas, M. K., "An algebraic approach to the specification and synthesis of digital designs," *Proc. 7th Intl. Symp. on Computer Hardware Description Languages and their Applications,"* Tokyo, Japan, August 1985

[Lupanov58] Lupanov, O. B., "A method of circuit synthesis," *Radiofizika*, 1, 1958

[Mano97] Mano, M. M., and Kime, C. R., *Logic and Computer Design Fundamentals*, New York: Prentice Hall, 1997

Chapter Four

Simulation

As with most computer topics, hardware specification and synthesis is a subject one learns by doing. So it is important to start in with the simulator at an early point. Although the principal procedural constructs are yet to come in Chapter 5, enough Verilog has now been introduced to write a simple module specifications and try out a simulator.

4.1 Types of Simulators

There are various types of simulators available:

interpreted: Like a software interpreter, this type is faster overall for small designs.

compiled: This type first parses the Verilog source and then calls on a regular 'C' compiler to construct an executable file. This type is slower to compile, but faster at runtime, especially for large designs.

In either category, in case the simulator is an *event simulator*, it operates in a simulated dimension of time in which it jumps from event list to event list as shown in Figure 4.1. As the event list corresponding to the current time is executed, it results in further additions to event lists further on in time. When the simulator is finished executing the current list it then jumps to the nearest next time for which an event list exists. As of now, all commercial computers and almost all digital designs are synchronous under the control of one or more regular clocks. So, as shown in the figure, some of the event lists correspond to active clock edges, and others, in between, correspond to the composition of propagation delays through the various intermediate gates and modules of the design.

Event simulators are between three and four orders of magnitude faster than *electrical simulators* (for example, Spice) which must solve a set of partial differential equations at each time step and trace out the form of analog voltages and currents. However, for large designs and current processor speeds, event simulation can still take a long long

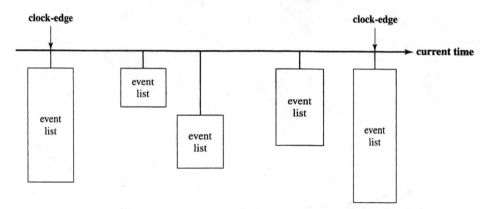

Figure 4.1   *Event Simulator Model of Time.*

time. For example, for a 200K-gate circuit designed to run at 50Mhz, event-based simulation of one minute of actual real time would take years. Typically event-based simulators are used for functional verification and timing verification of sections of a design, and are left to run overnight or through several days.

A design may be known to be strictly synchronous so that most of the action takes place at the clock transitions. Or it may be known from a static-timing analysis tool that the propagation delay through the worst electrical path (critical path) is less than the clock interval. In this case a *cycle-based simulator* might be satisfactory. This constructs event lists only for each clock edge and is limited to functional verification rather than timing. By limiting simulation to clock edges of interest and eliminating the overhead of event management in between it is possible to obtain a reduction of between one and two orders of magnitude in memory utilization and between one and three orders of magnitude in speed improvement. Cycle-based simulation is particularly suited to disciplined synchronous design styles.

For large designs even a cycle-based simulation of a whole design taken together will prove too time consuming. For the first few generations of integrated circuits, the final design verification was commonly done by putting together a prototype built from standard small and medium scale IC's on a breadboard. In this way a design was tested and debugged in its target system environment before the first silicon was fabricated. Since the design could be tested at almost full speed under close to real operating conditions, including (for processor designs), a boot of the operating system, this gave a high level of confidence in the design. As time passed, the increased chip complexity and limited time for design combined to render this option obsolete. However the advent of *field programmable gate arrays* (FPGAs) has made possible a return to a similar method, called *emulation*. In this method the design specifications, even if intended for custom IC, are first synthesized to FPGA chips in special emulation equipment. This process is similar to what will be described in Chapters 12 and 14. For large designs it requires a significant effort, because the design must be partitioned between multiple FPGAs and even multiple boards. So this method is typically used after the design has stabilized and before the final commitment to silicon. Finally, for the 50 million transistor chips of "sub-micron" fabrication, even this may be impractical, and recourse may have to be made to arrays of special purpose high-speed processors specifically designed for simulation.

4.2   Using the VCS Simulator

In this book, where we will be dealing with small- to medium-size modules only, we can use one of the available Verilog event simulators. The *vcs* simulator in particular is a compiled simulator which is now available through the Synopsys university program, and will serve to illustrate what is typically available. It is invoked by a command line such as:

```
vcs test_topmod.v topmod.v submod.v <options>
```

(To invoke this command in Unix it will first be necessary to set up a path in the user's .login file to wherever the simulator binaries have been installed on the user's system.)

   In this command line, *topmod.v* is the specification of the main (top level) module of the design, and is followed by any submodules which are necessary and have not been listed in '*include* statements in the *topmod* specification itself.

   The Verilog models are processed through 'C' language source into an executable in a similar manner to the 'C' compiler itself. The executable is named *simv* by default and can then be executed to produce a printing of the signals for which monitoring is called for in the testbench. Option -M will save 'C' sources to facilitate subsequent incremental compilation (for large designs). Option +cli will save information necessary for interactive source level debugging, which will be active after an *simv -s* command has been issued and a *$stop* system call has been encountered in the model. While in this stage a "?" or "help" command will cause a printing of the interactive command possibilities. At the completion of the interactive session a *$finish* system call will return control to the operating system.

   The foregoing should be sufficient to get the user started. For further information, or if some other simulator is to be used, the user should consult a local reference manual. Many simulators, including *vcs*, include a graphical back end which can be used to view simulated waveforms. The user should consult a corresponding manual for details. It could make the process of visually comparing outputs from the high-level and gate-level simulations easier. However for this type of comparison on larger designs it would probably be necessary to write a program which analyzes the tabular form of simulation output. For the small- to medium-size exercises in this book the tabular form is sufficient to do the exercises.

4.3   Testbenches

In the example invocation of the VCS simulator given above, the first quoted module, namely *test_topmod.v*, is the *testbench* specification. Although it would be possible to include the testing instructions in another module inside the same file as *topmod.v*, it is usually preferred to write the testbench in the form of a separate file. This way it will be easy to invoke a variety of simulations in cases where there are several different testbenches for a particular module under test or possibly the same testbench for more than one module specification (say at high level and gate level).

```
module test_alu;
   reg [3:0] func;
   reg [15:0] op_s, op_d;
   wire [15:0] result;
   alu #(16) ALU(func, op_s, op_d, result, ovfl);
initial
begin
  $display(``func  op_s  op_d  ovfl result´´);
  $monitor(``%b  %h  %h    %b    %h´´, func, op_s, op_d, ovfl, result);
  $display(``ADDU´´); func = 4´b0001; op_s=16´h7fff; op_d=1;
  #1                  func = 4´b0001; op_s=-1; op_d=1;
  #1 $display(``ADD ´´); func = 4´b0111; op_s=16´h7fff; op_d=1;
  #1                  func = 4´b0111; op_s=-1; op_d=1;
  #1 $display(``SUBU´´); func = 4´b0011; op_s=1; op_d=0;
  #1                  func = 4´b0011; op_s=-1; op_d=1;
  #1                  func = 4´b0011; op_s=1; op_d=-1;
  #1 $display(``SUB´´ ); func = 4´b0010; op_s=1; op_d=0;
  #1                  func = 4´b0010; op_s=-1; op_d=1;
  #1                  func = 4´b0010; op_s=1; op_d=16´h7fff;
  #1 $display(``SLTU´´); func = 4´b1011; op_s=1; op_d=0;
  #1                  func = 4´b1011; op_s=-1; op_d=0;
  #1                  func = 4´b1011; op_s=16´h7fff; op_d=16´h7fff;
  #1 $display(``SLT´´ ); func = 4´b1010; op_s=0; op_d=1;
  #1                  func = 4´b1010; op_s=16´h8001; op_d=1;
  #1                  func = 4´b1010; op_s=16´h7fff; op_d=16´h7fff;
  #1 $display(``OR  ´´); func = 4´b0101; op_s=16´h1441; op_d=16´h5555;
  #1 $display(``AND ´´); func = 4´b0100; op_s=16´hf00f; op_d=16´h5555;
  #1 $display(``XOR ´´); func = 4´b0110; op_s=16´h1441; op_d=16´h5555;
end
endmodule
```

Specification #1 Testbench for the ALU.

Let us illustrate the writing of a testbench specification for the case of the *alu* module described at the end of the previous chapter. Inasmuch as a fair number of testbenches may eventually accumulate, the user should try to keep the files easily recognizable by naming them accordingly: *test1_alu.v* and *test2_alu.v* to test the module "*alu.v*". Such a testbench is given in specification #1.

This specification begins with the declaration of necessary test variables, after which appears the invocation of the module under test. In the invocation, the construct #(16) sets the parameter(s) of the module under test in the same ordering as they appear in the parameter statement(s) of the specification of that module.

The *$monitor* statement is an example of a Verilog system task. All system tasks are preceded by the $ sign and thereby indicate to the simulator that it must call a program which implements the desired function. The monitor statement and the formatting it uses is modelled directly on the *printf* statement of the 'C' language. Thus it prints out the requested variables in the format specified by the string part (the part enclosed in double quotes). Another system task is *$display* with a similar syntax, and used here to set up the headings of the simulation output. The difference is that the *$display* statement just prints when execution reaches it, whereas the *$monitor* causes a printout whenever any of the requested variables change value. In cases where concurrent constructs are employed it will not always be apparent in which order the actions will be invoked. Different simulators may actually invoke the operations in different orders. To facilitate testing in such situations a variation of the *$display* task can be invoked by the system call *$strobe*. It will synchronize the printout to the screen to occur only after all the events in the list scheduled for that time slot have completed. Some other system tasks are:

- *$time*: used to keep track the simulator time in the units and accuracy requested in the *$timescale* statement.
- *$stop*: when encountered, stops the simulation and returns the user to the interactive mode of the simulator.
- *$finish*: when encountered, causes the simulator to exit to the operating system.

The **initial** statement indicates that the subsequent block of actions between the **begin** and **end** are to be executed just once at the outset (perhaps corresponding to when the power is turned on). The symbol "*#1*" indicates a delay of one unit of time before resuming with the actions following. The time units being used are those defined in the '**timescale** statement as described in Chapter 2.

Note that the **initial** statement and the delay constructs are unsynthesizable. Arguably the **initial** statement might have been, if a special charging and trigger circuit were available to the synthesizer to insert into the design to control the power-up. This is more a matter of policy. The delay constructs are not synthesizable for a more important reason, because the synthesizer attempts to generate the fastest circuit possible within the framework of the target technology. It then tells the user what are the resulting delays, not the other way round. So delay statements (#) in the specification are just ignored by the synthesizer (although not by the simulator). The simple testbench above applies a series of test vectors at one time unit intervals. Perhaps a better way of activating the test vectors is to time them from the clock of the module under test itself. This is done in the testbenches of the modules in Chapter 8 onwards. Extending this concept, it is even possible to synthesize portions of a testbench module too, as will be done in Chapter 15. In this way this portion of the testbench becomes a *built-in self-test*.

The selection of the test vectors themselves is perhaps an art rather than a science. For modules of any size, certainly those with parameterizations of thirty-two and greater, we will not have the luxury of being able to test exhaustively. So the test vectors are selected to include the so-called *corner cases*. These are the ones which exercise the boundary conditions in some sense, in the hope that the vectors in between will perform in rote, and that there are no important cases that have been forgotten. In this respect it is better for one person to make up the design specification and another to select the test cases, preferably someone with a motivation to break it. Even a partner (whose motivation is probably to whitewash) might be useful since the important missing test case is often one that simply never occurs to the person who designed it. In the case of the present example, the cases with the longest chains of carries (or borrows) have been selected, as well as vectors which distinguish the unsigned *alu* operations from the signed ones.

We are now ready to use this testbench to invoke the simulator by the command line given earlier. After the compile phase completes, the executable phase can be run. In the case of the *alu* there is another specification of the same function in Chapter 5 that can be exercised with the same testbench. So the executable could be run with the output redirected to a file to facilitate a later comparison:

```
simv > alu1.outh
```

```
Chronologic VCS simulator copyright 1991-1997
Contains Viewlogic proprietary information.
Compiler version 4.0.2; Runtime version 4.0.2; Sep 11 18:48 1998
```

func	op_s	op_d	ovfl	result
ADDU				
0001	7fff	0001	0	8000
0001	ffff	0001	1	0000
ADD				
0111	7fff	0001	1	8000
0111	ffff	0001	0	0000
SUBU				
0011	0001	0000	1	ffff
0011	ffff	0001	1	0002
0011	0001	ffff	0	fffe
SUB				
0010	0001	0000	0	ffff
0010	ffff	0001	0	0002
0010	0001	7fff	0	7ffe
SLTU				
1011	0001	0000	0	0001
1011	ffff	0000	0	0001
1011	7fff	7fff	0	0000
SLT				
1010	0000	0001	0	0000
1010	8001	0001	1	0000
1010	7fff	7fff	0	0000
OR				
0101	1441	5555	z	5555
AND				
0100	f00f	5555	z	5005
XOR				
0110	1441	5555	z	4114

```
            V C S    S i m u l a t i o n    R e p o r t
Time: 18
CPU Time:    0.467 seconds; Data structure size: 0.0Mb
Fri Sep 11 18:48:37 1998
```

Simulation Output for the ALU of Chapter 3.

The simulation output shown here has been labelled to distinguish it from that of the low-level simulation to come later. If it is compared with the output produced from the simpler procedural specification of Chapter 5, it can be seen that the only difference is the elimination of the high impedance overflow outputs for the three logical operations at the bottom of the table. Note that for the signed operations the leading bit of the result has the significance of sign and the overflow bit signifies that the absolute value of the result is too large to be encompassed correctly by the remaining bits in twos complement form.

4.4 Debugging

Most people do not expect to see their simulation working on the first try. In case your first programming courses have not yet cured you of this expectation, a few remarks on debugging are included here.[1] The worst thing that might happen after invoking the *simv* is nothing. Although this certainly indicates that no events requested in the *$monitor* command are being reached it doesn't mean that nothing is happening. So to avoid using up useless processor cycles you ought to do a control C. At this point interactive debugging facilities of the simulator could be used to query registers or wires manually, although this may have required a compiler switch to be set up ahead of time. At this stage it would probably be more useful to examine the initial part of the **initial** block of the testbench which almost certainly has failed to start the circuit in a known good state. Sequential modules (see Chapter 5 onwards) almost always have an explicit reset input for this purpose, which may not have been invoked or released in a timely fashion, or the clock may have simply failed to activate. The clock is also usually generated by the testbench.

After getting past the point of nothing, the next step is usually a whole table full of *x*'s (unknowns) of various varieties for which most simulators have a predilection. In this case it may be necessary to start at the inputs or signals supposed to be reset at the outset and follow the action successively through the internal points toward the misbehaving outputs. For this purpose, it may be necessary to dive into submodules, using the hierarchical dot notation described at the end of Chapter 2. This may be done interactively, or by separate runs with extra terms inserted into the *$monitor* statements of the testbench, or into extra *$display* statements inserted into the model. Probing internal points in this way is a privilege available at this stage of *high-level simulation* although not at the *post-synthesis* or *gate-level simulation* stage, which we will reach at the end of Chapter 14. If while trying to modify the design in order to get it working you find yourself simplifying it greatly, then you know you are on the right track.

After finally obtaining some output other than *x*'s beware of the temptation to jump to the conclusion that the operation is correct without careful scrutiny. While the output may look correct at first glance, a small unexplained signal in one corner can still indicate a whole load of trouble and extra debugging time. At this stage problems are nearly always caused by faulty timing. The clocking, and strict separation of updating and sensing actions, will need to be robust if the design is to survive through synthesis and gate-level simulation.

Exercises

4.1. Write a Verilog module for one of the four-output multiplexers of Figure 3.3, and a testbench module that tests it. Run it through the simulator. Then use the same testbench on the module *full-par* from Section 5.5, which implements an identical function using a functional specification. To keep the volume of output manageable it will be sufficient for this exercise to test whether toggling the selected input does indeed result in a toggling of the output for each state combination of the selects. The reader should not think that this will be considered a sufficient test when she gets a job.

---

[1]More notes on debugging are to be found in Chapters 6, 7, and 14. More examples of testbenches are given in Sections 7.4 and 8.3.

4.2. Write a Verilog module for a comparator based on one of the comparison operations of Table 3.1. Write a testbench and compare its functioning with comparator Specification #5 in Section 5.4 of the following chapter.

4.3. Write a Verilog module for a combinational shifter based on the shifter operation of Table 3.1. Write a testbench and compare its functioning with a module using the structured principle of Figure 3.6.

4.4. Write a parameterized Verilog module for a prioritizer based on the ripple method of Figure 3.9(c) together with a suitable testbench. (Hint: This can be constructed along similar lines to the comparator specification #5 in Chapter 5.) Compare its functioning with a specification in procedural behavioral form such as that of the prioritizer of Section 5.6.

4.5. Write a Verilog structural Verilog module for the not *one-hot* function of Chapter 3, Problem 3.7 with n = 3. Write a testbench and then compare its functioning with the parameterized behavioral *not-hot* module of Section 5.4.

4.6. Does the processor in your system have a 32-bit word? If so try to simulate the ALU with a parameterization of thirty two (which means the carry-out will be bit #33). Does your simulator give the right answers? Can you break it by increasing the vector size further? If it did break could you suggest a workaround?

Chapter Five

Procedural Specification

The continuous assignment style of the last chapter is limited in expressive power. The behavioral styles most used for synthesis use procedural constructs which are the main vehicle for synthesis. This type of specification is reminiscent of software, especially 'C' and so most people find this style easier to follow. The price for the expressive power is that all assignments must be made to a register (or part of) although it is possible that such registers may later be optimized away by the synthesizer. Verilog also allows assignments to **integer, real**, and **time** datatypes but synthesis does not. Another language requirement for procedural statements is that they must be enclosed within an **always** or **initial** block. The **initial** block has been discussed earlier in connection with testbenches, but for synthesis the only one allowed is the *always* block.

5.1 The *always* Block

The syntax of an *always* block is:

```
  ┌─► always @(event-expression [or event-expression*])
  └────(assignment) or (block)
```

The semantics are that execution starts at time 0 (power-on) and the execution of the assignment statement or block of assignment statements repeats endlessly unless or until a *$stop* or *$finish* system call is encountered. There is an implicit loop as indicated by the arrow. Intuitively this corresponds to hardware which is continuously active until an interrupt or a power-down.

The event expressions are optional. They may be either:

level type: eg: @(*a* or *b* or *c*): the block is triggered whenever a change occurs in the value of *a* or *b* or *c*. This usually results in the synthesis of a combinational net with the declared **reg**'s for the left hand sides of the assignments optimized away. A warning is issued if a variable is read which is not in the event trigger list.

45

edge type: eg: @(**posedge** *a* or **negedge** *b* . . .): At least one of the variables *a* and *b* . . . will usually be a clock, and a synchronous sequential circuit will be synthesized. The synthesizer also accepts @(posedge clk) statements instead inside the enclosed block instead of in the sensitivity list (but not both). See for example the multicycle subsection below.

For reasons of gate economy and clock skew, where possible it is recommended not to mix positive and negative edges as done here. If more than one assignment statement appears after the **always** then a *block* with **begin** and **end** statements is mandatory.

5.1.1   Blocks

A *sequential block* is a series of assignments enclosed between a **begin** and an **end** statement. Sequential blocks may be optionally named by placing a colon and an identifier after the **begin**, in which case the identifier may appear in the hierarchical naming convention discussed in Chapter 2.

The statement: **disable** *blockname*; transfers control to the next statement after the named block (see comparator, Specification #5). This is somewhat like the **break** statement in 'C', although the latter is used to exit from a control block such as a **while**. As in all structured languages, blocks may be nested. A *parallel* block is one enclosed instead by **fork** and **join** statements. Although this is unsynthesizable at present, this is not a severe handicap because there are many alternative constructs which can be used to model concurrency in Verilog:

- First, we could have multiple **always** blocks, all starting at time 0. This is often done, although it has the disadvantage that a separate sequential machine may be generated for each always block with possibly its own controller. Also, assignments made to common variables in different **always** blocks will result in warnings that multiple outputs are wired together, called wired-OR logic.
- Alternatively, the effect of concurrency at the statement level can be obtained within a sequential block by using the non-blocking assignments to be discussed.
- Finally structural invocations outside of **always** blocks are activated concurrently as seen in Chapter 2.

5.1.2   Always Blocks with Multicycle Execution Time

If the main block inside the always loop takes more than one clock time to complete its computation, the question arises as to how often the block will be restarted. For example in the following block:

```
reg [3:0] r;
always
 begin
 @(posedge clk) if (reset) r <= 0;
 @(posedge clk) r <= r+1;
 end
```

Simulation assumes that the block is not restarted until execution completes so that in this example the register will be incremented only on every other clock edge. The user should take care that this behavior corresponds with what is desired from synthesis. The examples of Chapter 10 are constructed with tests for odd and even cycles so that there will be no possible confusion.

5.2   Functions and Tasks

The Verilog **function** works in a very similar manner to the one in 'C' language and was introduced for the same reason—to make the software more understandable by modularizing it. In Verilog a **function** is declared in the following format (compare with that for **module** in Section 2.2):

```
function                      [range]
func_name;
  parameters
  input declarations
  reg declarations
   ... text body ...
endfunction
```

The order and ranges of the declarations must match the arguments in the invocation. As in 'C' the function's return bitvector is implicit with a width corresponding to [*range*] (default 1 bit). If it is desired to return more than a single argument, this could be done by bundling them inside func_name using a concatenation.

Functions are also limited in that they execute in zero time and cannot contain any timing control statements. So the Verilog designers elected to relax these limitations in a new type of subroutine called a **task**. Tasks may have the option of no **input**, multiple **output** or **inout** ports, and delay, timing, or event constructs. Outputs must be registered. The format of the invocation is:

```
            task_name(arguments);
```

The format of the task body is:

```
task task_name;
  parameters
  input    declarations
  output   declarations
  reg      declarations
    ... text body ...
endtask
```

Of course the order and ranges of the arguments in the invocation must match the input and output declarations in the task body.

As an example the 4-bit adder of Chapter 2 will be reformulated with the component fulladders represented as functions instead of submodules. This is possible because the behavior of *fulladd* is combinational, as it must to be represented as a function. In Specification #1, first the body of the function is declared, followed by the four invocations inside an always block. As a function has only one output allowed, so the two outputs of the fulladder must be bundled. Note that unlike the structured version of Chapter 2, the four invocations of

```
module add_4_r (A, B, C_in, SUM, C_out);
 input [3:0] A,B;
 input C_in;
 output [3:0] SUM;
 output C_out;

 function fulladd;
  input a, b, c_in;
   {c_out, sum} = a + b + c_in;
 endfunction

always @(A or B or C_in)
 begin
  {C0, SUM[0]} = fulladd (A[0], B[0], C_in);
  {C2, SUM[2]} = fulladd (A[2], B[2], C1);
  {C_out, SUM[3]} = fulladd (A[3], B[3], C2);
 end
endmodule
```

Specification #1: 4-bit Adder Using **Functions.**

```
module add_4_r (A, B, C_in, SUM, C_out);
 input [3:0] A,B;
 input C_in;
 output [3:0] SUM;
 output C_out;

 task fulladd;
  input a, b, c_in;
  output sum, c_out;
   {c_out, sum} = a + b + c_in;
 endtask

always @(A or B or C_in)
 begin
   fulladd (A[0], B[0], C_in,SUM[0], C0);
   fulladd (A[1], B[1], C0, SUM[1], C1);
   fulladd (A[2], B[2], C1, SUM[2], C2);
   fulladd (A[3], B[3], C2, SUM[3], C_out);
 end
endmodule
```

Specification #2: 4-bit Adder Using a Task.

the function must occur in the correct sequence. Actually the = sign indicates that these assignments are *blocking*—each one must complete before the next one commences. (Blocking versus non-blocking assignments will be contrasted in the very next subsection.)

Now the 4-bit adder is reformulated once again, this time using tasks (Specification #2). The property of tasks that allows multiple outputs can be well used for this example, although the possibility of memory will not.

The function is usually used for computing expressions that affect the parameterization of the specification rather than anything that will be itself synthesized. We do not use it in this book. It is possible for functions and tasks to be mapped to modules by the synthesizer but this usage is not recommended here. An exception is the experimental object-oriented Vpp writing style in Chapter 16. Other than this we have stayed consistently with the module formulation for all synthesizable objects.

5.3   Blocking and Non-blocking Assignments

Assignments indicated by the = sign are called *blocking assignments*, such as:

```
begin
  A = B;
  B = A;
end
```

The simulator completes each assignment action before starting the next even if no delay time is attached (the synthesizer does not accept the # delay construct anyway). The result here would therefore be that both *A* and *B* end up with the original value in *B*.

Non-blocking assignments are indicated by the <= symbol combination, which is reused for this purpose (it was also used for *less-than-or-equal* in a different context).

```
begin
  A <= B;
  B <= A;
end
```

The simulator collects all the right-hand sides of the assignments first into temporaries. Then it places the values in the left-hand sides. This gives the effect of concurrency. The result here would be the interchange of the values in *A* and *B*.

The selection of blocking or non-blocking assignments will also have an effect on the final synthesized result. Figure 5.1 shows possible results from synthesis[1] for corresponding examples of blocking and non-blocking assignments. For the non-blocking assignments (right-hand side of Figure 5.1) the variable *B* receives the previous value of *A*, a result achieved by the shift register configuration shown in the figure. Because of the **posedge** occuring in the **always** statement, the flipflops synthesized here would be D-type edge triggered, and the final result would be assured because the hold time of flipflop *B* would necessarily be shorter than the propagation time of flipflop *A* (see discussion on flipflop types in Section 5.7).

For the blocking assignments on the other hand, the result is the two latched variables ending up with the same final value, as shown on the left-hand side of Figure 5.1 by the parallel load. This result may initially seem counter intuitive, but it is due to the ordering of the two assignments, which for the blocking case is significant. Had this ordering been reversed, then a similar synthesis result to the right-hand side would have been produced, with the possible slight difference that the clocking of the first flipflop might be

---

[1]The synthesized result may also depend on how *A* and *B* are used elsewhere in the design.

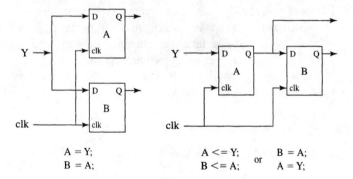

Figure 5.1   *Synthesized Result from Two Assignment Situations.*

delayed somewhat after that of the second. Note that it is not allowed to mix the two kinds of assignments within the same **always** block nor in assignments to the same register. Hardware is usually by nature concurrent, so when in doubt it is generally best to use the non-blocking assignments. This will be the preference in the examples that follow. If the function described should turn out to be purely combinational then no harm will be done.

5.4   Control Constructs

5.4.1   *IF Statements*

In procedural specifications the **?:** conditional operator of Chapter 3 is replaced by the more general **if** construct, which may have the following forms:

```
if (expression) block;
if (expression) block_1 else block_2;
if (expression) block_1 elseif (expression) block_2 elseif ... else block_n:
```

The first block is executed only if the expression evaluates to true, not if false or unknown.

5.4.2   *Looping Statements*

Verilog has four kinds, which may be nested:

repeat <n> <block>: Repeats the block *n* times. Not currently synthesizable.

for (*initial index; terminal index; step*) block: Usually used to iterate over space rather than time (such as modelling parallel hardware over vectors or arrays). In this case an integer should be declared for the index, not a register. In case the **for** iterates over time, the same remarks as to breaking the loop apply as in the **while** construct below.

while (*expression*) block: Executes the block until the expression becomes false (maybe no executions if *expression* starts out false). More general than the **for**, but is not synthesizable unless some *@(posedge clock)* statement breaks the loop.

forever: Same as above but loops forever. Similar semantics could be achieved alternatively by a separate **always** block. However the **forever** might be preferred in the

interest of minimizing the number of synthesized controllers and the test complexit̲
arising from the resulting state combinations. These choices are again a matter of
style.

Some prefer styles using many **always** blocks. In this text we have employed styles that
minimize the number of **always** blocks to a single-edge triggered one (with perhaps one or
two asynchronous ones, and no **forever** blocks).

5.4.3   *Examples*

The comparator is first modelled in the dataflow style of the last chapter in Specification #3. Superior to this from the point of view of synthesis is Specification #4 done in
the style of the present chapter. If this were synthesized for say a parameterization of
four and using only a library of elementary gates, the result would be optimized to
around twenty gates or so, depending on the gates available and the time and area constraints set by the user. If it were synthesized for a parameterization of sixty-four, the
synthesizer might take a long time and still fail to come up with a good result. If however a library is available, such as the Synopsys designware or the Altera LPM discussed in the next chapter, it will simply choose an appropriate part and do quite well.
Note that in a combinational function such as this the non-blocking assignments are not
really necessary, but again the habit does no harm.

```
module comparator(A, B, Cgt, Clt, Cne);
 parameter n = 4;
 input [n-1:0] A, B;
 output Cgt, Clt, Cne;
  assign Cgt = (A > B);
  assign Clt = (A < B);
  assign Cne = (A != B);
endmodule
```

Specification #3: Comparator.

```
module comparator(A, B, Cgt, Clt, Cne);
 parameter n = 4;
 input [n-1:0] A, B;
 output Cgt, Clt, Cne;
 reg Cgt, Clt, Cne;
 always @(A or B)
  begin
   Cgt <= (A > B);
   Clt <= (A < B);
   Cne <= (A != B);
  end
endmodule
```

Specification #4: Comparator.

```
module comparator(A, B, Cgt, Clt, Cne);
  parameter n = 4;
  input[n-1:0] A, B;
  output Cgt, Clt, Cne;
  reg Cgt, Clt, Cne;
  integer i;
    always @(A or B)
      begin: compare
      for (i = n-1; i >= 0; i = i-1)
        begin
         if(A[i]^b[i])
           begin
             Cgt <= A[i]; Clt <=~A[i]; Cne <=1;
             disable compare;      //stop looping
           end
        end
        //if this point is reached, A==B
        // if disable executes, the next line won't
        Cgt <= 0; Clt <= 0; Cne <= 0;
      end
endmodule
```

Specification #5: Comparator.

A third alternative formulation is that of Specification #5 which uses a **disable** of a named block to load the dice in favor of the ripple formulation of Figure 3.9(b). Although this might give more guidance to the synthesizer in the case where (a) a large parameterization is involved and (b) only elementary gates are available or a standard cell target is being used, more usually the synthesis does not do as well for the simple reason that this specification has inhibited the choice of a ready made comparator part from the library. In such cases results may differ according to whether the target is FPGA or standard cell and what library resources come with it. Probably the best advice is to start with the simplest possible specification and then try variations if the results do not satisfy.

We end this section with another module that is conveniently done in this style, for the *not-hot* function described in Problem 3.7, Chapter 3. The objective is to develop a signal that will flag an error when the elements of a bitvector become not *one-hot*, and to provide a specification that is generally parameterized on the bitvector length. The module will be utilized later and its Specification (#6) follows.

5.5   Synthesis of Conditional Constructs

The following two examples of the **if** construct are called *full* since all possible outcomes are accounted for:

```
if(select) out = A;                    out = B;
else       out = B;                    if (select) out = A;
```

```
module nothot(bv,onehot);
  parameter n=4;
  input [n-1:0] bv; // bitvector to test for one-hot
  output onehot; // one-hot indicator
  wire [n-1:0] bv;
  reg onehot, Chb; // Chb => one 1-bit encountered in bv so far
  integer i;
   always @(bv)
    begin: sweep
     onehot = 1; Chb = 0;
     for (i=n-1; i>=0; i=i-1)
      if (bv[i]==1)
       if (Chb==1)
          begin // this is second 1-bit
          onehot=0;
          disable sweep; // stop looping
          end
        else Chb = 1;
        // if this point is reached there are no multiple 1-bits
       if (Chb==0) onehot=0; // no 1-bits at all
    end
endmodule
```

Specification #6: Module Not-Hot.

As expected, synthesis of a full **if** statement will result in a multiplexer. As perhaps not quite so expected, the following **if** statement results instead in a D-type latch, with variable *A* connected to the *D* input and the variable *select* connected to the *clk* input. The synthesizer gives a warning flag that a latch has been inferred. This is because if *select* is false, there may be a need to preserve a previous value set onto the **wire** *out*.

```
                          if (select) out = A;
```

5.5.1 *Case Statements*

For more than about three alternatives, instead of the nested **if . . . elseif**, in terms of clarity, the **case** statement is often to be preferred. The semantics are similar to those in software engineering, but with many extra pitfalls. The syntax is as follows:

```
case (expression) // n-bit valued
  // case item : case action
  n´d0 : block_0;
  n´d1 : block_1;
  ...
  n´dm : block_m;
  [default: block_d;]
endcase
```

The default is optional. The block corresponding to the first match executes, and unlike most software languages there is then an implied break. The **case** statement compares its *expression* literally bit for bit with the *case items* and considers values of *x* or *z* in the *case items* to be distinct alternatives. Of course while *x* values may occur in simulation, they cannot occur in synthesized logic; in other words, real life. So the designers of Verilog have provided the following variations of the case statement for when *don't care* in a case item is really intended as such.

- The **casez** treats *z* or *?* symbols in the expression or case items as don't-cares.
- The **casex** treats *z* or *x* or *?* symbols in the expression or case items as don't-cares.

Since the simulator also assigns *x* to expressions when there is some ambiguity in the design, so of these, the **casez** would normally be considered the safer of the two for the purpose of representing an intended don't care.

It follows that the **case** constructs will have similar characteristics to the **if** statements regarding being full or parallel. A **case** statement is called *full* if all possible outcomes are accounted for and is called *parallel* if the stated alternatives are mutually exclusive. There are four possible cases (sic):

Full parallel: module *full-par.* Results in simple parallel logic (in this case a mux).

```
module full-par (slct, A, B, C, D, out);
  input [1:0] select;
  input A, B, C, D;
  output out;
  reg out; // optimized away
    always @(slct or A or B or C or D)
      case (slct)
        2'b11  : out <= A;
        2'b10  : out <= B;
        2'b01  : out <= C;
        default : out <= D; // 2'b00
      endcase
endmodule
```

Parallel, not full: module *par-not-full.* A latch is synthesized.

```
module par-not-full (slct, A, B, C, out);
... always @(slct or A or B or C)
      case (slct)
        2'b11 : out <= A;
        2'b10 : out <= B;
        2'b01 : out <= C
      endcase
//see also note in not-full not-par below
```

Full, not parallel: module *full-not-par*. Prioritizer synthesized, latch optimized away.

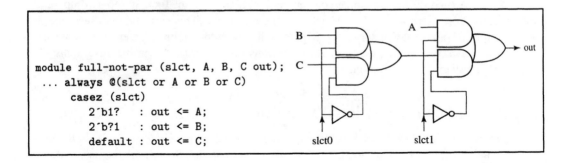

```
module full-not-par (slct, A, B, C out);
... always @(slct or A or B or C)
    casez (slct)
        2'b1?  : out <= A;
        2'b?1  : out <= B;
        default : out <= C;
```

In the example, if the case 2'b11 occurs, a choice has to be made. The synthesizer chooses the first outcome because it occurs highest in the list of cases. In the schematic this gets higher priority because it is closer to the output.

Not full, not parallel: module *not-full-not-par*. Prioritizer and latch synthesized.

```
module not-full-not-par (slct, A, B, out);
   ... always @(slct or A or B)
       casez (slct)
           2'b1? : out <= A;
           2'b?1 : out <= B;
// non-full if either case item missing
        // eg: if there is no default,
// or, if one of the variables is unassigned
// in a case action, eg:
               default : ;
    endcase
```

Although the synthesized result may also differ somewhat also depending on the given constraints, it can be seen from the examples that resulting schematics can be quite markedly and sometimes unexpectedly different. The user will be alerted by warnings in the synthesis reports in these cases.

Due to the nature of the application, the user may know that it is impossible for the missing case(s) to occur, or that the cases are really mutually exclusive. This fact can be indicated to the synthesizer by *pseudo-comments* to avoid the generation of unnecessary latches or priority logic. For example with Synopsys:

```
//synopsys full_case                    or
//synopsys parallel_case                or
//synopsys full_case parallel_case
```

This would synthesize more economically. But it has the disadvantage of being vendor-specific and outside the Verilog standard, as well as carrying the danger that synthesis might differ from simulation. To make a **case** *full* it is recommended instead to use a

default statement with dummy assignments to variables for which no latch is expected. In all these cases synthesizer warnings of unintentional latches should be heeded.

A final variation, permitted only in Verilog, is to place the fixed number comparand in the case expression, and the variables in the case items. This case style is illustrated in the *fifosl* design of Chapter 8. It is a situation in which the pragmas given may be necessary since here especially it may not be obvious that the variables in the case items are mutually exclusive and all-inclusive.

5.6   Example: Combinational Modules

As a first example we consider two specifications for a 3-bit prioritizer module. In the left-hand side of Specification #7, the case is full but not parallel. So a prioritizer is simulated and synthesized as expected—Verilog acts on the first line of the case that evaluates to true and ignores the rest. In the right-hand side of the specification the cases are mutually exclusive, hence parallel, and also full, so according to many Verilog manuals this is interpreted as parallel (multiplexer type) logic in simulation. However recent versions of DC and FPGA compilers generate a priority encoder as before! See Problem 5 at the end of the chapter for more specifications of the prioritizer function.

In the next example, Specification #8 ex.v describes a module that extends its input field by various amounts. It will be used later as part of the MIPS200 (sic) processor. The selector cases are drawn from the MIPS200 opcodes. Prioritizer logic will be inserted for the first two cases since these are not parallel. The *ex* unit is not used for the missing case 4'b0000 which will never occur, so a dummy default is used instead of a pseudo-comment to avoid synthesis of an extra unwanted latch.

As a final example, the ALU from Chapter 3 can now be rewritten as shown below in ALU Specification #9. In this ALU the **case** is parallel, so there is no priority logic generated. However there are some unimplemented opcodes. So a pseudo-comment has been included to prevent generation of an extra latch. (In the MIPS specification of Chapter 10 which uses this as a submodule there is already an adder-out latch explicitly included.) On the other hand the information that an unimplemented opcode was somehow encountered would be useful during simulation and test. So another pair of Synopsys pseudo-comments has been inserted to hide the default from the synthesizer! Notice in this

```
module prioritize(request, grant);        module prioritize(request, grant);
  input   [3:1] request;                    input   [3:1] request;
  output [3:1] grant;                        output [3:1] grant;
  reg [3:1] grant;                           reg [3:1] grant;
  always @(request)                          always @(request)
   casez (request)                            casez (request)
      3'b1?? : grant = 3'b100;                  3'b1?? : grant = 3'b100;
      3'b?1? : grant = 3'b010;                  3'b01? : grant = 3'b010;
      3'b??1 : grant = 3'b001;                  3'b001 : grant = 3'b001;
      3'b000 : grant = 3'b000;                  default: grant = 3'b000;
   endcase                                    endcase
endmodule                                  endmodule
```

Specification #7.

```
module ex (ec, Din, Dout);
  parameter n = 16;
  input    [3:0] ec;
  input    [n-1:0] Din;
  output   [n-1:0] Dout;
  reg      [n-1:0] Dout;
  wire     [n-1:0] Din;
  always@(ec or Din)
    casez (ec)
      4'b1111 : Dout = {Din[7:0],8'b0};         // for LUI instruction
      4'b1??? : Dout = {{8{Din[7]}},Din[7:0]};   // for immed & branch
      4'b011? : Dout = {{12{Din[3]}},Din[3:0]};  // for LW, SW
      4'b001? : Dout = {{4{Din[11]}},Din[11:0]}; // for jumps
      4'b0001 : Dout = {{4{Din[11]}},Din[11:0]}; // for trap
      default : Dout = {{4{Din[11]}},Din[11:0]}
    endcase
endmodule
```

Specification #8: Module Ex.

ALU specification that care has been taken to place into the trigger of the **always** statement all of the variables which are read. Any missing ones may also cause unintended latches.

5.7   Flipflops versus Latches

When a **reg** is declared in Verilog or when the synthesizer says it is infering a register or a latch, it is important to know what is being placed in the synthesized result. Assignment statements in procedural code will get implemented by *D-type* latches or flipflops which are capable of storing the binary digit from the data input wire. Figure 5.2 reviews the various kinds of D-type latches and flipflops that may result from synthesis, although of course, the choices may be constrained by the target technology. In particular, if that is a FPGA, there may only be only the edge triggered type available. In the types in the figure, the data will be stored in response to a positive going pulse on the control input. The control is said to be *active high*.

The first type in Figure 5.2(a), called a *latch*, is sufficient for many data retention applications but has the disadvantage that if the value on the data input changes while the enable control remains high, that change "flows through" to the stored value. This could cause race problems if such a flipflop were employed in the feedback path of a sequential machine. To prevent this, the "edge triggered" type in Figure 5.2(b) has been designed (called simply a "flipflop" in the synthesis community). It truly takes a "snapshot" of the data input at the instant of the control rising edge. If logical values are followed through this diagram it can be verified that successive changes in the data will not affect the storage outside of a small interval of time before and after this edge [Mano97]. This time interval will be dependent on the flipflops in the target cell library. It is characterized by the following time properties:

set-up time: The time that the *D* input must remain stable before the clock edge.

hold time: The time that the *D* input must remain stable after the clock edge.

```
`define ADD  4'b0111 // 2's compl add
`define ADDU 4'b0001 // unsigned add
`define SUB  4'b0010 // 2's compl subtract
`define SUBU 4'b0011 // unsigned subtract
`define AND  4'b0100 // bitwise OR
`define OR   4'b0101 // bitwise AND
`define XOR  4'b0110 // bitwise XOR
`define SLT  4'b1010 // set result=1 if less than 2's compl
`define SLTU 4'b1011 // set result=1 if less than unsigned
`define NOP  4'b0000 // do nothing

module alu(func, operand_0, operand_1, result, ovfl);
 parameter n = 16;
 input  [3:0] func;
 input  [n-1:0] operand_0, operand_1;
 output [n-1:0] result;
 output ovfl;
 reg    carry_out, ovfl;
 wire   [n-1:0] operand_0, operand_1;
 reg    [n-1:0] result, tmp;

always @(func or operand_0 or operand_1)
 case(func)
// synopsys full_case
   `ADD:  begin {carry_out, result} = operand_0 + operand_1;
                      ovfl = operand_0[n-1]&operand_1[n-1]&~result[n-1]
                             |~operand_0[n-1]&~operand_1[n-1]&result[n-1];
          end
   `ADDU: {ovfl, result} = operand_0 + operand_1;
   `SUB:  begin {carry_out, result} = operand_1 - operand_0;
                      ovfl = operand_0[n-1]&~operand_1[n-1]&result[n-1]
                         |~operand_0[n-1]&operand_1[n-1]&~result[n-1];
          end
   `SUBU: {ovfl, result} = operand_1 - operand_0;
   `SLT:  begin {carry_out, tmp} = operand_1 - operand_0;
                      ovfl = operand_0[n-1]&~operand_1[n-1]&tmp[n-1]
                             |~operand_0[n-1]&operand_1[n-1]&~tmp[n-1];
                    result = tmp[n-1]^ovfl;
          end
`SLTU: begin {carry_out, tmp} = operand_1 - operand_0; result = carry_out; end
   `OR :  result = operand_0 | operand_1;
   `AND:  result = operand_0 & operand_1;
   `XOR:  result = operand_0 ^ operand_1;
   `NOP:  result = operand_0;
 // synopsys translate_off
    default:  $display(``alu: unimplemented opcode encountered'');
 // synopsys translate_on
    endcase
endmodule
```

Specification #9: ALU.

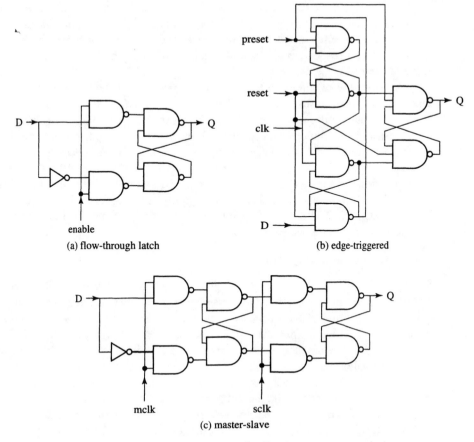

(a) flow-through latch   (b) edge-triggered

(c) master-slave

Figure 5.2 *D Flipflop Types.*

```
module ff_ar(d,clk,reset,Q);
 input d, clk, reset;
 output Q;
 reg Q;
  always @(posedge clk or negedge reset)
   if (!reset) Q <= 0;
   else         Q <= d;
endmodule
```

Specification #10: Flipflop with Asynchronous Reset.

The edge triggered flipflop may be augmented with asynchronous preset or/and asynchronous reset, (all the wires in the figure connected to the preset and reset nets). These inputs, active low, will cause the flipflop to be set or reset respectively at any time, overriding the data and clock lines if these are simultaneously activated. If the asynchronous reset is required, the specification should be written exactly as in Specification #10 above.[2] This positional format is used to indicate to the synthesizer that the signal named

---

[2]Some design groups discourage the use of asynchronous set or reset because they present difficulties for scan insertion (see Chapter 15).

reset is in fact the one to be connected to the asynchronous clear. Then it divines which signal is the clock by a process of elimination, and relates it to the final else clause of the always block. Note the mixed *posedge* and *negedge* that has been included in this specification just to correspond exactly with the diagram of Figure 5.2b where the *clk* is active high and the *reset* is active low.

A third type of flipflop in Figure 5.2(c) is the master-slave. When the data is originally loaded into the first stage, called the *master*, the *slave* stage retains the previous value. If the user codes master and slave registers explicitly then the synthesizer will generate master-slave flipflops with one member of the pair as edge triggered and the other member as a latch. For many target technologies all of this is not necessary, certainly in the context of the FPGA chips used for the examples in this book. In this case if the specification is done in the style that infers edge triggered flipflops, the synthesized result will handle the simultaneous load and sense satisfactorily at gate level. This is reflected in the following examples. The synthesis reports should be checked to confirm that flipflops and not latches have been selected.

5.7.1 *Examples Using Flipflops*

Some simple examples using flipflops are now illustrated. The issues involved in the design of single modules of the type of this section is discussed in somewhat greater detail in Chapter 6 following. So if the reader finds this section a little too succinct then there might be benefit to going to Chapter 6 first and returning to this section afterwards.

Just about the simplest binary counter is described in Specification #11 below. The reset and enable inputs are not in the sensitivity list of the **always** trigger so it is the user's responsibility to make sure that they are stable prior to the rising edge of the clock by more than the set-up time for the flipflops. The reset signal is a synchronous reset because as specified it is active only at the positive going edge of the clock. In the synthesized result it will be gated in through the D input. The carry_out signal can be used to trigger another counter of the same type.

This counter would be synthesized using an incrementer (limited adder) circuit and a register of edge triggered flipflops (Fig. 5.3). Compare this with Problems 2 and 3 at the end of Chapter 3, and the down-counter in Chapter 6.

In Specification #12 a slightly more complex counter is shown. This version has a terminal count parameter instead of waiting until the count rolls over to zero after the count reaches the state of all binary ones. This parameter is *static* because it is fixed in

```
module counter (clk, enable, reset, state, carry_out);
 parameter n = 4;
 input clk, enable, reset;
 output [n-1:0] state;
 output carry_out;
 reg     [n-1:0] state;
 reg carry_out;
 always @(posedge clk)
  if (reset) state <= 0;
  else if (enable) {carry_out,state} <= state + 1;
endmodule
```

Specification #11: Binary Counter.

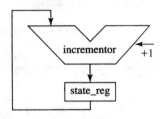

Figure 5.3   *Synthesized Counter.*

```
module countertc(clk, reset, enable, state, carry_out);
 parameter n=4;  // number of binary bits
 parameter r=12; // static range
   input clk, enable, reset;
   output carry_out;
   output [n-1:0] state;
   reg    [n-1:0] state;
   assign carry_out = (state==r-1);
 always @(posedge clk or negedge reset)
   if (~reset) state<=0;
   else begin
        if (enable)
           if (carry_out) state<=0;
           else state<=state+1;
        end
endmodule
```

Specification #12: Counter with Terminal Count.

the specification and cannot be varied during the operation as would a *dynamic* parameter which would need to be fed in through a module input argument. In this case the reset is asynchronous and will be synthesized into the asynchronous reset input shown in Figure 5.2(b) active low. This could be simpler to debug since it is active immediately, instead of waiting for the clock input, which might be slow in coming in a counter chain.

The synthesizer would also insert a comparator to detect the terminal count *r-1*. In this way the carry could be used as the enable of another counter providing that the set-up requirements are met (see the *aclock.v* example in Chapter 12).

A problem with the counters discussed so far is that they are based on rippling, both inside the incrementer and, via the *carry*, to any succeeding counter. Even if an incrementer with the carry-with-less-delay organization of Chapter 3 is employed, it will always be faster to use counters based on shift registers. In these the critical path is limited to the connection from one stage to the next. To build a shift register, some means must be employed to temporarily store each bit while the transition of data is taking place. This implies either master-slave latches as in Figure 5.2(c) or edge triggered flipflops as in Figure 5.1(b). There are a number of ways to use shift registers as counters. The first is a simple ring counter shown in Figure 5.4.

For a count of *n* the ring counter requires *n* master-slave stages as opposed to the $\log_2 n$ stages of a binary counter. But it is preferred in many applications because simpler

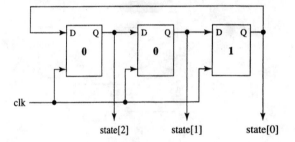

Figure 5.4   *Ring Counter with "One-Hot" Contents.*

```
module ringcount(clk,state);
  input  clk;
  output [2:0] state;
  reg    [2:0] state;
  wire a=state[2], b=state[1], c=state[0];
  wire error = ~a & ~b & ~c | a & b | a & c | b & c;
    always @(posedge clk)
      case (error)
        1'b0: state <= {state[0], state[2:1]};
        1'b1: state <= 3'b001;
        1'bx: state <= 3'b001;
      endcase
endmodule
```

Specification #13: Ring Counter.

decoding at the output can lead to less circuitry overall. Ring counters must be initialized to a condition called *one-hot* in which one and only one of the stages contains a logical '1'. Specification #13 includes logic to initialize or reinitialize the counter should ever the contents become not one-hot:

Apart from the fact that this scheme is limited to fixed $n = 3$, there is also a question in synthesis about the *case 1'bx*, included just to get the simulator started. The synthesizer always assumes that x is false. An approach without such questions is Specification #14 which eschews the *case* for a simple binary *if-else*. This is also more general in that it calls on the not-hot module from earlier in this chapter. To call it with the generalized parameter we have used the #( ) notation of Verilog to give a value to the parameter in the called module. Before moving on we note that there exists a variation called the *switch-tail* or *Johnson* counter which has the last output coming instead from ~Q and doubles the counting capacity to $2n$.

In situations where the order of the count is not important, the most efficient shift register counter is that of the maximal or near-maximal length *linear feedback shift register* (FSR) [Golomb 67]. For certain values of the number of stages, n, it is possible, using only a single **xor** gate, to cause it to cycle through all of the possible state combinations save the one with all binary *zero's*. The *fsr* must be intialized with a *seed* state which can be any member of the maximal sequence. Here we use the bitvector of all 1's. For values n for which maximal length sequences do not exist, it is still possible to obtain a near-maximal length sequence which is usually more than 99.9% of the maximal [Clark94].

```
`include ``nothot.v´´
module ringcount(clk,state);
 parameter n = 4;
 input clk;
 output [n-1:0] state;
  reg    [n-1:0] state;

  nothot #(n) NH(state, onehot);

  always @(posedge clk)
    if (onehot) state <= {state[0], state[n-1:1]};
    else         state <= 1;
endmodule
```

Specification #14: Improved Ring Counter.

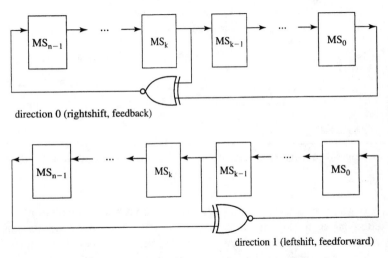

direction 0 (rightshift, feedback)

direction 1 (leftshift, feedforward)

Figure 5.5 *Operations of the Bidirectional FSR.*

In the example which is now given there is one other augmentation, this is a bidirectional shift register corresponding roughly to an up-down counter. In the bidirectional FSR, if the shift direction is reversed at any point, the identical states leading to that point will be retraced. The principle is illustrated in the schematic of Figure 5.5 and Specification #15. Of course if it were desired to retrieve intermediate binary counts from an FSR, some amount of additional decoding circuitry would be required.

It turns out that it is also possible to modify the register-incrementer counter model to actually reduce the critical delay to the equivalent of a single stage. This is done by progressively partitioning the counter into smaller ones at the least significant end so that the carry inputs to the upper counters are less frequent and they are given more time for the ripple [Tenca97]. The specification of this is left for an exercise at the end of Chapter 8.

A final example of a master-slave based module is included here because it is also a component which will be used later. The intended function of this module is as a data background generator (*dbg*) for use in testing embedded memories with multiple bit word lengths. A succession of data backgrounds (and their bit complements) can be generated

```
module fsrb(clk,direction,enable,reset,state);
 // maximal length bidirectional feedback shift register
 // will retrace previous states when direction is changed
  parameter n=4, k=1;//insert manually from table of trinomials below
 // (*indicates non-primitive: period not maximal but very close)
 // n = 2, 3, 4, 5, 6, 7, 8, 9, 10, 11, 12, 13, 14, 15, 16, 17, 18, 19,
        20, 21, 22, 23, 24, 25, 26, 27, 28, 29, 30, 31, 32
 // k = 1, 1, 1, 2, 1, 1,*3, 4, 3, 2, *1, *3, *1, 1, 7, 3, 7, *6,
        3, 2, 1, 5, *5, 3, *5, *8, 3, 2, *7, 3, *15
 input  clk, reset, direction, enable;
 output [n-1:0] state;
 reg    [n-1:0] newstate, state;

always @(state or direction)
   if (direction==0) // feedback, right shifting
        newstate <= {(state[k]^state[0]), state[n-1:1]};
   else    // feedforward, left shifting
        newstate <= {state[n-2:0], (state[k-1]^state[n-1])};

 always @(posedge clk)
   begin
     if (reset)            state <= -1;
     else if (enable) state <= newstate;
   end
endmodule
```

Specification #15: Counter (Bidirectional Feedback Shift Register).

such that any two bits occur in all four possible state combinations. In each state the asserted or negated signal can be steered to the output *Tout* under the control of the *invc* input. When not in test mode the circuit can be used as an ordinary register, storing from *Din* under the control of the *loadc* signal. For example for $n = 8$, after initialization the bitvectors shown in Specification #16 would be generated in sequence upon successive clockings of the *next* control signal.

5.8 Memory

In Verilog memories may be declared as arrays of **reg**'s with the decoder as implicit. Unless special directions are given to the synthesizer, such memories will end up as arrays of edge triggered flipflops (very expensive), or arrays of latches (only slightly less expensive). This is recommended only in small doses for such purposes as embedded scratchpad or small prototypes for test. For synthesis to FPGAs of memories of size 16×4 or bigger, the RAMs making up the truth tables of the logical elements can be enlisted into use for this purpose (see Chapter 14). Finally for synthesis to FPGAs with embedded RAMs, we could go a lot higher, up to 800 K bits per chip as of the fourth quarter of 1999. If this is not available then it might be better to use industry RAMs and use the synthesis only for the surrounding glue logic.

```
// generates vectors: 01010101
//                     00110011
//                     00001111
//                     11111111

module dbg(clk, init, invert, next, out, outinv);
 parameter n = 8; // wordsize
   input clk, init, next, invc;
   output [n-1:0] out, outinv;
   reg [n-1:0] state;
   integer i;
 assign out = (invert) ? state : ~state;
 assign outinv = (invert) ? ~state : state;
always @(posedge clk)
   begin
     if (init)       state <= {n/2{2'b01}};
     else if (next) for (i=0; i<n; i=i+2)
     begin state[i] <= state[i/2]; state[i+1] <= state[i/2]; end
   end
endmodule
```

Specification #16: Data Background Generator.

```
module aram(addr, data_in, we, data_out);
 parameter n=7, a=3, w=4; // number of words, addrsize, wordsize
 input we;
 input    [a-1:0] addr;
 input    [w-1:0] data_in;
 output [w-1:0] data_out;
 reg [ws-1:0] data_out;
 reg [ws-1:0] ram_data [n-1:0];

 always @(addr or data_in;
   if (we) ram_data[addr]<=data_in;
   else    data_out <= ram_data[addr];
endmodule
```

Specification #17: Asynchronous RAM.

We shall look at two RAMs, asynchronous and synchronous. This will serve to demonstrate the difference on a specification that is much smaller and simpler than readers will find in most libraries.

First the asynchronous RAM (Specification #17). It is continuously reading at the current address until the write enable WE is asserted, in which case a write is initiated.

In contrast, in a synchronous RAM (Specification #18), there is a definite cycle under the control of some incoming clock signal. The write enable control (*we*), the memory select (*slct*), input address (*addr*), and input data (*data_in*) must be guaranteed stable for the set-up time before the rising edge of this clock arrives.

In this variation the read-out word has been clocked into a buffer register at the output. This is roughly equivalent to the synchronous *iuor* RAM generated by the Altera

```
module ram(addr, clk, cslct, data_in, we, data_out);
 parameter nw=7, as=3, ws=4; // number of words, addrsize, wordsize
   input   clk, cslct, we; // chip select, write enable
   input   [as-1:0] addr;
   input   [ws-1:0] data_in;
   output  [ws-1:0] data_out;
   reg     [ws-1:0] data_out;
   reg     {ws-1:0] ram_data [nw-1:0];
     always @(posedge clk)
       if (cslct)  if (we) ram_data[addr] <= data_in;
                   else            data_out <= ram_data[addr];
endmodule
```

Specification #18: Synchronous RAM.

```
module atpr (D_in, raddr, waddr, we, D1_out, D2_out);
 parameter nw=7, as=3, ws=4; // number of words, addrsize, wordsize
  input   we;
  input   [as-1:0] raddr, waddr;
  input   [ws-1:0] D_in;
  output  [ws-1:0] D1_out, D2_out;
  reg     [ws-1:0] D1_out, D2_out;
  reg     [ws-1:0] tpr_data [n-1:0];

  always @(D_in or we or waddr or raddr)
    if (we) begin if(waddr!=0) tpr_data[waddr] <= D_in; end
    else
      begin
       if (raddr==0) D1_out<=0; else D1_out<=tpr_data[raddr];
       if (waddr==0) D2_out<=0; else D2_out<=tpr_data[waddr];
      end
endmodule
```

Specification #19: Asynchronous Two-Port RAM.

genmem program, which has the address input unclocked and the data output clocked (see Section 14.2). The embedded array blocks used for memory in the Altera flex10K chips have an output latch included for this purpose. The question of whether an implicit decoder (as here) or an explicit decoder is best used will depend again on the target technology and the available libraries. In general the simplest formulation for a specification is preferred. This is certainly true if embedded array blocks are being used.

The next example is a *two-port* RAM (Specification #19). True custom integrated two-port RAMs have the two address select lines fed to each of the cells in the array. Other versions are possible using duplicated arrays or a single array time multiplexed on a double frequency clock (as in the Synopsys and Altera libraries). One port is usually restricted to read-only (of course, two different contents cannot be written into the same row anyway). The particular two-port ram shown here[3] is specialized for the register bank of the MIPS processor architecture example of Chapter 10, in that the first word is read-only and always zero.

---

[3]In the Synopsys library this would be called a three-port RAM, to distinguish it from the version in which only one of the ports can be read and the other one only written.

Unless embedded RAMs are available, this memory array will synthesized into flipflops. To cause latches instead the sensitivity list should have only signal levels—**always** @(clk or WE or data_in) as in the asynchronous *aram* and *atpr*. Of course in the case that common FPGAs are the target, then the available registers are synchronous flipflops anyway.

5.9 Conclusion

This chapter has covered the procedural specification style which comprises the most important part of the Verilog subset as used for synthesis. The Verilog language requires procedural assignments to be directed to registers and most of the examples of this chapter have been sequential machines. Nevertheless procedural specifications can sometimes result in combinational networks. The present generation of synthesizers has been built to optimize the registers out whenever possible and so counteract what is a limitation of the language definition.

At this point in the course and book students may get a little glassy eyed at all the myriad qualifications which synthesis has brought to hardware design languages. So the next chapter steps back and takes a more liesurely approach to the methodology behind some of the modules we have been seeing.

Exercises

5.1. List three different ways that concurrent assignments can be described in Verilog. For each note whether this construct is synthesizable.

5.2. List three different mechanisms for effecting sequentiality in Verilog. For each note whether this construct is synthesizable. You may use short fragments of code if necessary to illustrate your answers.

5.3. Demonstrate that the circuit for the edge-triggered flipflop given in Figure 5.2 fulfills the required behavior; for example, at a positive edge of the signal *clk*, the value of D is transfered to Q: then Q is insensitive to further changes in D until the next positive going edge of *clk* occurs. Ignore the lines from the asynchronous inputs *preset* and *reset* (gray lines in the figure).

a. It used to be that the edge-triggered flipflops were composed from the simpler SR latch and JK flipflop. Now, however, some synthesis tools allow only the edge triggered D-type and ban combinational feedback (such as feedback of gate outputs to gate inputs without a clocked D-type flipflop in between). Show circuits for the clocked JK and set dominant flipflop types that would be satisfactory to these synthesis tools.

Truth Table for jk and sd Flipflops.

Q^n	S	R	Q_{jk}^{n+1}	Q_{sd}^{n+1}
0	0	0	0	0
0	0	1	0	0
0	1	0	1	1
0	1	1	1	1
1	0	0	1	1
1	0	1	0	0
1	1	0	1	1
1	1	1	0	1

5.4. The classical model of a sequential machine has feedback loops broken by latches either in the form of edge sensitive flipflops or two-phase level-sensitive clocking. Illustrate the textual equivalents by modifying the following Verilog fragment (unsynthesizable as written):

```
always while (x < y)
           x = x + 1;
```

5.5. Write a parameterized procedural specification for the 16-input prioritizer. Hint: One way is to use a named block similar to Specification #5 of the comparator in this chapter. Use a similar testbench as in **Problem** 3.14 of Chapter 3.

5.6. Write Verilog fragments which would cause the synthesis of
   a. A latch with asynchronous reset
   b. A flipflop with synchronous reset
   Explain why latches are not be suitable to in the feedback path of the classical model of a state machine.

5.7. For the following two Verilog fragments:

```
...reg A,B,C;              ...reg A,B,C;
always @(posedge clk)      always @(posedge clk)
 begin                      begin
 A=C; B=A; C=B;             C<=B; B<=A; A<=C;
 end ...                    end ...
```

   a. Draw a gate schematic for the expected synthesis result.
   b. In each case, is the ordering of the assignments significant?
   c. If the ordering of both were made the same as that of the second one, would the synthesis results then be identical?

5.8. For the following asynchronous Verilog fragment:
   a. Sketch a schematic of the synthesized hardware.
   b. Repeat part (a) for the synchronous version.
   c. Repeat part (b) with the "=" assignments replaced by "<=" assignments.
   In each case:
   i. State whether the order of the assignments matters.
   ii. Identify what should be the data types to which the assignments are made.

```
always @ (x or y or z)
 begin
  w = y & z;
  u = w | x;
 end
```

5.9. Write a parameterized specification for a priority encoder.

5.10. Sketch the expected outcome of synthesis for the following three source fragments:

| ```
wire A, B, a, b, c;
reg out;
always@(A or B or a or b
       or c)
  if(A&&B)      out = a;
  elseif(A&&!B) out = b;
  elseif(!A)    out = c;
``` | ```
wire A, B, a, b, c;
reg out;
always@(A or B or a or b
       or c)
  if(A&&B)       out = a;
  elseif(A&&!B)  out = b;
  elseif(!A&&!B) out = c;
``` | ```
wire A, B, a, b, c;
reg out;
always@(A or B or a or b
       or c)
  if(A&&B)       out = a;
  elseif(A||B)   out = b;
  elseif(!A&&!B) out = c;
``` |

5.11. What might be the difficulties for synthesis from the following code fragments?

| ```
always @(posedge clk)
  casez (op)
    2'b1? : // assignment block1
    2'b?1 : // assignment block2
  endcase
``` | ```
always @(posedge clk)
  if (push)  begin
             ptr  = ptr + 1;
             Dout = RAM[ptr];
             end
``` |

5.12. Sketch the gate circuits you would expect to result from synthesis of the following three Verilog fragments. What Z might result if say $s = 3'b110$, for each temperature, after simulation and after synthesis?

| ```
module one_warm (s,A,B,C,Z)
  input A,B,C;
  output Z;
  input [2:0] s;
  always @(s or A or B
         or C)
  case (s)
    3'b100 : Z<=A;
    3'b010 : z<=B;
    3'b001 : Z<=C;
  endcase
endmodule
``` | ```
module
one_notsohot(s,A,B,C,Z)
  input A,B,C; output Z;
  input [2:0] s;
  always @(s or A or B
         or C)
  case (s)
    s[2] : Z<=A;
    s[1] : Z<=B;
    s[0] : Z<=C;
  endcase
endmodule
``` | ```
module one_tepid (s,A,B,C,Z)
  input A,B,C; output Z;
  input [2:0] s;
  always @(s or A or B
         or C)
  case (s)
    4 : Z<=A;
    2 : Z<=B;
    1 : Z<=C;
    0,3,5,7: Z<=1'bx;
  endcase
endmodule
``` |

5.13. Write a Verilog fragment that captures the logic represented in the following truth table. You do not need to minimize the logic.

A[1:0]	B	C	Next1	Next2
11	x	x	1	1
10	1	1	0	1
01	0	0	0	0
00	1	x	1	1
otherwise			1	0

5.14. Change the logic design specified in Exercise 5.13 so as to capture the following synchronous truth table, where next1 and next2 change only after each positive clock edge.

A[1:0]	B	C	Next1	Next2
11	x	x	1	same
10	1	1	0	1
01	0	0	same	0
00	1	x	1	1
otherwise			same	same

5.15. Write a Verilog fragment that correctly describes the synchronous logic specified in the following truth table for a J-K (like) flipflop, where Q+ refers to the value of the output Q after the clock edge.

J	K	Q+
0	0	Q
1	0	1
0	1	0
1	1	~Q

5.16. Sketch a logic schematic equivalent to the following code:

```
reg E1, E2, E3, E4;
reg A, B, C, D;
reg [3:0] F;
always@(posedge clock)
  begin
    if(E4) A = 0;
      else A = B;
    C = A;
    D = B;
  end
always@(E1 or E2 or E3 or F)
  casez (F(2:1])
    2'b0? : B = E1;
    2'b?1 : B = E2;
    default : B = E3;
  endcase
assign E4 = E1? E2:E3;
```

5.17. An embedded module has unidirectional ports for operation activation (*remove*, *insert*) and status return (*empty, full*). If the surrounding environment needs information from the status return in order to determine the choice of the next operation, what would be the minimum clock period for the design in terms of common target cell library parameters?

5.18. The following are two different specs for a read-only table lookup. Discuss what hardware you would expect to be generated in each case if the table bits themselves are synthesized to flipflops. What if the specification included a write operation in addition to the read? How might synthesis be better directed if the table size increased?

```
module tablelookup1(read_enable, ptr,      module tablelookup2(read_enable, ptr,
                    outbit)                                    outbit)
input read_enable;                         input read_enable;
input [4:0] ptr;                           input [4:0] ptr;
reg [31:0] table1;                          reg table2 [31:0];
    always @(read_enable)                      always @(read_enable)
        outbit <= table1[ptr];                     outbit <= table2[ptr];
endmodule                                  endmodule
```

5.19. As part of an investigation into what difference an implicit or explicit decoder on a register bank makes to the synthesized result:

    a. Write Verilog specifications for a decoder in procedural behavioral style. This should be generally parameterized. Write a testbench for the decoder and test using a simulator. Choose a small test version such as 3:8.

    b. Write two parameterized versions of a RAM memory module, one with an implicit decoder and the other explicit with an instantiation of the above decoder.

    c. Write a single testbench for the two RAMs and test using the simulator.

5.20. Write a specification for a parameterized prioritizer module.

5.21. Write a Verilog specification for a fast 64-bit up/down partitioned up/down-counter in the style of Ercegovac and Tenca [Tenca97], [Stan98]. Twisted tail ring counter components as well as register-incrementer components are required for this.

References

[Golomb67] Golomb, S. W., *Shift Register Sequences,* Holden-Day, 1967

[Clark94] Clark, D. W., and Weng, L.-J., "Maximal and Near-Maximal Shift Register Sequences: Efficient Event Counters and Easy Discrete Logarithms," *I.E.E.E. Computer,* May 1994, pp. 560–568

[Tenca97] Tenca, A. F., and Ercegovac, M. D., "Synchronous up/down binary counter for LUT FPGA's with counting frequency independent of counter size," Intl. Symposium on FPGA, November 1997

[Stan98] Stan, M. R., Tanca, A. F., and Ergovac, M. D., "Long and fast up/down counters," *IEEETC* 47:7 July 1998, pp. 722–735

Chapter Six

Design Approaches for Single Modules

6.1 Introduction

Verilog is a powerful and flexible language. In addition, it has many similarities with 'C'. As a result, novice designers have a great tendency to use Verilog to capture behavioral intent and then try to make that intent look like synthesizable code. The results tend to be nonfunctional or inefficient designs that take a long time to debug. A far better approach is to spend effort to first determine the hardware structure and then capture that structure in code. The main purpose of this chapter is to teach the novice designer how to use and be successful with this approach.

With respect to sequential machines the specification style of this chapter is sometimes called *explicit*, to distinguish it from the *implicit* styles of Chapter 8 and those following. Although the explicit style is often recommended for beginning designers, both style families have their place, and the eventual style adopted by designer will be both a matter of preference as well as depending on the characteristics of a particular design project.

6.2 Basic Design Methodology

Modern designs tend to be very complex, consisting of thousands to millions of gates. Yet, in general, the first prototype of a silicon chip either works completely or has only a handful of bugs. First pass success is highly desirable as repairing and reimplementing a design is very time consuming, and time-to-market is a key factor in the eventual profitability of a new system. If the part being built is a CMOS chip, the fabrication facility will take eight weeks or more to return the chip after design submission. Even though the reimplementation delay is not as long if the design is implemented with an FPGA, it is a lot easier to debug a large design at the Verilog stage than at the hardware stage.

For this reason, good design teams enforce a disciplined approach to their design. This is usually referred to as a methodology—a method or process to be used during

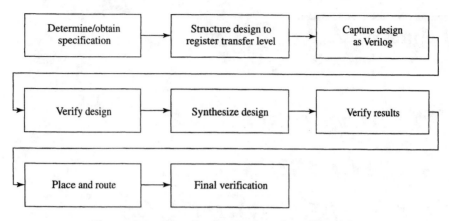

Figure 6.1   *Steps in the Design of Small Modules.*

design. This chapter is going to emphasize a simple methodology to be used for module level design. This process is summarized in Figure 6.1 and described in detail.

1. *Determine or obtain the specification.* The specification details the behavior and interface of each module being designed. This stage is discussed more in Section 6.3.
2. *Structure the design to the register transfer level.* This is the 'logic design phase' when the designer determines a "block diagram" for the design, including registers, functions of combinational logic, etc. A set of techniques for tackling this stage is the subject of Section 6.4.
3. *Capture the design as Verilog.* If the structuring step is done well, then this step is very straightforward, as described in Section 6.5.
4. *Verify the design.* A critical element in obtaining a working prototype is a spending a lot of time verifying the design via Verilog simulation. In today's chips, sometimes over half of the project resources are spent on verification. This topic is important enough to rate its own chapter (Chapter 7).
5. *Synthesize the design.* The synthesis tools are used to transform the Verilog design into a gate level design. Synthesis is not just a black box, the designer has to be aware of what synthesis tools can, and cannot, do well. The partitioning of the design into Verilog modules also has a big impact on synthesis. These issues are discussed more in Chapters 8 through 11.
6. *Verify the results of synthesis.* Every tool has bugs and thus the output has to be checked. A combination of gate-level simulation, timing analysis, and other techniques, are used to verify that the design produced by the synthesis tool is correct and consistent with the Verilog RTL design.
7. *Place and route.* This stage is often referred to as "physical design" because it is where the actual layout of the chip is determined. The gates in the chip are assigned to positions on the chip (placement) and then connected together with wires (routing).
8. *Final verification.* Before sending the chip to the fabrication facility, or burning the FPGA, a number of final checks are done to make sure that the chip is wired up correctly, is manufacturable, etc. The nature of these checks are beyond the scope of this book.

6.3   The Specification

The specification details the behavior and interface of each module in the design. It is a very important step. Many chips fail in the marketplace because the feature set was not well thought through. In addition, a surprisingly large number of chips pass stand-alone functional test but do not work when inserted in the system board because the chip interfaces were incorrectly or incompletely specified. The specification covers multiple levels of the design, all the way from the chip level functionality down to module level timing. In order to speed up time-to-market, detailed design often starts while the specification is still being formulated. Thus the module designer has to cope with a changing specification and also often plays a role in formulating its details.

At the module level, the specification should include the following:

- A description of the top-level behavior of the module
- A description of all its inputs and outputs, their timing, and constraints
- Performance requirements and constraints

Ideally, the top-level behavior of the chip and each module should be captured in a high-level language, such as C++, Java, Matlab, or Specification and Description Language (SDL—often used in communications system design). Such a high-level model is useful for a number of reasons. First, by being able to simulate and verify the behavioral specification, fewer bugs will be introduced at this level. Second, the results of these simulations can later be checked against the results of the Verilog RTL simulations. This comparison will give the module designer greater assurance that the design is correct. Finally, this high-level module could be used in place of some of the Verilog RTL modules when simulating the entire design at the chip level. Since the high-level language description simulates a lot faster than a Verilog description of the same module, final chip-level simulation can be speeded up by simulating only critical portions in Verilog, and the rest in a high-level language. Verilog's Programming Language Interface (PLI) is a useful mechanism for performing this type of co-simulation (see Chapter 17).

Note that the structure of the high-level language description of the module does not have to relate to the internal hardware about to be designed. However, also note that one cannot turn 'C' into Verilog simply by putting an `always @(posedge clock)` in front of blocks of 'C' code!

6.4   Structuring the Design

This is a very important step that neophyte designers are tempted to skip or combine with the actual coding. When this step is given short shrift, the resulting design is often buggy and inefficient in performance and/or area. Often the time saved in avoiding effort in the structuring step is more than compensated for by the time spent debugging or improving the design. The sub-steps are as follows:

1. *Determine the control strategy.* An important rule to follow is:

Clearly separate Control from Datapath.

The elements of the design that operate on the data (the *datapath*) must be clearly separated from the portion of the design that determines the sequence of events in the datapath (the *controller*). The datapath and controller are joined by clearly identified *control signals* and *status signals*. Together, these control and status signals are referred to as *control points* in the following chapters. Typically the controller consists of some combination of Finite State Machines and counters (or possibly a microcode ROM so as to avoid an overly large FSM). The datapath consists of a number of registers and combinational logic. The controller determines the sequence of events that take place on the datapath. It controls this sequence of events via the control lines. The datapath processes the data and reports a number of status bits back to the controller.

There are a number of key elements that must be considered when determining the control strategy and sequence, including the following:

- *What is the Reset strategy?* Every chip has a global reset. Reset usually becomes active on power up and when the reset button is pushed. Typically active low, the Reset signal sets the contents of various registers to a predetermined value to put the chip into a known state. Which registers to reset will be illustrated in the examples which follow in subsequent chapters.

- *What is to be performed in each clock period?* The purpose of the controller is to determine what events are to be performed on the datapath during each clock period.

- *Pay special attention to transitions.* Transitions between different modes of operation, for example, the start and finish of sets of operations, requires special attention.

2. *Determine the Register Transfer Level structure of the design.* At this stage, the following pieces of the design must be explicitly identified and labeled:

- *Module inputs and outputs.* Identify, name, and determine the function of each input and output signal.

- *Registers and register outputs.* Identify each register and give a signal name to its output(s). Obviously, the purpose of each register must be clear in the designer's head. Generally a register is necessary whenever a value has to be preserved across one or more clock edges. In most designs each register is clocked once every clock cycle. Usually it is dangerous to mix together registers that are clocked every clock cycle with registers that are clocked less or more frequently. There are several reasons why this practice is dangerous. First, it complicates synthesis, the designer will have to explicitly identify the multi-clock cycle registers. Second, it complicates the design. Let's say one register that is clocked every cycle is feeding another register that is clocked every other cycle, through some combinational logic. Then there is a requirement that the first register must hold its outputs stable for two clock periods to permit the second register to have the correct inputs when it is ready to latch. Similarly, asynchronous (unclocked or self-timed) design is not supported by commercial synthesis tools.

- *Combinational logic blocks and their functions.* Identify the blocks of logic, including arithmetic units, multiplexors, comparators, deselectors, coders, decoders, etc. Not a lot of detail is needed at this stage—you do not design these blocks down to the gate level.

During the RTL structuring phase, it is important to ensure that these control issues are properly addressed. However, above all, the following rule must always be obeyed:

Always design before coding.

Flipflops and Associated Input Logic

```
always @(posedge clock)
  case (sel)
    0 : E <= D + B;
    1 : E <= B;
  endcase
```

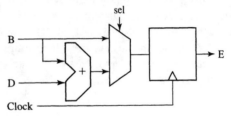

Simple Combinational Logic

```
assign H = C|F;
```

Complex Combinational Logic

```
always @(A or B or C)
  case (A)
    2'b00 : D = B;
    2'b01 : D = C;
    2'b10 : D = 1'b0;
    2'b11 : D = 1'b1;
  endcase
```

Figure 6.2   *Correspondence between Verilog and Hardware Being Modeled.*

3. *Capture the design as Verilog.* If the above steps are done correctly, then this step is straightforward, as different groupings of logic can be mapped onto groups of Verilog RTL descriptions with fairly unique mappings. The correspondence between different types of logic and their Verilog single or compound statement equivalents are illustrated using simple examples is given in Figure 6.2.
   - Edge-triggered flipflops and their associated input logic are built using procedural blocks containing `always @(posedge clock)` statements as was discussed in Section 5.6. Optionally, `@(posedge clock)` can also be used. Remember, every variable assigned in a procedural block triggered by a statement of the type `always @(posedge clock)` will become the output of a flipflop when synthesized.
   - Level sensitive latches (and associated input logic), if used, are built using procedural blocks headed with `always @(clock)` statements. (Latches are not illustrated in Figure 6.2 as latch usage is rare in modern design.)
   - Simple combinational logic is built using continuous assignment statements.
   - More complex combinational logic is built using procedural blocks that do not contain 'clock' in the timing sensitivity list.

   In general, these are the only types of construct that are needed in order to capture a design at the Register Transfer Language level.

Note how the explicit parallelism of hardware is captured. Since each procedural block or continuous assignment statement in Verilog executes independently of each other, by mapping groups of gates onto different blocks or statements, we are modeling each group of gates independent of the other groups.

Now two designs are used to illustrate steps 1 to 3 above, with an emphasis on the structuring step.

6.5   Design Example 1 – A Simple Down Counter

Counters are often used to count events or clock ticks so as to cause control lines to toggle at certain pre-arranged times. Fundamentally, a counter is a simple version of a finite state machine (FSM), in which the next state is simply the current state plus +/– X, often +/–1. In this section, a simple decrement (down) counter will be designed from specification through to verification.

6.5.1   *Specification*

For this module, the specification will be conveyed by a simple document identifying the module and specifying the behavior of the inputs and outputs. A simplified specification document is depicted in Figure 6.3. In this case, the specification only describes behavior, normally timing and other issues will also be addressed.

Count Down Timer

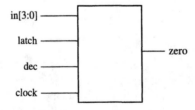

Overall Function

A count down with the following functions. When 'latch' is high, the value 'in' is loaded into the timer. When 'dec' is high, the internal value is decremented by one every clock period. The count down stops at zero, whereupon 'zero' goes high. The internal count down value stays at 0 then until the counter is reloaded.

Inputs

clock: Clock, frequency varies
   in: Initial number loaded into counter
latch: When latch is high, the counter is loaded from 'in'
  dec: Decrement the counter when 'dec' is high

Outputs

zero: Goes high when count reaches zero. Stays high until latch goes high.

Figure 6.3   *Specification Document for Count Down Timer.*

Step 1. Identify inputs and outputs

Step 2. Identify registers

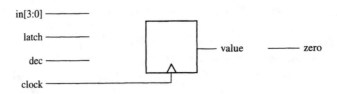

Step 3. Specify combinational logic

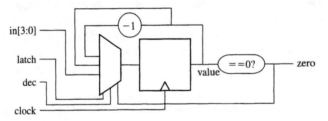

Figure 6.4   *A Sketch of the Structure of the Design at Each Stage.*

6.5.2   *Determine the Control Strategy*

In this case, there is no need to go through identifying the control strategy of this module, due to its simplicity.

6.5.3   *Determine the RTL Structure of the Design*

There are three steps in this stage, illustrated as a sequence in Figure 6.4. These steps are as follows:

1. *Identify the inputs and outputs.* These come directly from the specification.
2. *Determine what registers are needed and name their outputs.* In this case, this decision is straightforward. The current value of the count must be registered so as to preserve it across clock edges. In addition, the fact that the count value is fed back through the subtractor that produces it also dictates that a register is needed. Feedback of combinational logic is never permitted because that essentially creates a race condition. Consider what would happen without the register (Figure 6.5). The count would cycle down to zero as fast as the logic would permit. This point is

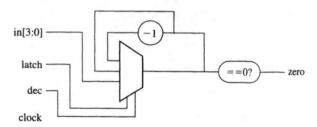

Figure 6.5   *With No Register in the Feedback Path, This Works Incorrectly.*

worth emphasizing and generalizing: *A register must always break feedback loops in a design.*

3. *Specify the function of the combinational logic.* In this case, we need a subtractor, a multiplexor, and some simple logic to produce the zero flag. Note the details are not specified, because at this stage, we are just producing a sketch.

6.5.4 *Capture the Design As Verilog*

Once the Register Transfer Level design is complete, capturing the design as Verilog is almost a straightforward translation of design to Verilog construct, as follows:

Registered outputs and their associated logic are described in procedural blocks starting with **always** @(posedge clock). In this case, the flipflops storing the count, the input multiplexor and the subtractor are captured in Verilog as in the first box:

```
always @(posedge clock)
  begin
    if (latch)value <= in;
    else if (dec && !zero) value <= value - 1´b1;
  end
```

Note, since the procedural block contains only one statement, the **begin** and **end** are not strictly necessary here. This implements the following hardware: A register with an output called 'value'; a priority-selector (latch has priority over dec and zero since the **if** statement is always executed if latch = 1, no matter the value of dec and zero) that connects to the data input of the flipflops, and a subtract-by-1 unit connected to one of the inputs to the selector. This logic could also have been implemented with a **casez** statement as in the next box:

```
always @(posedge clock)
  casez ({latch, dec, zero})
    3´b1?? : value <= in;
    3´b1?10: value <= value - 1´b1;
  endcase
```

Simple combinational logic is best captured as a continuous assignment statement. In this case, the logic that produces the 'zero' flag is captured in Verilog as follows:

```
assign zero = ~|value;
```

More complex combinational logic is captured in procedural blocks with no clock in the sensitivity list. In this example, this was not necessary.

Putting it all together, including variable declarations and appropriate comments to describe the module, the final module was as follows:

```
module counter (clock, in, latch, dec, zero);
  input     clock;/* clock */
  input  [3:0] in;/* input initial count */
  input     latch;/* `latch input` */
  input       dec;/* decrement */
  output     zero;/* zero flag */
  reg [3:0] value;/* current count value */
  wire    zero;

// Count Flipflops with input multiplexor and subtractor
  always @(posedge clock)
    if (latch) value <= in;
    else if (dec && !zero) value <= value - 1'b1;

  assign zero = ~|value;// combinational logic for zero flag
endmodule // counter
```

Down counter with Zero Flag.

6.5.5   *Verify Correctness of the Design*

Generally about half of the effort in design goes into verifying correctness. A test fixture must be written to determine if the design is correct. Verification approaches will be discussed more in Chapters 7 and 15. Shown on the next page is a simple test fixture to verify only the basic features in the above design. It is not a full verification of functionality.

As all of the syntax features included in this testbench are illustrated elsewhere in this book, a detailed review of this code will not be conducted here. However, the waveforms produced by this code are shown in Figure 6.6, and the reader should note the following:

- An **initial** statement is used as the testbench needs to start executing when the simulation starts.
- Delay (#) statements are used to determine when input vectors change.
- Correct behavior of the module being tested is checked within the test fixture. There is no need to view the waveforms if no errors are reported.
- The use of the **always** statement to invert the clock every five ns.

```
module test_fixture;
 reg clock, latch, dec;
 reg [3:0] in;
 wire zero;
 include (``count.v´´);
 initial // this following block executed only once
  begin
   // The next two lines are Cadence-specific
   $shm_open(``all.shm´´); // to save waveforms
   $shm_probe (``AS´´); // for Cadence waveform viewer
   // initialize inputs
   clock = 0; latch = 0; dec = 0;
   in = 4´b0010;
   // latch in input `2´
   #11 latch = 1; // wait 11 ns
   #10 latch = 0; // wait 10 ns
   #10 dec = 1; // start decrementing
   // It should take two clock cycles to reach `0´
   #10 if (zero==1´b1) $display(``count: Error in Zero flag\n´´);
   #10 if (zero==1´b0) $display(``count: Error in Zero flag\n´´);
   #20 $shm_close();  // close data base - Cadence specific
   $finish; // finished with simulation
  end

always #5 clock = ~clock;// 10ns clock
   // instantiate modules -- call this counter u1
   counter u1(.clock(clock), .in(in), .latch(latch),  .dec(dec), .zero(zero));
endmodule // test_fixture
```

Test Fixture for Down Counter.

Note in Figure 6.6 that the outputs of the flipflops do not respond to changes in their inputs until after the clock edge. This might seem obvious, but it is a common source of confusion to novice designers.

6.6   Example 2 — Unsigned Parallel-Serial Multiplier

The goals of this example are as follows:

- To illustrate the steps involved in structuring on a more complex design
- To illustrate some clock to clock timing issues
- To show how the 'control' and 'datapath' are clearly separated and identified

The example design is an unsigned parallel serial multiplier. Before proceeding with the design, it is necessary to review the basic parallel serial multiplication algorithm. This review will be used in place of a detailed specification in this example. Consider the example of multiplying two 4-bit numbers:

```
Multiplicand: 1011 (11 in base 10)
Multiplier:   1011 (11 in base 10)
```

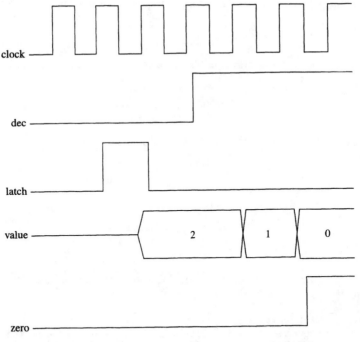

Figure 6.6   *Waveforms Produced by Test Fixture and Counter.*

The product is formed by a series of four adds. At each stage, the multiplicand is added to the high order 4-bits of the product if the least significant bit of the multiplier is 1 or zero is added to the product if the least significant bit of the multiplier is 0. The multiplier and multiplicand are then both shifted to the right.

The first step in the example is to clear the product register:

Product: 0000 0000

Since the least significant bit (lsb) of the multiplier is '1', the multiplicand is added to the high-order 4-bits of the product in the first cycle to give the result:

```
Multiplicand:    1011
Product:         0000 0000
New Product:     01011 0000
```

Note how the carry-out of the sum is included in the add. To finish the first cycle, the multiplier and product are both shifted to the right:

```
Multiplier:      101
Product:         0101 1000
```

In the second cycle, the lsb of the multiplier is 1, so the multiplicand is added again to the product:

```
Multiplicand:    1011
Product:         0101 1000
New Product:     10000 1000
```

The carry-out is 1 this time. The multiplier and product are again both shifted to the right:

```
Multiplier:   10
Product:    1000 0100
```

In the third cycle, the lsb of the multiplier is 0, so zero is added to the product:

```
Zero:        0000
Product:     1000 0100
New Product: 01000 0100
```

The multiplier and product are again both shifted to the right:

```
Multiplier:    1
Product:    0100 0010
```

In the final cycle, the multiplicand is added again:

```
Multiplicand: 1011
Product:      0100 0010
New Product:  01111 0010
```

The multiplier and product are both shifted to the final time and the 8-bit result is left in the product:

```
Multiplier:
Product:     0111 1001   (121 in base 10, as expected)
```

The design procedure of a multiplier that can execute this algorithm is described next.

6.6.1 *Determine the Control Strategy*

Since the multiplier requires nine steps (one step to load the required registers and eight steps to do the actual multiplication), a counter-based controller makes the most sense.

6.6.2 *Determine the RTL Structure of the Design*

The three steps to this stage are as follows (see the structure of the design sketched in Figure 6.7):

1. *Identify the inputs and outputs.* These are simply as expected. We need to input the multiplicand and multiplier under the control of a 'load' signal, and output the product.
2. *Determine what registers are needed and name their outputs.* Remember to clearly separate the datapath from the controller. The following need to be registered in the datapath:
   - The multiplicand and multiplier, as their values are needed over several clock cycles
   - The product, as it is determined through steps over many clock cycles

     However, we note that there is potential here to save some flipflops. Note that at each stage of the multiply, both the low order bits of the product register and the high order bits of the multiplier contain 0. They are not actually being used. We can safely use the low-order half of the product register to store the multiplier when loading the inputs. Then, as the algorithm progresses, the product and multiplier will shift right in unison until at the end only the product is stored in this register.

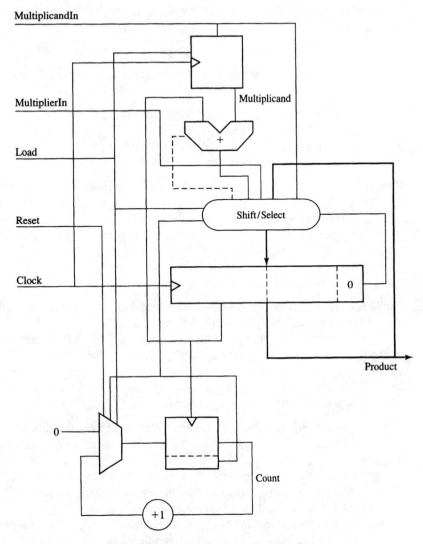

Figure 6.7   *Structure of Multiplier.*

The following registers are needed in the controller:
- A register to store the count

3. *Specify the function of the combinational logic.* Again the details of the datapath are determined before those of the controller.

The first thing to note is that there is no reason not to perform the add and the shift in the same clock cycle. A novice designer would most likely have been tempted to do the add and the shift in two separate clock cycles, thinking naively that the shift *has* to be done in a shift register. Instead we do the shift in a logic block, thus halving the time necessary to perform the multiplication.

Thus, the logic consists of an adder, and a combinational logic block to use the result of the add, to perform the shift and the initial load. Note that Verilog recognizes that adding two 8-bit numbers actually produces a 9-bit result, and the code can capture the ninth bit (the carry-out) explicitly as follows:

```
{next_E, AdderOut} = multiplicand + Product[15:8];
```

It is necessary to explicitly identify the control inputs to the datapath. They are as follows:

- 'load' from an input
- The most significant bit, bit 3, of count to tell the logic that the multiply is finished and product should be left unchanged
- The low order bit of the multiplier (stored in the product register) to determine whether to use the result of the add to the multiplier or not

Then it is necessary to determine the details of the controller. A novice designer might think that a 3-bit counter would suffice to count the eight clock cycles needed to do the multiplier. However, a ninth state is needed to 'hold' the product output until load goes high again. Thus, a 4-bit counter is needed, with the fourth bit being the 'finish' control bit.

6.6.3   Capture the Design As Verilog

The Verilog code that captures this design is presented on the next page, as "Unsigned Parallel Serial Multiplier" (in a parameterized form).

This example illustrates each of the three types of constructs that are generally used to capture synthesizable designs. In this design, there are two procedural blocks, one for the registers (including smaller input selectors) and one for the large selector and shift logic. There is also a continuous assignment statement to build the adder including carry out. The design also has the following features:

- It is parameterized. By varying the parameters *N* and *Cycles*, different sized multipliers can be built easily and quickly. Thus, the design can be easily modified and reused in later chips.
- Because of the use of non-blocking assignment ('<=') in the procedural block building the flipflops, all the statements in this block execute 'in parallel' and thus the registers being defined are all independent of each other.
- In the non-clock procedural block, all of the logical inputs are included in the timing sensitivity list; in other words, every variable on the right-hand side of an assignment statement that is not produced internally to the block has to be in this list. Otherwise, when it changes, the execution of this block will not be triggered. Since, in the real hardware, the logic does reevaluate whenever an input to the hardware changes, the Verilog model would not accurately capture the hardware without an accurate timing sensitivity list. Unfortunately, if a variable is accidentally left out of this list the Verilog simulator will not complain, though the synthesis tool will do so when you read in the Verilog.
- The larger input multiplexor and shifter could have been captured in the **always** @(posedge clock) statement as in the code shown that depicts "Combining All Datapath Operations into a Single **always** Block."

Note that with the case statement included in the clocked procedural block, there is no need for a default statement. We are building memory, so accidentally building memory

```
module ParallelSerialMult (clock, reset, load, multiplicandIn, multiplierIn,
                           Product);
 parameter N=8; // Number of bits in inputs
 parameter Cycles=3; // # cycles to compute = log(N)
 input clock; // clock
 input reset; // global reset
 input load; // =1 => load multiplicand and multiplier
 input [N-1:0] multiplicandIn; // Multiplicand
 input [N-1:0] multiplierIn; // Multiplier
 output [2*N-1:0] Product; // Product = Multiplicand * Multiplier
 reg [N-1:0] multiplicand; // stores MultiplicandIn
 reg [2*N-1:0] Product; // Stores Product and MultiplierIn
 reg [Cycles:0] Count; // counter that controls end of multiply
 reg [2*N-1:0] next_Product;  // input to Product register
 wire    next_E;        // Carry out of adder
 wire [N-1:0] AdderOut;      // `sum` output of adder

 always @(posedge clock)
  begin // Build the registers and their input logic
    if (load) multiplicand <= multiplicandIn;
    Product <= next_Product;
  end

 always @(posedge clock) // Build controller
    if (!reset) Count <= 0;
    else if (load) Count <= 0;
    else if (~Count[Cycles]) Count <= Count + 1'b1;

 // Adder to provide next partial product
 assign {next_E, AdderOut} = multiplicand + Product[2*N-1:N];

 // Input mux and shifter for product register
 always @(next_E or AdderOut or Product or Count[Cycles] or multiplierIn or load)
   casez ({Product[0], Count[Cycles], load})
     3'b??1 : next_Product = {N'b0, multiplierIn[N-1:0]};
     3'b100 : next_Product = {next_E, AdderOut[N-1:0], Product[N-1:1]};
     3'b000 : next_Product = {1'b0, Product[2*N-1:1]};
     default: next_Product = Product;
   endcase
endmodule
```

Unsigned Parallel Serial Multiplier.

by not having a default statement is not a concern! Also note that because the **casez** statement uses the output of the counter, non-blocking assignment is essential for correct operation. In this design this block was coded separately mainly to illustrate the use of a procedural block to capture combinational logic only rather than for any more fundamental reason.

```
always @(posedge clock)
  begin
  . . .
  casez ({Product[0], Count[Cycles], load})
    3'b??1 : Product <= {N'b0, multiplierIn[N-1:0]};
    3'b100 : Product = {next_E, AdderOut[N-1:0], Product[N-1:1]};
    3'b000 : Product = {1'b0, Product[2*N-1:1]};
  endcase
  . . .
  end
```

Combining All Datapath Operations into a Single always Block.

6.7   An Alternative Approach to Specifying Flipflops

In the previous code, flipflops are built by placing the names of their outputs in a procedural block starting with `always @(posedge clock)`. An alternative approach to specifying flipflops is to place `@(posedge clock)` triggers within procedural blocks. For example, the following Verilog fragment is equivalent to the fragment that built the flipflops in the counter example given earlier.

```
always
  begin @(posedge clock)
    if (latch) value <= in;
    else if (dec && !zero) value <= value - 1'b1;
  end
```

In this case the always statement specifies a continuous loop and the `@(posedge clock)` 'trigger' results in the body of the procedural block only executing when there is a positive edge of the clock; thus capturing the behavior of a flipflop.

It is also possible, though sometimes a little dangerous, to embed multiple `@(posedge clock)` statements into a block and thus specify a series of events on a set of flipflops. For example, consider the following code fragment.

```
always
  begin
    @(posedge clock)
    if (dec1) value <= value - 1'b1;
    @(posedge clock)
    if (dec2) value <= value - 2'b10;
  end
```

This code fragment actually specifies a downcounter that includes an implicit small 1-flipflop finite state machine, as well as the specified 'value' register. On every odd phase of the clock, it decrements value by one if dec1 is true. On every even phase of the clock, it decrements value by two if dec2 is true. Though this is a perfectly legal style for purposes of both synthesis and simulation, it does carry its dangers, especially for neophyte designers. In the example above, there is specified an implicit, unnamed one-bit finite state machine now buried in the datapath. This approach thus violates two of the guidelines above: The datapath and controller are not clearly separated and we have not explicitly identified the output signals of all flipflops. However, many designers do use this technique successfully, and since it reduces the labor of specifying the controller, this style will also be developed in succeeding chapters.

6.8 Common Problems and Fixes

There are many common patterns to the errors that neophyte designers make. This section presents some of these common problems and discusses how to avoid them.

6.8.1 *Accidental Instantiation of Latches*

As introduced in Sections 5.5 and 5.6, latches are inferred whenever a non-clocked procedural block intended to model combinational logic does not give a fresh assignment to each and every variable assigned to it every time it is executed. This is such a common source of problems that the topic merits additional emphasis here. One common situation when this occurs is when all possible combinations of 'control' variables are not covered in a **case** or **if–else** statement. For example:

```
reg A,B,C,D;
always @(A or B or C)
 casez ({B,C})
  2'b1? : D=A;
  2'b?1 : D=~A;
 endcase
```

Here, if {B,C} changes to {0,0}, this procedural block will execute but neither of the assignments to D will execute; in other words, the block is implicitly specifying that D should remain unchanged whenever {B,C} = 2'b00. This is what was called a *not-full* **case** in Chapter 5. For D to remain unchanged requires that its value be stored in a memory element. As there are no edge-triggers here, that memory element will be a latch 'clocked' through some combined value of B and C. The fix to this problem is to make sure that every case statement not in a clocked procedural block has a default. In this case, the designer does not care what value D takes when B or C is not equal to 1, and so D is specified as a don't care. Remember, the appropriate use of don't cares often leads to smaller, faster logic. A correct version follows:

```
reg A,B,C,D;
always @(A or B or C)
 casez ({B,C})
  2'b1? : D=A;
  2'b?1 : D=~A;
  default : D = 1'bx; // default to prevent latches
 endcase
```

Another common way latches are accidently inferred occurs when a procedural block has multiple outputs, and not every output is assigned for all possible combinations in which the block could be executed. For example:

```
reg A,B,C,D,E;
always @(A or B or C)
 casez ({B,C})
   2'b1? : D=A;
   2'b?1 : E=~A;
   default : E = A;
 endcase
```

This problem is best fixed by assigning defaults to all the outputs at the start of execution of the procedural block. Again, use don't cares if they are appropriate. The solution is:

```
reg A,B,C,D,E;
always @(A or B or C)
 begin
  D = 1'bx; E = 1'bx; // default to prevent latches
  casez ({B,C})
   2'b1? : D = A;
   2'b?1 : E = ~A;
   default : E = A;
  endcase
 end
```

Remember that a procedural block like this describes the behavior of a block or logic, not
a sequence of events. You can reassign the outputs as often as you want within the block.

When you read your Verilog file into Synopsys, it provides a listing of all flipflops
and latches described within the code. For example:

```
Inferred memory devices in process in routine counter line 27 in file
    `/afs/eos.ncsu.edu/users/p/paulf/ece520/examples/countbad.v'.
```

Register Name	Type	Width	Bus	MB	AR	AS	SR	SS	ST
D_reg	Latch	1	-	-	N	N	-	-	-

Always take a moment to look at the Synopsys log output to make sure that you are not
building unintentional latches.

6.8.2 *Incomplete Timing Specifications (Sensitivity Lists)*

Another common problem that is easy to fix occurs when the designer forgets to make sure that
all inputs to a block are specified in the timing control block or sensitivity list. For example:

```
reg A,B,C,D,E;
always @(A or B)
 begin
  D = A^B;
  E = C | D;
 end
```

In this case, if C changes, the execution of this block will not be triggered. Since synthesis will build the XOR and OR gate as described, the result will be an inconsistency between the pre-synthesis Verilog and the post-synthesis logic, that can lead to a bug in the design. Remember, in the actual hardware, whenever C changes the OR gate will 'execute' and change state if appropriate. The fix is to include C in the sensitivity list:

```
reg A,B,C,D,E;
always @(A or B or C)
 begin
  D = A^B;
  E = C | D;
 end
```

In this example, that there is no need to include D in the sensitivity list, even though it is an input to the OR gate because D is produced internally within this block. Synopsys will generate a warning about this type of problem, when the Verilog file is read in, as follows:

```
Warning: Variable `D' is being read in routine counter line 24 in file
`/afs/eos.ncsu.edu/users/p/paulf/ece520/examples/countbad.v',
but does not occur in the timing control of the block which begins there.(HDL-180)
```

6.8.3   *Unintentional Specification of Wired-Or Logic*

This is a more subtle problem that typically occurs when a designer does not design before coding as discussed in the methodology presented in Section 6.2. This type of problem commonly occurs when the designer is thinking of terms of C software coding instead of specifying hardware. It is best illustrated by an example:

```
reg A,B,C,D;
always @(posedge clock)
 C <= A^B;
always @(posedge clock)
 if (D==1) C <= A | B;
```

The logic being described here is illustrated in Figure 6.8. The designer has unintentionally specified that the outputs of two different flipflops are actually the same signal, in a

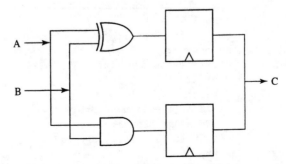

Figure 6.8   *Improper Logic Resulting from Incorrect Verilog Usage.*

sense specifying wired-or logic. Most CMOS logic families do not permit wired-or logic and so this specification can not be synthesized. To fix this problem, the designer has to make sure that C is assigned only within one procedural block. The details of the fix depend on the logical intent, but one possibility is described here.

The existence of this general problem leads to the specification of a general rule: *Every variable must be assigned only within one procedural block or continuous assignment statement.*

```
reg A,B,C;
reg [1:0] D;
always @(posedge clock)
  if (D==2`b01) C <= A | B;
  else if (D==2`b10) C <= A^B;
```

Again, Synopsys will warn you about this problem when you read the Verilog file in:

```
Warning: Variable `Z` is driven in more than one process or block in file
/afs/eos.ncsu.edu/users/p/paulf/ece520/examples/countbad.v.
This may cause mismatch between simulation and synthesis. (HDL-220)
```

6.8.4   *Improper Use of Loop Constructs*

This is another problem that commonly occurs when the designer is thinking in terms of software constructs instead of hardware is the improper use of loop constructs. For example, consider the code fragment below:

```
reg [7:0] A, B;
reg [7:0] C [0:7];
integer i;
always @(posedge clock)
  for (i=0; i<=7; i=i+1)
    if (A[i]==1) B <= B+C[i];
```

This fragment describes a chain of eight adders that eventually reach a register. It can be seen that this is a slow and inefficient implementation. There is a logic depth of at least eight adders between the input registers and the output register B, giving a slow clock cycle. In addition, the eight adders that are built will take up considerable area. One solution is to 'break' the **for** loop with a clock edge.

```
reg [7:0] A, B;
reg [7:0] C [0:7];
integer i;
always @(posedge clock)
  for (i=0; i<=7; i=i+1)
    begin
      if (A[i]==1) B <= B+C[i];
      @posedge(clock);
      \\ wait for clock edge before proceeding
    end
```

This code fragment is implicitly combining datapath and control in that an implicit 8-bit counter is now specified to determine which of C[i] is presented on each clock cycle. This code is potentially confusing. For example, a novice designer might not realize that this 8-cycle operation is looping continuously. However, this implementation will not have the speed and area penalties of the previous one. A better solution still is to explicitly separate control and datapath and redesign it without a **for** loop, either as a pipeline or as a single adder and accumulator. This is illustrated below, as controlled by a simple counter.

```
reg [7:0] A,B,C;
reg [4:0] countAccumB;
always @(posedge clock)
  begin
    if (clear==1) countAccumB <= 4'b0; // counter = controller
    else if (countAccumB[3] != 1) countAccumB <= CountAccumB + 1'b1;
    if (clear==1) B <= 0;    // accumulator B
    else if (countAccumB[3] != 1)
    B <= B+C[countAccumB[2:0]];
  endmodule
```

In general, loop structures (**for, while**, and **repeat**) are best used for iterating over the variables of an array, rather than for describing a sequence of operations on the same variable, as above. An example of good use of a **for** loop, a simple odd parity generator (generating an output of '1' if A contains an odd number of 1's), is coded below:

```
reg [7:0] A;
reg    OddParity;
always @(A)
 begin
  OddParity = 1'b0;
  for (i=0; i<=7; i=i+1)
   if (A[i]==1) OddParity = ~OddParity; // Inverse parity
  end
```

Note, however, that the loop must have a constant termination. Consider the next example:

```
reg [7:0] A,N;
reg    OddParity;
always @(A)
 begin
  OddParity = 1'b0;
  for (i=0; i<=N; i=i+1)
   if (A[i]==1) OddParity = ~OddParity; // Inverse parity
  end
```

Since N is a variable, the synthesis tool will not know how much hardware to build. Loops that do not have a constant termination can not be synthesized.

6.9   Debugging Strategies

Getting bugs out of a design is often a difficult and tiresome task. There are rarely short-cuts to make the designers job less difficult. Debugging strategies that generally work well include the following:

- *Localize the bug.* This is a very important step. It is necessary to keep narrowing down the search until the line that is toggling at the wrong time, or the state machine that is spending too long in the wrong state, is found. Obviously, turning on trace mode, viewing all relevant waveforms and judicious use of **$display** and **$monitor** are all helpful. Divide and conquer strategies must sometimes be used to localize the problem.
- *Trace the offending code in your head.* Trace the code by hand as a Verilog simulator would. Often the problem will appear when you notice a branch incorrectly specified or other inconsistency.
- *If all else fails, try something different.* Sometimes the cause of the problem is still elusive after a lot of effort. In this case, simply trying a different approach to coding the offending piece of the design will often lead to a solution. For example, redesign a case statement so that it is different. Other examples are converting an if-then-else statement to a case statement and changing a filename if there seems to be an Operating System problem, etc.
- *Check the manual.* Often an incorrect approach to coding a particular example can be discovered by reviewing the Language Reference Manual or Synthesis manual. Alternatively, it is possible to glean some ways of doing 'something different' by looking at the manual.[1]

6.10   Conclusion

The purpose of this chapter was to instruct the reader on how to convert a module-level hardware concept into Verilog RTL. Some important principles enumerated in this chapter include:

- *Clearly separate control and datapath.* They are separated by the 'control points': control lines and status lines. The controller is generally some combination of FSM and counters.
- *Design before coding.* Create a sketch of the design before writing any Verilog. Clearly identify all registers. Give names to all important signals, including all register outputs.
- *Convert areas of the design to blocks of Verilog code.* Each area of the design becomes one procedural block or one continuous assignment statement. The behavior of registers and their connected input logic is described in a procedural block starting with `always @(posedge clock)`. The behavior of large combinational logic blocks is coded in non-clocked procedural blocks, while the logic required for small pieces of combinational logic is coded using continuous assignments.

---

[1]Other debugging tips may be found in Section 4.4, Chapter 7, and Section 15.1.

Watch out for the following common problems:

- Accidently instantiating latches by not using defaults in combinational procedural blocks.
- Incomplete sensitivity lists in combinational procedural blocks.
- Assigning the same variable in two different procedural blocks of continuous assignment statements.
- Improperly using loop constructs, resulting in inefficient hardware.
- Assigning the same variable in two different procedural blocks or continuous assignment statements.
- Improper loop constructs, resulting in incorrect or inefficient hardware.

Exercises

6.1. What signals, if any, are latched in the following code fragment? Recode the design to remove any latches.

```
always @(foo or fred)
  if (foo = 2`h2) bar = fred;
```

6.2. What signals, if any, are latched in the following code? Recode to remove any latches.

```
always @(foo or hal or tron)
  begin
  case (foo)
   2`b00 : fred = hal;
   2`b01 : fred = tron;
   2`b10 : mike = hal;
   2`b11 : mike = tron;
  endcase
  end
```

6.3. Redesign the counter described above to count-up instead of a count-down. Design it so that it halts when the count reaches 4'hF and replace the *zero* flag with a *ones* flag.

6.4. A sequential piece of logic is designed to check to see if any register in a 32-entry register file is equal to zero. It continuously scans port *A* of the register file, setting the zero flag if any entry contains 32'h0. The zero flag is changed only after register 32 is reached. A piece of C code describing the function of this unit is:

```
temp_zero = 0;
for (i = 0; i <= 31; i++)
 if (RegisterFile [i] == 0) temp_zero = 1;
zero = temp_zero;
```

and a Verilog description of the top-level interface to this module is provided as follows:

```
module CheckForZero (clock, AddressA, DataA, zero);
input   clock; // 10 ns clock
output [4:0] AddressA; // Address sent to Register File
input [31:0] DataA; // Data from register file
output zero; // zero flag
```

Assume that the Register File is asynchronous—whenever the address input changes, the data output (for the port) changes half a clock period later. Then do the following:

a. Sketch the logic for this unit, explicitly identifying each register you plan to implement.

b. Write the Verilog capturing your logic, completing the module *CheckForZero*. Hints:
   - No Reset is needed.
   - If your answer contains a 'for' loop, you are probably wrong.

6.5. Redesign the counter module as an 8-bit downcounter. In addition, add the input *divide-by-two*. Whenever *divide-by-two* is high and *latch* is low and *dec* is low, divide the current contents of the counter by two (by doing a right shift).

6.6. Design logic to do the following:
   - There are two 8-bit counters. Counter 1 is loaded from *in1[7:0]* when the signal *load1* is high, and is decremented by 1 when *dec1* is high. Counter 2 is loaded from *in2[7:0]* and is decremented by the amount specified in *in3[7:0]* when *dec2* is high.
   - Whenever the contents of the two 8-bit counters become the same as each other, then the output flag *ended* goes high AND the counter contents must remain the same until one of them are reloaded from *in1* or *in2*.
   - Also, if either counter overflows (the counters contain unsigned numbers), then *ended* should go high AND the counter contents must remain the same until one of them are reloaded from *in1* or *in2*. (Overflow is indicated simply by a carry out =1 in this case.)
   - The value on *in3* will be held constant for you. You do not need to register it. Design and implement your solution. Make sure you include a block diagram sketch of your design, as well as a timing diagram. Also, make your solution consistent with the input/output declarations below.

```
module count_compare (clock, in1, in2, in3, load1, load2, dec1, dec2,
                      count1, count2, ended);
input      clock;
input [7:0] in1, in2, in3;
input      load1; // when load1 goes high, in1 is registered into count1
input      load2; // when load2 goes high, in2 is registered into count2
input      dec1;  // decrement count1 by 1
input      dec2; // decrement count2 by in3
output [7:0]  count1; // contents of counter 1
output [7:0]  count2; // contents of counter 2
output     ended; // goes high when count1=count2, or either counter
// experiences an unsigned overflow
// note: count1 and count2 will not change
// after same goes high until load1 or load2 forces one of them to be reloaded.
```

6.7. Design and implement an interval counter in Verilog which works by monitoring an incoming data stream and counts the number of clock cycles between occurances of 'Fx', or, any eight-bit data in which the first four bits are 1's.

```
Sample Timing:
Clock     1  0   1  0  1  0  1  0  1  0  1  0  1  0  1  0  1  0  1  0  1
Data      01     FF    22    34    F1    01    F0    23    45    AB    D0
Interval  ?      1     2     3     1     2     1     2     3     4     5
```

We *do care* if Interval overflows. The overflow flag must go high in the clock cycle it overflows. It does need to stay high, however. There is no need for a reset, clear, or any other type of initialization. Draw a block diagram of your hardware design and capture it as a Verilog module.

6.8. Design and implement a communications interface in Verilog. Often data sent over a data link are organized as *packets* of data, each packet containing some identification bits, data, and some check bits used to determine if a transmission error has occurred. Your hardware must meet the following specification:

```
Inputs:
 Clock;
 Reset;  // reset is active low
 Clear;  // clears output registers - active high
 InData[11:0] // Input data, organized as follows:
         // InData[11:8] contains the `header´
         // InData[7:4] contains the `data payload´
         // InData[3:1] are not used
         // InData[0] is a parity bit.
         //  it is `1´ if InData[18:4] is meant to
         //  be Even Parity
         // A new `InData´ arrives every clock
Outputs:
 All outputs are registered and are cleared when
  `reset´ is low or `clear´ is high.
 Payload[3:0];// is changed to contain the
         // `data payload´ when `InData´ is of type 1
 Count[7:0]; // Total count of type 1 datas
 Error[7:0]; // Number of type 1 datas of WRONG parity


Clock 1 0 1 0 1 0 1 0 1 0 1 0 1 0 1 0 1 0 1 0
Clear 1 0 0 0 0 0 0 0 0 0 0 0 0 0 0 0 0 0 0 1


InData 1F1 0E0 171 0E0
(i.e. 1F1 = `type 1´ payload=F, parity should be even
     0E0 = `not type 0´, payload=E, odd parity
     170 = `type 1´ payload=7, payload should have even parity)
Payload 0  F   F   7   7                     0
```

This piece of hardware checks *InData* on each clock cycle. If *InData[12:9]=1*, then it transfers the middle four bits of *InData* to payload and increments *count*. At the same time it checks the parity of the middle four bits and see if it is as expected. If it is not, then there is a transmission error, and *error* is incremented.

6.9. Design, and implement in Verilog, a piece of hardware that meets the following specification:

A datastream is presented on the port *data_in*. While the input *go* is high, you are to count the number of words in that datastream that have even parity, and separately, the number of words that have odd parity. These counters are cleared when *go* is low. Don't worry about the counters overflowing.

```
A sample timing diagram is as follows:
```

clock	1	0	1	0	1	0	1	0	1	0	1	0	1	0	1	0	1	0	1	0	1	0
go	0	1	1	1	1	1	1	0	0	0	0	0	0	0	0	0	0	0	0	0	0	0
data_in	1		3		2		4		5													
odd	0		0		1		2		0													
even	0		1		1		1		0													

The module header is as follows:

```
module parityCount (clock, data_in, go, odd, even);
  input clock, go;
  input [7:0] data_in;
  output [7:0] odd, even;
```

6.10. Design a module that accumulates statistics on an incoming data stream consisting of two individual bytes. The I/O to the module is as follows:

```
input        clock;    // Clock
input        reset;    // synchronous reset - active low
input        clear;    // Clears statistics when high (synchronous)
input [7:0] DataIn1;   // Input Data 1
input [7:0] DataIn2;   // Input Data 2
// all outputs are registered
output [7:0] EvenParity; // # of data with Even parity
output [7:0] GreyCode;   // # of data with pattern 10101010 or 0101010101
output       overflow;   // =1 if any of the counters above overflow
```

Thus, an example of how this module running might behave is as follows:

Clock	1	0	1	0	1	0	1	0	1	0	1	0	1	0	1	0	1	0	1	0
start	0	1	1	0	0	0	0	0	0	0	0	0	0	0	0	0	0	0	0	0
DataIn1	02		AA		04	...			02											
DataIn2	02		03		01	...			03											
EvenParity	00		00		01	01	...				FF	01								
OddParity	00		02		03	05	...													
Overflow	0								0		1									

Design, implement in Verilog, verify, and synthesize a module that meets these specifications.

6.11. Saturating accumulators are often used in multimedia applications. The idea is that if instead of overflowing when the number that is being accumulated tries to go beyond

FF...FF, it just remains at FF...FF. That way if a "white" pixel stays a "white" pixel if you are trying to make it light, instead of becoming a "black" pixel that has overflowed.

Design a saturating accumulator that is performing a series of adds on an incoming datastream. Every eight clock cycles, the accumulator is to start over again. The I/O specification for the module is as follows:

```
module SaturatingAccumulator (clock, go, in, out);
input clock;
input go; // Accumulate inputs while go is high, clear when low
input [7:0] in;
output [7:0] out;
```

```
clock  1 0 1 0 1 0 1 0 1 0 1 0 1 0 1 0 1 0 1 0 1 0 1 0
go     0 1
in     1   1   1    FF  1   6   7   8   9   A   B
out    0   1   2    FF  FF  FF  FF  FF  FF  9   13
```

Your design is going to consist of a counter, and a saturating accumulator. The signal *out* must come from a register, and obviously the counter needs a register.

HINT: You need to be able to detect unsigned overflow in this design. You an detect overflow by realizing that an 8-bit adder really produces a 9-bit output (*sum* and *Cout*). This fact can be captured in Verilog as follows:

$$\text{assign } \{Cout, Sum\} = A + B;$$

The *Cout* is the unsigned overflow.

6.12. What is wrong with the following code fragment? Rewrite it so it correctly describes and simulates the logic drawn.

```
reg [1:0] Sel2;
reg     in1, in2, out1, out2;
always @(in1 or Sel2)
  case (Sel2)
    2'b1x : out1 = in1;
    default : out2 = in2;
  endcase
```

Assume the multiplexer inputs are in order of the select: 00 01 10 11, with 11 at the top:

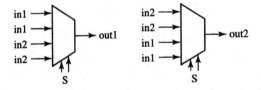

Chapter Seven

Validation of Single Modules

7.1 Introduction

Verification refers to the process of determining that the design is 100 percent functionally correct. In this chapter, the focus will be on pre-synthesis verification, making sure that the Verilog-level design has no latent bugs within it.

Generally, about half of the effort that goes into a design is spent on verifying correctness. So much effort is spent because of the time and expense involved in debugging a chip after it is made. If a fault is found after fabrication, at best it will be necessary to go through one or more rounds of chip prototyping. At more than six weeks per round (assuming a CMOS ASIC implementation), the eventual delay in product release can accumulate quickly. Product profitability decreases dramatically when the product is introduced late to the market. At worst, the chip will be released and sold with the bug still within it, possibly requiring field replacement of customers' products later, a very expensive situation. Even for an FPGA-based implementation, where the design cycles are shorter, fixing bugs in the prototype hardware is much more complex than discovering them in the Verilog code. In either case, a thorough and disciplined verification effort is very valuable.

This chapter will focus on some basic strategies for verification of relatively small designs. Two important aspects will be covered: sources of verification vectors and coding strategies for testbenches. Examples will be presented at the end.

7.2 Sources of Verification Vectors

A design is verified for correct functionality by presenting a suitable set of inputs to it and checking that the outputs are as expected. These inputs and expected outputs are referred to as 'verification vectors.' Ideally, the designer would verify the design for every possible input and check the outputs against a perfect specification of expectations. Unfortunately, such an approach is rarely practical as the input vector set would be impossibly large. Instead, practical approaches focus on generating a representative vector set and having multiple sources of vectors.

The following sources of test vectors are available to the designer:

- *Comparison with the results produced by a higher-level model.* Often the designer has available or produces, a 'C', Java or Verilog description capturing the behavior of the intended function. Alternatively, she can use one of the emerging languages for specification capture. This piece of code should capture input and output behavior only—it has no 'hardware' structural detail within it. Once this piece of code has been verified for correctness (generally by running real test cases through it), it can be used as a source of verification vectors. Sometimes, it is also useful to run random vectors into this higher-level model, in order to capture some of the unusual behaviors that running real test cases might not produce.
- *Constructing 'pathological' test cases.* The approach above tends to permit verification only of the main function of the module or group of modules. It is also important to construct cases that specifically verify unusual modes of functionality, including error modes, unusual transitions, etc.
- *Complete code coverage.* Many CAD tool suites contain tools that report on the percentage of code lines, branch alternatives, and paths that have been exercised during verification. This reporting can be used to determine which pieces of code are lightly tested or not tested at all. Special verification cases can then be constructed in order to verify these code pieces. Be careful to not use high code coverage numbers as an excuse not to produce other sources of vectors.
- *Regression testing.* A design is often modified many times before final completion. An important set of test vectors is the 'regression test' set, or test set that verifies that previously deloused bugs have not been accidently reintroduced as a result of a more recent modification.

Other sources of verification vectors (such as details from an IEEE specification, logic analyzer waveforms from real hardware) might be used as appropriate. Variety is the spice of quality in verification.

7.3   Verification Testbench Coding Approaches

In Verilog, the verification is conducted from a piece of code referred to as a 'testbench' or 'test fixture.' Simple examples were given in Chapters 4 and 6. Further examples are given here, illustrating other approaches to building testbenches.

7.3.1   *Absolute versus Relative Timing*

The example given in Chapter 6, reproduced here, used relative timing, in that the delay statements (#10, etc.) are cumulative. For example, the signal latch is changed back to '0', 10 ns after it was set to '1', i.e., at absolute time 11 ns + 10 ns = 21 ns after the simulation started (assuming a 1 ns timebase).

Unfortunately, this approach becomes unwieldy when a long sequence of transitions have to be studied. The designer must spend a lot of time keeping track of accumulated delay. An alternative approach is to use the **fork-join** statement instead of **begin-end**.

Between the **begin** and the **end**, the enclosed statements are executed in sequence. Between a **fork** and **join**, the statements are executed in parallel. Thus, absolute timing

```
initial // following block executed only once
 begin
  clock = 1, latch = 0, dec = 0;// initialize inputs
  in = 4´b0010;
  #11 latch = 1; // wait 11 ns, latch in input `2´
  #10 latch = 0; // wait 10 ns
  #10 dec = 1; // start decrementing
  // It should take two clock cycles to reach `0´
  #10 if (zero==1´b1) $display(``count: Error in Zero flag\n´´);
  #10 if (zero==1´b0) $display(``count: Error in Zero flag\n´´);
  $finish; // finished simulation
 end
```

```
parameter CP = 10; // clock period is 10 ns
 initial // following block executed only once
  fork
   clock = 1, latch = 0, dec = 0; // initialize inputs
   in = 4´b0010;
   #(CP+1) latch = 1; // wait 11 ns, latch in input  `2´
   #(2*CP+1) latch = 0; // wait 10 ns
   #(3*CP+1) dec = 1;
   // It should take two clock cycles to reach `0´
   #(4*CP+1) if (zero==1´b1) $display(``count: Error in Zero flag\n´´);
   #(5*CP+1) if (zero==1´b0) $display(``count: Error in Zero flag\n´´);
   $finish; // finished with simulation
  join
```

can be used. The above box has recoded the test fixture as a **fork-join** statement *and* with the clock period parameterized. Here, an extra nanosecond is added to each transition so that it is clear that the inputs are changing just after the relevant clock edge. Again, note the 'self-checking' nature of the test fixture (the if . . . statements). There is no need to view the waveforms in order to verify correctness as incorrect behavior is reported during simulation.

Another approach is to derive the timing of the testbench from the same clock as used in the design under test (see Chapter 8 onward).

7.3.2   *Reading in Verification Vector Files*

If the designer is verifying the RTL file against a higher-level simulatable model, then a common verification approach is to use the higher-level model to produce files containing input vectors and expected output vectors. These can be read into the test fixture and either verified in place or verified later by performing a 'diff' between the expected output vectors and the actual simulator output vectors. This approach is illustrated here using the multiplier designed in Chapter 6 as an example.

```
module test;
 parameter N = 5; // number of test vectors
 reg clock, reset, load;
 reg [7:0] multiplicandInArray [0:N];
 reg [7:0] multiplierInArray [0:N];
 reg [15:0] ExpectedResult [0:N];
 reg [7:0] multiplicandIn, multiplierIn;
 wire [15:0] Product;
initial begin
        $readmemh(``source1_vec.txt´´, multiplicandInArray);
        $readmemh(``source2_vec.txt´´, multiplierInArray);
        $readmemh(``result_vec.txt´´, ExpectedResult);
        end
initial
 begin
  reset = 1, clock = 0, load = 0;
  for (i=0; i<=N; i=i+1)
   begin
    multiplicandIn = multiplicandInArray[i];
    multiplierIn = multiplierInArray[i];
    #10 load = 1;
    #10 load = 0;
    #120 if (Product != ExpectedResult[i])
        $display(``Error Iteration %i\n´´,i);
   end
  $finish;
 end
 always #5 clock = ~clock;
 ParallelSerialMult u1 (clock, reset, load,
    multiplicandIn, multiplierIn, Product);
endmodule
```

An example of the input file, "source1_vec.txt" is given below.

```
// Multiplier inputs
73hf   // first vector
beef   // second vector
1234
5678
9ABC
DEF0
FFFF
0000
7923
8943
```

7.4 Post-Synthesis Verification

After synthesis, it is necessary to simulate the resulting gate-level netlist with actual
timings back-annotated from the output of synthesis. This step is important to catch any
synthesis errors and to verify correct initialization (reset) of the hardware. Pre-synthesis,

Verilog initializes all signals to unknown ('x'), potentially leading to reset-related bugs being masked as the unknowns can persist for even hundreds of clock cycles. One way to catch these bugs is a with a post-synthesis verification since, with actual gates in the design, the gate outputs settle to either logic-0 or logic-1 well before the first clock period is complete. Some details are given in Section 14.7. Typically, a lot of post-synthesis simulation time is also done to verify that the synthesized design is operating correctly, using the test vector sets that were employed pre-synthesis. However, a lot of that simulation time can be eliminated by using formal verification.

7.5   Formal Verification

The continuing advance of chip complexity has now passed the million gate level. Such chips are tested by high-performance simulators running in server ranches of hundreds of processors. Accordingly IC and CAD vendors are putting much effort into the development of methods based on verification by theorem proving. Present commercial verification tools are not practical at more than about 20,000 gates. To get a feel for these numbers, note that most of the synthesis exercises in these notes in small parameterizations are all below 5,000 gates, except for the MIPS example of Chapter 10 which is around 50,000 gate equivalents not including the embedded memory.

The formal verification tools come in two varieties, namely equivalence checkers and model checkers, outlined in the following sections.

7.5.1   *Equivalence Checkers*

Equivalence checkers compare a design to a reference design. The method works by using logical equivalence theorems to successively transform one description until the other one is reached, much in the way that mathematical theorems are proved by successive substitutions to the right-hand side of an equation until the form of the left-hand side is reached. Current commercial equivalence checkers can accept the specifications to be checked in Verilog, VHDL, or EDIF. These are converted internally to the symbolic logic form in which the manipulations are actually performed. In this way a logic equation is developed for every state bit and every primary output. For the process to succeed it is necessary that the two descriptions being compared have the same synchronous functionality and correlated state holding data types. If the process succeeds it can be much faster than simulation and can divine the equivalence irrespective of different identifiers and hierarchy. The output from the equivalence checker lists which signals in the two designs are equivalent. If a discrepancy is discovered, then a test vector is generated which exercises it. Some checkers will even output a list of nets that are possible sources of the discrepancy, together with corresponding estimates of the probabilities.

Of course the process may also fail to prove equivalence. Possible reasons might be:

- A state machine has different encodings in the two specifications, which will lead to completely different logic. This could be a particular problem for the implicit writing styles of Chapters 8 and 9, because the synthesizer will be generating a state machine and encoding it on its own.
- If authorized, the synthesizer may have optimized the logic across logic boundaries, which changes the logic equations coming into those state bits.
- The use of in-line compiler directives (pragmas) may cause different synthesizer interpretations of the specification (e.g., *//synopsys full case, one-hot*, etc.).

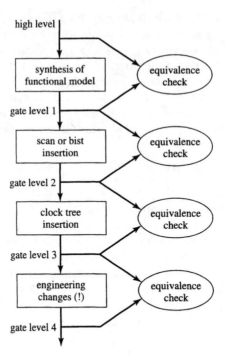

Figure 7.1   *Applications of Equivalence Checking.*

- Parts of the design may be produced by a generator (like the Altera *genmem* program of Chapter 14).
- The two descriptions may have the same function but different architectures. Multipliers are notable examples of this.

Most of these problems apply to the synthesis step and reduce the probability that an equivalence check between pre- and post-synthesis will be successful. Besides, there is some question as to whether this is even a valid concept if the synthesis were constructive, or if some of the routines of the synthesizer and the equivalence checker are shared (notably the parsing of the Verilog or VHDL source and the conversion to symbolic logic). But there are other comparisons for which the equivalence checker may be much more effective as shown in Figure 7.1. In general the rule is that the less similar the two representations are, the more time and memory the equivalence checker will take, and the higher the probability that it will fail. So the moral is, verify in small steps as the design stages proceed. Still, there remain questions about the applicability of an equivalence checker. To wit: If the gate level description is changed, by insertion of DFT circuits, or by late engineering changes, should not the design be resynthesized instead? Finally how is it known whether the first (*golden*) specification being used as a yardstick itself truly meets the design intentions? It is such reasoning that leads to the expectation that the second type of formal verification may ultimately be more effective.

7.5.2   *Model Checkers*

Model checkers are used to prove that certain assertions about a design are true. The designer captures assertions about the design, such as "signals A and B can never be true at the same time" and the model checker proves that these assertions are correctly implemented. Model checkers accept input of the assertions and seek to prove that these assertions are a necessary consequence of the high-level source description—or, if not, generate test vectors which exercise the violation. This process is closer to the notion of checking that the specification truly meets the designer's intentions. Actually the same philosophy can often just as well be applied in simulation as in formal verification. It also suffers from the same difficulty, that coming up with such "assertions" useful for this purpose might sometimes be a hit or miss affair.

Examples of assertions which can be checked within the context of present HDL and simulator technology are the following:

- Set of signals required to be one-hot
- Read and write never simultaneously true
- Initiation of a handshake is always eventually followed by its completion
- Deadlock or livelock
- *Register leaks*: A shared register has new data loaded before the previous data has been read to any destination
- *Register corruption*: Data is enabled into the register while either no source or multiple sources are connected

The advantage of this kind of assertion checking is that it can be flagged immediately as it occurs, as opposed to the usual simulation situation in which the effect may not be seen at the output pins until after an extended time. After a long time separation it is more difficult to trace back to the cause. The contrast between the end-to-end checking and assertion checking methodologies is illustrated in Figure 7.2.

Finally, there are packages that seek to generate candidate assertions automatically from the HDL specification. This is done by scanning for crucial shared registers.

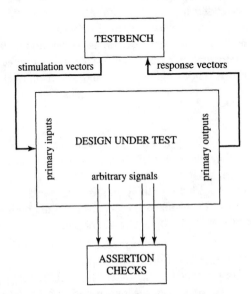

Figure 7.2   *Distinction between End-to-End and Assertion Checking.*

7.6   System-level Verification

Before a chip is sent for fabrication, considerable effort is expended to ensure that it functions correctly as an integrated unit. Simulation is slow at this stage of the design, making this task time-consuming. In addition, it is not enough to just run test vectors through the model of the entire chip. Often, misunderstandings of the specification can mean that the test vectors have subtle bugs in them. There have been many cases of designs that pass all their test vectors but the actual chip does not work when inserted into the system board.

Some form of system verification is needed—the entire system in which the chip is to be used needs to be verified as a whole. One approach to system verification is to obtain or build Verilog models for all of the other system components and simulate the board as a whole. Though often used successfully, this approaches can result in overly long simulation sessions. In addition, effort must be spent to make sure that the models for the peripheral chips are in themselves correct.

Another approach is emulation—synthesize the chip onto an array of FPGAs and "plug" the resulting emulator into the actual system board. Though this approach makes the discovery of subtle interface bugs more likely, it does require a significant engineering effort to make the rest of the system work correctly at the slower speed of the FPGAs.

7.7   Conclusion

Verification of correct operation is a very important part of the chip design process, often consuming almost 50 percent of the project resources. Time-to-market pressures force design teams to try to achieve 100 percent correct functionality in only one or two rounds of prototyping.

Simulation is heavily used to verify correctness. Verification vectors are applied to the design and the results observed for correctness. Ad-hoc approaches to the production of verification vectors will generally leave unexercised bugs in the design. A disciplined methodology is needed to make sure that all possible bugs are tested for. Elements of a good methodology will include obtaining different sources of test vectors, making sure that all functionality, normal and extreme, is tested, and making proper use of code coverage and formal verification tools. Good testbench coding techniques can reduce the agony associated with verification and improve bug-reduction rates.

Exercises

7.1. Generate a "complete" test fixture for verifying the correctness of the counter example used in Chapter 6. For example, make sure that it operates for different loaded values, determine if it operates correctly when a load occurs before the count completes, when it is loaded initially with 0, etc. Make sure that you have complete code coverage in that every line and every if-else branch alternative is executed during the execution of your test fixture. Use a fork-join style coding technique.

7.2. Assume you are verifying a signed 8-bit adder designed by someone else in your group. Generate a set of input and output vectors that verify correct operation of the overflow flag produced by the adder. Does it correctly predict overflow for all combinations of positive and negative numbers? Do not exhaustively test the adder (meaning, try all possible numbers) as that is very wasteful of simulator time. Instead, generate an appropriately representative vector set.

7.3. Design, implement and test a complete verification approach for Exercise 6.7 in Chapter 6. Approach this problem by building a 'C' module that generates a variety of sample inputs and expected results for a wide variety of data streams, predetermined, random, correct, and with errors. Design a test fixture that uses these files as a comparison point to a simulation of the actual Verilog module.

7.4. Write a test fixture to verify the correctness of your solution to Exercise 6.8 of Chapter 6. Use a 'C' or C++ program to generate a random set of numbers for DataIn1 and DataIn2 and expected correct results. Write these numbers to a suitable file. Then write a Verilog test fixture to compare these files with the results of your actual circuit running.

7.5. Write a test fixture to verify the FSM you designed to solve Exercise 8.9 in Chapter 8. It should test for every possible sequence of states.

Chapter Eight

Finite State Machine Styles

8.1 Introduction

In Chapters 5 and 6, we started to encounter some simple sequential machines, ones where the behavior involves memory. As we now progress towards sequential machines that are more complex; the synthesizer implements the various operations called for in the specification using a collection of functional submodules. These functional submodules in turn need to be sequenced by a *controller*, which is itself another specialized sequential machine, called a *state-machine* in this context. This is the point where writing styles really begin to diverge. This chapter and the next lead the reader through some of the styles that are possible. Although there are state machine editors, such as the Synopsys FSM compiler, that create code directly from a state diagram, this chapter remains oriented toward the Design Compiler and similar synthesis tools.

8.2 Synthesis of State Machines

8.2.1 Classical Model

The classical method of deriving the control section of a design is via a state diagram and a state assignment. But there are several methods for specifying a state machine for synthesis. These are first illustrated with the aid of a simple example of a state machine which controls the output of successive words from a RAM using a pointer p. The state diagram for this machine is shown in Figure 8.1. This machine outputs the next word if the *read* control is high at the positive edge of the clock, unless a *reset* input is high in which case the pointer is reset to zero.

8.2.2 Explicit Specification Style

The *explicit* state specification style closely follows the classical method. A bitvector is assigned to each state and tested so as to sequence the states as required. It is shown as explicit Specification #1.

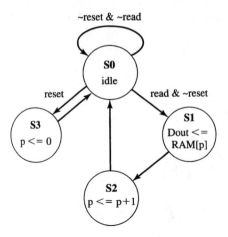

Figure 8.1   *Simple State Machine.*

```
module state_machine(clk, reset, read, data_out)
 input clk, reset, read;
//********datapath stuff-not part of controller state machine *
 parameter ws=4, as=3, nw=8;    //                            *
 reg [ws-1,0] ram_data [n-1:0]  // RAM                        *
 reg [ws-1,0] data_out;         // output buffer              *
 output [ws-1,0] data_out;      //                            *
 reg [as-1:0] p;                                              *
//***************************************************************

 parameter S0=0, S1=1, S2=2, S3=3; // state assignment
 reg [1:0] present_state, next_state;
   always @(reset or read or present_state)
   case(present_state)
    S0: if (reset)                  next_state<=S3;
        elseif (read)               next_state<=S1;
        else                        next_state<=S0;
    S1: begin data_out<=ram_data[p]; next_state<=S2; end
    S2: begin p<=p+1;               next_state<=S0; end
    S3: begin p<=0;                 next_state<=S0; end
   endcase
   always @(posedge clk) present_state <= next_state;
endmodule
```

Explicit Specification #1 of Simple State Machine.

The resulting synthesis of the controller state machine uses a multiple-output network of combinational gates in the classical synchronous feedback form shown in Figure 8.2.

In general the outputs from the combinational network to the inputs of the state register are functions of both the present state vector and the external inputs. Then it is called a Mealy machine. But if the combinational network is such that these outputs are functions only of the state vector then it is called a Moore machine. It follows that Specification #1

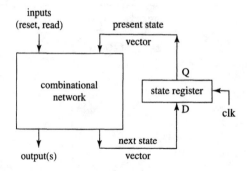

Figure 8.2   *Classical Sequential Machine.*

```
module state_machine(clk, reset, read, data_out)
  ...
 parameter S0=0, S1=1, S2=2, S3=3; // state assignment
   reg [1:0] state;
     always @(posedge clk)  // state sequencing
       case(state)
         S0:  if(reset)                       state<=S3;
              elseif(read)                    state<=S1;
              else                            state<=S0;
         S1:  begin data_out<=ram_data[P];    state<=S2; end
         S2:  begin p<=p+1;                    state<=S0; end
         S3:  begin p<=0;                      state<=S0; end
       endcase
endmodule
```

Explicit Specification #2 of Simple State Machine.

corresponds to a Moore machine because the outputs (causing the actions inside the circles) depend only on the states. In early computers, the combinational network of the figure was realized as a network of gates, called *random logic* because of the somewhat inscrutable appearance of the haystack of wires on the old backplanes. Later it was most likely implemented as a *programmed logic array* (PLA), which is an organized array structure suited to integrated circuit layout. However, with current synthesis tools it can now be implemented once again as a network of gates.

The register in the feedback path could be either edge-triggered or master-slave. Either would ensure that the machine changes state once only on each clock strike. In either case, it is actually redundant to specify a register for both the present state and the next state, and the same synthesized result could be obtained from the slightly simpler second explicit Specification #2.

The previous specifications are highly encoded and the area resulting from synthesis may depend on the state assignment chosen. An alternative prefered by many designers is to employ one-hot vectors for state assignment. Even though the one-hot coded state vector uses more flopflops, the simpler output coding will usually result in a smaller synthesized area. Plus, the area will be independent of state assignment. An example is shown in explicit Specification #3.

```
module state_machine(clk, reset, read, data_out)
 . . .
reg [3:0] state, next_state;
parameter S0=3´b0001, S1=3´b0010, S2=3´b0100, S3=3´b1000;
  always @(posedge clk)  // state sequencing
    begin
    case(state)
      S0: if (reset)                        next_state<=S3
             elseif (read)                  next_state<=S1
             else                           next_state<=S0
        S1: begin data_out<=ram_data[P];    next_state<=S2; end
        S2: begin p<=p+1;                   next_state<=S0; end
        S3: begin p<=0;                     next_state<=S0; end
        default: next_state<=S0; // if not one-hot
        endcase
      end
  always @(posedge clk) present_state <= next_state;
endmodule
```

Explicit Specification #3 of Simple State Machine.

```
module state_machine(clk, reset, read, data_out)
    . . .
   always @(reset or read)
     begin
       @(posedge clk)
         if (reset) p<=0;
         elseif (read)
          begin
           data_out<=ram_data[p];
           @(posedge clk)
           p<=p+1;
          end
  endmodule
```

Specification #4: Implicit Simple State Machine.

8.2.3 *Implicit Specification Style*

For situations involving a simple linear sequence of states, such as the S0-S1-S2 sequence on the right-hand side of the state diagram of Figure 8.1, a still more economical *implicit style* can be employed as in the following implicit Specification #4.

In this style a (*posedge clk*) statement sends the machine to the next state. The specification is much shorter and the synthesized hardware the same. Unlike the situation in the state diagram of Figure 8.1 and the specifications so far, a proper *reset* should be preemptive from inside all other states. The standard method using a loop disable has been suggested [Knapp95], as illustrated in implicit Specification #5.

```
module state_machine(clk, reset, read, data_out)
  ...
 always
        begin: loop_with_reset
         if(reset) p<=0; // all reset action(s) here
         elseif(read)
         forever
          begin
           data_out<=ram_data[p];
           @(posedge clk)
           //this next line goes after every @(posedge clk)
             if(reset) disable loop_with_reset;
             p<=p+1;
          end
        end
endmodule
```

Specification #5: Implicit Simple State Machine.

```
module state_machine(cphA, cphB, reset, read, data_out)
  ...
  always
    begin
      @(posedge cphA)
      if(reset) p<=0;
      elseif(read)
      begin
        data_out<=ram_data[p];
        @(posedge cphB)
        p<=p+1;
      end
endmodule
```

Specification #6: Implicit Simple State Machine.

Finally, as another alternative, instead of using a series of (*posedge clk*) statements, a similar effect could be achieved by using a multiphase clock, as shown in implicit Specification #6 above. If non-overlapping clock phases are employed this will be logically equivalent to the one-hot state assignment described earlier in this chapter.

Of course, the state diagrams used in the above examples only describe the control function. What is in fact being controlled are other sequential machines, such as the pointer and the RAM in this case. These modules together with the necessary data interconnections are gathered together in a *datapath* in the extension called *finite state machine with datapath* (FSMD) [Gajski92], as shown in Figure 8.3.

Datapaths consist of modules like the examples in previous chapters, interconnected by busses. Each module has control inputs associated with it, which cause some kind of

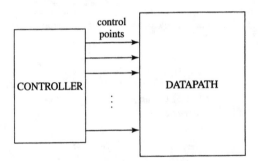

Figure 8.3   *FSMD Machine.*

action or operation to take place, such as *reset, read*. These inputs are the *control points*. They are driven in some kind of appropriate sequence by the controller which is the FSM in the FSMD. These *control points* would emanate from the register in Figure 8.2, sometimes called a *microinstruction* register in this context. The point is that in the explicit versions above, this register actually appears in the specification, and the synthesized result includes it as part of the controller. In the implicit versions, the controller parts do not appear in the specification but are synthesized automatically. The example specifications in the next section illustrate the concept.

8.3   Example Specifications

Example 1: Booth multiplier

The first example is the Booth multiplication algorithm. This is an extension of the simple multiplier of Chapter 6 to handle two's complement numbers. The corresponding FSMD is shown in Figure 8.4. This is the simplest version of the Booth algorithm, called radix 3. The next higher (radix 4) version has the multiplier bits examined three at a time (see Problem 8.5), Commercial multipliers usually use the radix 4 but with the shifted multiplands all added in parallel rather than serially.

The product is accumulated in a double-length register which is initialized with zero in the left half and the multiplier bits in the right half. The Booth technique essentially examines pairs of bits of the multiplier from right to left to see where runs of 1's begin and end. For each position corresponding to a *run-beginning*, a corresponding shifted version of the multiplicand (M) is *subtracted*, and for each position just after a *run-end* a corresponding shifted version of the multiplicand is *added*. Also at each clock the whole double-length contents are arithmetically shifted one position to the right. The final result is ready after the *nth* multiplier cycle, where *n* is the number of bits in the operands.

Specification #7 is given in the next box. During the load cycle a new multiplicand and multiplier are loaded. Thereafter, the multiplier goes through as many multiply cycles as there are bits in the operands. Here there is only one clock per cycle of the multiplier so we do not see multiple @(*posedge clk*) statements as in Implicit Specification #4.

For completeness and as an example of a suitable test, a specification for a corresponding testbench follows on page 118.

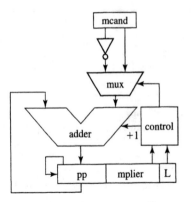

Figure 8.4 *Hardware for Sequential Multiplier.*

```
module booth(clk, load, mc, mp, pr);
 parameter w=4;          // small wordsize for test
 parameter csize=2;      // cycle counter size = log2(w)
  input  clk, load;
  input [w-1:0] mc, mo;
  output [2*w:1] pr;
  reg [2*w:0] pp; // extra bit on right end
  reg [w-1:0] mcand;
  reg [csize:0] cc;
  wire [w-1:0] mc, mp, sum, diff;
  assign sum = pp[2*w:w+1]+mcand;
  assign diff = pp[2*w:w+1]-mcand;
always @(posedge clk)
 if (load) begin cc<=0; mcand<=mc; pp<={{w+1{1´b0}},mp,1´b0}; end
 else if (~cc[csize])
  begin
    cc<=cc+1;
    case (pp[1:0])
     2´b01: pp<={sum[w-1], sum, pp[w:1]};     // add mcand & arithmetic Rshift
     2´b10: pp<={diff[w-1], diff, pp[w:1]};   // sub mcand & arithmetic Rshift
     2´b00, 2´b11: pp<={pp[2*w], pp[2*w:1]};  // arithmetic Rshift alone
    endcase
  end
endmodule
```

Specification #7: Simple Booth Multiplier.

Note the cycle length of the master clock is set up using a parameter. In this way it will be easy to change if the timing constraints are violated in the synthesis timing report. In this and following testbenches, (*posedge clk*) statements are inserted inside the **initial** block rather than the using integral delay (#) constructs in order to relate the test timing to the clock of the module under test. Display statements have been added to enhance the readability of the simulation output. In the present case these set up the heading and insert spaces between successive multiplications.

```
`timescale 1 ns / 100 ps
module test_booth;
 parameter w = 4;
 parameter dt = 20;
 integer i;
 reg load, clk; // master clock
 reg [w-1:0] mcand, mplier;
 wire [2*w-1:0] product;

 booth BTH(clk, load, mcand, mplier, product);

 always begin clk=1; #dt clk=0; #dt; end

 initial
  begin  clk<=0; load<=1;
   $display(``time load mcand mplier product-b product-d´´);
   $monitor(``%5g %b %h      %h     %b  %d´´,
   $time, load, mcand, mplier, product, product);
   @(negedge clk);
   mcand<=7; mplier<=3; load<=1; @(negedge clk);  load<=0;
   for (i=0; i<4; i=i+1) @(negedge clk);
    $display(`` ´´);
   mcand<=7; mplier<=-3; load<=1; @(negedge clk); load<=0;
   for (i=0; i<4; i=i+1) @(negedge clk);
    $display(`` ´´);
   mcand<=-7; mplier<=3; load<=1; @(negedge clk); load<=0;
   for (i=0; i<4; i=i+1) @(negedge clk);
    $display(`` ´´);
   mcand<=-7; mplier<=-3; load<=1; @(negedge clk); load<=0;
   for (i=0; i<4; i=i+1)  @(negedge clk);
    $display(`` ´´);
   mcand<=7; mplier<=7; load<=1; @(negedge clk); load<=0;
   for (i=0; i<4; i=i+1) @(negedge clk);
   $finish;
  end
endmodule
```

Testbench for the Booth Multiplier.

One of the ambiguities of the finite state machine with datapath (FSMD) model is just exactly where the dividing line is between the datapath and the controller. If all the flipflops of the total design were included in the model of Figure 8.2 then the number of states would be around 2^{4w}. On the other hand, if the controller just contained the counter, as in the specification of Chapter 6, then the number of states in the controller of Figure 8.4 would be n. Finally, if the design were coded as in Specification #7, then the controller would be purely combinational and would contain no states. So whether this specification is called implicit is somewhat debatable. The following design will be a more "explicit" example of the implicit style.

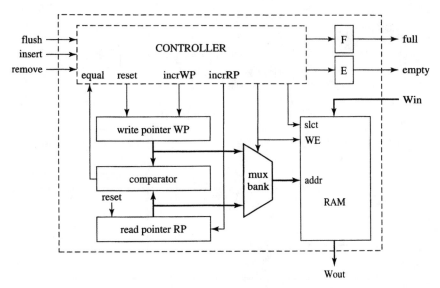

Figure 8.5   *Organization of FIFO.*

Example 2: First-in first-out buffer (FIFO)

The *first-in first-out* (FIFO) buffer is a common component in architectures for interfacing and communication. It has operations for *flush, insert,* and *remove*. Although other formulations are possible, it is commonly implemented as a RAM with associated pointers. For the illustrations here, these pointers will be feedback shift registers similar to the previous *fsrb* specification except shifting only in one direction. The FIFO will be introduced here and then also used in other chapters to illustrate other specification styles. A diagram of the hardware involved is given in Figure 8.5.

Most commercial FIFOs use ring counters for the pointers, thus avoiding the necessity for a RAM decoder and its associated propagation delay, besides simplifying the comparator. Other variations are possible, for example using the two-port ram of Chapter 5, producing a FIFO capable of simultaneous *insert* and *remove* operations (see Chapter 9, Problem 9.2), or even a totally different design using a unidirectional shift registers for each data bit and a bidirectional shift register in the controller (see Chapter 8, Problem 8.7). Unless special efforts are made, common Verilog usage assumes an implicit decoder (see Chapter 5, Problem 5.19). More important, the embedded RAMs available in our target technology have the decoders built in. So for the purposes of the following examples we will stick with the implicit decoders.

In the simplest formulation a FIFO would use two cycles for each of its operations as reflected in the controller state diagram for the FSMD of Figure 8.6.

In words:

* *insert*: write to memory; then increment the write pointer
* *remove*: read from memory; then increment the read pointer

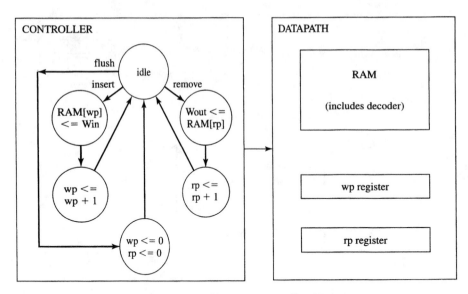

Figure 8.6   *FSMD Diagram for FIFO.*

A corresponding specification is given on the next page and employs the multiple @(*posedge clk*) statements exactly like those in the Implicit Specification #4. As a result the entire functionality of both datapath and controller is described in the single **always** block and the controller details are synthesized automatically.

Another feature of the first (*fifosl*) specification is the way that the flush-insert-remove control is treated as a one-hot vector in the case items. This case style puts the fixed comparand in the case expression and the variables in the case items. Such a role reversal is permitted only in Verilog. Although many designers use this style success-fully, it has been eschewed in the *fifosc* and the specifications to follow because the necessity for the fullcase parallel-case pragma carries the danger that synthesis might differ from simulation.

The full/empty flags are computed by comparing the write and read pointers for equality combined with the knowledge of whether the previous operation had been an *insert* or *remove*. As specified the full and empty indicators are available at the pins. In some FIFO's it is the responsibility of the external environment to use this information to ensure correct protocol and sometimes it is used internally to prevent over-writing or over-reading. In the timing diagram of Figure 8.7 (upper section) the arrows show that the information could be available in time for either purpose. However, the operation of this FIFO is hardly speed efficient since it is only possible to initiate a new operation every other clock time.

The lower section of Figure 8.7 shows that it might be possible to speed up the oper-ation to one operation per clock and still have the full/empty information available in time to decide on the next operation. The following specifications achieve the speedup possibil-ity implied by this diagram. In order to achieve this speedup, have the pointer increment and the RAM reference executed at the same clock time, and do it in a robust manner for synthesis and different target technologies, it is necessary to have some sort of shadow register for each pointer. An example of this type is shown in Specification #9 (*fifosc*). This is really our first example of a module with pipeline registers.

```
module fifosl(clk, flush, insert, remove, Win, empty, full, Wout);
 parameter nw=7, as=3, ws=4; // capacity, addrsize, wordsize
 parameter  k = 2; // from table of irreducible trinomials
  input  clk, flush, insert, remove;
  input  Win;
  output Wout;
  output full, empty;
   reg full, empty;
   reg [ws-1:0] ram_data [nw-1:0];
   reg [as-1:0] wp, rp;
   reg [ws-1:0] Wout;
   wire [ws-1:0] Win;
 always
  begin
   @(posedge clk)
   if (flush)
          begin
            full<=0; empty<=1;
            @(posedge clk);
            rp<=0; wp<=0;
          end
    else
     case(1'b1)
      remove:begin
            full<=0; Wout <= ram_data[rp];
            if (wp==rp) empty<=1;
            @(posedge clk);
            rp <= ~{(~rp[k]^~rp[0]), ~rp[as-1:1]};
            end
      insert: begin
            empty<=0; ram_data[wp] <= Win;
            if (wp==rp) full<=1;
            @(posedge clk);
            wp <= ~{(~wp[k]^~wp[0]), ~wp[as-1:1]};
            end
      default: @(posedge clk); // idle
     endcase
   end
endmodule
```

Specification #8: FIFO (fifosl).

This module has a further important improvement. By employing a two-port RAM array instead of a simple RAM, simultaneous insert and remove operations are now possible, so the control sequence has been upgraded to exploit this—as long as we do not allow simultaneous reads and writes at the same TPR address! Finally note that the all zero location is unwritable in the submodules used here for both the *fsr* pointer and the *tpr* two-port RAM.

The final specification of this chapter is a testbench for the *fifosc*. This tests that the correct sequence of words emerges at the output, and that the design is capable of invoking one operation every clock cycle, while getting the full/empty information back in time to make an appropriate decision on the next operation.

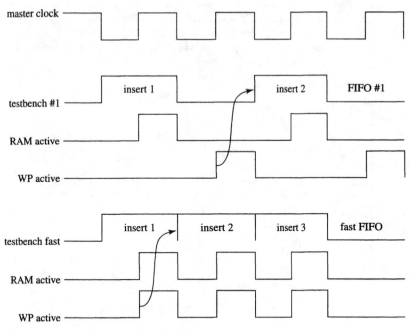

Figure 8.7   *FIFO Timing.*

It is desirable to use the same testbench for the presynthesis specification and also the gate level netlist that results after synthesis. In that case the testbench shown below needs to incorporate the following features, as does the specification for the *fifosc* itself:

- Separation of the test vectors into bits for the low level simulator. At gate level the bitvectors are always separated into their constituent bit lines since they are not all guaranteed to have the same capacitance (and consequently, delay times) after routing. For example, if a bus has a bend, then the outer wires on the turn would be longer than the inner ones. So in what follows, all top-level module specifications and their testbenches will include a mapping to the separate bit lines. While this is a little user unfriendly now, it will be a distinct convenience at low-level simulation time, when we will need all the help we can get.
- For the Altera FPGAs all module argument lists emerge from the fitter ordered with inputs first, then followed by outputs, and within these groups, ordered lexigraphically. So it is desirable to set up the source modules the same way. In this book we have gotten into this habit since Chapter 2 in order to reduce the clutter in the example specifications. For larger modules, the paired port naming convention is recommended in which case the ordering is not a problem (see Section 2.3).

The specification for the testbench now follows. Note how the testbench is timed from the same clock as the circuit under test. This technique will be followed from this point onward. With minor variations this same testbench will serve for all the FIFO variations to follow.

```
module fifosc (clk, flush, insert, remove,
       Win_0, Win_1, Win_2, Win_3, empty, full,
       Wout_0, Wout_1, Wout_2, Wout_3);
 parameter nw=7, as=3, ws=4; // capacity, addrsize, wordsize
 parameter  k = 1; // from table of irreducible trinomials
  input  clk, flush, insert, remove;
  input  Win_3, Win_2, Win_1, Win_0;
  output Wout_3, Wout_2, Wout_1, Wout_0;
  output full, empty;
  reg full, empty;
  reg  [ws-1:0] tpr_data [nw-1:0];
  reg  [as-1:0] wp, rp,  wpo, rpo; // pipelined pointers
  reg  [ws-1:0] Wout;
  wire [ws-1:0] Win;
 assign Win = {Win_3, Win_2, Win_1, Win_0};
 assign Wout_3= Wout[3], Wout_2=Wout[2], Wout_1=Wout[1], Wout_0=Wout[0];
always @(posedge clk)
 if (flush)
  begin
   full<=0; empty<=1; wp<=-1; rp<=-1; wpo<=-2; rpo<=-2;
  end
 else
    begin
     case ({remove,insert})
       2`b00 : ;
       2`b01 : if (~full)
             begin                    // insert only
               tpr_data[wp] <= Win;
               wp <= {(wp[k]^wp[0]), wp[as-1:1]};
               empty<=0; wpo<=wp; if(wp==rpo) full<=1;
             end
       2`b10 : if (~empty)
             begin                    // remove only
               Wout<=tpr_data[rp];
               full<=0; rpo<=rp; if (rp==wpo) empty<=1;
               rp <= {(rp[k]^rp[0]), rp[as-1:1]};
             end
       2`b11 : if (~full && ~empty)
             begin                      // concurrent insert-remove
               tpr_data[wp]<=Win; Wout<=tpr_data[rp];
                wpo<=wp; rpo<=rp;
               wp <= {(wp[k]^wp[0]), wp[as-1:1]};
               rp <= {(rp[k]^rp[0]), rp[as-1:1]};
             end
     endcase
   end
endmodule
```

Specification #9: FIFO (*fifosc*).

```verilog
`timescale 1ns / 100ps
module test_fifosc;
 parameter nw=8, ws=4, as=3, k=2, dt=20; // capacity, wordsize, addrsize, clk
  wire [ws-1:0] Wout;
  wire [as-1:0] wp, rp;
  reg   [ws-1:0] Win;
  integer i;
  reg clk, FLUSH, INSERT, REMOVE;
  wire empty, full;
  wire Wout_3,Wout_2,Wout_1,Wout_0;  // separate wires for low level sim
  wire Win_3=Win[3], Win_2=Win[2], Win_1=Win[1], Win_0=Win[0];
  assign Wout = {Wout_3, Wout_2, Wout_1, Wout_0};

   fifo FI(clk, FLUSH, INSERT, REMOVE, Win_0, Win_1, Win_2, Win_3,
              empty, full, Wout_0, Wout_1, Wout_2, Wout_3);
  always begin #dt clk=1; #dt clk=0; end

initial begin INSERT<=0; REMOVE<=0; FLUSH<=0; Win<=0;
 $display (``time flsh ins rmve Win Wout E F'');
 $monitor (``%4g  %b    %b    %b    %h    %h    %b %b'',
             $time, FLUSH, INSERT, REMOVE, Win, Wout, empty, full);
 @(negedge clk) FLUSH<=1; @(negedge clk) FLUSH<=0;

INSERT<=1; REMOVE<=1;         // attempt concurrent insert-remove
 @(negedge clk) Win<=Win+1;   // when empty

REMOVE<=0;
for (i=0 ; i<=8 ; i=i+1)      // attempt to insert seven words
 @(negedge clk) Win<=Win+1; // - test for full at 6th, err on 7&8

INSERT<=1; REMOVE<=1;
 @(negedge clk) Win<=Win+1;   // attempt concurrent when full

INSERT<=0; REMOVE<=1;
for (i=0; i<=8; i=i+1)        // attempt to remove seven words
 @(negedge clk);             // - test for empty at 6th, err on 7&8

  REMOVE<=0; INSERT<=1;
  for (i=0; i<=2; i=i+1)      // insert three words
   @(negedge clk) Win<=Win+1;

  REMOVE<=1;
  for (i=0; i<=3; i=i+1)      // concurrent insert/remove four
   @(negedge clk) Win<=Win+1; // test 7&8,inserted in error,missing

  INSERT<=0;
  for (i=0; i<=3; i=i+1)      // attempt to remove four words
   @(negedge clk);           // - test for empty on 3rd
  $finish; end
endmodule
```

Testbench for FIFO (test-fifosc).

Exercises

8.1. Draw a state diagram for a 2-bit maximal length FSR.
  a. Give a Verilog specification in the explicit FSM style.
  b. Give a Verilog specification in the Synopsys implicit FSM style.
  c. Do you think either of these as written would result in an efficient synthesis?

8.2. a. Draw a flowchart for the control of the simple (radix 3) Booth multiplier considered as an FSM with datapath (FSMD).
  b. Assuming an input signal available to initiate each new multiplication, draw a state diagram for the controller.
  c. When synthesized, the resulting report shows only one flipflop above those needed for the partial product shift register, bit counter, and multiplicand storage. Explain this.

8.3. The successive approximation analog-to-digital converter is built from an analog part (D-to-A converter feeding an analog comparator) and a digital part. The purpose of the digital part is to accumulate the digital result and to sequence the action so as to:
  • First compare the unknown against a voltage half way up the range.
  • Then if comparison indicates LT (less than), select new comparand 1/4 up the range, or if comparison indicates GE (greater than or equal), select new comparand 3/4 up the range.
  • Continue this process with 1/8, 3/8, 5/8, 7/8, and so on, until the requisite number of bits has been accumulated.
  a. For a 4-bit accumulation, draw the state diagram of the digital part considered as an FSM.
  b. Draw a state diagram for a controller if the digital part is considered as an FSMD (finite state machine with datapath), where the datapath consists of the accumulator register, a shift register containing a "one-hot" bitvector, and an adder/subtractor. For example, your state diagram now just controls these components.
  c. Is the full complexity of an adder/subtractor necessary in this application? If not, why? Would a synthesizer have any way of knowing this?

8.4. Redo the Booth multiplier or FIFO specifications of this chapter in explicit state machine style.

8.5. Booth originally intended his algorithm to save time, but it only really started to do so in its multiple-bit formulations. The fact that the algorithm also handled negative numbers came as a bonus. The radix 4 version compares three bits at a time, and shifts two bits at a time. This time the action table has eight alternatives as follows:

Mplier Bits	Corresponding Action	Remarks
111	+0	this is in the middle of some run of 1's
110	+2M − M = +M	a run starting in the middle of triple
101	−2M + M = −M	a run ending and another starting
100	−2M	a run starting at the left of triple
011	+2M	a run ending at the left of triple
010	+2M − M = +M	a run starting and another ending
001	+M	a run ending in the middle of triple
000	+0	no run in sight

Write a specification for the radix 4 multiplier, a testbench, and test using the simulator.

8.6. Recast the FIFO design of this chapter in the style of [Zorian94]. This uses ring counters for pointers (no decoder) and requires a specialized comparator design.

8.7. Specify a FIFO using shift registers for each bit of the data word and a bidirectional shift register to control the "fill point" (analogous to the indicator tube on an oil tank). This kind of FIFO is more economical for small capacities and synthesis to the flipflops in FPGA logical elements.

8.8. In the brave new world it has become necessary to employ combination locks on every room in order to retain a semblance of equipment, furniture, or even potted plants, and to change the combinations every few weeks. One popular lock marketed for this need has twelve buttons similar to a digital phone. The lock is opened by a sequence of button pushes which may include multiple (simultaneous) button pushes. For this purpose "simultaneity" is defined as "within a concurrent timeout period" from the time any button push is first sensed. A further (longer) timeout determines when a renewed opening attempt may be commenced (audio visual indicator).

   We will assume that a suitable internal clock is available that may be counted down for the timeouts and that a carry output from a counter can be used as a state machine clock.

   a. For a given combination setting, draw a suitable state diagram for the lock opening function (we will skip the combination resetting functions). Sketch the datapath of a corresponding FSMD machine.

   b. Add a combination sequence counter to the FSMD datapath and draw a state diagram for the new controller.

   c. Write a specification for either model (a) or (b) and test.

8.9. Write a Verilog module that correctly captures the following Moore machine state diagram, where *taken* is the input and *predict* is the output. In this case would it be more efficient to employ the one-hot state encoding? Could this machine be specified in implicit style?

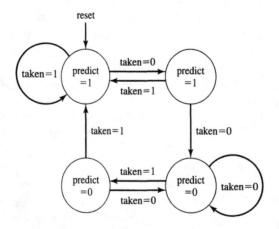

References

[Gajski92] Gajski, D., et al, *High Level Synthesis,* Kluwer, 1992

[Knapp95] Knapp, D., Ly, T., MacMillen, D., and Miller, R., "Behavioral synthesis methodology for HDL-based specification and validation," *Proc. ACM/IEEE Design Automation Conference,* 1995

[Zorian94] Zorian "FIFO built-in self test," *Proc. IEEE Intl. Test Conf.,* 1994, pp. 378–387

Chapter Nine

Control-Point Writing Style

9.1   Introduction

As designs become still more complex than the ones in the last chapter it would seem easier to build them from submodules which have already been designed and tested. The difficulty is that unless the module interfaces are very well described this could lead to more trouble instead of less. Nobody likes to work through somebody else's problems, and most students, given somebody else's design as a starting point, will end up redoing the whole thing out of preference. For industrial designers this has now become a luxury that can no longer be afforded. This issue of design reuse is one of great current interest and will be revisited in Chapter 17. On a modest scale and for some types of applications, one standardized way of handling the interface issue is the *control-point* style described in this chapter.

This style might be summarized as follows: Each module is designed to offer a repertoire of legal operations to the outside world. Inside the module each such operation is described as a composition of operations selected from the repetoires of modules at the next hierarchical level down; in other words, its submodules. This composition is specified in the form of a sequence of operations in the implicit style of the last chapter. Thus this writing style is a mixture of procedural behavioral and structural at each hierarchical level, although a mixture of a prescribed type.

In order to use previously designed modules to speed up the design process in this way we will need to make a small compromise on the controller being completely implicit. The compromise is that the control points are explicitly specified as **reg**'s but the rest of the controller state machine is still in the implicit style of Chapter 8. So all the remaining details of the controller are synthesized automatically from the datapath specification.

To describe the control point style it will be illustrated on variations of the FIFO and Booth multiplier designs from the last chapter. Of course, the very simplicity of these, which is the reason using them for an initial introduction, means that the complexity of a design hierarchy is not really justified. In particular we incur a half cycle time penalty for the interface to each new hierarchical level, although in the case of these FIFOs this does not prevent us from executing a new operation and getting status back every clock cycle.

This is somewhat comparable to the need for the insertion of extra *posedge clock* statements in the BC styles of Chapter 16.

9.2   Instantiation of Parameterized Modules

The modules that we are now starting to encounter are *parameterized*. In them, one or more dimensions are defined by the use of **parameter** statements, each of which set the size of a corresponding dimension to some number. In case the user wishes to utilize such a module in a design with some other dimension, or even use several instantiations of the same module, Verilog provides a calling mechanism that can override the values in the body. For this purpose the # symbol is used followed by a list of arguments that evaluate a numeric quantity and must be in the same order that the parameter statements appear in the body of the called module. For example, the *fsrb* and *ram* modules of the preceding chapters could be instantiated in versions identified as FSR1, FSR2, and MEM1 as follows:

```
fsrb #(NumStages, TapPoint)    FSR1(clk, left-right, enab1, rst, freg1);
fsrb #(5, 2)                   FSR2(clk, left-right, enab2, rst, freg2);
ram  #(NumWords, WidthAd,
       WidthData)              MEM1(clk, select, WE, addr1, data_in, data_out)
```

Here we assume that the variables NumWords, WidthAd, and so on are given numeric values in the parent specification.

9.3   Control-Point Style

To use the FIFO of the previous chapter as an illustration, we take the principal components generated by the synthesis of the previous *fifosc* specification and break them out as separate modules. The organization of such a FIFO store using a two-port RAM (TPR) and two pointers is shown in Figure 9.1. Separate specifications of these components have already been encountered in the two previous chapters.

A Verilog control-point style description of the FIFO is shown in Specification #1.

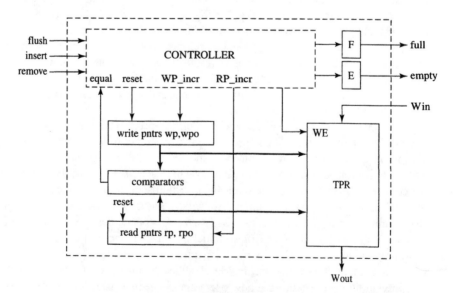

Figure 9.1   *Organization of Concurrent Operation FIFO.*

```
`include ``fsr.v´´
`include ``atpr.v´´
module fifo (clk, flush, insert, remove, Win_0, Win_1, Win_2, Win_3,
               empty, full, Wout_0, Wout_1, Wout_2, Wout_3);
 parameter nw=7, as=3, ws=4; // capacity, addrsize, wordsize
 parameter k=1;           // tap point for fsr
  input  clk, flush, insert, remove;
  output empty, full;
  input  Win_0, Win_1, Win_2, Win_3;
  output Wout_0, Wout_1, Wout_2, Wout_3;
   reg full, empty;            // status
   reg reset, RP_incr, WP_incr; // control points
   wire [ws-1:0] Win, Wout;
   wire [as-1:0] wp, rp, wpo, rpo; // insert and remove pointers, and their shadows
 assign Win = {Win_3, Win_2, Win_1, Win_0};
 assign Wout_3=Wout[3], Wout_2=Wout[2], Wout_1=Wout[1], Wout_0=Wout[0];
  atpr #(nw+1,as,ws) TR (Win, rp, wp, insert&&~full, Wout,);
  fsr #(as,k)        RP (~clk, reset, RP_incr, rp);
  fsr #(as,k)        WP (~clk, reset, WP_incr, wp);
always @(posedge clk)
  if (flush)
   begin
     full<=0; empty<=1; wpo<=-2; rpo<=-2;
     reset<=1; RP_incr <=0; WP_incr <=0;
   end
  else
   begin  reset<=0;
    case ({remove,insert})
     2'b00 : begin WP_incr<=0; RP_incr<=0; end               // idle
     2'b01 : if (~full)
               begin                                          // insert only
                 empty<=0; wpo<=wp; if(wp==rpo) full<=1;
                 WP_incr<=1; RP_incr<=0;
               end
             else WP_incr<=0; // abort insert
     2'b10 : if (~empty)
               begin                                          // remove only
                 full<=0; rpo<=rp; if(rp==wpo) empty<=1;
                 RP_incr<=1; WP_incr<=0;
               end
             else RP_incr<=0; // abort remove
      2'b11 : if (~full && ~empty)
                begin                                 // concurrent insert-remove
                  WP_incr<=1; RP_incr<=1;
                  wpo<=wp; rpo<=rp;
                end
              else begin WP_incr<=0; RP_incr<=0; end
    endcase
   end
endmodule
```

Specification #1: FIFO—Control-Point Version.

The submodules are instantiated to the sizes required as described in Section 9.2. The FIFO itself is also parameterized so that this process can be iterated through higher hierarchical levels in which the FIFO itself will form one of the components. Note the control points listed in a **reg** statement line and the interconnections between the submodules, which are listed in **wire** statements. These may be compared against the block diagram of Figure 9.1 to aid in understanding how the components are organized.

The essence of the control-point style appears in the procedural part (**always** block). The control points are set high (active) and low (inactive) as necessary while in the control sequences corresponding to each operation of the FIFO. The way that the **always** block is set up corresponds to the implicit style of Section 8.2. It results in control points implemented as edge-triggered flipflops with synchronous set and reset.

Of course the operations of the submodules themselves are also generally edge triggered, and they cannot be expected to activate at the same edge that the control point is actually rising. In other words, there must be a delay equal to the set-up time between the control points going high and the submodule activation clock. To achieve this, the submodule

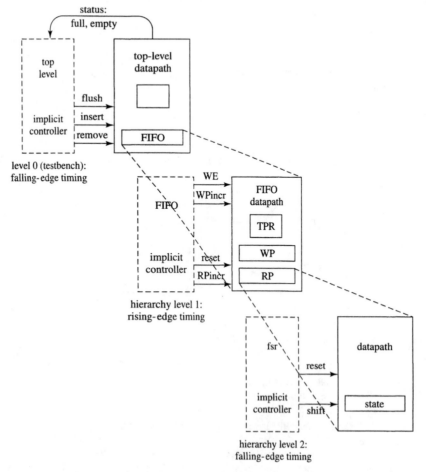

Figure 9.2   *Control Hierarchy for FIFO.*

actions in the successive hierarchical levels are delayed a half clock cycle from that of the preceding level. In the simple examples this has been done by alternating activation on the rising and falling edges on each succeeding level. For now we are talking about a two-level hierarchy on the synthesized chip, or a total of three levels counting the testbench module. Figure 9.2 illustrates the hierarchy.

The testbench is similar to the one used for the *fifosc* specification of Chapter 8.

9.4   Using Vendor's Components

Many organizations have already accumulated their own libraries of components similar in principle to the homebrew ones used in the examples so far. These include:

1. CAD vendors, who usually have a selection of reusable components integrated within their synthesis environment.
2. ASIC fabrication companies and FPGA vendors, with components designed to work within the context of their cell arrays.
3. Third-party *intellectual property providers*, who design and test large macromodules or *cores* (see Chapter 17).

An example of category 1 is the Synopsys *DesignWare* library. Examples of category 2 are those produced by module generators such as the Altera *genmem* program. We will discuss the synthesis aspects of this in Chapter 14, in particular, how to target efficient RAMs. For now we will concentrate on the simulation models. These are provided to assist the user to verify the correctness of the design specification before synthesis.

In order to give a concrete example we will consider the DesignWare modules. On the system the library is located in the directory $SYNOPSYS/dw wherein the families corresponding to our discussion so far are *basic alu* (dw01) and *basic sequential* (dw03). Within each of these are separate directories for synthesis (*lib*, machine readable) and the VHDL and Verilog simulation models (*src_vhd* and *src_ver*).

As an example, the FIFO specification is now repeated once again, this time substituting for the *fsr* module the "*DW03_lfsr_scnto*" module from the DesignWare library. This module has a static *count-to* feature, so that some of the arguments go unused here. When unused arguments are made equal to constants, the synthesizer is supposed to optimize out the corresponding unused circuitry of the submodule. The included file *DW03_lfsr_scnto.v* is the simulation model, used only to check the soundness of the design by high-level simulation. At synthesis time these *include* statements are removed and the compiler picks up the presynthesized modules from the *lib* directory. This is shown in FIFO Specification #2 (*fifodw*).

As a final comparison, one of the several FIFO modules already available in the DesignWare library could just be enclosed in a wrapper and nearly all of the specification above dispensed with. This is shown in Specification #3 (*fifoDW*). Structural instantiation of library modules as in this last example are completely general and of course not limited to the control-point style (Problem 9.2 at end of the chapter).

In comparing the results from synthesis, the single-level *fifosc* specification of the previous chapter might be expected to result in savings since the separate controllers are rolled into one, but this does not seem to be a major factor. In fact the control-point Specification #1 turns out slightly faster. The *fifoDW* from the library gives somewhat poorer results perhaps due to the extra overhead of the wrapper and almost-full flags. Note that

```
`include ``atpr.v``
`include ``/usr/local/pkg/cad/synopsys/dw/dw03/src_ver/DW03_lfsr_scnto.v``

module fifodw(clk, flush, insert, remove,
      Win_0, Win_1, Win_2, Win_3,
      empty, full,
      Wout_0,Wout_1,Wout_2,Wout_3
     );
 parameter nw=7, as=3, ws=4; // capacity, addrsize, wordsize
 parameter k=1;            // tap point for fsr
  input  clk, flush, insert, remove;
  input  Win_3, Win_2, Win_1, Win_0;
  output Wout_3,Wout_2,Wout_1,Wout_0;
  output full, empty;
   reg full, empty;
   reg RP_reset, RP_incr, WP_reset, WP_incr;
   wire [ws-1:0] Wout, Win;
   wire [as-1:0] wp, rp;   // insert and remove pointers
   reg  [as-1:0] wpo, rpo; // pipelined pointers
   wire [as-1:0] ZERO = 0;
 assign Win = {Win_3, Win_2, Win_1, Win_0};
 assign Wout_3=Wout[3], Wout_2=Wout[2], Wout_1=Wout[1], Wout_0=Wout[0];
 atpr   #(nw+1,as,ws)        TR (Win, ~rp, ~wp, insert&&~full, Wout,);
 DW03_lfsr_scnto #(as,nw+1)  RP (ZERO,1´b1,RP_incr,~clk,~RP_reset,rp,);
 DW03_lfsr_scnto #(as,nw+1)  WP (ZERO,1´b1,WP_incr,~clk,~WP_reset,wp,);
 always @(posedge clk)
   //... control part same as before
```

Specification #2: FIFO—Using Submodule from Library.

```
`include ``/usr/local/pkg/cad/synopsys/dw/dw03/src_ver/DW03_fifo_a_sf.v``
module fifoDW(clk,flush,insert,remove,
       Win_0, Win_1, Win_2, Win_3,
       empty, full,
       Wout_0, Wout_1, Wout_2, Wout_3);
 parameter data_width = 4, depth = 7, level = 2, addr_width = 3;
  input  clk, flush, insert, remove;
  input  Win_3, Win_2, Win_1, Win_0;
  output Wout_3, Wout_2, Wout_1, Wout_0;
  output full, empty;
   wire [data_width-1:0] Win, Wout;
 assign Win = {Win_3, Win_2, Win_1, Win_0};
 assign Wout_3=Wout[3],Wout_2=Wout[2],Wout_1=Wout[1],Wout_0=Wout[0];
  DW03_fifo_a_sf   #(data_width, depth, level)
                   U0(Win,~insert,~remove, 1´b0,~flush,Wout,full,empty,);
endmodule
```

Specification #3: FIFO—Using Whole Module from Library.

```
module ashft(clk, init, load, shift, m_in, a_in, state);
 parameter n = 16;
 input  clk, init, load, shift;
 input [n-1:0] a_in, m_in;
 output [2*n:0] state;
 reg    [2*n:0] state;
 always begin @(posedge clk)
  if (init)     state <= {{n{1'b0}}, m_in[n-1:0], 1'b0};
    elseif (load) state <= {a_in[n-1:0], state[n:0]};
    @(posedge clk)
    if (shift) // long arithmetic right shift
    state <= {state[2*n],state[2*n:1]};
  end
endmodule
```

Specification #4: Submodule for Long Right Arithmetic
Shift of Partial Product.

even for the small memory size used here (7,3,4), over half of the area counts at this point are due to the RAMs being inefficiently constructed from arrays of flipflops. This will be made apparent when embedded RAM is substituted in Chapter 14.

9.4.1   Booth Multiplier

As the next example, the Booth multiplier of the last chapter is translated into control-point form. This shows how the control-point style can be applied to designs with looping. The homebrew submodules *ashft* and *shiftcount* are used, which are specialized registers that accomplish the long right arithmetic shift of the partial product with test bit, and a shift register which acts as a counter. Their function is similar to that described in the single-level example in Chapter 8. To illustrate, the *ashft* submodule is shown in Specification #4.

Specification #5, the Booth multiplier in control-point form then follows on the next page.

9.5   Conclusion

In summary, the control-point style makes it easy to incorporate submodules for users or vendors libraries and, like other implict styles, lets the synthesizer do most of the work of building the controller. For submodule hierarchy depths greater than two or three, the method would start to suffer from an accumulation of controller set-up delays in general. Although for the designs considered here there was little or no penalty in either time or area performance, clearly one method does not fit all. Some designs will benefit from a particular style and some not. One situation in which the control-point style works well is in pipelined designs with submodules that operate on two cycles: An active cycle and a recovery cycle. Then the control points can be set and reset in the alternate cycles. The cache and MIPS processor designs of Chapter 10 are of this nature and it is in such complex designs where the benefits of this style are more apparent.

```
`include ``mux.v´´
`include ``register.v´´
`include ``adder.v´´
`include ``ashft.v´´
`include ``shiftcount.v´´

module boothcp(clk, mult, mcand_in, mplier_in, product_out);
 parameter w=4; // small wordsize for test
  input  clk, cphase, mult;
  input  [w-1:0] mcand_in, mplier_in;
  output [2*w-1:0] product_out;
  reg PP_init,PP_ld,PP_shft,MCAND_ld, CNT_rst, CNT_shft, C_in;
  wire clk, cph=~clk;
  wire [w-1:0] count, lbus, rbus, add_out, mcand_out;
  wire [2*w:0] pps;
  assign lbus = pps[(2*w):w+1];
  assign product_out = pps[2*w:1];
 adder #(w) ADD(lbus, rbus, C_in, add_out);
 mux   #(w) MUX(C_in, mcand_out, ~mcand_out, rbus);
 ashft #(w) PP(cph,PP_init,PP_ld,PP_shft,mplier_in,add_out,pps);
 shiftcount #(w) CNT(cph, CNT_init, CNT_shft, count);
 register   #(w) MCAND(cph, MCAND_ld, mcand_in, mcand_out);
 always
 begin @(posedge clk)
  PP_shft<=0; CNT_shft<=0;                    // reset control points
  if (mult) begin // load operands for a new operation
            PP_init<=1; CNT_init<=1; MCAND_ld<=1; PP_ld<=0;
            @(posedge clk);
            CNT_int<=0;  PP_init<=0;  MCAND_ld<=0;
            end
   else if (count[0]) // have not yet reached last bit
     begin
       case (pps[1:0])
         2´b01: begin C_in<=0; PP_ld<=1; end   // add mcand
         2´b10: begin C_in<=1; PP_ld<=1; end   // subtract mcand
         2´b00, 2´b11: ;                       // no operation
       endcase
       @(posedge clk);
       PP_shft<=1; CNT_shft<=1; PP_ld<=0;
     end
 end
endmodule
```

Control-Point Specification #5: Booth Multiplier.

Exercises

9.1. Modify the FIFO of this chapter so as to replace the homebrew two-port RAM with the *DW_ram_r_w_a_dff* or the *DW_ram_r_w_s_dff* from the Synopsys DW-06 DesignWare library. Simulate using the DesignWare Verilog simulation models and test using a link to the *lib* version.

9.2. The following FIFO variations are possible:
- Use ring counters and explicit addressing for pointers. Can use a simplified comparator (see [Zorian96]).
- Use single-port or two-port RAM.
- Provide for concurrent *insert* and *remove* operations (possible with two-port RAM only) or not.
- Use binary up-counters or maximal length feedback shift registers for the pointers.
- Use homebrew submodules, or DesignWare submodules, or no submodules.
- Use indicators for full or 3/4 full, empty or 1/4 full. Use internal interlock to prevent overfilling, or rely on user (surrounding circuitry).

Specify an alternative FIFO in the control-point style, and simulate with a corresponding test module.

9.3. Write a specification for a stack module with push and pop operations. Try to get your version as close as possible to that of the stack in the DesignWare library (with a wrapper around it in the style of *fifoDW*) so that hopefully a single testbench can be used for both.

9.4. Another project with a similar flavor to the FIFO or stack is the Pico-Java stack with spill-fill [McGhan99]. This could be specified with a two-port RAM from the homebrew or DesignWare library now and replaced with an embedded FPGA RAM after reaching Chapter 14.

9.5. The family of *content addressable* memories are addressed with a key instead of a numeric value as in the RAM. They include those in which the stored fields are simply the keys themselves (plus a row occupancy bit) strictly called CAM, and those in which an associated field is read out, called *associative memories*. For the CAM, the output is binary, simply indicating if the presented key is present in the memory or not.

In custom VLSI CAM, the array cells themselves are augmented with extra transistors to handle the search accesses, but for synthesis this is not easily effected. Instead a variant of the well-known hash methods [Knuth75] can be employed in a hardware context. One possibility is a variation on algorithm D of this reference, called double hashing. In the following such variation, *KEY[i]* are the key fields stored in a RAM, *TABLE[i]* is a vector of occupancy bits, K is the presented key, and M is the RAM capacity in number of words.

```
D0: N<=0
D1: (first hash and probe): set i <=h_1(K);
    if (TABLE[i] empty) goto D3, elseif  (KEY[i]=K)return success
D2: (second hash and probe): set i <= h_2(i);
    if (TABLE[i] empty) goto D3;
    elseif  (KEY[i]= K) return success; else go back to D2
D3: if (N = M-1) return overflow;
    else begin N=N+1; mark TABLE[i] occupied; set
        KEY[i] <=K; end
```

One possibility is for the synthesized hardware module to handle operations *flush, search, enter,* and *repeat* (second hash and probe), and for the testbench to handle the tests and sequencing above. For a small model the first hash $h\_1(K)$ could be a combinational hash based on folding [Lum71] with bitwise exclusive *or* instead of decimal add. The second hash $h\_2(i)$ could be based on a feedback shift register if provision is made to EXOR an extra 1 bit into the feedback path in the event the first hash produces all zeros.

a. Design such a CAM and write a specification. You may use methods similar to those employed on the FIFO in this chapter, which will facilitate synthesis later. Parameterize as much as possible, and select a small version for testing.

b. Design a testbench that will exercise the various steps of the modified algorithm D above and verify the correct operation by simulation.

9.6. Good exercises at this stage are the floating point add/subtract, or the floating point multiply. For the latter the Booth multiplier from the text could be incorporated. The IEEE single precision standard should be followed, see Appendix A of [H&P90]. A priority encoder could be used to detect the first non-zero bit in the result to be normalized, and the output could be used to feed a barrel shifter (Chapter 3, Problem 3.16, or select from the DesignWare library).

9.7. In practice both the Booth technique and the carry save adders are combined to produce a fast multiplier. For example a version for the 32X32 bit multiply uses fourteen CSA modules in the form of a tree (called a Wallace tree) [H&P90]. The last stage is a carry propagate adder (CPA). The hardware is extensive since the adders must accommodate up to sixty-four bits as the bottom of the tree is reached. However, the equivalent number of fulladder components required is only about half of that required for the equivalent array multiplier, while the equivalent ripple delay is reduced to about one quarter. Specify and test such a multiplier (see also [Ciminiera96]).

References

[Ciminiera96] Ciminiera, L., and Montuschi, P., "Carry-Save Multiplication Schemes without final addition," *IEEETC* 45:9 (Sept. 1996), pp. 1050–1055

[Knuth75] Knuth, D. E., *The Art of Computer Programming—Vol 3: Sorting and Searching,* Addison Wesley, p. 521, 1975

[Lum71] Lum, V. Y., et al., "Key-to-address transform techniques: A fundamental performance study on large existing formatted files," *Communications of the Association for Computing Machinery,* pp. 228–239, 1971

[McGhan99] McGhan, H., and O'Connor, M., "PicoJava: A direct execution engine for Java bytecode," *IEEE Computer* 31:10 (Oct. 1998), pp. 22–30

Chapter Ten

Managing Complexity – Large Designs

Chapters 6 through 9 focused on designs containing only a few hundred gates. How does one approach designs that contain thousands or even tens of thousands of gates? The intent of this chapter is to give the reader insight into the design and partitioning of more complex digital subsystems.

10.1   Steps in High-Level Design

Given a design specification, novice designers are often tempted to start coding straight away. This is a poor approach to generating a quality design. In general, time spent generating a "paper" design before coding is more than rewarded with a smaller, faster design, and a much quicker debugging cycle. In this section, a structured approach is provided for generating a paper design.

An important guiding principle in high-level design is to clearly separate the datapath from the controller. The "datapath" refers to the collection of arithmetic and logic units, registers, multiplexors, and buses that process the data so as to produce the desired result. The controller refers to the sequencing logic (finite state machines [FSMs] and/or counter[s]) that determines what happens on the datapath. They are interconnected by clearly defined *control points*—control lines and status lines. Novice designers may want to separate the datapath and controller so as to avoid confusing the relationship between "cause" and "effect" in the design, and thus ease debug and modification. For this purpose:

Always clearly separate datapath from controller.

This important principle can be easily followed if the designer takes a disciplined approach to design as follows:

Step 1. Structuring the Datapath

From the structural and performance specification, determine the functional units needed and their connectivity. Examples of functional units would include adders, multipliers, shifters, memory interfaces, data coders and decoders, and so on. Connectivity is provided by wires, buses, and multiplexors.

The quality of the design at this stage will largely determine the overall performance and area of the function. It is important for the designer to determine the degree of parallelism and pipelining required. Alternative design approaches often need to be explored to provide an efficient design. General steps and guidance as to how to design a datapath are given in Chapter 6.

In more complex designs, especially microprocessors, a useful initial step in structuring the datapath is the determination of the *micro-operations* that have to be performed on the datapath—for example, a list of register-to-register transfer operations that the datapath must perform in order to deliver its required functionality. A simple example will be given later in the on-line addendum to this book.

Step 2. Identify Control Points

As discussed in Chapter 9, the control points consist of control lines and status lines. Control lines originate in the controller and determine the detailed operations to be performed on the datapath during any one clock cycle. Status lines originate in the datapath and indicate the status outputs of important units, for example zero and overflow flags.

Step 3. Determine Transition Points in Control Flow

It is important to identify critical points in the control sequence. For example, start, stop, and transitions between different modes of operation. These points generally require special attention to get them right.

Step 4. Determine Control Strategy and Control Flow

Generally, control sequences are generated by a combination of the following:

- *FSM*s. This was introduced in Chapter 8 and is repeated for completeness in Figure 10.1. One or more such machines might be necessary to control events.

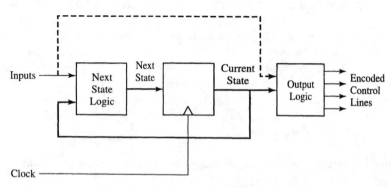

Finite State Machine (FSM). In a Moore machine, the inputs are not connected to the output logic block. In a Mealy machine, they are.

Figure 10.1   *Elements Used in Building Controllers—Finite State Machine (FSM).*

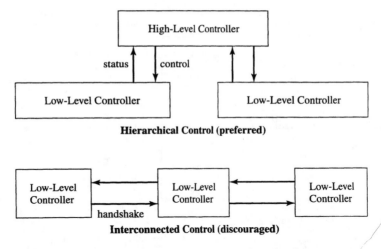

Figure 10.2   *Top-down Interconnected Control Strategies.*

When more than one FSM is needed, either from a functional point of view or to limit the number of states for speed reasons, a top-down control approach is better than an interconnected one (Figure 10.2).

- In a top-down approach, higher-level controllers control lower-level ones. This is better than an interconnected approach, as in the latter, the state of the lower-level machines depends on the state of several other FSMs, while in the former, it depends only on the state of the higher-level machine. A top-down strategy is easier to design and debug.
- *Microcode.* Sometimes instead of a large FSM, a microcoded controller is used as the design can be made smaller and faster. The elements of a microcoded controller are illustrated in Figure 10.3. It consists of a microcoded ROM (which is sometimes RAM), a micro program counter (uPC), and next uPC address logic. The next microcode address is either the previous address plus one (sequential addressing through the microcode) or determined from the 'jump' field of the microcoded ROM.
- *Counters.* Often it is necessary to count events making counters useful in the control strategy (Figure 10.4).
- *Combinational Decoders.* Often decode logic is needed that takes the output of one of the above and decodes it into the separate control points (Figure 10.5).
- By using these decoders, the sequential control portion (FSM, microcode, or counter) can often be made smaller than if these decoders were not present.

Step 5. Determine the Reset Strategy

Reset is a global signal distributed across the entire chip that initializes the chip to a known state. It is generally toggled on power-up or when a reset button is depressed. Its purpose is to bring the chip to a known state so that subsequent operation will be correct. Without reset, the chip would power up in a random state and the controllers would have to collaborate to reach a known start state on their own, an obviously difficult task.

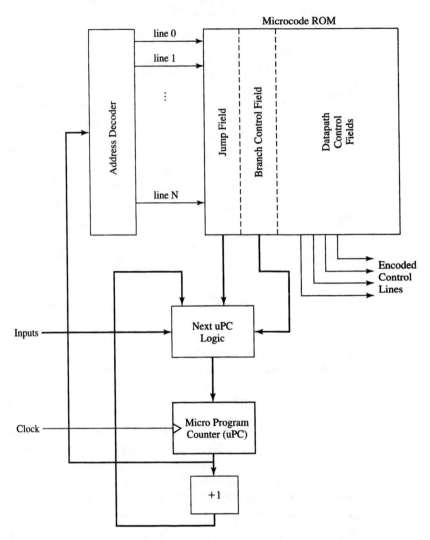

Figure 10.3   *Elements in Building Controllers—Microcoding.*

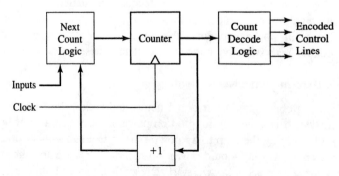

Figure 10.4   *Elements Used in Building Controllers—Counter.*

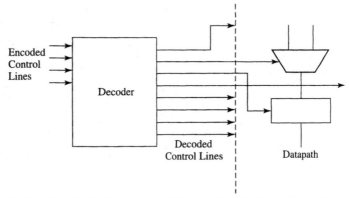

Combinational logic decoders are used for generating the final control points

Figure 10.5   *Elements Used in Building Controllers—Decode Logic.*

Reset is generally distributed to registers which collectively determine the state of the machine. Examples include state registers in FSMs, controlling counters, status registers, and so on. Reset is a global signal that should not be modified locally.

Step 6. Verify Before Coding

Generally, it is a useful practice to hand-simulate the design before coding. Draw a timing diagram capturing critical events to help you find potential bugs early.

10.2   Design Partitioning

The design has to be partitioned into separate modules, leading to the question as to how to decide what goes in which module. This issue is mainly related to synthesis, as the main goal of design partitioning is to make synthesis fast, efficient, and likely to lead to optimal results. When completed, the design will consist of a hierarchy of modules. For example, the hierarchy depicted in Figure 10.6 consists of three modules: module controlA instantiated as u1, module dataA instantiated as u2, and the module top which contains only u1 and u2 and is instantiated as uu1. Some general rules regarding design partitioning are as follows:

- *Only modules at the bottom of the hierarchy should contain logic.* The higher level modules should consist of only instantiations of lower-level modules and wires. No gates should appear in the higher-level modules (for example, module top in Figure 10.6). This way, the synthesis tools can work on one module at a time, leading to a faster synthesis run.
- *Critical paths should be contained entirely within one module.* "Critical path" refers to the slowest path of combinational logic that exists between registers (see Chapter 12). By keeping critical paths entirely contained within a module, synthesis will be able to concentrate on optimizing its timing.
- *Whenever possible, register the outputs of modules.* Whenever possible, the output of a module should be a flipflop output. That way, the synthesis tools can easily

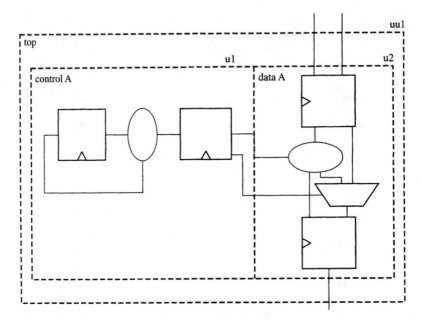

Figure 10.6   *Design Hierarchy.*

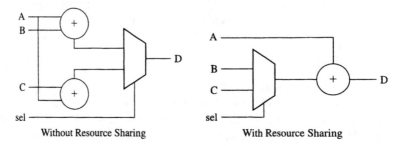

Figure 10.7   *Example of Resource Sharing.*

determine the timing of connections to the inputs of other modules (being solely the clock-to-output delay of a flipflop).

- *Potentially sharable resources should be within one module.* Sometimes, the synthesis tools determine how to share potentially common resources, such as adders. Whenever there is potential for such sharing, all of the related logic should be contained in one module, or even better, within one procedural block. In general, keep closely related portions of the design within one module. For example, synthesis will usually produce one adder and one multiplexor for the design below, even though two adders are 'specified' (Figure 10.7):

```
always @(A or B or C or sel)
    D = sel ? A+C : A+B;
```

- *Separate modules that will have different synthesis strategies.* Only one synthesis strategy can be used per module.
- *Keep modules as small as possible consistent with the above guidelines.* Synthesis has a better chance of optimizing small designs than large ones. However, don't take this to the extreme. Partitioning each design so that each flipflop and input logic is in its own module will make the design unnecessarilly unwieldy.

10.3   Controller Design Styles

The remainder of this chapter contains examples that illustrate these design principles via examples. Two of the major high-level design styles discussed in previous chapters are used. The first example uses an explicit control-design style. In this style, the control and datapath portions of the design are explicitly separated and joined via well-identified control points. This is the simplest style to use, especially for designers who are just learning their trade. The other two examples use an implicit control style. In this style, the control flow is specified in the same blocks as the datapath and the control points are thus implicit within these blocks. This design style generally leads to more compact and elegant code but requires a more sophisticated understanding of the relationship between code and hardware.

In many cases the area and performance can turn out to be very similar irrespective of the design style, but not always.

10.4   Example of Explicit Style—Motion Estimator

This is a typical example of an ASIC function—a piece of hardware purpose built to accelerate a function that would be performed too slowly in even the fastest general purpose microprocessor. The example is taken from multimedia hardware and would be found in a digital movie production system designed to produce MPEG video, such as a digital camcorder or videocam.

If recorded and transmitted in its raw format, TV-quality video would require about 6 Mb of storage or transmission bandwidth for every second. A number of compression techniques are used that when combined can reduce this number by a factor of four or more. One of these techniques is motion estimation.

Motion estimation is best illustrated by a simple example. Consider the two subsequent video frames shown in Figure 10.8. In this case, the black image that is common to the frames is moved one up and one to the right in the second frame, with respect to the first. Thus, the second frame can be recorded as being the same as the first frame except for having a motion vector of (1,1) between them. It takes a lot less storage to store this motion vector than the raw video bandwidth for the second frame.

Candidates for compression via motion estimation are found by doing a search on a set of possible motion vectors between two subsequent frames and looking for a good match. This is illustrated in Figure 10.9. Two frames are compared by taking each 16 pixel by 16 pixel reference block in the first frame and searching for a good match for it within a search window in the second frame. (The term "pixel" stands for "picture element" and is essentially one "dot" on the screen. It is encoded with color and intensity information.) In this case, the search window in the second frame is a 31×31 window centered around the position of the reference block in the first frame.

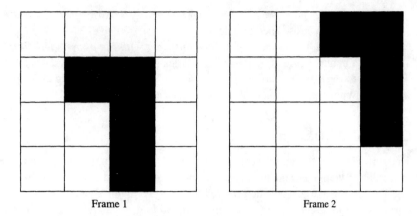

Frame 1   Frame 2

Figure 10.8   *Consecutive Frames in Which the Second Can Be Coded As a Motion Vector Applied to the First.*

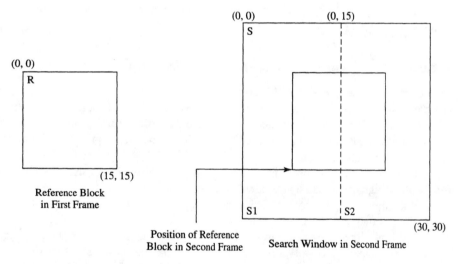

Figure 10.9   *Search Is Performed by Comparing the Reference Block in the First Frame with a Set of Possible Positions of the Reference Block in the Second Frame.*

Thus a total of $(31 - 15) \times (31 - 15) = 256$ comparisons must be performed, one for each possible match of a candidate to the reference block, from the candidate block in the top left corner to the candidate block in the bottom right corner of the search window. For each possible comparison block (starting at position (i,j)), a distortion figure is calculated.

$$D(i, j) = \sum_{m=0}^{15} \sum_{n=0}^{15} \left| r_{m, n} - S_{m+i, n+j} \right|$$

Where (i, j) is the position of the candidate block being evaluated, the index (i,j) will take on values from (0,0) to (15,15), that being all possible top left coordinates of the candidate blocks. If the value for $D(i, j)$ is zero, then a perfect match has been found and the appropriate motion vector can be calculated. In practice, if $D(i, j)$ is small enough, then the difference between the two frames is often still encoded as a motion vector, as the human eye will not notice the resulting small irregularities in the video picture.

Since the reference block position is at the center of the search window, a coordinate transformation is needed in order to obtain the actual motion vector. For example, the position of the (0,0) candidate block with respect to the reference block is (−8,−8). Thus if $D(i, j)$ provides the best match, the potential motion vector is $(i − 8, j − 8)$.

Determining motion vectors requires high levels of performance. For each comparison, 256 additions have to be performed. For each reference block, there are 256 possible candidate blocks, and there might be as many as 4096 reference blocks in each frame of video data. Thus over 268 million additions have to be done for each frame of data. At thirty frames per second, the required processing rate becomes over eight billion additions per second, clearly beyond any current microprocessor. However, a motion estimator capable of performing at this rate can be custom-built in a small amount of parallel logic.

One possible architecture for a motion estimator is shown in Figure 10.10 and is taken from [BK97]. The architecture consists of three small memories (one for the

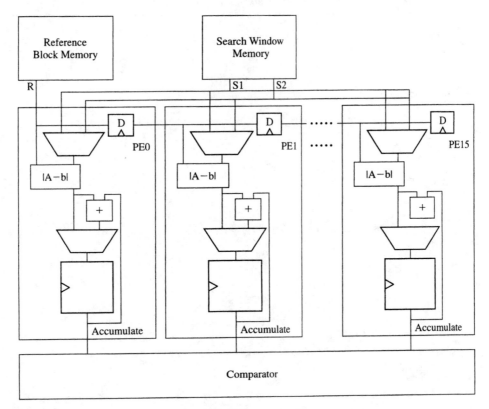

Figure 10.10   *Architecture for Motion Estimator.*

reference block data, and one each for the left- and right-hand sides of the search window data), sixteen processing elements (PEs), a comparator unit, and a control unit. The idea is that each PE will produce a new distortion figure $D(i,j)$ for candidate block (i,j) each 256 clock cycles. To do this, the reference block data is continuously fed into the left-hand PE and pipelined through the "D" registers from left to right. On each clock cycle, a datum from the search window is subtracted from the current datum from the reference window. The sequence of data from the search window memories, together with the pipelining of data from the reference block memory, is cleverly arranged to make sure that all of the PEs are 100 percent busy for most of the time. The sequencing of data from the memories, and the current subtract being done in each PE is given in Table 10.1.

The sequence of operations is clearly shown in Table 10.1. The first PE starts computing $D(0,0)$ on clock cycle 0 and finishes the computation on cycle 255. (Not shown is how it will start computing $D(1,0)$ on cycle 256.) Similarly, PE $- 1$ starts computing $D(0,1)$ on cycle 1 and finishes it on cycle 256, and PE $- 15$ starts computing D(0,15) on cycle 15 and finishes it on cycle 270.

Consider the performance of this structure. Note that it takes fifteen cycles for all the PEs to become busy after the search is started. Thus, in this pipelined fashion, all 256 possible block comparisons can be completed in $16(16 \times 16) + 15 = 4111$ cycles,

Table 10.1   *Memory Sequencing and Pixel Computation Sequence for Producing the First Sixteen Distortions.*

Clk Cyc	Input R	Input S1	Input S2	PE-0	PE-1	...	PE-15
0	$R_{0,0}$	$S_{0,0}$		$|R_{0,0} - S_{0,0}|$			
1	$R_{0,1}$	$S_{0,1}$		$|R_{0,1} - S_{0,1}|$	$|R_{0,0} - S_{0,1}|$		
2	$R_{0,2}$	$S_{0,2}$		$|R_{0,2} - S_{0,2}|$	$|R_{0,1} - S_{0,2}|$		
...	...	...		...	...		
15	$R_{0,15}$	$S_{0,15}$		$|R_{0,15} - S_{0,15}|$	$|R_{0,14} - S_{0,15}|$		$|R_{0,1} - S_{0,15}|$
16	$R_{1,0}$	$S_{1,0}$	$S_{0,16}$	$|R_{1,0} - S_{1,0}|$	$|R_{0,15} - S_{0,16}|$		$|R_{0,1} - S_{0,16}|$
17	$R_{1,1}$	$S_{1,1}$	$S_{0,17}$	$|R_{1,1} - S_{1,1}|$	$|R_{1,0} - S_{1,1}|$		$|R_{0,2} - S_{0,17}|$
...	...	...		...	...		...
31	$R_{1,15}$	$S_{1,15}$	$S_{0,31}$	$|R_{1,15} - S_{1,15}|$	$|R_{1,14} - S_{1,15}|$		$|R_{1,0} - S_{1,15}|$
...	...	...		...	...		...
240	$R_{15,0}$	$S_{15,0}$	$S_{14,16}$	$|R_{15,0} - S_{15,0}|$	$|R_{14,15} - S_{14,16}|$		$|R_{14,1} - S_{14,16}|$
...	...	...		...	...		...
255	$R_{15,15}$	$S_{15,15}$	$S_{13,31}$	$|R_{15,15} - S_{15,15}|$	$|R_{15,14} - S_{15,15}|$		$|R_{15,0} - S_{15,15}|$
256			$S_{15,16}$		$|R_{15,15} - S_{15,16}|$		$|R_{15,1} - S_{15,15}|$
...	...	...		...	...		...
270			$S_{15,30}$				$|R_{15,15} - S_{15,30}|$

and 4096 reference blocks could be searched for in $4096 \times 4111 = 16,429,056$ cycles. To achieve a frame rate of thirty frames per second, would require a clock frequency of almost 500 MHz. If the hardware could not be built to operate that fast, then two of these units could be used in parallel to achieve the required throughput at 250 MHz, or four units at 125 MHz, etc.

10.4.1   Datapath Design

Now that the algorithm, architecture, and performance of the design has been determined, it is necessary to produce the detailed design. In this case, the micro-operation sequence corresponds to that shown in Table 10.1. A useful approach is to first determine the detailed structure of the datapath elements, from that determine the control points, and finally design the controller to toggle the control points correctly. The details of the processing element were seen in Figure 10.10. It consists of an accumulator register and some input logic comprising an absolute subtractor, a saturating adder, and two multiplexors. A saturating adder is an absolute adder (no negative numbers) that never overflows. Instead of overflowing, it simply saturates with all "1"s. A saturating adder is used because it would be undesirable if the distortion produced was 0 since two larger numbers were added such as to cause an overflow and a zero result. Overflow in unsigned addition can be detected by looking at the carry flag. The reference memory data pipeline is illustrated at the top of the processing element. A possible Verilog level design for the PE is shown below.

```
module PE (clock, R, S1, S2, S1S2mux, newDist, Accumulate, Rpipe);
input clock;
input [7:0] R, S1, S2;// memory inputs
input S1S2mux, newDist;// control inputs
output [7:0] Accumulate, Rpipe;
reg [7:0] Accumulate, AccumulateIn, Difference, Rpipe;
reg       Carry;

always @(posedge clock) Rpipe <= R;
always @(posedge clock) Accumulate <= AccumulateIn;

always @(R or S1 or S2 or S1S2mux or newDist or Accumulate)
  begin  // capture behavior of logic
    difference = R - S1S2mux ? S1 : S2;
    if (difference < 0) difference = 0 - difference;
// absolute subtraction
    {Carry,AccumulateIn} = Accumulate + difference;
    if (Carry == 1) AccumulateIn = 8'hFF;// saturated
    if (newDist == 1) AccumulateIn = difference;
// starting new Distortion calculation
  end
endmodule
```

Motion Estimator Processing Element (PE).

Note the following features in this design:

- There are no need for "else" statements in the non-clocked procedural block. Every output is assigned for all possible input variations, so there are no implicit latches.
- The fact that the addition of two 8-bit numbers produces a 9-bit result is captured in the assignment of the add to {Carry, AccumulateIn}.

The comparator is a simple structure. It mainly consists of registers to keep track of the best distortion and associated motion vector detected so far; some initialization logic for these registers, and an input multiplexor. It can be described in Verilog as shown below.

```
module Comparator (clock, CompStart, PEout, PEready, vectorX,
                        vectorY, BestDist, motionX, motionY);
input clock;
input CompStart; // goes high when distortion calculations start
input [8*16:0] PEout; // Outputs of PEs as one long vector
input [15:0] PEready; // Goes high when that PE has a new distortion
input [3:0] vectorX, vectorY; // Motion vector being evaluated
output [7:0] BestDist; // Best Distortion vector so far
output [3:0] motionX, motionY; // Best motion vector so far
reg [7:0] BestDist, newDist;
reg [3:0] motionX, motionY;
reg       newBest;

always @(posedge clock)
  if (CompStart == 0) BestDist <= 8´hFF;  //initialize to highest value
  else if (newBest == 1)
    begin
      BestDist <= newDist;
      motionX <= vectorX;
      motionY <= vectorY;
    end

always @(BestDist or PEout or PEready)
  begin
    newDist = PEout [PEready*8+7 : PEready*8];
    if (((|PEready == 0) || (start == 0)) newBest = 0; // no PE is ready
    else if (newDist < BestDist) newBest = 1;
    else newBest = 0;
  end

endmodule
```

Comparator Module.

Now that the datapath has been designed, the control points can be established. Though a designer would not normally do this, they are explicitly listed below to emphasize this point.

```
PE control lines:
S1S2mux [15:0]; //S1-S2 mux control
NewDist [15:0]; //=1 when PE is starting a new distortion calculation

Comparator control lines:
CompStart;// = 1 when PEs running
PEready [15:0]; //PEready[I]=1 when PEi has a new distortion vector
VectorX [3:0];
VectorY [3:0];// Motion vector being evaluated

Memory control lines:
// Memories organized in row-major format
// e.g. R(3,2) is stored at location 3*15+2 - 1 = 46
AddressR [7:0];  // address for Reference memory (0,0)...(15,15)
AddressS1 [9:0];  // address for first read port of Search mem
AddressS2 [9:0]; // second read port of Search mem (0,0)-(30,30)
```

Control Points.

The natural control strategy for this design is counter-based, not FSM-based. There are a number of reasons for this choice:

- Every control signal is generated on a cyclic basis. For example, PEready[0] goes high every 256 clock cycles.
- There are no inputs to the controller apart from a start signal. Since no other decisions have to be made, there is no need for an FSM.

The Verilog for the controller is listed in the two boxes following:

```
module control (clock, start, S1S2mux, NewDist, CompStart, PEready,
                VectorX, VectorY, AddressR, AddressS1, AddressS2);
input clock;
input start; // = 1 when`going`
output [15:0] S1S2mux;
output [15:0] NewDist;
output  CompStart;
output [15:0] PEready;
output [3:0]  VectorX, VectorY;
output [7:0]  AddressR;
output [9:0]  AddressS1, AddressS2;
reg [15:0] S1S2mux;
reg [15:0] NewDist;
reg        CompStart;
reg [15:0] PEready;
reg [3:0]  VectorX, VectorY;
reg [7:0]  AddressR;
reg [9:0]  AddressS1, AddressS2;
reg [12:0] count;
reg     completed;
integer    i;
```

Controller Module: Declarations.

```
always @(posedge clock)
  if (start == 0) count <= 12'b0;
  else if (completed == 0) count <= count + 1'b1;

always @(count)
  begin
    for (i=0; i<15; i = i+1)
      begin
        NewDist[i] = (count[7:0] == i);
        PEready[i] = (NewDist[i] && !(count < 8'd256));
        S1S2mux[i] = (count[3:0] > i);
      end
    AddressR = count[7:0];
    AddressS1 = (count[11:8] + count[7:4]>>4)*5'd32 + count[3:0];
    AddressS2 = (count[11:8] + count[7:4]>>4)*4'd16 + count[3:0];
    VectorX = count[3:0] - 4'd7;
    VectorY = count[11:8]>>4 - 4'd7;
    complete = (count = 4'd16 * (8'd256 + 1));
  end

endmodule
```

Controller Module: Procedural Part.

When designing a controller, simplicity is often a key to success. In this case, the simplest controller design strategy is to build one counter and decode logic to toggle the various control lines. Just about any other alternative will involve multiple counters and/or shift register and will neither be as small nor as simple to design and understand as this alternative. The counter has to go high enough to calculate all of the distortion vectors.

10.5   Example of Implicit Style—Cache Store

The next example to be developed is a direct mapped, write-through cache store with sub-block placement [H&P94]. It will be tested with the parameterized size reduced to match the reduced size MIPS processor which is the example to follow.

The organization of the cache is shown in Figure 10.11.

If all requested addressed words were present in the cache, called *cache-hits*, then the data references would be provided to the central processor (CPU) at a rate of one every two clock cycles. The control of this cache is timed explicitly on an odd-even cycle basis so that it could be used as a component in the MIPS processor to follow, since in the MIPS the two cycles have to be unambiguously identified. If the cache misses, for example if the addressed word is not represented by a currently valid copy in the cache, then reference has to be made to the main-memory which is slower. Our example testbench will also play the roles of both CPU and main memory.

Since this is a *write-through* cache, if the requested operation is a write, then the data word is both written to the cache and also to the main memory. Since writes are usually rarer than reads, and so as not to hold up the regular operation of the cache, a *write-buffer* (WB) is used to temporarily store these data words destined for the main memory. This is concurrently active with the regular operation of the cache.

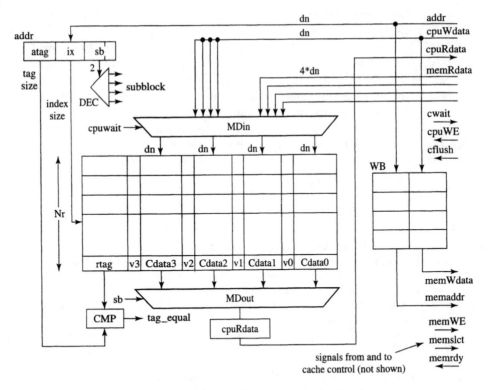

Figure 10.11   *Cache Store Organization.*

The division of the cache blocks into sub-blocks has two advantages. First, it reduces the number of bits needed for tag storage. Second, if the sub-block size is a single word, it allows a speed-up of the write hit cycle as follows. In the first (odd) clock cycle, the word is always written into the cache and sent to main memory anyway, before the outcome of the tag comparison is even known. Then if:

- tag match and sub-block valid (write-hit): Writing the sub-block was correct and no harm is done by setting the sub-block valid bit again.
- tag match and sub-block invalid (write-merge): This was the proper main block, and it is now appropriate to set the valid bit for the new word just written.
- tag mismatch or ~tag_valid (write-miss): The new word needs a new tag written, and the other sub-blocks in this row should be invalidated.

What if the miss is a read-miss? Then a new block must be brought to the cache from main memory and the cpu must be directed to idle in *wait states* until the fetch is complete. In order to compensate for the slow speed of the main memory somewhat, a wider bandwidth path is used. In the present case a whole block (four sub-blocks) is fetched. When the fetch is complete, a new tag is written, all four valid bits are set, and the cache completes the cycle as a *read-hit*.

There is one final case when the CPU has to be directed to wait, and that is if a word is presented to the write-buffer when it is found to be full.

The specification of the cache and its testbench is given in the next six boxes, although the description of the essential behavior takes up only two of these. The boxes are, in order: the cache declarations part (#1), the submodule part #2, and the odd- and even-cycle body parts (#3, #4), then the testbench declarations part (#5) and test schedule part (#6). In this specification either the homebrew RAMs from Chapter 5 or the embedded RAMs of Chapter 14 can be employed as shown. For the write-buffer, the fast *fifosc* from Chapter 8 has been employed, with the minor modification of using *switch-tail* instead of *fsr* pointers, in order to give the even buffer size of four required in Figure 10.11.

```
module cache(aaclk,aaoddeven,addr,cflush,cpuWdata,cWE,memRdata,memrdy,
             cpuRdata,cwait,hitmonitor,memaddr,memslct,memWdata,memWE);
 parameter tagsize=7, indexsize=6;
 parameter dn=16, an=tagsize+indexsize+3;   // data size, address size
 parameter Nr = 1<<indexsize;               // number of cache rows
 input aaclk,aaoddeven,cflush,memrdy,cWE;   // cWE = CPU wants to write
 input [an-1:0] addr;                       // address from cpu
 input [dn-1:0] cpuWdata;                   // write data from CPU
 input [4*dn-1:0] memRdata;                 // 4*bandwidth from main mem
 output [an-1:0] memaddr;                   // address to main memory
 output [dn-1:0] memWdata, cpuRdata;        // data: mem write & cpu read
 output memslct, memWE, cwait;              // cwait = cpu wait state
 output [2:0] hitmonitor;                   // to indicate write/read /miss/hit
 wire [dn-1:0] Din3,Din2,Din1,Din0;            // cache:write sub-block data
 wire [dn-1:0] Dout3,Dout2,Dout1,Dout0,mdout;  //        :read sub-block data
 reg [dn-1:0] cpuRdata;
 reg [Nr-1:0] v3, v2, v1, v0;                  // valid bits on 4 sub-blocks
 reg tagWE, WBinsert, WBremove, lull,
     cwait, memslct; // control points & handshakes
 reg [2:0] hitmonitor;                         // indicates read/write-hit/miss
 wire [tagsize-1:0] Stag;                      // stored tag vs presented tag
 wire [tagsize-1:0] Ptag = addr[tagsize+indexsize+2:indexsize+3];
 wire [indexsize-1:0] ix = addr[indexsize+2:3]; // index to cache blocks
 wire [1:0]          sb = addr[2:1];           // index to sub-blocks
 wire [3:0] subblock, SBslct;                  // ditto-decoded
 wire WBempty, WBfull, tag_equal;              // write buffer, tag compare
 wire allor1 = ~cWE && memrdy;                 // write one or all sublocks?
 wire wt = aaclk && aaoddeven;                 // cache data timing
 wire dataWE = cWE && wt || cwait && ~cWE;     // cache write enable
 assign memWE = WBremove;                      // logically equivalent
 wire sb_valid ={v3[ix], v2[ix], v1[ix], v0[ix]} & subblock != 4'b0000;
 wire tag_valid = v3[ix] || v2[ix] || v1[ix] || v0[ix];
```

Cache Specification Part #1: Declarations.

```
`include ``comparator.v´´
`include ``decoder.v´´
`include ``mux2.v´´
`include ``mux4.v´´
//`include ``ram.v´´            // if simulation, using home brew ram
`include ``fifosc.v´´
`include ``asyn_ram_64x16.v´´ // if simulation, using embedded ram
`include ``asyn_ram_64x7.v´´  // ditto
// else if synthesis:
//module asyn_ram_64x16 (Q, Data, WE, Address);
// parameter LPM_FILE = ``UNUSED´´;
// parameter Width = 16, WidthAd = 6, NumWords = 64;
// input [WidthAd-1:0] Address;
// input [Width-1:0] Data;
// input WE;
// output [Width-1:0] Q;
//endmodule
// instantiate submodules see block diagram
mux2  #(4*dn) MDin(allor1, {4{cpuWdata}}, memRdata, {Din3,Din2,Din1,Din0});
mux4  #(dn)   MDout(sb, Dout0, Dout1, Dout2, Dout3, mdout);
mux2  #(4)    Msb(allor1, subblock, 4´b1111, SBslct);
comparator #(tagsize)         CMPR(Stag, Ptag, tag_equal);
decoder    #(2)               DEC(sb, subblock);
fifosc     #(4,2,an+dn)       WB(~aaclk, cflush, WBinsert, WBremove,
              {addr,cpuWdata}, WBempty, WBfull, {memaddr,memWdata});
//ram_a #(dn,indexsize,Nr) Cdata3(ix, wt&&SBslct[3], Din3, dataWE, Dout3);
                                                    //home brew ram
//ram_a #(dn,indexsize,Nr) Cdata2(ix, wt&&SBslct[2], Din2, dataWE, Dout2);
//ram_a #(dn,indexsize,Nr) Cdata1(ix, wt&&SBslct[1], Din1, dataWE, Dout1);
//ram_a #(dn,indexsize,Nr) Cdata0(ix, wt&&SBslct[0], Din0, dataWE, Dout0);
//ram_a #(tagsize,indexsize,Nr) TAG(ix, ~aaoddeven, Ptag, tagWE, Stag);
asyn_ram_64x16 Cdata3(Dout3, Din3, dataWE&&SBslct[3], ix); // or embedded ram
asyn_ram_64x16 Cdata2(Dout2, Din2, dataWE&&SBslct[2], ix); // (see chapter 14)
asyn_ram_64x16 Cdata1(Dout1, Din1, dataWE&&SBslct[1], ix);
asyn_ram_64x16 Cdata0(Dout0, Din0, dataWE&&SBslct[0], ix);
asyn_ram_64x7 TAG(Stag, Ptag, tagWE, ix);
```

Cache Specification Part #2: Submodules.

In the odd control cycle, the requested address is loaded from the cpu into the *address_in* register, which is divided up into *tag, index,* and *subblock* fields. This cache uses a structure in which each cache block is divided into four sub-blocks. In the simple example cache here a sub-block size of one word, or two bytes only, is used.

For each new presented address, the index field is used to point to a row of the cache. If the stored tag field in that row matches the tag field in the presented address, *and* the valid bit corresponding to the sub-block is set, then the reference will be a cache-hit.

```
always
  begin : process_cpu_request
  @(posedge aaclk)
 if (aaoddeven)                             // start on odd clock
    begin  // odd even clock sequence
    tagWE<=0; hitmonitor<=0;

    if (cflush)
     begin  // cache flush
      WBinsert<=0; WBremove<=0;             // clear control points
      cwait<=0; memslct<=0; lull<=0;        // reset handshakes
      v3<=0; v2<=0; v1<=0; v0<=0;           // clear all valid bits
      @(posedge aaclk); disable process_cpu_request;
     end

    else if (cwait)                         // cpu is in wait state
     if (memrdy)
      begin                                 // main memory has now become free
      cwait<=0; memslct<=0;                 // reset handshakes
      if (cWE)
        begin                               // wait was to earlier WB full
         if (~WBfull) WBinsert<=1;
         else begin WBremove<=1; memslct<=1; cwait<=1; end
      end
       //else wait was due to read miss-will finish as read-hit
      end
     else begin WBremove<=0;                // main memory still not ready
          disable process_cpu_request;
         end

    else          // cpu not in wait state, so process as if a hit:
     begin        // read tag and read or write sublock regardless
        if (cWE)                            // if cpu wants to write
         if (~WBfull) WBinsert<=1;          // also insert into write buffer
        else begin             // WB is full, so remove word and send to mem
           WBremove<=1; memslct<=1; cwait<=1;
           @(posedge aaclk) WBremove<=0;
           disable process_cpu_request;// resume when mem rdy
          end

        else      // cache read: use membus lull to deal with WB backlog
        if (lull) begin WBremove<=1; memslct<=1; lull<=0; end
        else      begin memslct<=0; end
     end // of odd clock sequence
```

Cache Specification Part #3: Odd Cycle Procedure.

```
@(posedge aaclk)                    // even clock-clear control points
  WBinsert<=0; WBremove<=0; lull<=0;
  if (cWE)                // write: but data write already done in odd clock

    if (~tag_equal || ~tag_valid)
     begin hitmonitor<=7;       // write-miss
      {v3[ix],v2[ix],v1[ix],v0[ix]}<=subblock;
        tagWE<=1;               // invalidate other subblocks, write new tag
     end

    else begin hitmonitor<=3; // write-hit/merge
              {v3[ix],v2[ix],v1[ix],v0[ix]} <=
              {v3[ix],v2[ix],v1[ix],v0[ix]} | subblock;
             end // set valid bit of selected subblock

    else if (~tag_equal || ~sb_valid)
     begin hitmonitor<=2;       // read-miss
      // replace all 4 subblocks & set valid
      {v3[ix],v2[ix],v1[ix],v0[ix]}<=4'b1111;
      cwait<=1; memslct<=1; tagWE<=1;    // write new tag
     end

    else
     begin  // second phase of read hit
       hitmonitor<=1; cpuRdata<=mdout;
       if (~WBempty && memrdy)               // if write buffer not empty:
       lull<=1;                  //take advantage of mem lull
     end                         //to remove a word from WB on next odd cycle
  end // of oddeven clock sequence
 end // of process_cpu_request
endmodule
```

Cache Specification Part 4: Even Cycle Procedure.

For the testing, a monitor register has been used to make the hit information viewable both at the high- and the low-level simulation time. However, for low-level simulation it is necessary to modify the test specification so that the cache is called with the bitvector elements separated into distinct arguments.

To debug a complex design like this it is best at first to turn off the concurrent parts (in this case the write-buffer and main memory actions) and get the basic timing of the machine correct. Then turn on the concurrent parts and debug the remainder. The output from simulation shown in #7 shows the series of hits, misses, and wait cycles that occur. The comments on the right-hand side are annotations added in afterwards in order to ease the burden of the grader (something students hardly ever do).

```
`timescale 1 ns / 1 ns

module test_cache; //plays role of external world ie: CPU & main-mem
 parameter tn=7, ixn=6;                   // tag size, index size
 parameter dn = 16, an = tn + ixn + 3;  // datasize, addrsize
 parameter N = 1<<ixn, dt=20;            // number of cache rows
  reg  clk, toggle, cWE, cflush, memrdy;
  reg  [4*dn-1:0] memrdD;
  reg  [an-1:0] MAR;                      // cpu memory address register
  reg  [dn-1:0] MDRout;                   // cpu memory data register
  wire [dn-1:0] MDRin, memwrD;
  wire [an-1:0] memaddr;
  wire [ixn-1:0] ix = MAR[ixn+2:3];
  wire [2:0] hitmonitor;                  // write/read, hit/miss
  integer i, im;

// cache invocation:
// for low level simulation remove parameters and redo args with separated bits
 cache #(tn,ixn,an,dn,N) C(clk,toggle,MAR,cflush,MDRout,cWE,memrdD,memrdy,
                        MDRin,cwait,hitmonitor,memaddr,memslct,memwrD,memWE);

 always  begin #dt clk=1; #dt clk=0; end  // master clock

 always  @(negedge clk) toggle <= ~toggle; // for odd even cycle

 always  @(negedge clk)                   // simulate main memory
         if(memslct)                      // with access time 8*cache access
           begin
            memrdy<=0; // if read from mem,give recognizable pattern
            if (~cWE) memrdD<= memrdD + 64`h1000010000100001;
             for (im=0; im<16; im=im+1) begin @(negedge clk); end // delay
             memrdy<=1;
            end

 always  @(hitmonitor)
  case (hitmonitor)
   3`b111: $display(``write miss´´);
   3`b011: $display(``write hit/merge´´);
   3`b010: $display(``read miss´´);
   3`b001: $display(``read hit´´);
   default:;
 endcase
endmodule
```

Cache Specification Part 5: Testbench Declarations and Stub for Main Memory.

```
initial begin
  clk<=0; toggle<=0; cWE<=0; memrdD<=0; memrdy<=1; cflush<=0;
    $display(``cyc MAR MDRin slct mrdy cwait´´);
    $monitor(``%3g %h %h  %b    %b    %b´´,
                    $time/80, MAR, MDRin, memslct, memrdy, cwait);
    @(negedge clk); cflush<=1; $display(``flush complete´´);
    @(negedge clk); @(negedge clk); cflush<=0; memrdD<= 64´h0000000000000000;

// write miss/write merges
    MAR<=0; cWE<=1; MDRout<=0; @(negedge clk); @(negedge clk);
  for (i=1; i<8; i=i+1) // two rows of subblocks
    begin while (cwait) begin @(negedge clk); @(negedge clk); end
     MAR<=MAR+2; MDRout<=MDRout+1; @(negedge clk); @(negedge clk);
     end
    while (cwait) begin @(negedge clk); @(negedge clk); end

// read hits
  MAR<=0; cWE<=0; @(negedge clk); @(negedge clk);
  for (i=1; i<8; i=i+1)
    begin  while (cwait) begin @(negedge clk); @(negedge clk); end
     MAR<=MAR+2; @(negedge clk); @(negedge clk);
     end
    while (cwait) begin @(negedge clk); @(negedge clk); end

// write miss/write merges
  MAR<=1024; cWE<=1; @(negedge clk); @(negedge clk);
  for (i=1; i<8; i=i+1) // two rows of subblocks
    begin while (cwait) begin @(negedge clk); @(negedge clk); end
     MAR<=MAR+2; MDRout<=MDRout+1; @(negedge clk); @(negedge clk);
    end
    while (cwait) begin @(negedge clk); @(negedge clk);end

// read hits
  MAR<=1024; cWE<=0; @(negedge clk); @(negedge clk);
  for (i=1; i<8; i=i+1)
    begin while (cwait) begin @(negedge clk); @(negedge clk); end
     MAR<=MAR+2; @(negedge clk); @(negedge clk);
     end

// read misses
  MAR<=0; cWE<=0; @(negedge clk); @(negedge clk);
  while (cwait) begin @(negedge clk); @(negedge clk); end
  for (i=1; i<8; i=i+1)
    begin while(cwait) begin @(negedge clk); @(negedge clk); end
     MAR<=MAR+2; @(negedge clk); @(negedge clk);
     end
    $finish;
  end
endmodule
```

Cache Specification Part #6: Testbench Schedule.

```
Compiler version 4.0.2; Runtime version 4.0.2;   Jun  6 10:50 1999

cyc MAR MDRin slct mrdy cwait // annotations
...flush complete
write miss                    // comment generated by hit monitor
 2  0002  xxxx    0  1  0     // 1st write after flush is a miss
write hit/merge               // tag valid but sub-block invalid
 3  0004  xxxx    0  1  0
write hit/merge
 4  0006  xxxx    0  1  0
write hit/merge
 5  0008  xxxx    0  1  0
 5  0008  xxxx    1  1  1     // wait caused by write-buffer full
 5  0008  xxxx    1  0  1
13  0008  xxxx    1  1  1     // nothing happens until mem is ready
14  0008  xxxx    0  1  0
write miss
...                           // etc (another 4 writes occured here)
read hit
45 0000   0000    0  1  0     // first read of 8
...                           // etc
read hit
52 000e   0007    0  0  0     // last read of 8
53 0400   0007    0  0  0
write miss
54 0402   0007    0  0  0     // now write in new area-new tag
...                           // etc (7 more writes as before)
read hit
117 0402  0007    0  1  0     // now these reads hit-1st new read
...                           // etc
read hit                      // last read of 8 into new area
123 040e  000e    0  0  0
124 0000  000e    0  0  0
read miss                     // now when we revert to original address
124 0000  000e    1  0  1     // the tag is wrong and we get a miss
125 0000  000e    1  1  1     // so wait due to main mem read delay
126 0000  000e    0  1  0
read hit
134  0000  0002   0  1  0     // new read word appears from
....                          // main mem simulator-first of 4
read hit
137 0006  2000    0  0  0     // last of 4, word already fetched so a hit
...
read miss
138 0008  2000    1  0  1     // new miss of second block of 4 subblks
...
read hit
155 000e  3000    0  0  0     // last of second block
$finish at simulation time          112000
```

Cache Part #7: Simulation Output.

10.6 Another Implicit Style Example: MIPS200

For an example of a pipelined processor we have chosen a variation of the progenitor of the MIPS series of processors—the MIPS2000. This is because first, it is such a clean simple design, and second, because treatments of it are so readily available in standard textbooks, such as [H&P94]. In the following example, simply to make the synthesis more tractable, we have reduced the word length and the register file size to sixteen. This leaves the pipeline and control virtually unchanged but entails some minor changes in the instruction set. For example, ALU instructions are now two-address, and as a consequence, a MOVE instruction is now necessary. Other than this, the flavor of the MIPS2000 instruction set is more or less preserved. Therefore, we call our example "the MIPS200." The changes are illustrated in Figure 10.12.

type	instruction fields				example instructions	action
					SUBU rd, rs	rd = rd − rs
ALU	4	4	4	4	SLTU rd, rs	if (rd < rs) rd = 1 else rd = 0
	opcode	rs	rd	funct	MOV rd, rs	rd = rs
immed	opcode	rs	immed		ADDI rd, 127	rs = rs + 127
LW	opcode	rs	rd	displ	LW rd, (7)rs	rd = MEM(7 + rs)
SW	opcode	rs	rd	displ	SW rd, (15)rs	MEM(−1 + rs) = rd
branch	opcode	rs	displacement		BNEZ rs, −126	if (rs! = 0) PC = PC + 2 − 126
JMP	opcode	displacement			J 1047	PC = PC + 2 + 1047
LUI	opcode	rs	immed		LUI rs, 127	rs = {127, 8'h00}

Figure 10.12 *Instruction Fields in the MIPS200.*

The instruction pipeline of the MIPS2000 and MIPS200 is illustrated in Figure 10.13. Note that the fixed point instruction pipeline has five stages, although, as in the MIPS2000, three of them are two-cycle: IF, *instruction-fetch*; EX, *instruction-execute*; and MEM, *data-reference*. The one cycle stages are ID, *instruction-decode* and *register-read*; and WB, *register write-back*. The machine is a *load/store* general register architecture, which means that arithmetic operations are supported only from the register bank. An operand in memory must be transferred to or from a register using separate instructions. The machine has a split cache, which means a separate cache for the instructions. The cycle time of the caches in such machines is engineered to coincide with that of the ALU, called the *CPU cycle*, equal here to the duration of ph1 and ph2 clock phases together. Providing no wait states (cache misses) are encountered, the machine completes one instruction every such cpu cycle. Otherwise a pipeline stall should be generated. The MIPS2000 relied on the compiler to insert *no-operation* (NOP) instructions in such situations. In the following model the caches are represented by small RAMs.

Besides the instruction pipeline itself, the interesting thing about this architecture from a modeling point of view is the *pipeline forwarding*, otherwise known as *bypasses*. These are extra 16-bit pathways that supplement the shared register-bank communication between instructions. They lead directly between active submodules and are capable of avoiding a pipeline stall in many cases where the result of one instruction is used as an operand in a following instruction. Such an operand would otherwise have to await a read from the register bank using a WB and ID stage in between. Our model incorporates two such bypasses for the ALU and SET instructions, one for the LW (load word) instruction, two for the SW (store word) instruction, and one for the BRANCH instruction. These are symbolized by the arrows in Figure 10.13. They may be alternatively seen in a physical way in the architectural block diagram of the datapath shown in Figure 10.14.

Since, for a given instruction, the WB machine is one CPU cycle delayed after the MEM machine, which is in turn one cycle delayed after the EX machine, so three versions of the IR register which holds that instruction are necessary. These are called *shadow* registers. For similar reasons a shadow PC (program counter) and a shadow SMDR (storage memory data register) are needed.

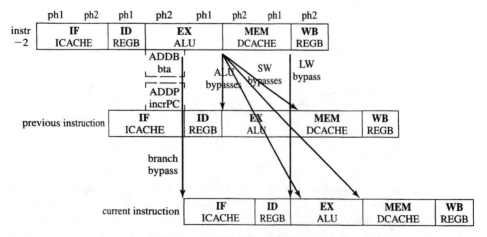

Figure 10.13   *MIPS200[0] Instruction Pipeline.*

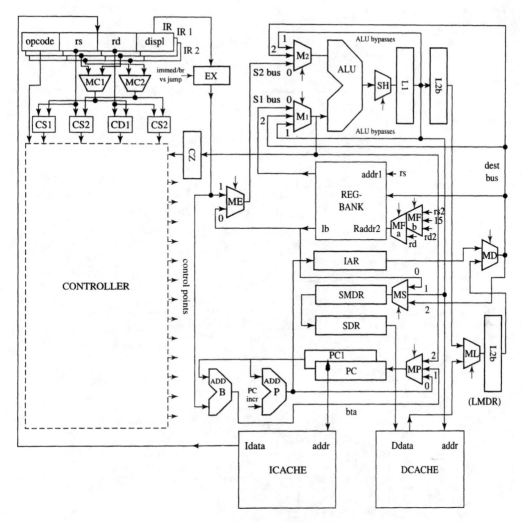

Figure 10.14   *MIPS200 Datapath Organization.*

To specify this example in the control-point style, one controller-datapath pair for each pipe-stage will be needed. Although these have all been merged together in the datapath diagram of Figure 10.14, synthesis from Verilog actually generates a separate controller for each **always** block. Figure 10.15 illustrates the concept. There are four concurrent machines corresponding to the four **always** blocks of the specification. For this purpose the ID and WB stages are combined since they are short (single phase) stages, active on alternate phases of the clock. From another point of view this might be regarded as eight machines, one corresponding to each clock phase. In fact the specification might equally well have been written with eight **always** blocks, by splitting each double-phase block into two single-phase ones. However there would still remain only four concurrent activities on each phase.

Yet another way of viewing the pipelined architecture is as a series of combinational logic blocks separated by registers which store the information from one pipeline stage to the next. This is illustrated in Figure 10.16. The register IR stores the information

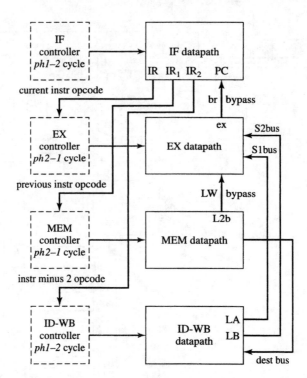

Figure 10.15 *MIPS200 Pipeline Viewed As Concurrent Machines.*

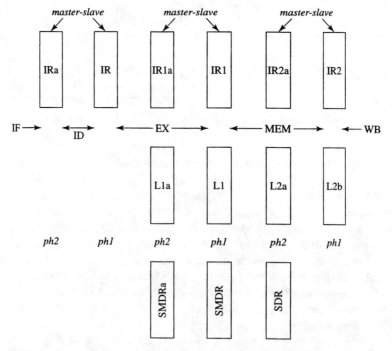

Figure 10.16 *MIPS200 Pipeline Registers.*

from pipestage IF *ph1* to EX *ph2* (These are master-slave registers, so they store for a full *ph1–ph2* cycle). Similarly, registers IR1 and L1 store the information from stage EX *ph1* to MEM *ph2*, and single-phase registers L2a and L2b together store the information from stage MEM *ph1* to stage WB *ph2*.

In Figure 10.14 the datapaths of the concurrent machines are all merged together, but for the control-point style, the control points must be kept strictly separated into disjoint sets. For example the *load L1* control point is cleared in machine EX *ph1*, and set only in machine EX *ph2*, while *load L2a* is set only in machine MEM *ph2*. Note that only registers that have their outputs connected to *busses* (nets with more than one driver) have a control point for a *sense* operation.

Returning to Figure 10.14, the purpose of the set of comparators CS1, CS2, CT1, CT2 is to detect the various possible operand collisions in the pipeline and to activate the corresponding bypasses. A separate adder ADDP is necessary for the update of the PC because the main ALU is already continuously busy with instruction execution. Similarly a separate adder ADDB is necessary to compute the *branch-taken* or *jump* address, which is calculated as early as possible in the instruction cycle in order to minimize the number of *branch* or *jump delay slots*. In the case of the MIPS2000 and MIPS200, this number can be reduced to one—regardless of the branch condition only one extra instruction will be executed before the branch takes effect. There is a similar *load delay slot* for the LW instruction (see Figure 10.13). It is the responsibility of the code generator to fill these delay slots, hopefully with something useful, but otherwise with a NOP instruction. For further details refer to [H&P94].

The specification of the MIPS200 processor follows in the next ten boxes. This version implements twenty-eight instructions using four controllers, and thirty-five submodules.

We start with a list of includes for the required generic submodule types.

The selection for the MIPS200 is given in Specification Part #1.

```
`include ``register.v´´  // plain register
`include ``rregister.v´´  // register with reset
`include ``reg_msr.v´´  // master-slave with reset
`include ``comparator.v´´  // equality comparator
`include ``ex.v´´  // sign extender
`include ``mux2.v´´  // selects one of two busses
`include ``mux2s.v´´  // ditto with one hot select
`include ``mux4.v´´  // selects one of four busses
`include ``adder.v´´  // adder for address computations
`include ``alu.v´´  // ten function arithmetic and logic unit
`include ``shft.v´´  // one bit combinational shifter
`include ``ram.v´´  // ram with separate input and output data
`include ``tpr.v´´  // two port ram
`include ``syn_rom_32x16_iuor.v´´  // embedded memories-see ch 9
`include ``syn_ram_32x16_iuor.v´´
```

MIPS Specification Part #1: Generic Submodule Includes.

These are the homebrew submodules already encountered in previous chapters, like the *alu, comparators, multiplexers,* and others that are minor variations. Library memory modules are used to represent the two caches, but the homebrew *tpr* module is used for the register bank because of the special treatment needed for register R0. Submodules such as *reg_msr* have been included even for the registers instead of just using Verilog **regs** in order that special resets or timing could be incorporated. Of course, in an industrial setting, instead of homebrew submodules, the submodules would be selected from vendors libraries of parameterized modules.

Next, in Specification Part #2 comes a list of defined identifiers for the subfields of the instruction register and its shadows. These are included just for convenience to simplify the rest of the specification.

```
`define op      str[15:12]
`define opa     ira[15:12]
`define op1     instr1[15:12]
`define op1a    ir1a[15:12]
`define op2     instr2[15:12]
`define op2a    r2a[15:12]
`define rsa     ira[11:8]
`define rs1a    ir1a[11:8]
`define rs2     instr2[11:8]
`define rs2a    ir2a[11:8]
`define rd      instr[7:4]
`define rda     ira[7:4]
`define rd1a    ir1a[7:4]
`define rd2     instr2[7:4]
`define rd2a    ir2a[7:4]
`define funct   instr[3:0]
`define funct2  instr2[3:0]
```

MIPS Specification Part #2:
Instruction Subfields.

After this the specification continues with a list of the implemented instructions in numerical order of their codes in the *opcode* and *funct* fields. The reduction of the three-address MIPS2000 to the two-address MIPS200 has necessitated the addition of a MOVE instruction in order to retain assembly programming flexibility. Otherwise, the remainder of the implemented instructions are similar to those of the MIPS2000 except for the shifts which are limited to one bit only. The LUI instruction and a few instruction codes have been left unassigned for the problems at the end of the chapter. The MIPS200 instruction list is shown in Specification Part #3.

```
//instruction opcodes (opcode 1111 still free)
  `define ALUr       4`b0000 // R-type instructions
                             // (differentiated in funct field)
  `define TRAP       4`b0001 // transfer of control instructions:
  `define J          4`b0010
  `define JAL        4`b0011
  `define BEQZ       4`b0100 // branches:
  `define BNEZ       4`b0101
  `define ADDI       4`b1000 // I-type alu instructions:
  `define ADDUI      4`b1001
  `define SLTI       4`b1010
  `define SLTIU      4`b1011
  `define ORI        4`b1101
  `define ANDI       4`b1100
  `define XORI       4`b1110
  `define LW         4`b0110 // data transfer instructions:
  `define SW         4`b0111
//funct field for ALUr (funct codes 1100, 1101 still free)
  `define MOVE       4`b0000 // MOVE/NOP
  `define SRL        4`b1110 // only one bit right shift
  `define SRA        4`b1111 // only one bit arith right shift
  `define JR         4`b1000 // jump register
  `define JALR       4`b1001
  `define ADD        4`b0111 // R type alu instructions:
  `define ADDU       4`b0001
  `define SUB        4`b0010
  `define SUBU       4`b001
  `define AND        4`b0100
  `define OR         4`b0101
  `define OR         4`b0110
  `define SLT        4`b1010 // set if less than
  `define SLTU       4`b1011

  `define nop        2`b00// for shift unit control
  `define srl        2`b01
  `define sra        2`b10
```

MIPS Specification Part #3: Instruction Opcodes and Function Fields.

Next, Specification Part #4 starts with the MIPS200 top-level module header line with its list of arguments. At least one output argument must be included to satisfy the synthesizer. For debugging purposes we have chosen the program counter, instruction register, and the adder-out bus. The header line is followed by a list of the internal datapath interconnection busses (**wire** declarations), and a list of the control points (**reg** declarations). These are separated into disjoint sets corresponding to the four controllers of Figure 10.15.

```
module mips200(clk, oddeven, reset, ao, ira, pc)
  input clk, oddeven, reset;
  output [15:0] ao, ira, pc;
// interconnection busses between submodules:
  wire [3:0]  Raddr2, mfb, dest1, dest2;
  wire [15:0] instr, instr1, instr2, ira, ir1a, ir2a, destbus, bypass1;
  wire [15:0] s1bus, s2bus, sdr, Ddata, Idata, Rdata1, Rdata2, l2b, iar;
  wire [15:0] bta, addp, mp, ms, m1, m2, ao, smdr, ml, sh, pc, pc1, lb, l2a, ex;
  wire cs1, cs2, cd1, cd2, eqz;
  wire clkd = ~clk;
  wire ph1d = ~clk && oddeven;
  wire ph2d = ~clk && ~oddeven;
// control points of the 4 submachines:
  reg R_rst, IR_ld, PC1_ld;                    // IF control points
  reg MFA_s0, MB_s;                            // ID control points
  reg [1:0] M1_s, MS_s, M2_s;                  // ID control points
  reg PC_ld, L1_ld, SMDR_ld, IAR_ld;          // EX control points
  reg [1:0] MP_s,  SH_s;                       // EX control points
  reg L2a_ld, L2b_ld, ML_s, SDR_ld, DCACHE_WE; // MEM control points
  reg IAR_sns, MFA_s1, RF_write;              // WB control points
  reg [1:0] MFB_s;                            // WB control points
  reg [3:0] alufunc;
```

MIPS Specification Part #4: Declarations of Busses and Control Points.

Specification Part #5 lists the actual submodule instantiations in the number of repetitions and sizes needed. The given identifiers of these instantiations may be compared to the ones in the block diagram of Figure 10.14. Note that these are not divided into disjoint sets here because many of them are loaded by one controller and sensed by another.

Now begins the specification of the pipestages. In order for the four controllers to interact correctly with each other it is important for them to adhere to the corresponding odd-even or even-odd phase timing. For this purpose a signal *oddeven* is brought in as an argument from the testbench along with the clock itself.

As was shown in Figure 10.13, the IF stage is on a *ph1–ph2* timing cycle so this is the order of the events in its **always** statement line. Like all good home computers the MIPS200 has a reset button, which is connected to the reset input of all the crucial registers. The PC and PC1 registers together act like a single master-slave. The PC master is loaded on the *ph1* pipeline phase and the PC1 slave or shadow is loaded on the *ph2* pipeline phase. Why could this not simply be implemented by a single master-slave submodule like the IR? The reason is that the PC part is loaded in the EX specification in order to incorporate the *branch-taken-address* (bta) (see Figure 10.13). From a timing point of view this makes no difference since the *ph2* phases of all the pipeline stages will be concurrently active, but it is necessary to keep the control points in disjoint sets because each **always** block results in a separate controller (see Figure 10.15). The specification of the IF stage is given in Part #6.

```
//instantiate submodules:
 reg_msr     #(16) IR(ph2d,R_rst,IR_ld,Idata,ira,instr);      //instruction register
 reg_msr     #(16) IR1(ph2d,R_rst,IR_ld,instr,ir1a,instr1); //and its shadows
 reg_msr     #(16) IR2(ph2d,R_rst,IR_ld,instr1,ir2a,instr2);//.
 mux2        #(4)  MC1((`op1a==`ALUr||`op1a==`LW),`rs1a,`rd1a,dest1);
 mux2        #(4)  MC2((`op2a==`ALUr||`op2a==`LW),`rs2a,`rd2a,dest2);
 comparator  #(4)  CS1(`rsa,dest1,cs1);               // comparators to detect
 comparator  #(4)  CS2(`rsa,dest2,cs2);               // pipeline hazards
 comparator  #(4)  CD1(`rda,dest1,cd1);               //.
 comparator  #(4)  CD2(`rda,dest2,cd2);               //.
 ex          #(16) EX(`op,instr,ex);                  // extend immed/displ field
 mux4        #(16) M1(M1_s,s1bus,bypass1,destbus,16`h0000,m1);  // ALU input mux1
 mux4        #(16) M2(M2_s,s2bus,bypass1,destbus,16`h0000,m2);  // ALU input mux2
 alu         #(16) ALU(alufunc,m1,m2,ao,);            // ALU with 10 operations
 shft        #(16) SH(SH_s,ao,sh); // combinational 1 bit shift
 register    #(16) L2a(ph2d,L2a_ld,bypass1,l2a);          // 1/2 pipestage delay
 reg_msr     #(16) L1(ph2d,1`b0,L1_ld,sh,,bypass1);       // 1 pipestage delay
 mux2        #(16) ML(ML_s,l2a,Ddata,ml);                 // mux for LMDR register
 register    #(16) L2b(ph1d,L2b_ld,ml,l2b);               // LMDR reg for load data
 comparator  #(16) CZ(m1,16`h0000,eqz);                   // comparison against zero
 mux2        #(16) MB(MB_s,ex,lb,s2bus);                  // mux onto S2 bus
 mux2s       #(4)  MFA(MFA_s0,MFA_s1,`rd,mfb,Raddr2);     // REGBANK addr2
 mux4        #(4)  MFB(MFB_s,`rd2,4`b1111,`rs2,4`b0000,mfb); // REGBANK addr2
 register    #(16) IAR(ph2d,IAR_ld,pc1,iar);             // interrupt address reg
 mux2        #(16) MD(IAR_sns, l2b, iar, destbus);        // mux to dest bus
 mux4        #(16) MS(MS_s,lb,bypass1,destbus,16`h0000,ms); // SMDR input mux
 reg_msr     #(16) SMDR(ph2d,1`b0,SMDR_ld,ms,,smdr);     // store data
 register    #(16) SDR(ph2d,SDR_ld,smdr,sdr);            // 1/2 pipestage delay
 adder       #(16) ADDB(ex,pc1,bta);                    // address adder for br/jmp
 adder       #(16) ADDP(pc1,16 h0002,addp);             //address adder for PC incr
 register    #(16) PC(ph2d,R_rst,PC_ld,mp,pc);          // program counter
 rregister   #(16) PC1(ph1d,R_rst,PC1_ld,pc,pc1);       // shadow PC
 mux4        #(16) MP(MP_s,addp,bta,m1,16 h0000,mp);    // PC input mux
 tpr         #(16,4,16) REGFILE(ira[11:8], Raddr2, clkd, destbus, RF_write, s1bus, lb);
 syn_rom_32x16_iuor
         ICACHE(.Q(Idata),.Address(pc[5:1]),.MemEnab(1`b1),.Outclock(ph1d));
 syn_ram_32x16_iuor
DCACHE(.Q(Ddata),.Data(sdr),.WE(DCACHE_WE),.Address(bypass1[5:1]),.Outclock(ph2d));
```

MIPS Specification Part #5: Submodule Instantiation.

```
always  // pipeline stage IF
  begin @(posedge clk)
    if(oddeven) // ph1-start only odd clock
        begin
         IR_ld<=0; // reset control point of ph2
         if (reset) R_rst<=1; else R_rst<=0;  // reset all crucial registers
         PC1_ld<=1; // activate control point at ph1
         @(posedge clk) // ph2 cycle
         PC1_ld<=0; IR_ld<=1;
        end
  end
```

MIPS Specification Part #6: IF Pipeline Stage.

The specification of the ID stage follows in #7. The two main functions ascribed to the ID stage in the textbooks are in fact implicit here: The instruction decode (because of the subfield defines) and the register bank fetches (coming from the instantiation of the REGFILE module). In fact all the complication appearing in this specification is due to the necessary interlocks required for the bypasses when pipeline hazards occur. These involve the set of comparators CS1, CS2, CD1, CD2, which are continually checking to see if the result of the last instruction is called for as an operand in either of the next two. There are further complications: for example, if either of the previous two instructions was a control type then the bypass must be aborted.

In Specification Part #8 the EX stage is reached which is the one that executes most of the instructions. It consists mostly of a giant **case** construct on the instruction types. This stage is on a *ph2–ph1* cycle.

```
always // pipeline stage ID
 @(posedge clk)
 if (oddeven) // ph1 cycle-start only on odd clock
 begin
   MFA_s0<=1; // activate control point at ph1:
   // drivebusses:
   if (ira[15]||(ira[14:13]==2´b11)) MB_s<=0;   // immed/datatran
   else                              MB_s<=1;   // ALUr instr
   // bypasses: abort if either of 2 prev instr were control type
   if (reset ||
        ((`op1a==`ALUr)&&(ir1a[3:1]==3´b100)) || //instr-1 = jump reg
        ((`op2a==`ALUr)&&(ir2a[3:1]==3´b100)) || //instr-2 = jump reg
         (~ir1a[15]&&(ir1a[14]^ir1a[13])) ||   //instr-1 = j or br
         (~ir2a[15]&&(ir2a[14]^ir2a[13]))      //instr-2 = j or br
       )
       begin M1_s<=0; M2_s<=0; MS_s<=0; end
     else
       begin // detect pipeline collisions
        casez ({cs2, cs1})
          2´b?1:   M1_s<=1;
          2´b10:   M1_s<=2;
          default: M1_s<=0;
        endcase
        casez ({`opa, cd2, cd1})
          6´b0111?1: MS_s<=1;     // SW only
          6´b011110: MS_s<=2;     // SW only
          6´b0110??: M2_s<=0;     // LW only
          6´b0????1: M2_s<=1;     // all unless immed, LW or SW
          6´b0???10: M2_s<=2;     // all unless immed, LW or SW
          default:   begin M2_s<=0; MS_s<=0; end
        endcase
       end
       @(posedge clk) // ph2 cycle just to deactivate control point
       MFA_s0<=0;
   end
 end
```

MIPS Specification Part #7: ID Pipeline Stage.

```
always // pipeline stage EX
 begin @posedge(clk)
  if (~oddeven) // ph2 cycle-start only on even clock
     begin // activate control points at pipe phase 2:
     PC_ld<=1; L1_ld<=1;
     case(`op) // instructions
        `ALUr:
           case(`funct)
             `MOVE: begin alufunc<=`funct;   SH_s<=`nop; MP_s<=0; end
             `SRL:  begin alufunc<=`NOP;  SH_s<=`srl;   MP_s<=0; end
             `SRA:  begin alufunc<=`NOP;  SH_s<=`sra;   MP_s<=0; end
             `JR:    MP_s<=2;
             `JALR: begin MP_s<=2; IAR_ld<=1; end
             `ADD,`ADDU,`SUB,`SUBU,`AND,`OR,`XOR,`SLT,`SLTU:
                       begin alufunc<= `funct; SH_s<= `nop; MP_s<=0; end
            default : $display(``unimplemented funct code´´);
            endcase
         `TRAP:      begin    MP_s<=1; IAR_ld<=1; $stop;  end
         `J:                  MP_s<=1;
         `JAL:      begin    MP_s<=1; IAR_ld<=1; end
         `BEQZ:     if (eqz)  MP_s<=1; else MP_s<=0;
         `BNEZ:     if (~eqz) MP_s<=1; else MP_s<=0;
         `ADDI:     begin alufunc<=`ADD;  SH_s<=`nop; MP_s<=0; end
         `ADDUI:    begin alufunc<=`ADDU; SH_s<=`nop; MP_s<=0; end
         `ORI:      begin alufunc<=`OR;   SH_s<=`nop; MP_s<=0; end
         `ANDI:     begin alufunc<=`AND;  SH_s<=`nop; MP_s<=0; end
         `XORI:     begin alufunc<=`XOR;  SH_s<=`nop; MP_s<=0; end
         `SLTI:     begin alufunc<=`SLT;  SH_s<=`nop; MP_s<=0; end
         `SLTIU:    begin alufunc<=`SLTU; SH_s<=`nop; MP_s<=0; end
         `LW:       begin alufunc<=`ADDU; SH_s<=`nop; MP_s<=0; end
         `SW:       begin alufunc<=`ADDU; SMDR_ld<=1; SH_s<=`nop; MP_s<=0; end
        default:      $display(``unimplemented opcode´´);
      endcase
     @(posedge clk) // phase ph1 just to deactivate the ph2 control points:
        PC_ld<=0; L1_ld<=0; SMDR_ld<=0; IAR_ld<=0;
     end
 end
```

MIPS Specification Part #8: EX Pipeline Stage.

Next, in Specification Part #9 is shown the MEM pipeline stage which interfaces with the DCACHE memory. Results from the ALU and shifter are progressively delayed as they pass through the pipeline registers L2b and SDR so that they are ready for the MEM stage at the appropriate time.

The last stage is WB in Specification Part #10. This where the instruction result is written back into the register bank. Care has been taken to separate the control points used from those in the ID stage where reading from the same register bank is performed.

```
always  // pipeline stage MEM
 begin @(posedge clk)
  if (~oddeven) // ph2 cycle start only on even clock
    begin
       DCACHE_WE<=0;  L2b_ld<=0; // reset control points of ph1:
       L2a_ld<=1;  SDR_ld<=1;     // activate control points of ph2:
       @(posedge clk) // ph1 cycle
       L2a_ld<=0;  SDR_ld<=0;
       case (`op1)              //activate control points of ph1:
         `LW:      begin ML_s<=1;  L2b_ld<=1;  end
         `SW:      DCACHE_WE<=1;
         default:  begin ML_s<=0;  L2b_ld<=1;  end
       endcase               // L2b delays ALUout until WB stage
    end
 end
```

MIPS Specification Part #9: MEM Pipeline Stage.

```
always  // pipeline stage WB
  @(posedge clk)
  if (~oddeven)
    begin
    casez (`op2) // activate control points of ph2
     `ALUr: begin // type1 alu
             if(`funct2==`JALR) begin IAR_sns<=1; MFB_s<=1;end
             else MFB_s<=0;
             MFA_s1<=1; RF_write<=1;
           end
     `JAL:  begin IAR_sns<=1; MFB_s<=1; MFA_s1<=1; RF_write<=1; end
     `LW:   begin MFB_s<=0; MFA_s1<=1; RF_write<=1; end
     4`b1???: begin MFB_s<=2; MFA_s1<=1; RF_write<=1; end // ALU immed
     default:  // do nothing
     endcase
     @(posedge clk) // deactivate control points of ph2
     IAR_sns<=0; MFA_s1<=0; RF_write<=0;
     end
  end
endmodule
```

MIPS Specification Part #10: WB Pipeline Stage.

10.6.1   Testing the MIPS200

Since the pipeline stages described above are all concurrently active it would not be sufficient to test each instruction in isolation, although that could certainly be done as an initial
step. To adequately test the model it is necessary to execute machine code programs at full
speed to check that concurrently active instructions do not interfere with each other and to

```
0000  // Zero   test data in Dcache
1155  // INUM
8000  // LB
 test instructions in I cache follow
6022  // LW    R2, 2(R0)     load test number INUM
6034  // LW    R3, 4(R0)     load comparand LB-leading bit 1
0010  // MOV   R1, R0        initialize R1 with 0
0240  // MOV   R4, R2        copy R2 to R4
034B  // SLTU  R4, R3        R4 < R3?
5406  // BNEZ  R4, 3         if yes-skip 3 instr (6 bytes)
0000  // NOP                 (branch delay slot)
9101  // ADDUI R1, 1         increment partial result
0323  // SUBU  R2, R3        erase leading bit
0221  // ADDU  R2, R2        shift left one
52F0  // BNEZ  R2, -8        branch -8 instr (16B) if not finished
7016  // SW    6(R0), R1     (branch delay slot) store answer in RSLT
1018  // TRAP  12            (usual) exit to OS, (actual) traps to self
```

MIPS200 Test Program #1—Count Binary 1's in a Number.

```
0050  // MOV   R5, R0        initialize R5 with 0
950a  // ADDUI R5, 5*2       load R5 with address of subroutine
200a  // J     +5*2          jump to first subroutine call
0010  // MOV   R1, R0        (br/jmp delay slot) initialize R1 with 0
1000  // TRAP  0             (usual) exit to OS, (actual) traps to self
9101  // ADDUI R1, 1         subroutine-increment partial result
0f08  // JR    R15           return from subroutine
0000  // NOP                 (br/jmp delay slot)
3ff8  // JAL   -4*2          jump #1 to subroutine
0000  // NOP                 (br/jmp delay slot)
0509  // JALR  R5            jump #2 to subroutine
0000  // NOP                 (branch delay slot)
2fee  // J     -9*2          jump to TRAP
0000  // NOP                 (br/jmp delay slot)
```

MIPS200 Test Program #2—Subroutine Calls and Jumps.

see if various consecutive instruction pair situations indeed operate correctly. The following two assembly programs were among those used to debug the model. The first Test Program (#1) tests arithmetic, branching, and store instructions and also the LW, ALU, and branch bypasses and interlocks. It inputs a test number from the data cache and counts the number of binary ones in it. A second Test Program (#2) tests the jumps and subroutine calls.

10.6.2   *Notes on the MIPS200 Testbench*

A testbench for the MIPS200 processor follows. The *$readmemh* system-calls are present in order to load the test program and data in hexadecimal form into the respective RAMs. A different scheme for doing this will be necessary for the Altera embedded memories and gate-level simulation (see Chapter 14). The test sequence proper starts by holding down the reset button for five cycles while the pipe flushes out, and then releasing it.

```
`timescale 1ns/100ps
module test1_mips200;
 parameter dt = 25;
 reg clk, toggle, Treset;
 integer Ti;
 wire [15:0] ao,ira,pc;
 wire alpha = toggle & ~clk;

  mips200 M200(clk, Treset, ao,ira,pc);

   always begin  clk=1; #dt clk=0;  #dt;  end

   always @(negedge clk) toggle <= ~toggle;
   initial
     begin // read test program and data into memories
       $readmemh(``test_program´´, M200.ICACHE.ram_data);
       $readmemh(``test_data´´, M200.DCACHE.ram_data);
       $display(``time     pc   IR   AO´´);
       $monitor(``%5g    %2g    %h    %h´´,
                 $time,   pc[8:1],  ira,  ao);
       Treset = 1; clk<=0;
       for (Ti=0; Ti<5; Ti=Ti+1) @(posedge alpha);   // flush pipe
       @(posedge alpha)  Treset = 0;                 // start the processor
       for (Ti=0; Ti<128; Ti=Ti+1) @(posedge alpha); // time to finish
       $finish;
       end
endmodule
```

Testbench for MIPS200.

10.6.3 *RTL and Control-Point Specifications of MIPS*

The following table (10.2) compares the model above written in the control-point style against two other Verilog specifications of the MIPS2000 processor done in the explicit style [GM92], [Olukotun94]. The GM version was a full pipelined version. For the comparison in the table we have tried to excerpt sections of the specification equivalent in scope to the control-point model here. The Stanford version was not pipelined. Of course neither the GM or the MIPS-Lite was written to be synthesizable. The synthesized area shown for the MIPS200 is in terms of Altera logical elements (multiply by about two orders of magnitude for the number of gates—see Chapter 12) and does not include the three memories.

Table 10.2   *Comparison of MIPS Specifications.*

Model	Spec Lines	Area
GM research	3600	—
Stanford MIPS-Lite	1118	—
Control-point MIPS200	400	861

Normally, a large hierarchical design is synthesized by a combination process in which the component parts are compiled first bottom-up, and then constrained (*character-ized*) top down in a final compile. This is because the design synthesizer has an effective limit on the size of design which can be compiled in one shot. On the other hand the synthesis process will not be able to take advantage of cross boundary optimizations if the component designs are too small. The optimum size granularity has been recommended to be in the region of 4k–10k gates, although the 98-02 release of the Synopsys Design Compiler is reputed to be able to handle up to 100k gates at a time. As can be seen from the table, the MIPS200 is small enough not to require a hierarchical compile. The synthesis process itself is described in more detail in the next chapter.

10.7 Conclusion

The purpose of this chapter is to attempt to give a feel for more industrial-sized projects. Although these designs are necessarily still very modest compared with the million gate designs of current industry practice, they can nevertheless illustrate the problems in real life design.

The successful execution of large, complex designs requires a disciplined methodology. Key elements are the clear separation of datapath and controller, and the explicit identification of control points—control lines that originate in the controller and status lines that originate in the datapath. By taking this approach, the designer separates cause and effect, and thus makes design and debug significantly easier.

Another very important issue for synthesized designs is that of partitioning—answering the question of what goes into what module. A quality partitioning approach is critical to synthesis success. Using modules that are too large leads to long synthesis runs while overly atomizing a design results in an unwieldy design hierarchy. In general each module should be just large enough to contain functions that share common logic and no larger. In addition, each module should use registers as the final stage of their output, so as to ensure that the timing interface to the next module is easy to understand and characterize.

The reuse of modules designed for previous chips in future designs is rapidly growing as chips grow in size while the length of the design cycle decreases. As chip designs get larger and larger, there is considerable concern that design teams will get too large and design cycles too long. One technique that will be used to address this potential concern is design reuse—reuse of designs previously implemented by others. Design reuse methodologies involve a large number of issues and concerns. Reuse is discussed at greater length in Chapter 17.

Exercises

10.1. Test the MIPS200 processor in high-level simulation with a small assembly program of your own. You may create new instructions or modify existing ones for this purpose. Some suggestions for test programs (there are one or two opcodes and function codes in the model still free):

a. Unsigned multiply with 8-bit operands. Optional: add the LUI instruction (as in Figure 10.12) to the model and test.

b. Ditto with 16-bit operands. In order to obtain a long right shift you may need to augment the model with a right shift instruction which takes the shifted-in bit from a MS flipflop and saves the shifted-out bit in the same.

c. Ditto with radix 2 Booth signed multiply or non-restoring division.

d. Assembly code version of the bidirectional fsrb of Figure 5.5.

10.2. A somewhat more up-to-date version (than the MIPS200) of a suitable processor for specification and synthesis at this stage is the integer subset of the Java virtual machine [Tanenbaum98] reproduced in Table 10.2. A Verilog specification could implement the instruction set architecture directly (not via microcode as in the reference). In that case we would need the stack from Chapter 9, Problem 9.3 for the operands, supplemented with two special registers so that the top two words are readily available to feed into the two sides of the ALU. Similar to the treatment of the MIPS200 in this chapter, a toy specification could use a small RAM to represent the cache for the method area, and another small RAM to represent two levels of the local variable frame. A final small RAM would represent the constant pool. The machine sounds a little more complex than the MIPS200 and it is. On the other hand it could be implemented in a non-pipelined version which would make it a lot simpler. Also there are only twenty instructions. To give the flavor, we reproduce the instruction set here (Table 10.3), with the admonition that you must buy Tanenbaum's book for more details. One further augmentation to this jvm subset would be a right shift instruction, which would do a lot for its usability.

Table 10.3   *The IJVM Instruction Set from [Tanenbaum98].*

Hex	Mnemonic	Action
10	BIPUSH byte	push byte onto stack
59	DUP	copy top word of stack and push onto stack
A7	GOTO offset	unconditional branch
60	IADD	pop two words from stack and push their sum
7E	IAND	pop two words from stack and push Boolean AND
99	IFEQ offset	pop word from stack and branch if zero
9B	IFLT offset	pop word from stack and branch if less than zero
9F	IF_ICMPEQ offset	pop two words from stack and branch if equal
84	IINC varnum const	add a constant to a local variable
15	ILOAD varnum	push local variable onto stack
B6	INVOKEVIRTUAL disp	invoke a method
80	IOR	pop two words from stack and push Boolean OR
AC	IRETURN	return from method with integer value
36	ISTORE varnum	pop word from stack and store in local variable
64	ISUB	pop two words from stack and push their difference
13	LDC_W index	push constant from constant pool onto the stack
00	NOP	do nothing
57	POP	delete word from top of stack
5F	SWAP	swap the two top words on the stack
C4	WIDE	prefix instruction; next instruction has a 16 bit index

10.3. Design hardware that will produce the sequence, F_D, where each successive number in the series is the sum of the two previous numbers:

$$F_N = F_{N-1} + F_{N-2}$$

(For example, for the third number in the series, $N = 3$, $F_3 = 2 + 3 = 5$). Design and implement a module that whenever its input N changes, it produces F, at latest N clock cycles later. N will be any 32-bit number (meaning that F has to be 64-bits long). N will not change while a new F is being calculated. F must be held after the series has been calculated until N changes again.

a. Sketch your design. Clearly identify your datapath and control sections. Clearly identify your control strategy, explicitly labeling control lines and status lines. This design does not need a reset or any kind of "start" signal. Include a timing diagram showing the operation of important signals. N will not change during the calculation of the series.

b. Write Verilog capturing this design. The module header is: module Fib (clock, N, Fib).

c. Redesign the counter used in Chapter 6 so that it is parameterized with respect to the number of bits in the counter and the number at which it stops counting.

10.4. Design and implement, in Verilog, the following function:

There are two 32-entry memories, each with different data in it. Design and write a module called "match" that determines if any of the entries in the two memories are identical. Upon finding an identical match, the module is to assert (active high) the "found" flag and stop the search. If there is no identical match, then assert the "not_found" flag (active high). The search starts when "start" goes high. "start" will remain high during the entire search and will go low one clock cycle after found or not_found goes high. In 'C', the function would be captured as follows:

```
while (!start);/* wait for start to be true */
found = 0;
not_found = 0;
for (i=0; i<31; i++)
  {for (j=0; j<31; j++)
     {if (m1[i] == m2[j])
        {found = 1;
         break;
         }
     }
   if (m1[i] == m2[j]) break; /* inner loop was broken */
   }
if (m1[i] != m2[j]) not_found = 1;
```

The overall Verilog description is shown below:

```verilog
module top (clock, address1, address2, data1, data2, rw1, rw2, found, not_found,
            start);
input    clock;
inout [4:0] address1, address2;
inout [7:0] data1, data2;
input    rw1, rw2;
output    found, not_found;
input    start;
wire // I skipped declaring all the wires for brevity
buffer m1 (.clock(clock), .address(address1), .data(data1), .rw(rw1));
buffer m2 (.clock(clock), .address(address2), .data(data2), .rw(rw2));

match  u1 (.clock(clock), .address1(address1), .data1(data1), .data2(data2),
.start(start), .found(found), .not_found(not_found);
endmodule

module buffer (clock, address, data, rw);
input      clock;
input [4:0] address;
input [7:0] data;
input      rw;
reg [7:0] mem [31:0];
tri [7:0] data;

always @(posedge clock)
  if (!rw) mem [address] <= data;

assign data = rw ? 8´hzz : mem[address];
endmodule
```

a. Sketch a block diagram design of the module *match*, giving full details of any finite state diagrams, and so on.

b. Draw a timing diagram that shows correct functionality of the logic you designed.

c. Give a Verilog description for the module *match*. Make sure it is consistent with your design in part (a).

References

[BK96] Bhaskaran, V., and Konstantides, K., *Image and Video Compression Standards, Algorithms, and Architectures*, Kluwer, 1997

[GM92] D'Ambrosio, Joseph, G., "DLX core Verilog model," Technical report, GM Research Laboratories, EE Dept., May 1992

[H&P94] Patterson, D. A., and Hennessy, J. L., *Computer Architecture: A Quantitative Approach, 2nd edition*, Morgan–Kaufman, 1994

[Olukotun94] Olukotun, Kunle, A., "MIPS-lite," in notes for course ee282, Stanford University

[Tanenbaum98] Tanenbaum, Andrew S., *Structured Computer Organization*, 4th edition, Prentice Hall, 1998, pp. 203–232

Chapter Eleven

Improving Timing, Area, and Power

11.1 Introduction

The use of automatic synthesis tools does not automatically guarantee a high-quality design. The tools largely operate at the gate level. If the designer poorly structures the design, automatic synthesis can only minimally improve it. For example, if you specify two multipliers where only one multiplier and a multiplexor would have sufficed, you will often see two multipliers in the final design. As a rough characterization, it is sometimes best to think of synthesis tools as simply giant logic minimization engines that can also manage the details of the timing. For this reason, the designer needs to be aware of performance and efficiency issues as the design and RTL capture is proceeding. The purpose of this chapter is to introduce the reader to timing, power, and area issues as they relate to RTL-level design.

11.2 Timing Issues in Design

Obviously, performance and implementation area are of fundamental importance in the design of a digital system. Timing-related design issues have a big influence on both of these.

Fundamentally, performance is measured by one or both of the following metrics:

- *Latency.* How long does it take to complete a particularly operation?
- *Throughput.* How many operations can be completed per second?

As a gross generalization, latency is the domain of the system designer while throughput is the concern of the logic designer. For example, consider an Internet packer router. The function of the router is to determine where incoming packets of data should be directed for their next hop. The packet is transmitted through several routers in order to complete its journey. The latency of each router is important as the delays accumulate. A target latency might be in the few-millisecond range. However, this translates to the logic designer as a throughput requirement. Routing is done by table lookup. The more table lookups that can be done per second, the better the ability of the router to route a large amount of packet traffic with minimal delay.

In general, the throughput of an ASIC is defined as a function of two factors:

$$Throughput = f_{clock}/CPO \qquad (11.1)$$

where f_{clock} is the clock frequency, measured in megahertz, and *CPO* is the cycles per operation—in other words, how many clock ticks transpire between the completion of each operation.

The clock frequency is determined directly by the logic design, specifically the worst case delay between any pair of connected flipflops. The logic path taken to determine this worst path delay is called the critical path. Though the synthesis tools try to minimize the length of the critical path, the details of the design often have a large influence on the length of the path. For example, consider the following code fragment:

```
always @(posedge clock)
  begin
  result <= A + B + C + D;
  compare <=A ^ B;
  end
```

In this case, the chain of three adders is the critical path as shown in Figure 11.1 and is likely to lead to a fairly slow clock period. Also note, that the design is not very well balanced. The other paths in the design are much faster than the critical path and are thus sitting idle for most of the clock cycle. In addition, each adder is only busy for approximately one-third of each clock cycle. In this case, let's say the clock frequency came out to be 10 MHz and the code above specified a complete operation, then

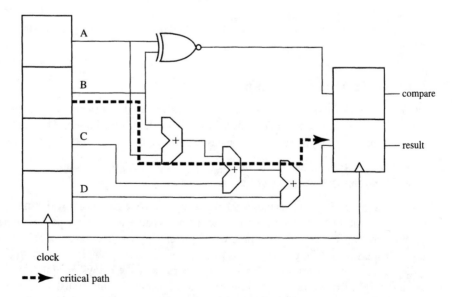

Figure 11.1 *Critical Path.*

```
always @(posedge clock)
 begin
  interimResult1 <= A + B;
  Cint <= C;
  Dint <= D;
  Dnew <= Dint;
  interimResult2 <= InterimResult1 + Cint;
  Result <= InterimResult2 + Dnew;
  InterimCompare1 <= A^B;
  InterimCompare2 <= InterimCompare1;
  Compare <= InterimCompare2;
 end
```

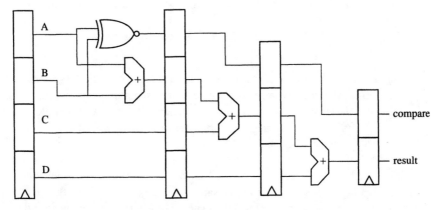

Figure 11.2   *Pipelined Design.*

the resulting throughput would be 10 million operations per second (for the triple-add).

A more efficient design (as measured in performance/gate) is given above. The design has been pipelined (Figure 11.2) so that the hardware is actually performing three calculations at the same time. Each stage of flipflops shown in Figure 11.2 holds a different computation, a partial result for the first two stages and the final result in the last stage. The inputs also need to be fed into the pipeline so that they can change every clock cycle. Now the clock cycle is about one-third that of the previous design. For the cost of a few flipflops, the throughput has been increased by a factor close to three. (The clock cycle is not exactly one-third than it was before because of the fixed overhead of the delays associated with the flipflops.) Note the use of non-blocking assignment to correctly describe the pipeline.

The next section describes how to calculate a clock period in detail.

11.2.1   *Delay Calculations*

Every piece of logic—gate, flipflop, or latch—introduces additional delay into the timing paths within a circuit. The actual delay depends on the transistor parameters produced when the circuit was manufactured, the operating temperature, and the load that the gate is driving. This load consists of the input capacitance of all of the gates driven by a particular

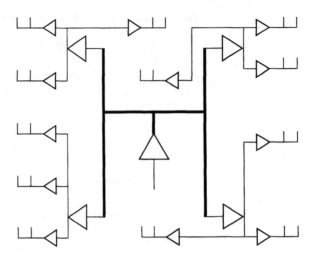

Figure 11.3   *Typical Clock Distribution Scheme.*

circuit and the capacitance of any wiring to those gates. The designers of the cell library or FPGA family conduct a number of simulations and measurements to obtain the equations or tables of delay as a function of these parameters. These delay calculators are then used by timing analysis tools, during and after synthesis, in order to obtain the actual delay of the critical path(s) in the circuit.

As well as logic delays, it is also necessary to account for the effects of imperfect clock distribution. Ideally, the clock edges would arrive at each synchronous logic element (flipflop or latch) at exactly the same time. To try to achieve this, a clock distribution tree, a typical example of which is shown in Figure 11.3, is designed to attempt to ensure that the delay from the clock source to each of the clock leaves is identical. In practice, this goal is impossible as the different buffers in the clock tree have slightly different delays and the capacitive loading (gates and wires) of all of the branches are not identical. The clock tree might be feeding hundreds of thousands of loads, which are very unlikely to be evenly distributed over the chip. The differences between the clock arrival times at different leaves of the tree is referred to as the clock skew. Though in principal, the skew between different leaves could be predicted, it is far simpler simply to guarantee a maximum skew figure and provide that figure to the timing tools. Note that clock skew can be either positive or negative—for example, the clock input to one flipflop might be either advanced or delayed with respect to the clock input at another flipflop. The worst case "direction" has to be assumed, as appropriate, for each calculation.

11.2.2   *Timing Design with Edge-Triggered Flipflops*

The basic behavior of an edge-triggered D (or delay) flipflop is illustrated in Figure 11.4. For a rising edge-triggered flipflop, the signal at the D input is sampled at the rising edge of the clock and transferred to the Q output after a delay, t_{clock_Q}. The input signal must be stable during the setup and hold period of the flipflop. That is, the signal must be correctly "setup" before the setup time and remain unchanged, at a logic_0 or logic_1, until the

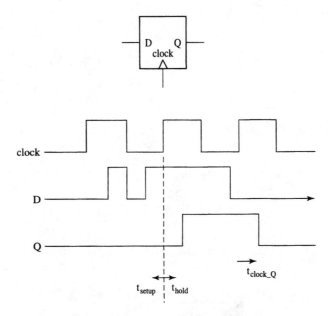

Figure 11.4   *Basic Flipflop Operation.*

expiration of the hold period after the clock edge. If the D input changes during this period, the flipflop can become metastable, leading to incorrect operation of the logic.

Referring to Figure 11.5, there are two main timing concerns that the timing analysis tools check for on all the paths in the circuit. The first concern is that the clock period is long enough to account for the output delay of the flipflops, all the logic delays and for the setup time of the "input" flipflop. The necessary clock period is calculated as follows:

$$t_{clock} \geq t_{clock\_Q\_max} + \sum t_{logic\_max} + t_{setup\_max} + t_{skew} \tag{11.2}$$

where $t_{clock\_Q\_max}$ is the maximum delay from the clock edge on the "transmitting flipflop" (left-hand side of Figure 11.5) to the Q output changing, $\sum t_{logic\_max}$ is the sum of the logic delays of the gates between successive flipflops, t_{setup_max} is the longest possible setup time requirement and t_{skew} is the worst-case clock skew. Note that the worst "direction" for clock skew is that when the clock arrives at the "receiving" flipflop before it arrives at the "sending" flipflop.

The timing analysis tools check this equation for all possible legitimate logic paths in the synthesized design (in any design there can be "false" paths, or logic paths that can never be exercised). For paths that satisfy this equation it calculates the "clock slack" or the amount that could be added to the right-hand side of Equation (11.2) to produce an equality. Logic paths that do not satisfy this equation are referred to as having "setup violations." These paths need to be redesigned to remove gates or wiring delay. Ideally, the synthesis, and other tools used to produce a design, would not introduce setup violations.

The circuit should also be designed to prevent race conditions. With reference to Figure 11.6, a race occurs when a logic change at the flipflops to the left occurring on any particular clock edge races through the circuit so that the flipflops on the right are responding

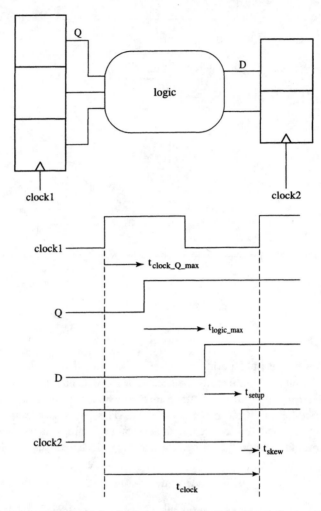

Figure 11.5   *Timing Calculations for Clock Period and Setup Violations.*

to this data on the same clock edge that the data passed through the flipflops on the left. On a particular clockedge, changes at Q propagate quickly through the logic from Q to D in less than the hold time associated with that clock edge. A race can occur when the skew and hold time is greater than the minimum logic delay. To ensure race conditions are not present, the timing tools test the following condition for each logic path through the circuit:

$$t_{hold\_max} + t_{skew} \le t_{clock\_Q\_min} + \sum t_{logic\_min} \qquad (11.3)$$

where $t_{clock\_Q\_min}$ is the fastest possible delay from a clock edge occurring at a flipflop to the output Q changing and $\sum t_{logic\_min}$ is the shortest possible accumulated delay through a path of combinational logic gates. Note, that the worst-case clock skew here is when the clock at the "receiving" flipflop arrives after the clock at the "transmitting" flipflop. When this equation is not satisfied, the problem is referred to as a "hold violation" and the design is fixed by inserting extra logic in the violating path (such as pairs of inverters). On command, synthesis tools can identify and correct hold violations automatically.

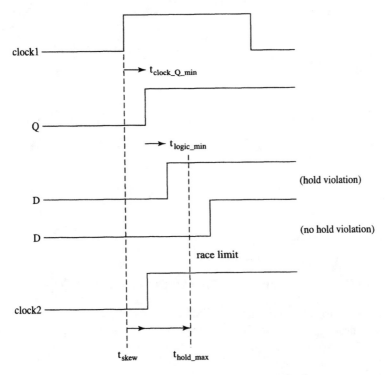

Figure 11.6   *Race Conditions in D Flipflops.*

11.2.3   *Timing Design with Latches*

The basic behavior of a D- or data-latch is shown in Figure 11.7. The output, Q, of the latch tracks the input, D, while the clock is high. When the clock falls low, the last value at D is stored on the output of the latch until the clock goes high again. The setup and hold times are referenced to the falling ("latching") edge of the clock.

Timing considerations are different in latch based designs than in flipflop based designs. Consider the two stages of logic and associated timing diagrams shown in Figure 11.8. Theoretically, the delay between two stages of latches can be longer than a clock period because the high time of the clock is available for logic transitions to occur at the input at the latch on the right. As long as the Q output on the left of Figure 11.8 is stable at the start of the clock period, satisfying the following equation ensures correct operation,

$$t_{clock} + t_{clock\_high\_min} \leq t_{clock\_Q\_max} + \sum t_{logic\_max} + t_{setup\_max} + t_{skew} \qquad (11.4)$$

where $t_{clock\_high\_min}$ is the minimum time for which the clock is high. Using the high period of the clock, $t_{clock\_high\_max}$, to allow a longer logic path in part of the design is referred to as cycle stealing. Cycle stealing, however, can not be used everywhere in a design. For example, consider the two stages of logic shown in Figure 11.8. Cycle-stealing is clearly shown here. The logic delay for stage one has been increased by using part of the second clock cycle shown. If cycle-stealing is used in the left-hand stage to the extent that Equation (11.4) becomes an equality, the second stage cannot do any cycle stealing and has to

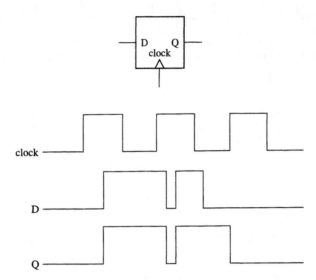

Figure 11.7   *Basic Operation of D-latch.*

satisfy Equation (11.2) instead. In Figure 11.8, it can be seen that $t_{logic\_2\_max}$ is significantly shorter than $t_{logic\_1\_max}$ as the first stage of logic has used up most of the available $t_{logic\_high\_min}$. Within any continuous chain of interconnected flipflops and logic (e.g., through a complete pipeline) the accumulated "stolen" time has to add up to $t_{clock\_high\_min}$ or less. As a result, cycle-stealing has relatively little utility in practice. Again, the lack of satisfaction of the appropriate equations is referred to as a "setup violation." If cycle stealing is not permitted, then Equation (11.4) becomes the same as Equation (11.2).

Race-through conditions are a lot more difficult to prevent in latch-based designs. Race through does not occur if the following equation is satisfied (Figure 11.9):

$$t_{hold\_max} + t_{skew} + t_{clock\_high\_max} \leq t_{clock\_Q\_min} + \sum t_{logic\_min} \tag{11.5}$$

where $t_{clock\_high\_max}$ is the maximum time for which the clock is high. Again, situations where this equation are not satisfied are referred to as hold violations. This inequality is more difficult to satisfy than Equation (11.3), especially if the nominal high period of the clock is long. This is the main reason why flipflop based designs are generally preferred over latch-based designs.

11.2.4   Timing-Aware Design

The structure of the design, and its RTL-level capture, have a major impact on the clock frequency and the overall performance. For example, the potential benefits of pipelining was previously described. *The biggest mistake that novice designers make in regards to timing is to lose awareness of the logic depth they are specifying.* A simple example was given previously in which the logic depth in the critical path became large, and therefore the path was broken up to take three clock cycles. Many more subtle examples exist. In some cases, the choice of the algorithm to implement has a large impact on the efficiency of the design. For example, consider the case where four inputs have to be compared and

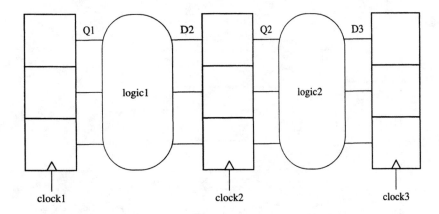

Setup Violations:

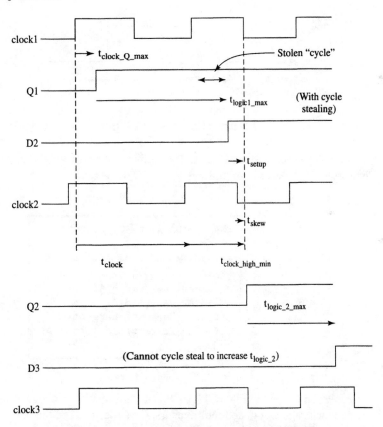

Figure 11.8   *Timing Considerations in D-Latch Design.*

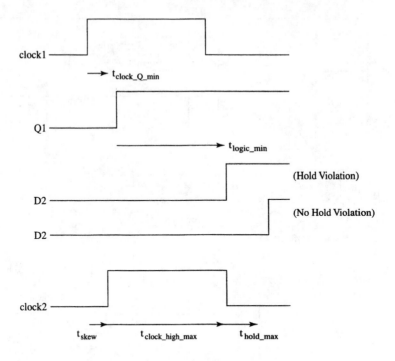

Figure 11.9   *Race in Latch-Based Design.*

the largest presented as an output. The designer's first thought might be to implement a linear search. A description follows.

```
reg [15:0] A, B, C, D, Largest;

always @(A or B or C or D)
begin
 if (A>B) Largest = A;
 else Largest = B;
 if (C > Largest) Largest = C;
 if (D > Largest) Largest = D;
end
```

As can be seen in Figure 11.10, this design results in a logic depth of three ">" comparison units and associated multiplexors. Consider instead the implementation that could be obtained by using a binary search technique (on the next page).

Now the logic depth is two ">" compare units and associated multiplexor as illustrated in Figure 11.11. The design is almost 30 percent faster with no additional area or pipeline stages. Very often, a little thought put into the algorithm results in a faster design.

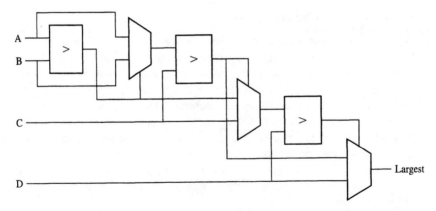

Figure 11.10   *Slow (Linear Search) Comparator Design Implementation.*

```
reg [15:0] A, B, C, D;
wire [15:0] Large1, Large2, Largest;

assign Large1 = (A>B) ? A : B;
assign Large2 = (C>D) ? C : D;
assign Largest = (Large1 > Large2) ? Large1 : Large2;
```

Often, the designer knows a smart way to structure the design. Specifying that structure, rather than expecting the synthesis to "discover" it, will facilitate a fast design. (See also the shift example in Section 3.6.) Other examples are arithmetic units. In many synthesis tools, simply specifying "+" leads to a ripple-carry adder. To obtain a carry-lookahead or carry-save adder, the designer might have to explicitly call it from a library of designs, or design it by hand down to the gate level.

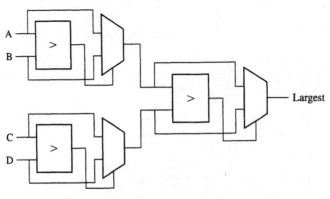

Figure 11.11   *Fast Binary Search Structure.*

11.3   Low Power Design

Power consumption is an important system issue in integrated circuit design. Obviously, low power circuits are desirable in battery-operated applications, in order to maximize battery life. Power-per-operation is an important metric in these applications. However, power consumption can also be important in wall-powered applications as the expense and difficulty of cooling the electronics increases with the power consumed. For example, inexpensive plastic packaging cannot be used when a chip consumes more than 1–2 watts. Instead, expensive ceramic packaging and (at higher powers) cooling fans become necessary. Even though power supply voltages have been shrinking with decreasing device dimensions, chip dissipations have continued to rise due to increasing complexities and switching speeds. Some have reached more than 50 watts, although most current processor chips do not exceed 10 watts.

This section discusses power consumption in digital CMOS circuits and then presents strategies for reducing power consumption.

11.3.1   *Power Consumption in CMOS Circuits*

In general, the loads driven by CMOS digital gates are best modeled as capacitive ones. Most of the power consumed in static CMOS logic consists of the power dissipated when charging and discharging these capacitive loads. Consider a CMOS gate driving a capacitive load over one logic cycle on that node (Figure 11.12). The energy dissipated during the logic cycle can be calculated solely as that drawn from the power supply when the capacitance is being charged (i.e., the potential energy removed from *Vdd* during the cycle).

During the charging the instantaneous current, i_{supply} is equal to:

$$i_{supply} = C_L \, dV/dt \tag{11.6}$$

where C_L is the load capacitance and V the instantaneous voltage across that capacitance. Now, if the supply voltage is *Vdd*, then the instantaneous power being consumed in the circuit consisting of the gate and the capacitive load is given as:

$$P = i_{supply} \, Vdd = Vdd \, C_L \, dV/dt \tag{11.7}$$

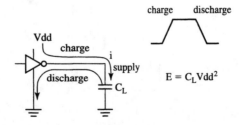

Figure 11.12   *Circuit Model for Power Dissipated in a CMOS Gate.*

Therefore the energy drawn from the power supply for a 0 to *Vdd* transition (and thus the energy consumed for both rising and falling transitions together), over a period of time 0 to *T*, is given by:

$$E = \int_0^T P(t)dt = 2 \int_0^{Vdd} C_L dV = C_L Vdd^2 \qquad (11.8)$$

and the power dissipated will be given by the energy per transition multiplied by the number of transitions per second. Now an actual chip consists of a large number of nodes, each transitioning at different rates. Only the clock node itself toggles up and down at the clock frequency, f_{clock}. The other nodes in the circuit toggle at a rate equal to some fraction, N_{node}, of the clock frequency, e.g., if a node changes state every clock period then $N_{node} = 0.5$ (it charges only on every other clock cycle). For most nodes the actual fraction would be much lower than 0.5. Thus the power consumed for the circuit as a whole is given as:

$$Power = \sum_{nodes} Nnode C_L V_{dd}^2 f_{clock} \qquad (11.9)$$

where f_{clock} is the clock frequency and N_{node} is the fraction of clock cycles that each nodes switches, hereafter referred to as the *switching activity*.

11.3.2   *Design for Low Power*

Equation (11.9) leads directly to strategies for low power design by considering how to reduce each term in the equation. Generally the capacitance of standard loads and the supply voltage are decided by the processing technology, thus most designers can not use the C_L and V_{dd} terms as leverage for reducing power consumption. (Though a small number some fabrication technologies now permit multiple *Vdd*'s, even for dynamic charging of *Vdd*, their use is not yet widespread.[1])

Thus most practical power reduction techniques concentrate on reducing the clock frequency, f_{clock}, when appropriate, and eliminating unnecessary switching activity, reducing N_{node}. A very effective strategy is to turn off or slow down the clock to sections of the chip that are not needed or can go slow while waiting for an event. For example, notebook computers slow down if the only activity is waiting for a key stroke from the user, and most of the CPU turns itself off after a certain period of inactivity. Usually referred to as clock gating, the clock reduction or elimination (gating) circuits are not designed by the logic designer, but by the clock circuit designer. This is mostly due to the intricacies involved in the clock network design required to keep clock skew low. Clock gating is usually done to complete functional units, for example, an ALU, and is usually not implemented down to the module level. In other words, use of clock gating is usually determined by the system designer, not the logic designer. However, the logic designer might be asked to provide the clock designers with signals that request when to slow down or stop the clock. For example, to detect when the inputs to a module are not changing.

---

[1]Dynamic Vdd reduction is used when the circuit does not need to function at full performance, as the circuit delay increases proportionally to the reduction Vdd. Thus Vdd reduction is usually associated with a reduction in clock frequency and would be applied to large sections of the chip, not individual circuits.

The logic designer can make a big difference in power consumption by reducing unused switching activity within his or her modules. The key strategy is to look for large circuits that have a large ΣC (usually correlating to a large number of transistors) and are switching uselessly. For example, consider the following multiplier design:

```
reg [31:0] C;
reg [15:0] A,B;

always @(posedge clock)
  C = A * B;
```
(11.10)

This is illustrated in Figure 11.13. Let's say that in this case, signals A and B are actually buses in that they go to many functional units beside the multiplier. Let's assume that the output of the multiplier is only actually used on only 10 percent of the clock cycles. Now note that whenever A or B change, the multiplier calculates a new result A*B. For 90 percent of the time this calculation is not used and thus the power consumed in producing it is wasted! Since multipliers are large, power hungry units (ΣC is large), this design is very power-wasteful. It is desirable to prevent the nodes within the multiplier switching when the multiplication result is not needed. A circuit needs to be designed that minimizes logic changes at the input to the multiplier when the multiplictaion is not needed. Note that if the input to the multiplier is left unchanged, the multiplier consumes no power. (It is useful to point out here that, in this case gating the clock would not produce useful power savings. Gating the clock only prevents the flipflops from operating, the multiplier simply continues to operate.)

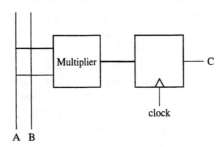

Figure 11.13   *Potentially Power-Inefficient Multiplier Design.*

```
reg [31:0] C;
reg [15:0] A,B;
tri [15:0] Ain, Bin,

always @(posedge clock)
  C = Ain * Bin;

assign Ain = GoForthAndMultiply ? A : 16´hzzzz;
assign Bin = GoForthAndMultiply ? B : 16´hzzzz;
```

In order to achieve this design change, it is first necessary to design a signal, *GoForthAndMultiply* that is active only when the multiplication is actually needed. The power consumption would be improved by modifying the multiplier input signals so that they change only when needed. For example, tristate units could be used.

Whenever the control signal is low, the output of the tristate gates become high impedance and the inputs to the multiplier stay unchanged.

However, large-scale use of tristate buffers is generally considered undesirable because they can make production debug and test difficult. Use of tristating is generally limited to important system buses (and some design groups forbid its use entirely). In this situation, a better compromise strategy might be to use multiplexors, as follows:

```
reg [31:0] C;
reg [15:0] A,B;
wire [15:0] Ain, Bin;

always @(posedge clock)
 C = Ain * Bin;

assign Ain = GoForthAndMultiply ? A : 16'h0;
assign Bin = GoForthAndMultiply ? B : 16'h0;
```

This is shown in Figure 11.14. Although this strategy almost doubles the power consumption over the previous strategy (every useful multiply is followed by a zero-multiply unless *GoForthAndMultiply* stays high for two clock cycles in a row), it is a good compromise between power consumption and practical design issues.

A third alternative would have been to place registers at the input to the multiplier and permit their contents to change only when needed, as illustrated in the code on the next page.

Many opportunities for reducing switching activity are available to the power-aware designer. Other techniques which have been suggested include:

- Reduce switching activity at the pins. This may be done by allocating an extra pin to signal the following situations on each cycle: (a) More than half of the pins are supposed to change state—then output instead all the inverted values. (b) The vector

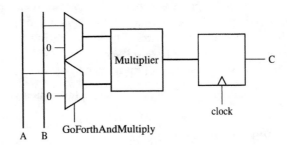

Figure 11.14   *More Power-Efficient Multiplier Design.*

represented on the pins is merely incrementing—then freeze the pins and let the destination chip compute the incremented value itself.

```
reg [31:0] C;
reg [15:0] A,B;
wire [15:0] Ain, Bin;

always @(posedge clock)
 begin
  C <= Ain * Bin;
  if (GoForthAndMultiply == 1)
   begin
    Ain <= A;
    Bin <= B;
   end
 end
```

- Replace arithmetic modules with lesser strength (for example, replace multiplier with shift, or shift and add).

11.3.3   CAD Tools in Low-Power Design

There is now a variety of power design tools from the the CAD vendors that can be placed in the following categories [Frenkil97]:

1. *Transistor and switch level*: These can estimate the power to within a few percent of silicon but are limited to a few hundred devices at the transistor level (although more at switch level) at the cost of long compute times. Such tools also have the disadvantage that power overruns will be revealed only after the design has progressed through layout and extraction.
2. *Gate level*: Given a gate-level netlist in Verilog, VHDL, or EDIF and a gate-level library graded for power, these tools can incorporate the actual switching activities from a simulation testbench to produce power estimates to within about 10–15 percent of silicon. Also at this level power compilers are available which use expression factoring, technology mapping, and cell sizing to achieve power reductions of 10–15 percent. Still designers would prefer information earlier in the design cycle.
3. *Architectural and RTL level*: Statistical techniques for power estimation at this level is still an active area of research. Tools are starting to appear that link power estimates to source code in RTL-level Verilog or VHDL to within about 20–25 percent of silicon. It is also an order of magnitude faster than the gate level.

A good survey of emerging techniques at various levels is given in [Macii98].

11.4   Area Issues in Design

Again, remember that at a crude level of understanding the synthesis tools only take the logic design implied by the Verilog and try to minimize it using Karnaugh-map style techniques. Generally if the designer poorly structures a design, the final netlist is inefficient in area, timing, and power. It is common to see a two-to-one difference in area between different designers implementing the same function. The purpose of this section is to introduce some techniques for structuring designs for minimizing area.

During the design process, it is important to be "area aware." The designer should constantly think about the number of large units being specified (adders, multipliers, registers, and so on), the complexity of the FSMs, and also whether there is a known structure that leads to a smaller area.

Consider the following trivial example:

```
wire [15:0] A,B,C;
wire [7:0] In1, In2, In3;
wire    MultSelect;

assign A = In1 * In2;
assign B = In1 * In3;
assign C = MultSelect ? A : B;
```

In this example, two multipliers are specified and will be built. However, it is fairly obvious that, because of the output multiplexor, only one of the multipliers is being used at a time. A more area-efficient solution would be to multiplex the input, as follows:

```
wire [15:0] C;
wire [7:0] In1, In2, In3, InSelect;
wire    MultSelect;

assign InSelect = MultSelect ? In2 : In3;
assign C = In1 * InSelect;
```

This is a simple and slightly contrived case. More subtle cases generally occur where designer knowledge leads to a smaller, more efficient implementation. For example, consider the following register file:

```
module RegFile (clock, WE, WriteAddress, ReadAddress, WriteBus, ReadBus);

input clock, WE;
input [4:0] WriteAddress, ReadAddress;
input [15:0] WriteBus;
output [15:0] ReadBus;

reg [15:0]  RegisterFile [0:31];   // thirty-two 16-bit registers

always @(posedge clock)
  if (WE) RegisterFile [WriteAddress] <= WriteBus;

assign ReadBus = RegisterFile [ReadAddress];

endmodule
```

This design will synthesize correctly but is not the most efficient implementation; the synthesis tools are not very good at implementing the implied address decoder. Instead, think about what the designer would do if she had to implement the above register file to the gate level by hand. The designer would explicitly design address decode logic separately from the register array itself. Here, the human designer does a better job of structuring the design than the tool does.

Consider the following design with explicit address decode logic (as captured in the signals "WElines"):

```
module RegFile (clock, WE, WriteAddress, ReadAddress, WriteBus, ReadBus);
  input clock, WE;
  input [4:0] WriteAddress, ReadAddress;
  input [15:0] WriteBus;
  output [15:0] ReadBus;
  reg [15:0]  RegisterFile [0:31];   // thirty-two 16-bit registers
  // provide one Write Enable line per register
  wire [0:31] WElines;
  integer i;
  // explicitly build the individual Write Enable lines by
  // shifting WE into correct line
  assign WElines = (WE << WriteAddress);
  assign ReadBus = RegisterFile [ReadAddress];

  always @(posedge clock)
    for (i=0; i<=32; i=i+1)
    if (WEline[i]) RegisterFile [i] <= WriteBus;
endmodule
```

When synthesized, this design is 20 percent smaller and 4 percent faster than the simpler, implicit design (when implemented in the standard cell library discussed in the next three chapters). Unfortunately (as it increases coding effort), it is often the case that adding detail of this nature leads to a smaller, more efficient design.

11.5   Conclusion

Synthesis tools, in and of themselves, do not produce good designs. All they do is save the human designer the drudgery of applying logic minimization techniques by hand and making sure that the timing is correct. If a design is poorly structured or designed hastily, the result is often an implementation that is slower, bigger, and more power-hungry than a carefully structured design would be. Often the difference between well-structured and poorly-structured designs is two to one or more in speed, area, and/or power consumption. The purpose of this chapter was to introduce you to fundamental design issues as related to timing, power, and area and illustrate some basic techniques that are used to arrive at better designs. A compendium of further case studies may be found in [Kurup97].

Exercises

11.1.   Consider a latched circuit consisting of D-latches and intermediate combinational logic. There are no false paths in the logic. (A false path is a logic path that exists between the timed elements but in practice is never exercised). The circuit has the following timing parameters:

- The latches have a set-up time of 3 ns, and a zero hold time. The clock to output delay is (in Verilog timing syntax) #(3:4:5).
- The combinational logic has the delay parameters #(2:7:9).
- The clock has a period of 20 ns, a 50 percent duty cycle (or, the clock is high for 50 percent of the period), and a clock skew of 1 ns.

Determine if any extra delay has to be inserted in order to prevent a race. If an inverter has a delay of #(2:3:4), how many are needed?

11.2. A multiplier is operating at 100 MHz with a supply voltage of 1 V. The sum of all of internal node capacitances is 10 fF. If, on average, 10 percent of the nodes switch during any one clockcycle, what is the power consumed in the multiplier?

11.3. Consider the following Verilog fragment:

```
reg     [31:0] bus1, bus2;
reg     [31:0] snoop;
reg            flag;

always @(posedge clock)
  if ((snoop == bus1) || (snoop == bus2))
     flag = 1´b1;
  else flag = 1´b0;
```

Use the following data in your answers:

- Each bit of the "= =" unit has a switching capacitance of 100 fF.
- The RS flipflop has a switching capacitance of 100 fF.
- $f = 100$ MHz, $Vdd = 5$ V
- Half of the bits in the bus change every clock cycle on average.
- The flipflop changes for 60 percent of the clock cycles.

Then answer the following questions:

a. Estimate the power consumed in the '= =' units and flipflop.

b. Assume a signal called *snoopon* can be provided. When *snoopon* is low, this unit does *not* need to be monitoring the bus. Rewrite the code so that the equivalent logic consumes less power.

11.4. Why is the design below bad from a power consumption point-of-view if the signal *En1* is only high 10 percent of the time? Show how it could be improved. Your answer should be in Verilog.

Assume that the potential savings in the adder is not worth the effort to change that part of the design.

```
reg En1;
reg [31:0] A, B, DataOut, MultOut, AddOut;
wire [31:0] A,B;
always @(posedge clock)
   if (En1 == 1) DataOut <= MultOut;
   else DataOut <= AddOut;
assign MultOut = A * B;
assign AddOut = A + B
```

11.5. Sketch the logic described in the following Verilog fragment.

```
reg A,B,C,D,E;
always @(posedge clock)
  begin
    A <= B^C;
    D <= E&F;
    G <= H | J;
    K <= G ? ~&{A,D} : ^{A,D}
  end
```

Then answer the following questions:

- If the cell library specified that the delay from every input of a gate to every output of a gate was written in Verilog as #(1 : 2.5 : 3) what does this mean (timescale is in ns)?
- If the clock period is 10 ns, the clock skew 1 ns, the max clock-Q delay is 2 ns, and maximum setup time 2 ns, is there a potential setup violation if this logic was synthesized exactly as described and the delays above apply?

If the max hold time is 1 ns, and the min clock-Q delay is 0.5 ns, is there a potential hold violation?

References

[Frenkil97] Frenkil, J., "Issues and directions in low-power design tools: An industrial perspective," Proc. ISLPED97 (*International symposium in low power electronics and design*), August 1997, Monterey, CA, pp. 152–157

[Kurup97] Kurup, P., and Abbasi, T., "Logic Synthesis using Synopsys," Kluwer, 1997

[Macii98] Macii, E., Pedram, M., and Somenzi, F., "High level power modelling, estimation, and optimization," IEEE Trans. CAD, 17:11, (November 98), pp. 1061–1079

[Sylvester98] Sylvester, D., and Keutzer, K., "Getting to the bottom of deep submicron," Proc. Intl. Conf. on CAD (ICCAD98), pp. 203–211

Chapter Twelve

Design
Compilation

12.1   Introduction

The subset of Verilog to which we have been introduced is now sufficient to start in with synthesis. If this were a book on software compilation it would be possible to cover the subject and provide examples without being vendor specific. Most 'C' compilers are similar to each other and the language accepted is standard ANSI. As of now, this is not true of hardware compilation, although this may change eventually with the current movement toward standards for synthesizable subsets of Verilog and VHDL. Until then, users must select a synthesis vendor and a target technology vendor and study the particulars for that combination.

To use the tools the first choice a user must make is that of the operating system. Although CAD tools started out in the workstation/Unix environment, most of the vendors are now making them available in the PC/NT environment and a few in PC/Linux. So far, the NT conversions do not seem as stable as the Unix, and the so-called "student editions" are more limited. We have elected to continue with the Unix version for now, although no doubt we will eventually have to change our ways.

A further choice is that of using the visual user interface style with sequences of menus and buttons, or the batch style with prewritten scripts. This is a matter of taste. The following material is oriented more toward the script style where possible. This is often preferred by designers because the development of a typical design involves a number of repeat runs with bug fixes or slightly different parameters. The script style makes it easier and faster to rerun these without making mistakes.

In this book the examples are couched in terms of the Synopsys, Altera, and Xilinx tools. Hopefully this should be illustrative of the kinds of questions users will face with other vendor combinations such as those from Cadence, Exemplar, Synplicity, Actel, or ATT, and so on. Suggestions for getting started with lists of vendors and Web sites are given in the preface. The flow of synthesis for the tools used here is illustrated in Figure 12.1 in a magnification of the central part of the sequence from Figure 1.2. As discussed in the previous chapter, use of modules from a library will certainly speed up the design process.

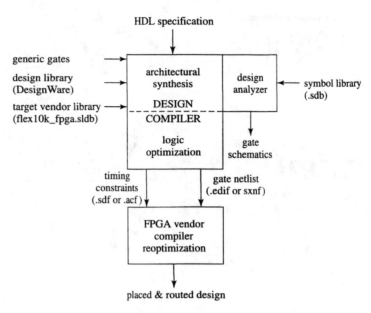

Figure 12.1   *Synthesis Flow.*

Where a similar module is available from more than one library as for example in memories, we will prefer the generator provided by the target vendor (see Chapters 13 and 14).

The form of the specification starting point is the dominant factor in the quality of results from synthesis. And this is the single point to which the designer must return either to remove verification errors or to improve the performance. This is the reason for the emphasis in this text on different ways of specifying the same behavior. One way of acquiring these skills is through documentation from vendors' Web sites and on-line help. This material (especially the manuals) can be somewhat intimidating in its sheer total volume. Second, for this book, the treatment shortcuts the normally long synthesis learning curve by using a cookbook approach keyed to particular HDL writing styles. In this approach the multitudinous choices of switches have been largely preselected, resulting in a feel more akin to casual software compilation. Corresponding to this, the emphasis is on the relation of errors to the source code rather than to gate schematics. It is possible to use the Synopsys design analyzer to produce views of the resulting schematics. Most users will not be much wiser if they do. For example, the illustrative design used in this chapter produces more than forty pages of such. Sufficient information about the resulting design is usually obtainable from the synthesis and fitter reports.

Another factor to be noted is the size of compiled (mapped) design files. Each of these can easily run to many megabytes even for modest designs (CAD vendors have typically placed memory conservation low on their list of priorities). Leave many of these files lying around in an educational environment and the user's disk allocation will be rapidly trashed. Similar remarks apply to the effect on available compute cycles of running multiple background compiles, a tendency of students that needs constant discouragement. So it is strongly recommended to run a single well-motivated compile at a time and keep just one other result with which to compare it. Certainly the best current result should never be overwritten. It has been well said that one might never get that lucky again.

In order to illustrate the functioning of the tools it is necessary to use some kind of running example, and this example has to be reasonably simple. So it will not make a lot of use of the two principal algorithms of the DC compiler, namely combinational minimization and finite state machine reduction. But it will show what the compiler is doing as it analyzes the input specification and builds the design in terms of cells available to it from the libraries.

12.2   Running Example: Alarm Clock

The example design chosen for this chapter is an alarm clock, very similar to a certain other well-known alarm clock.[1] This alarm clock has a different specification although its behavior is similar. We have added features that orient it toward the commonly available *design laboratory packages* available from the Altera and Xilinx university programs. In the case of Altera the count down factor is just a little off, so our alarm clock is only in fact accurate to sixteen seconds per day. Otherwise, the functioning corresponds fairly closely with that of the Synopsys tutorial and that of the familiar bedside instrument. Its datapath organization is shown in Figure 12.2 and discussed in the following paragraph.

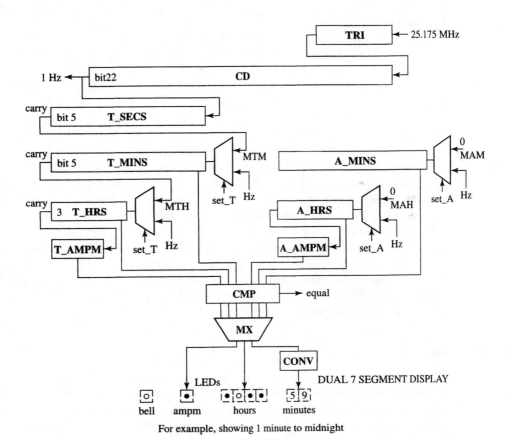

For example, showing 1 minute to midnight

Figure 12.2   *Aclock Datapath.*

---

[1]Done in the explicit state machine style in the Synopsys tutorial.

The TRI and CD modules together count down the Altera 25.175 MHz VGA quartz clock by the necessary ratio to give the seconds at the output. An alternative specification counts down the 12 Hz clock of the Xilinx XS40, although this board will need to be supplemented with a couple of extra seven-segment displays connected from the FPGA pins at the edge. In normal operation the timing part on the left half of the datapath counts the seconds down through the minutes, hours, and a.m./p.m. using carries connected in a rippling fashion through the uppermost inputs of the multiplexers MTM and MTH. Alternatively, when the clock time is being set, the inputs to either the minutes and hours counters are swept at a seconds rate. The alarm portion on the right-hand side of the datapath operates in a similar fashion except that in the normal mode it stays stationary. Other control logic is not shown in Figure 12.2, such as whether minutes or hours or alarm are being set. This will be inferred by the synthesizer from the specification.

In the Altera UP-1 board we are limited to two seven-segment display characters and these are used up for the minutes, so individual LEDs are used for the rest of the outputs. In this case we use an embedded ROM for the seven-segment converter. For the Xilinx version the minutes digits are fed instead through two instantiations of a BCD counter *count2d.v* feeding into combinational converter *enc7seg.v*. These details are reserved until Chapter 14.

In the following we have separated off the counters as submodules within a purely structural top-level specification. Besides making the specification much shorter (about 16 percent of the characters compared to that of the Synopsys tutorial) this is a reasonable convenience since most vendors libraries make such sequential functional modules available and the resulting synthesized area and time reports are also better. There is general evidence for this [Chaud96]. The specification is given in the box below using the *countertc* module from Chapter 5.

The discussion of the ROM converter module is delayed until Chapter 14.

An appropriate testbench for the alarmclock follows in the next box. Consistent with the methodology set out in Chapter 8 this has been written with the top-level module arguments in lexical order and separate bus bit lines. Then the same testbench can be used for the gate level netlist that emerges from synthesis and fitting. The timescale will result in a simulation print-out in units of seconds. While this may not appear to be much of a challenge for nanosecond FPGA technology, the synthesis time report will still show the propagation delays in the critical paths from the edges of the twenty-five MHz input clock. The various control inputs can be routed from rocker switches: *set_A* and *set_T* to set the alarm and time respectively and *hrs-mins* to control which counter is being set. During the setting modes the counters advance at the 1 Hz rate.

12.3   Setting Up

Before starting operations a setting-up procedure will be necessary which will be specific to the combination of operating system, synthesis vendor, and target vendor. The following illustrations are given for Unix/Synopsys, Altera, and Xilinx. While other combinations will need some kind of similar setup procedure, the user would need to consult vendor documentation or application notes.

The user should first establish a directory system having one subdirectory for each project, each having subdirectories for the principal files as listed in the Specification for the *aclock* project. Such an example directory structure is shown in Figure 12.3 on page 203.

```
module aclock(clk,clr,hrs_mins,set_A,set_T,toggle_sw, bell, hz,
              led_ampm, led_hrs0, led_hrs1, led_hrs2, led_hrs3,
              segm0a,segm0b,segm0c,segm0d,segm0e,segm0f,segm0g,
              segm1a,segm1b,segm1c,segm1d,segm1e,segm1f,segm1g);
parameter LPM_FILE = ``converter.hex´´;
parameter r = 1<<23, s = 1<<3;
input clk, clr, hrs_mins, set_A, set_T, toggle_sw;
output bell, led_ampm, led_hrs3, led_hrs2, led_hrs1, led_hrs0, hz;
output segm1a,segm1b,segm1c,segm1d,segm1e,segm1f,segm1g;
output segm0a,segm0b,segm0c,segm0d,segm0e,segm0f,segm0g;
wire [5:0] A_MINS_state, T_MINS_state; // counter states
wire [3:0] A_HRS_state, T_HRS_state;
wire [10:0] outbus;  // drives converter for 7 seg displays
wire [15:0] mseg; // converter output drives 7 seg displays
wire equal, bell, hz;

assign {segm1a,segm1b,segm1c,segm1d,segm1e,segm1f,segm1g,
        segm0a,segm0b,segm0c,segm0d,segm0e,segm0f,segm0g} = mseg;
assign {led_ampm,led_hrs3,led_hrs2,led_hrs1,led_hrs0} = outbus[10:6];
assign bell = equal && toggle_sw;
countertc #(2,3)  TRI(clk,clr,1´b1,,clk3); // divides by 3
// countertc #(23,r) CD(clk3,clr,1´b1,,hz);//cntdn to 1Hz for hardware
countertc #(3,s)  CD(clk3,clr,1´b1,,hz); //cntdn to 1Hz for simulation
countertc #(6,60) T_SECS(hz,clr,1´b1,,TScarry);
countertc #(6,60) T_MINS(mtm,clr,etm,T_MINS_state,TMcarry);
countertc #(4,12) T_HRS (mth,clr,eth,T_HRS_state,THcarry);
countertc #(1,2)  T_AMPM(THcarry,clr,1´b1,T_AMPM_state,);
countertc #(6,60) A_MINS(hz,clr,eam,A_MINS_state,);
countertc #(4,12) A_HRS (hz,clr,eah,A_HRS_state,AHcarry);
countertc #(1,2)  A_AMPM(AHcarry,clr,1´b1,A_AMPM_state,);
mux       #(11) MX(set_A,{T_AMPM_state,T_HRS_state,T_MINS_state},
                {A_AMPM_state,A_HRS_state,A_MINS_state},outbus);
comparator #(11) CMP({T_AMPM_state,T_HRS_state,T_MINS_state},
                {A_AMPM_state,A_HRS_state,A_MINS_state}, equal);
mux        #(1)   ETM(set_T,1´b1, ~hrs_mins, etm); //muxes
mux        #(1)   ETH(set_T,1´b1, hrs_mins, eth); //for
mux        #(1)   EAM(set_A,1´b0, ~hrs_mins, eam); //counter
mux        #(1)   EAH(set_A,1´b0, hrs_mins, eah); //enables
mux        #(1)   MTM(set_T, TScarry, hz, mtm); // muxes for
mux        #(1)   MTH(set_T, TMcarry, hz, mth); // counter inputs
syn_rom_64x16_iuor
  //synopsys translate_off
   #(LPM_FILE)
  //synopsys translate_on
    converter(.Q(mseg),.Address(outbus[5:0]),.MemEnab(1´b1),.Outclock(hz));
endmodule
```

Aclock Specification: Pure Structural Style.

```verilog
    ´timescale 1ns / 100ps
module test_aclock;
 parameter SET_ALARM=2´b10, SET_TIME=2´b01, RUN=2´b00;
  reg [1:0] setv;
  reg [3:0] m1,m0;
  wire set_A, set_T, BELL, Hz, ph;
  wire led_ampm, led_hrs3, led_hrs2, led_hrs1, led_hrs0;
  wire [10:0] outbus;
  reg hrs_mins,toggle,clk,clr;
  integer i;
  assign set_A = setv[1], set_T = setv[0], ph = ~HZ;
  assign outbus[9:6] = {led_hrs3,led_hrs2,led_hrs1,led_hrs0};

  aclock   AC(clk, clr, hrs_mins, set_A, set_T, toggle, BELL,
             led_ampm, led_hrs0, led_hrs1, led_hrs2, led_hrs3, HZ,
             segm0a,segm0b,segm0c,segm0d,segm0e,segm0f,segm0g,
             segm1a,segm1b,segm1c,segm1d,segm1e,segm1f,segm1g);

always begin #20 clk=1; #20 clk=0; end // 25 MHz/Hz  clock
always @(posedge clk)
 begin //convert 7 seg back to decimal for simulation output
  case ({segm1a,segm1b,segm1c,segm1d,segm1e,segm1f,segm1g})
   7´b1111110: m1<=0; 7´b0110000: m1<=1; 7´b1101101: m1<=2; etc...
  endcase
  case ({segm0a,segm0b,segm0c,segm0d,segm0e,segm0f,segm0g})
   7´b1111110: m0<=0; 7´b0110000: m0<=1; 7´b1101101: m0<=2; etc...
  endcase
 end

  initial begin toggle<=0; clr<=1; clk<=0;
    $display(``time(secs/10) setv bell ampm hours m1 m0´´);
    $monitor(``    %5g     %b   %b   %b   %d    %d%d´´,
     $time,setv,BELL,led_ampm,outbus[9:6],m1,m0);
    @(posedge clk) clr<=0;           //clear complete
    setv<=SET_TIME; hrs_mins<=1; @(posedge ph);
    for (i=0; i < 15; i=i+1) @(posedge ph); //set time
    hrs_mins<=0; @(posedge ph);
    for (i=0; i < 16; i=i+1) @(posedge ph); //to 4.16pm
    setv<=SET_ALARM; hrs_mins<=1; @(posedge ph);
    for (i=0; i < 15; i=i+1) @(posedge ph); //set alarm
    hrs_mins<=0;
    for (i=0; i < 20; i=i+1) @(posedge ph); //to 4.20pm
    toggle=1; setv<=RUN; //run for three mins 10 secs
    for (i=0; i < 200; i=i+1) @(posedge ph);
    $finish;
  end
endmodule
```

Testbench for *Aclock*.

Starting at the top of this diagram and proceeding downwards, the third level, inside the corresponding project subdirectories, is where we will execute the synthesis compiles (Testbench). The fourth level *hdl* subdirectory of course contains the source files, and is the directory in which the simulations are executed. In the case a Verilog simulator is being used for post-routing netlists, then the final gate-level netlist file *aclock.vo* which is the final result of synthesis and fitting, should also be moved to this directory. The mapped subdirectory is used here to receive the results of Synopsys compiles and it is in this directory that the FGPA fitting runs are executed. The *work* subdirectory is used for the intermediate non-textual files generated by the synopsys synthesizer.

Returning now to the project directory, this may also contain *setup* files. Typically a general version or *system-wide* setup file is available with a vendor's software installation. A second *user* setup file can be in the user's home directory, and a third *project-specific* version will be looked for in the current working directory. If present it is this last one that will be given precedence. The *.synopsys_dc.setup* file tells the synthesizer where to look for the various files it needs. The example below illustrates what is needed for both Altera and Xilinx. It should be copied into the working directory as shown in Figure 12.3, and the sections for the unneeded vendor should be commented out. In the following files, the aliases $SYNOPSYS, $ALT_HOME, $XILINX are used for the home paths of the corresponding vendor installation. In the Unix environment these may be defined in the users *.cshrc* file, such as: setenv SYNOPSYS = /usr/local/cad/synopsys.

12.3.1   *Notes on the Setup File*

An example setup file is shown on the next page. The *target library* specifies the cells from an ASIC or FPGA vendor that will be used to make up the netlist during the mapping and optimization phases of the synthesis. Such a vendor may have several technologies available with corresponding libraries. The FPGA chip families being used here are *flex10k* or *4005XL*. These may be further differentiated as to speed grade, for example, –4.

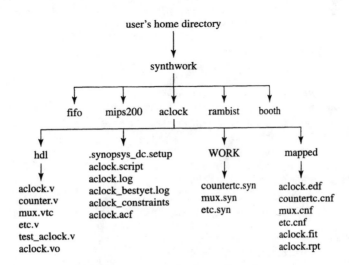

Figure 12.3   *Directory Structure.*

```
SynopsysInstall = get_unix_variable(SYNOPSYS);
AlteraInstall = get_unix_variable(ALT_HOME);
XilinxInstall = get_unix_variable(XILINX);
search_path = {. \
          ./hdl \
        SynopsysInstall + /libraries/syn \
        AlteraInstall + /synopsys/library/alt_syn/flex10k/lib \
        XilinxInstall + /synopsys/libraries/syn \
        SynopsysInstall + /dw/dw01/lib + /dw/dw03/lib }

hdl_keep_licenses = FALSE
synlib_evaluation_mode = FALSE
synlib_disable_limited_licenses = TRUE
bus_naming_style = ``%s<%d>´´
bus_dimension_separator_style = ``><´´
bus_inference_style = ``%s<%d>´´
define_design_lib WORK -path ./WORK

/* libraries for Altera */
link_library = {flex10k-4_fpga.sldb}
link_library = link_library + dw01.sldb + dw03.sldb
target_library = {flex10k-4_fpga.db}
symbol_library = {altera.sdb}
synthetic_library = {flex10k-4_fpga.sldb}
define_design_lib DW_FLEX10k-4_FPGA -path AlteraInstall + \
      /synopsys/library/alt_syn/flex10k/lib/dw_flex10k-4_fpga

/* libraries for Xilinx
link_library = {xprim_4005xl-3.db xprim_4000xl-3.db xgen_4000xl.db \
      xfpga_4000xl-3.db xio_4000xl-3.db}
target_library = {xprim_4005xl-3.db xprim_4000xl-3.db \
            xgen_4000xl.db xfpga_4000xl-3.db xio_4000xl-3.db}
symbol_library = {xc4000ex.sdb}
synthetic_library = {xdw_4000xl.sldb standard.sldb}
define_design_lib xdw_4000xl -path XilinxInstall + \
          /synopsys/libraries/dw/lib/xc4000xl */

/* EDIF variable settings for Altera */
edifout_netlist_only = true
edifout_power_and_ground_representation = net
edifout_power_net_name = ``VDD´´
edifout_ground_net_name = ``GND´´
edifin_power_net_name = ``VDD´´
edifin_ground_net_name = ``GND´´
edifout_no_array = false
edifout_write_properties_list={LUT_FUNCTION}

/* XNF settings for Xilinx */
xnfout_constraints_per_endpoint = 0
xnfout_library_version = ``2.0.0´´
```

The Synthesizer Setup File (*.synopsys_dc.setup*) for Altera or Xilinx.

The *symbol library* is of importance only if the generated schematics from the Synopsys *Design Analyzer* tool are wanted.

The *synthetic library* is the nontextual database of compiled parts. It is used by the synthesizer for combinational operator inference.

The *link library* is used when the HDL source itself has instantiations from a library as for example in the *fifodw* module of Chapter 9 which uses the Synopsys *DesignWare* library. For the *aclock* design of this chapter, this is not needed.

The *design_lib* entry indicates a directory where intermediate files corresponding to the submodules will be placed. It avoids cluttering up the main project directory with these. If it is desired to make use of the Synopsys *DesignWare* then the path to the appropriate libraries in this collection are also added here.

The *bus naming and separator style* chosen here is appropriate for the combination of FPGAs and Verilog gate-level simulation. Other target combinations may require a different selection, for which vendor's literature should be consulted.

Power and ground net names: Occasionally constant arguments are encountered in the source, or there are arguments corresponding to unused functionality. If the synthesizer has not been able to optimize them out, it may connect these fixed or unused ports to power or ground as appropriate.

A cache section provides an area in file memory that the synthesizer can use to cache its files and speed up the execution. On the first run, the synthesizer takes extra time to set this up.

12.4   Invoking Synthesis

In the style adopted here a script file is used to guide the synthesis rather than a sequence of menus and buttons. The following script file can be used to run the *aclock* example for the Altera or Xilinx targets. With only minor changes it can be used to run any other design which has been specified in the writing styles of Chapters 5 through 10.

12.4.1   *Notes on the* Aclock *Script File*

analyze: In this stage the synthesizer parses the HDL source. It is somewhat similar to the syntax check of the simulator except that also checks for constructs that are outside of the synthesis policy. The low-level submodules are analyzed first, followed by the top-level module.

elaborate: This replaces the synthesizable operators (see Table 5.1) with the synthetic operators and determines the correct register and bus sizes. At this stage an initial estimate of the network depth is made from the Boolean equations in terms of elementary gates from the GTECH library. The acronym is an abbreviation of *generic technology*, which means to say that this estimate is independent of the eventual target technology.

clock: If given the choice, the synthesizer attaches primary importance to minimizing the delays. Clock inputs have a special significance for the synthesizer because the defined edges will determine the start and finish points for the propagation paths through the sections of combinational logic between registers. In this script there are

```
 TOP = aclock
/* Analyze designs in the second hierarchy level */
 analyze -format verilog -lib WORK {comparator.v, mux.v, countertc.v, count2d.v}
/* Analyze and elaborate the top-level design */
 analyze -format verilog -lib WORK TOP + ``.v´´
 elaborate TOP -lib WORK -update
 current_design = TOP

/* set design constraints */
 set_max_area 100  /* 50 for Xilinx */
 create_clock clk -period 40
 set_input_delay 1 all_inputs() -clock clk
 set_output_delay 15 -clock ``clk´´  all_outputs()

/* pad details for Xilinx */
 set_operating_conditions ``WCCOM´´
 set_port_is_pad ``*´´
 set_pad_type -no_clock all_inputs()
 set_pad_type -clock find(port, ``clk´´)
 set_pad_type -slewrate HIGH all_outputs()
 insert_pads */

 set_dont_touch syn_rom_64x16_iuor  /* for Altera embedded memory */
 link
 replace_synthetic -ungroup
 uniquify

 current_design = TOP /* compile the design */
 compile -map_effort low -verify -verify_effort low
 check_design

/* Generate desired reports */
 report_area
 report_timing
 report_cell

/* write out netlist for Altera in EDIF format */
 write -f edif -hier -o TOP + ``.edf´´
/* and convert timing constraints into .acf format */
current_design = TOP
include get_unix_variable(ALT_HOME) + /synopsys/bin/syn2acf.cmd
sh $ALT_HOME/synopsys/bin/syn2acf TOP

/* write out netlist for Xilinx in xnf format */
 ungroup -all -flatten
 replace_fpga
 set_attribute TOP ``part´´ -type string part
 set_attribute find(design,``*´´) ``xnfout_write_map_symbols´´ -type boolean FALSE
 write -format xnf -hierarchy -output TOP +``.sxnf´´ */
quit
```

no explicit time constraints such as max or min delays from point to point, so the synthesizer takes its timing goals from the time durations between clock transitions.

set-max-area: After the time constraint is met, the synthesizer attempts to minimize the area. The area constraint might be a hard limit imposed by the designer. Otherwise the synthesizer does its best work when this constraint is realistic, such as just a little tighter than the results achieved in a previous run (though the synthesizer will still seek to minimize area with this set to zero). Normally Xilinx cells have about twice the gate content of an Altera cell so this figure would need to be adjusted accordingly. In this case the overall totals come out about equal because the converter is a black box in the Altera version.

set-load or **set-delay:** The load on the outputs will affect the time and area reports because higher capacitive loads may require a cascade of graduated buffer stages. A load of 1 unit corresponds to that required to drive a typical gate input. Hence the load of 3 units specified here will allow for the equivalent of a fanout connection of 3.

set-don't-touch: The details of the generated memory here will be known only to the FPGA vendor tool and so must be passed on untouched by the synthesizer. If synthetic modules are infered from the operations or if there were any DesignWare modules linked into the design (as in the *fifodw* module of Chapter 9) then the command *replace synthetic-ungroup* might be given. The ungrouping of submodules essentially collapses the hierarchy and allows the design compiler to optimize across their boundaries.

check-design: This command often finds situations that will cause problems in the compile stage.

uniquify: If the design hierarchy includes multiple copies of some submodule then the *uniquify* command is needed to alert the synthesizer to distinguish between them.

compile: Here is where the compiler proper is launched. In the *mapping* phase the generic GTECH gates are replaced with cells from the target technology. Then in the *optimization* phase the compiler attempts to find multiple output—multiple-level combinational networks of the target components which best meet the time and area constraints that have been set. During this phase the compiler will be *structuring* the Boolean expressions and corresponding gate networks into trial hierarchies. In an educational environment the burden on the computing infrastructure (not to mention the wait for the results) will be minimized if the *low effort* options are selected.

report: There are many synthesis reports that can be called for. In this script, three of the most important ones have been illustrated.

write: If the compilation is successful, the result is written out in a standard form which the target vendor software can accept (the *EDIF* netlist language for Altera or the *sxnf* netlist language for Xilinx. FPGA vendors used to throw away the Synopsys fpga-cell efforts and start again from GTECH gates, although now syntheizers like the Synopsys FPGAII compiler are very knowledgeable on the logical elements of the FPGA vendors and the flow is smoother. For *back-annotation* of delays into the netlist Xilinx generates a file in the *.sdf* standard delay format (SDF), a standard industry format for representing delays. Altera requires a conversion to its own *acf* format.

The Log File

In UNIX synthesis is invoked with a command such as:

fpga_shell -f aclock.script > aclock.log

then the warnings of errors and the reports will all be merged into a single log file. This could be used as a record and consulted at leisure. This is again a matter of taste. Some may prefer to keep report files separate—at least, after the bugs are out. A *synopsys* (uncapitalized) of such a log file for the *aclock* run is appended below. This kind of *synopsys* makes use of an *ellipsis* (three dots) every place a large chunk has been edited out. The progress of the synthesizer can be followed from the commands of the script file, which are reproduced in it. Our comments are interspersed between log excerpts.

```
          Version 1999.05-Dec 18, 1998
          Copyright (c) 1988-1998 by Synopsys, Inc.
             ALL RIGHTS RESERVED
    This program is proprietary and confidential information of Synopsys, Inc.
    and may be used and disclosed only as authorized in a license agreement
    controlling such use and disclosure.

/* Analyze designs in the second hierarchy level */
...
/* Analyze and elaborate the top-level design */
analyze -format verilog -lib WORK aclock.v
... elaborate aclock -lib WORK -update
...
Information: Building the design `countertc´ instantiated from design `aclock´ with
the parameters ``6, 60´´. (HDL-193)
Inferred memory devices in process
in routine countertc_n6_r60 line 9 in
    file `/home/facfs1/drs/max2work/aclock/hdl/countertc.v´.
===============================================================================
|    Register Name      |   Type   | Width | Bus | AR | AS | SR | SS | ST |
===============================================================================
|      state_reg        | Flipflop |   6   |  Y  | Y  | N  | N  | N  | N  |
===============================================================================
```

This indicates that this counter has been implemented with edge-triggered flipflops (rather than latches) with output gating to a bus. An asynchronous reset is used but no set or synchronous set/reset connections.

```
...
/* Set design attributes and constraints*/
set_max_area 120
set_load 3.0 all_outputs()
Performing set_load on port `Hz´.
...
create_clock -period 40 clk
Performing create_clock on port `clk´.
...link
```

```
Linking design:
  aclock
Using the following designs and libraries:
  flex10k_fpga.sldb (library), dw01.sldb (library)
...
replace_synthetic -ungroup
Loading db file `/usr/local/pkg/cad/maxplus2/synopsys/library/alt_syn/flex10k/
    lib flex10k_fpga.db`
Information: Checking out the license `DesignWare-Foundation`. (SEC-104)
  Loading target library `flex10k_fpga`
...
 Allocating blocks in `A_MINS`
...
Information: Read implementation `rpl` for synthetic design `DW01_inc_6`
from design library `DW01`. (SYNH-2)
  Allocating blocks in `DW01_inc_6`
  Structuring `DW01_inc_6`
  Mapping `DW01_inc_6`
Information: Modeled DW01_inc_6(rpl).
```

The ripple version of an incrementer is used in this trial. Other alternatives may also be tried.

```
...
  Transferring Design `countertc_n6_r60` to database `countertc_n6_r60.db`
...
check_design
Warning: In design `aclock`, a pin on submodule `CD` is connected to logic 1 or
logic 0.(LINT-32)
   Pin `enable` is connected to logic 1.
```

In our design of Figure 12.2 this counter was intended to be continuously enabled, so this warning can be disregarded.

```
...
/* uniquify any multiple instances */
uniquify
  Uniquifying cell `A_MINS` in design `aclock`. New design is `countertc_n6_r60_0`.
```

The synthesizer allocates its own identifiers using as indexes the parameters in the order in which they occured in the source specification of that submodule. Then it adds a final distinguishing index count starting at zero.

```
...
 /* compile design */
compile -map_effort low -verify -verify_effort low

 Loading target library `flex10k_fpga`
 Loading design `aclock`
Warning: In design `aclock`, there are 9 submodules connected to power or ground.
                                                                    (LINT-30)
Warning: In design `countertc_n1_r2_1`, there is 1 cell that doesn't drive any
                                                              nets. (LINT-30)
```

In Figure 12.2 this is the last counter in the chain, and it was intended that its output does not continue anywhere, so this warning can be disregarded.

```
. . .

Warning: Cell `converter` is an empty subdesign in design  `aclock`.
 The inputs of the cell will be ignored, not treated as verification endpoints.
                                                                   (FV-22)
```

This module is being passed through as a black box until it reaches Altera, when it will be fleshed out.

```
. . .
  Beginning Mapping Optimizations (Low effort)
  . . .
Optimization complete
  . . .
  Verifying Designs aclock (Low effort)
  VerificationvSucceeded
. . .
```

In such a log file the first thing to look for are the lines headed "error". As in software engineering, perusal should start from the top since later errors are usually caused by earlier ones. These indicate an immediate problem, which will prevent completion and have to fixed before proceeding. In this example the early errors have already been removed during high-level simulation.

Next the file should be scanned for the tables near the beginning indicating the details of the flipflop and latch types the synthesizer has selected for the declared registers, as well as for those nondeclared registers which it has inferred. If these types are not what was intended, it may indicate further modifications to be made in the source. In this example, the tables show that flipflops (edge-triggered) have been selected as a result of the posedge statements in the source.

After the errors have been purged, then the lines headed "warning:" should be heeded. Many of these may not be significant. The basic rule is that it is alright to disregard them if what produced them is thoroughly understood and it is certain that the warned situations are safe. For example the warnings about the CD input of logical 1 and the MAM input of logical 0 were deliberate in order to make the countdown always count and the alarm setting stay constant while the clock is running.

The area count depends on the target library used. In the case of custom design it really means chip area. To get a count in terms of two-input gate equivalents one would have to divide by the area of such a typical gate. For current .35um libraries this might be a factor of around fifty, while for .25um libraries it might be half of that. In the present case the given count is directly in terms of FPGA logical elements which might have fifty to 100 gates each, so one would have to multiply by this factor.

The timing report is a statistical estimate prior to actual routing. It has selected the longest electrical path (critical path) for display here.

The designer's cell hierarchy may be recognized in the cell report on page 212.

Finally, the compilation process is complete and the requested reports are generated: The cell report prints out a listing of the cells used and their areas. In addition it reports the

```
/* Generate desired reports */

************************************************************
Report : area
Design : aclock
Version: 1999.05
Date    : Mon Jul 19 14:18:56 1999
************************************************************
Combinational area:            104.000000
Noncombinational area:           0.000000
Net Interconnect area:         undefined   (Wire load has zero net area)

Total cell area:               104.000000
Total area:                    undefined
```

```
************************************************************
Report : timing
Design : aclock
Version: 1999.05
Date    : Mon Jul 19 14:18:56 1999
************************************************************
Startpoint: TRI/state_reg0 (rising edge-triggered flipflop clocked by clk)
  Endpoint: TRI/state_reg1 (rising edge-triggered flipflop clocked by clk)
  ----------------------------------------------------------------------

  aclock
  Point              ALL           flex10k-4_fpga       Incr       Path
  ----------------------------------------------------------------------
  clock clk (rise edge)                                20.00      20.00
  clock network delay (ideal)                           0.00      20.00
  TRI/state_reg0/CLK (DFFE)                             0.00      20.00 r
  TRI/state_reg0/Q (DFFE)                               1.10      21.10 r
  TRI/*cell*125/
CO (FLEX_CARRY_INC)                     2.56          23.66 r
  TRI/add_15/U13_1/S (FLEX_ADD)                         1.97      25.63 r
  TRI/U50/Y (LUT)                                       2.37      28.01 r
  TRI/state_reg1/D (DFFE)                               0.67      28.68 r
  data arrival time                                               28.68

  clock clk (rise edge)                                60.00      60.00
  clock network delay (ideal)                           0.00      60.00
  TRI/state_reg1/CLK (DFFE)                             0.00      60.00 r
  library setup time                                   -2.50      57.50
  data required time                                             57.50
  ----------------------------------------------------------------------
  data required time                                             57.50
  data arrival time                                             -28.68
  ----------------------------------------------------------------------
  slack (MET)                                                    28.82
```

```
*****************************************
Report : cell
Design : aclock
Version: 1999.05
Date   : Mon Jul 19 14:18:56 1999
*****************************************
Attributes:
    b - black box (unknown)
    d - dont_touch
    h - hierarchical
    n - noncombinational
    p - parameterized
    u - contains unmapped logic


Cell                    Reference  Library             Area   Attributes
------------------------------------------------------------------------------
A_AMPM                  countertc_n1_r2_0               2.50   h, n
A_HRS                   countertc_n4_r12_0             9.00   h, n
A_MINS                  countertc_n6_r60_0            14.00   h, n
CD                      countertc_n3_r8               7.00   h, n, p
CMP                     comparator_n11                8.00   h, n, p
EAH                     mux_n1_2                       1.00   h, n
EAM                     mux_n1_4                       1.00   h, n
ETH                     mux_n1_5                       1.00   h, n
ETM                     mux_n1_0                       1.00   h, n
MTH                     mux_n1_3                       1.00   h, n
MTM                     mux_n1_1                       1.00   h, n
MX                      mux_n11                       11.00   h, n, P
TRI                     countertc_n2_r3               5.00   h, n, p
T_AMPM                  countertc_n1_r2_1              2.50   h, n
T_HRS                   countertc_n4_r12_1            14.00   h, n
T_SECS                  countertc_n6_r60_2            14.00   h, n
converter               syn_rom_64x16_iuor             0.00   b, d

    ----- FPGA Look-up-table (LUT) Cells -----
...
U10             LUT             flex10k-4_fpga     1.00
  Output Pin    Function
  ----------    --------------
     Y          (IN1 IN2)
     Pin        Net
     ---        ---
     IN1        equal
     IN2        toggle_sw
     IN3        n222 (logic 0)
     IN4        n222 (logic 0)
     Y          bell
------------------------------------------------------------------
Total 20 cells                                        104.00

/* convert timing constraints into maxplus2 .acf format */
 current_design = TOP
Current design is `aclock'.
``/home/facfs1/drs/max2work/aclock/aclock.db:aclock''
 write_sdf TOP +``.acf''
Information: Annotated `cell' delays are assumed to include load delay. (UID-282)
Information: Writing timing information to file `/home/facfs1/drs/max2work/
                                       aclock/aclock.acf'. (WT-3)
quit
1
dc_shell>
Thank you...
```

functionality for each LUT and the nets feeding the LUT. Much information can be gleaned from this, in particular where most of the area is consumed. In this case, the memory, which would have been the largest, has been passed to the FPGA fitter as a black box to be implemented as embedded ROM. Other than this, any black box in the cell report merits attention. It may be indicative of some earlier unnoticed error in the log file.

The timing report is actually a kind of statistical estimate prior to actual routing. By default it gives just the worst propagation delay (critical path) between each set of clock edges. A slack violation in this report is a definite indication that the post-route simulation will not work. Since these are prerouting estimates it may very easily not work even without a slack violation. In attempting to trim the clock period or eliminate a slack violation, bear in mind that the result of a new simulation with a different clock period may not produce a new timing report that is linearly related! For example, the following two reports were obtained for the FIFO design of Chapter 9:

First try:

```
Report : timing
***********************************************
Design              Wire Loading Model      Library
-------------------------------------------------------------------

fifo                      ALL               flex10k_fpga

Startpoint: RP/state_reg2
        (rising edge-triggered flip-flop clocked by clk)
  Endpoint: RAM/data_out_reg0
        (rising edge-triggered flip-flop clocked by clk)
  Path Group: clk
  Path Type: max

  Point                                      Incr       Path
  ---------------------------------------------------------------
  clock clk (rise edge)                      0.00       0.00
  clock network delay (ideal)                0.00       0.00
  RP/state_reg2/CLK (DFFE)                   0.00       0.00 r
  RP/state_reg2/Q (DFFE)                     0.90       0.90 r
  RP/state2 (fsr_n3_1)                       0.00       0.90 r
  MUX/Din02 (mux_n3)                         0.00       0.90 r
  MUX/U21/Y (LUT)                            8.65       9.55 r
  MUX/Dout2 (mux_n3)                         0.00       9.55 r
  RAM/addr2 (ram_n7_a3_w4)                   0.00       9.55 r
  RAM/U107/Y (LUT)                           5.40      14.95 r
  RAM/U156/Y (LUT)                           4.70      19.65 r
  RAM/U118/Y (LUT)                           3.06      22.72 r
  RAM/data_out_reg0/D (DFFE)                 1.46      24.18 r
  data arrival time                                    24.18

  clock clk (rise edge)                     30.00      30.00
  clock network delay (ideal)                0.00      30.00
  RAM/data_out_reg0/CLK (DFFE)               0.00      30.00 r
  library setup time                        -0.20      29.80
  data required time                                   29.80
  ---------------------------------------------------------------
  data required time                                   29.80
  data arrival time                                   -24.18
  ---------------------------------------------------------------
  slack (MET)                                           5.62
```

Second try:

```
Report : timing
     Point                               Incr      Path
----------------------------------------------------------
clock clk (rise edge)                    0.00      0.00
clock network delay (ideal)              0.00      0.00
RP/state_reg2/CLK (DFFE)                 0.00      0.00 r
RP/state_reg2/Q (DFFE)                   0.90      0.90 r
RP/state2 (fsr_n3_1)                     0.00      0.90 r
MUX/Din02 (mux_n3)                       0.00      0.90 r
MUX/U21/Y (LUT)                          8.65      9.55 r
MUX/Dout2 (mux_n3)                       0.00      9.55 r
RAM/addr2 (ram_n7_a3_w4)                 0.00      9.55 r
RAM/U137/Y (LUT)                        11.02     20.58 r
RAM/U174/Y (LUT)                         3.06     23.64 r
RAM/U142/Y (LUT)                         3.06     26.70 r
RAM/data_out_reg0/D (DFFE)               1.46     28.17 r
data arrival time                       28.17

clock clk (rise edge)                   25.00     25.00
clock network delay (ideal)              0.00     25.00
RAM/data_out_reg0/CLK (DFFE)             0.00     25.00 r
library setup time                      -0.20     24.80
data required time                                24.80
----------------------------------------------------------
data required time                                24.80
data arrival time                                -28.17
----------------------------------------------------------
slack (VIOLATED)                                  -3.37
```

Such timing discrepencies at this level are due to the fact that the synthesizer has taken different optimimization routes. Further discrepencies are to be expected after routing when the true interconnect capacitances are known.

The *aclock* will be augmented with display outputs and pursued to an FPGA implementation in the next chapter. Only at this point will the actual delays be known and incorporated into the low-level simulation.

As device dimensions get further down into the submicron region, the propagation delays due to the interconnect continue to increase perhaps even to the point where they eventually exceed those of the gates themselves. However, recent estimates are that this point will not be reached soon. In fact, due to the changeover from aluminum to copper and improved dielectrics it is expected that, down to 0.1 micron features, interconnect delays will be held to 25–40 percent of gate delays for circuit blocks of 50–100K gates [Sylvester98].

Exercises

12.1. For the shifter and any of the comparator functions, compare synthesized area and time results from module specifications using the operations of Table 3.1 without library calls (Chapter 4, Problems 4.2 and 4.3) against equivalent modules instantiated from the Synopsys *DesignWare* library. Try gradually increasing the parameterization to see how synthesis has more and more difficulty unless it has some structure to draw upon.

12.2. Synthesize the two prioritizer specifications developed in Chapter 4, Problem 4.4 and compare the area and time results as the size parameter increases. A comparison could also be made with the prioritizer from the *DesignWare* library.

12.3. Compare the synthesis area and time results from the FIFO Specification #1 from Chapter 9, if the compiler is called with *-low_effort, -medium_effort,* and *-boundary_optimization*. Compare your results with that of the *DesignWare* library called with a wrapper as in Chapter 9 Specification #3.

12.4. At a time when the system is not in heavy use, synthesize a design selected from Chapter 10 or the problems from Chapters 9 or 10.

References

[Chaud96] Chaudhuri, S., and Quayle, M., "Synthesis using sequential functional modules," *ICCAD* 1996

[Sylvester98] Sylvester, D., and Keutzer, K., "Getting to the bottom of deep submicron," *Proc. Intl. Conf. on CAD (ICCAD98)*, pp. 203–211

Chapter Thirteen

Synthesis to Standard Cells

13.1 Introduction

The previous chapter covered general synthesis issues although motivated by FPGA implementation. This chapter covers issues related to synthesizing a design to a standard cell library. A standard cell is a full custom design of a simple gate function, such as an inverter or a flipflop. The design is targeted towards a particular IC fabrication process. Generally an engineering group designs one hundred to two hundred different cells down to the mask level that are familiar with the fabrication process being targeted. The synthesis tools then choose amongst these cells to produce a design that meets the required functional and performance specifications.

Examples of two standard cells, an inverter and a D flipflop are given in Figures 13.1 and 13.2. These cells are taken from the CMOSX 0.8 μm library distributed by Advanced Microelectronics [1]. The first page of each specification sheet describes the functionality and timing performance of the cell. The second page shows the cell layout that would be used to generate the mask information employed to fabricate the chips. Note the horizontal features on the top and bottom of the layout view of both cells. These are the Vcc (power) and ground rails (metalization) for the cells. The power and ground rail in each cell has identical width and vertical separation to those in other cells. This feature permits the cells to be placed in rows side by side with power and ground continuity.

After synthesis determines which cells will be used, a place and route tool forms the cells into rows, thus automatically connecting their power and ground, and connects the cells up by placing wires in the wiring channels between the cells. It is this layout that is later used to generate the mask information.

The next section will describe a sample synthesis strategy and illustrate that strategy using the Synopsys synthesis scripting language.

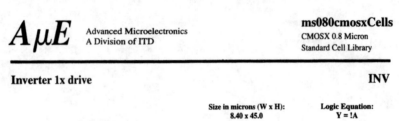

$A\mu E$ Advanced Microelectronics
             A Division of ITD

ms080cmosxCells
CMOSX 0.8 Micron
Standard Cell Library

Inverter 1x drive   **INV**

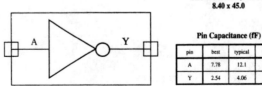

Size in microns (W x H):
8.40 x 45.0

Logic Equation:
Y = !A

Pin Capacitance (fF)

pin	best	typical	worst
A	7.78	12.1	21.3
Y	2.54	4.06	5.73

Truth Table

A	Y
0	1
1	0

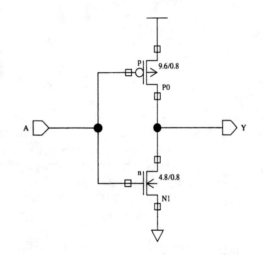

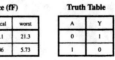

Delay Information

Path	Timing		best, 5.5V, −55C, load:0.35pF tr:0.584ns, tf:0.638ns			typical, 5V, 25C, load:0.35pF tr:1.15ns, tf:1.12ns			worst, 4.5V, 125C, load:0.35pF tr:2.78ns, tf:2.27ns		
			0.25 * load	1 * load	4 * load	0.25 * load	1 * load	4 * load	0.25 * load	1 * load	4 * load
a->y	10->10	PD	0.101	0.291	0.862	0.269	0.642	1.91	0.750	1.70	5.06
			0.0741 + 0.569 * CL			0.189 + 1.23 * CL			0.517 + 3.26 * CL		
		TR	0.305	0.579	1.76	0.554	1.16	3.88	1.08	2.77	9.90
a->y	01->10	PD	0.170	0.408	1.32	0.302	0.726	2.19	0.596	1.52	4.33
			0.0998 + 0.868 * CL			0.206 + 1.42 * CL			0.461 + 2.80 * CL		
		TR	0.311	0.675	2.31	0.539	1.15	3.84	1.05	2.34	7.47

Revision 1.0   December 20, 19941

Note: Advanced Microelectronics is a division of the Institute for Technology Development, Jackson, Miss.

Figure 13.1   *Sample Specification of an Inverter Cell.*

$A\mu E$ Advanced Microelectronics
A Division of ITD

ms080cmosxCells
CMOSX 0.8 Micron
Standard Cell Library

Inverter 1x drive   **INV**

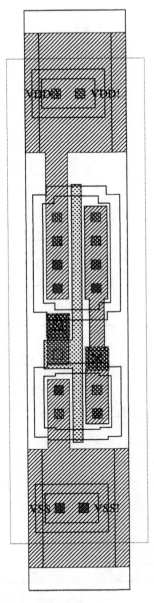

Revision 1.0   December 20, 19942

Figure 13.1   (*Continued*).

$A\mu E$ Advanced Microelectronics
A Division of ITD

ms080cmosxCells
CMOSX 0.8 Micron
Standard Cell Library

D flipflop   DFF

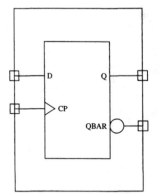

Logic Equation:
Q = [(D & CP[rise]) | (Q' &
!CP[rise])]
QBAR = !Q

Truth Table

CP	Q	QBAR
01	D	!D
10	Q'	QBAR'

Size in microns (W x H):
63.4 x 45.0

Pin Capacitance (fF)

pin	best	typical	worst
CP	14.7	21.6	30.9
D	10.4	13.5	18.4
Q	5.04	10.6	11.7
QBAR	11.4	12.7	22.3

Delay Information

Path	Timing		best, 5.5V, −55C, load:0.35pF tr:0.584ns, tf:0.638ns			typical, 5V, 25C, load:0.35pF tr:1.15ns, tf:1.12ns			worst, 4.5V, 125C, load:0.35pF tr:2.78ns, tf:2.27ns		
			0.25 * load	1 * load	4 * load	0.25 * load	1 * load	4 * load	0.25 * load	1 * load	4 * load
cp->qbar	01->10	PD	0.249	0.315	0.647	0.553	0.679	1.18	1.52	1.76	2.61
			0.213 + 0.308 * CL			0.517 + 0.478 * CL			1.46 + 0.831 * CL		
		TR	0.0697	0.206	0.811	0.144	0.354	1.29	0.281	0.668	2.32
cp->q	01->01	PD	0.211	0.266	0.545	0.459	0.624	1.25	1.24	1.70	3.34
			0.180 + 0.258 * CL			0.416 + 0.609 * CL			1.12 + 1.59 * CL		
		TR	0.0874	0.229	0.847	0.198	0.517	1.89	0.456	1.33	4.86
cp->qbar	01->01	PD	0.222	0.258	0.440	0.506	0.613	1.03	1.44	1.72	2.80
			0.202 + 0.169 * CL			0.475 + 0.403 * CL			1.35 + 1.03 * CL		
		TR	0.0669	0.154	0.565	0.140	0.347	1.26	0.364	0.901	3.24
cp->q	01->10	PD	0.209	0.316	0.797	0.429	0.631	1.37	1.16	1.59	2.91
			0.162 + 0.451 * CL			0.378 + 0.714 * CL			1.09 + 1.32 * CL		
		TR	0.107	0.310	1.19	0.210	0.537	1.92	0.441	1.06	3.55

Special Timing Information

	best, 5.5V, −55C	typical, 5V, 25C	worst, 4.5V, 125C
Setup-time on D	0.3	0.6	1.4
Hold-time on D	0.1	0.05	0.01
Minimum-pulse-width-low on CP	0.2	0.3	0.9
Minimum-pulse-width-high on CP	0.08	0.2	0.6
Minimum-period on CP	0.4	0.8	2.2
Maximum-fall-time on CP	4	39	3.8e+02

Revision 1.0   December 20, 19941

Note: Advanced Microelectronics is a division of the Institute for Technology Development, Jackson, Miss.

Figure 13.2   *Sample Specification for a D Flipflop Cell.*

$A\mu E$ Advanced Microelectronics
A Division of ITD

ms080cmosxCells
CMOSX 0.8 Micron
Standard Cell Library

D flipflop   **DFF**

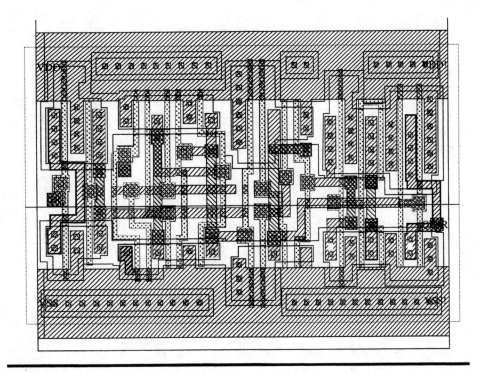

Figure 13.2   (*Continued*).

13.2   Synthesis Flow

A simple Synopsys synthesis script is given on the following pages. This will be used to illustrate the major steps in synthesis. The purpose of this section is to explain and illustrate the major steps in any synthesis strategy, not to teach the reader the details of the Synopsys scripting syntax.

```
/* Read in Verilog file and map (synthesize)  onto a generic library
MAKE SURE THAT YOU CORRECT ALL ERRORS & ALL WARNINGS THAT APPEAR during the execution
of the read command are investigated or understood to have no impact
ALSO CHECK your latch/flipflop list for unintended latches */

Read -f Verilog count.v

/* Our first Optimization `compile` is intended to produce a design
  that will meet hold-time under worst-case conditions:
  -slowest process corner(.XXW)
  -highest operating temperature (125C) and lowest Vcc(4.5V)
  -expected worst case clock skew */

/* Specify the worst case (slowest) libraries and slowest temperature/Vcc conditions */

target_library = {``ms080cmosxCells_XXW.db´´}
link_library = {``ms080cmosxCells_XXW.db´´}
set_operating_conditions -library ``ms080cmosxCells_XXW´´ ``T125_V4.5´´

/* Specify a 10 ns clock period with 50% duty cycle and a skew of 0.3 ns */
Create_clock -period 10 -waveform {0 5} clock
set_clock_skew  -uncertainty 0.3 clock

/* Most libraries have bugs in them. This library has cells that don't have a
 layout version-PULLUP and PULLDOWN cells are two of them */

set_dont_use ms080cmosxCells_XXW/PULLUP
set_dont_use ms080cmosxCells_XXW/PULLDWN

/* Now set up the `CONSTRAINTS` on the design:
 1. How much of the clock period is lost in the modules connected to it?
 2. What type of cells are driving the inputs to this module?
 3. What type of cells and how many (fanout) must it be able to drive (out of the
                                                              module)? */

/* ASSUME that the module is being driven by a slowest D-flipflop in the library.
The DFF cell has a clock-Q delay of 1.75 ns. Allow another 0.25 ns for wiring delay
NOTE: THESE ARE INITIAL ASSUMPTIONS ONLY */

set_input_delay 2.0 -clock clock all_inputs() clock
```

(*Contd.*)

```
/*ASSUME this module is driving a D-flipflop where the DFF cell has a set-up
time of 1.4 ns and another 0.25 ns is allowed for wiring delay
NOTE: THESE ARE INITIAL ASSUMPTIONS ONLY     */

set_output_delay 1.65 -clock clock all_outputs()

/* ASSUME being driven by a D-flipflop      */

set_driving_cell -cell ``DFF´´ -pin ``Q´´ all_inputs()-clock

/* ASSUME worst case output load is 3 D-flipflop(D-inputs) and 0.5 units of wiring
capacitance*/

port_load = 0.5 + 3 * load_of (ms080cmosxCells_XXW/DFF/D)
set_load port_load all_outputs()

/* Now set the GOALS for the compile.
 In most cases you want minimum area, so set the goal for maximum area to be 0   */

set_max_area 0

/* During the initial map (synthesis),
 Synopsys might have built parts (such as adders) using its DesignWare(TM) library.
 In order to remap the design to our CMOSX library AND to create scope for logic
reduction, it is necessary to `flatten out´ the DesignWare components, i.e., make one
flat design.
 `replace_synthetic´ is the cleanest way to do this     */

replace_synthetic -ungroup

/* check the design before otimization                   */

check_design
check_timing

/* Now resynthesize the design to meet constraints, and try to best achieve the goal,
   and using the CMOSX parts. In large designs, compile can take a lllooonnnnggg time!

 -map_effort specifies how much optimization effort there is, i.e., low, medium, or
high. Use high to squeeze out those last picoseconds.
 -verify_effort specifies how much effort to spend on making sure that the input
and output designs are logically equivalent     */

compile -map_effort medium -verify -verify_effort medium

/* Now trace the critical (slowest) path and see if the timing works.
 If the slack is NOT met, you HAVE A PROBLEM and need to redesign
 or try some other minimization tricks that Synopsys can do */
```

(Contd.)

```
report_timing
```

```
/* This is your section to do different things to improve timing or area-RTFM
Now resynthesize the design for the fastest corner making sure that hold time
conditions are met
 Specify the fastest process corner and lowest temp and highest (fastest) Vcc
(-55C,5.5V). The `translate` converts the design from the old library to the new. */
/*-------------------------------------------------*/
target_library = {``ms080cmosxCells_XXB.db``}
link_library = {``ms080cmosxCells_XXW.db``}
translate
set_operating_conditions -library ``ms080cmosxCells_XXB`` ``T-55_V5.5``
```

```
/* Since we have a `new` library, we need to do this again    */
```

```
set_dont_use ms080cmosxCells_XXB/PULLUP
set_dont_use ms080cmosxCells_XXB/PULLDWN
```

```
/* Set the design rule to `fix hold time violations` Then compile the design
again, telling Synopsys to only change the design if there are hold time violations.
 The -only_design_rule means only change the logic
to correct hold problems and -incremental means apply
only techniques that assume that a `from scratch`
synthesis has already been performed    */
```

```
set_fix_hold clock
compile -only_design_rule -incremental
```

```
/* Report the fastest path. Make sure the hold is actually met.  */
```

```
report_timing -delay min
```

```
/* Write out the `fastest` (minimum) timing file in Standard Delay Format.
 We might use this later in verification.                 */
```

```
write_timing -output count_min.sdf -format sdf-v2.1
```

```
/* Since Synopsys has to insert logic to meet hold violations,
 we might find that we have setup violations now. So recheck with the slowest
                                                       corner, etc. */
```

```
/* The target library is the new `target`
The link library describes the *current* design      */
```

```
/*   YOU have problems if the slack is NOT MET         */
/* `translate` means `translate to new library`         */
```

```
target_library = {``ms080cmosxCells_XXW.db``}
link_library = {``ms080cmosxCells_XXB.db``}
```

```
(Contd.)

translate
set_operating_conditions -library ``ms080cmosxCells_XXW´´ ``T125_V4.5´´

report_timing

/* Write out the resulting netlist in Verilog format     */

write -f verilog -o count_final.v

/* Write out the `slowest´ (maximum) timing file in Standard Delay Format.
  We might use this in later verification.        */

write_timing -output count_max.sdf -format sdf-v2.1
```

The major steps illustrated in this synthesis script are:

1. **Read in the design.** The "read" command parses in the Verilog file, checks it for errors and other potential problems, and maps it onto the GTECH logic library native to Synopsys. This initial logic mapping might take a long time for a large design. It is very important to understand, and fix if needed, all errors and warnings generated as a result of the read. As Synopsys also reports the flipflops and latches specified in the design, take a moment to make sure that there are no unintentional latches.

2. **Specify the slowest library and operating conditions.** The first goal in synthesis is to optimize the design so it will work when the chip is operating in its possible slowest state. The library and operating conditions specified here produce and model the cells in that state.

3. **Describe the clock.** The clock and the clock skew is specified. Synopsys needs this information in order to conduct a detailed timing design and analysis.

4. **Set up the "constraints."** It is necessary to have an accurate description of what the design being synthesized is connected to as the loads and delays in the neighboring modules determine the timing details within the module being synthesized. This section describes the constraints on the design about to be synthesized.

5. **Establish the goal.** Usually the goal of synthesis is to meet the clock period and timing constraints while minimizing area. The "set_max_area" command specifies the latter goal.

6. **Determine the pre-optimization steps.** Various checks and other commands are performed pre-optimization. The details are beyond the scope of this text.

7. **Carry out optimization.** This is the purpose of the "compile" statement. Synopsys applies various routines to try to minimize the logic while meeting timing constraints.

8. **Report the timing.** Asks Synopsys to report the timing to determine if the clock period and timing constraints were satisfied. If a "SLACK VIOLATED" message is given by the timing analyzer, then the timing constraints are not met and the

designer might have to explore alternative synthesis strategies and/or redesign the module to make it faster.

9. **Fix potential race-through conditions.** If the chip is operating in the fast corner and a low temperature there is potential for race-through or "hold violations" to occur (see Chapter 11 for details). A number of steps here (translate, compile, incremental, etc.) are inserted in the script to allow Synopsys to determine if extra logic has to be inserted so as to prevent race-through. After inserting that logic, the design is rechecked for correct timing in the slow corner at high temperature.

10. **Write out the design.**

The output of Synopsys in this case is a Verilog netlist and two Standard Delay Format (SDF) files; one for the slow corner of the design, one for the fast. These can be used for various post-synthesis simulations and timing checks. In the case of the counter, designed in Chapter 6, the Verilog netlist was as follows:

```
module counter ( clock, in, latch, dec, zero );
input   [3:0] in;
input   clock, latch, dec;
output zero;
  wire \value[3] , \value[1] , \value53[2] , \value53[0] , \n54[0],
    \value[2] , \value[0] , \value53[1] , \value53[3] , n95, n96, n98, n99,
    n100, n101, n102, n103, n104, n105, n106, n107, n108;
  DFF \value_reg[0] ( .Q(\value[0] ), .QBAR(n95), .CP(clock), .D(n96) );
  DSEL2 \value_reg[0]/U3 ( .Y(n96), .D0(\value[0] ), .D1(\value53[0] ),
    .S0(\n54[0] ) );
  DFFR \value_reg[1] ( .Q(\value[1] ), .CP(clock), .R(1´b1), .D(n98) );
  DSEL2 \value_reg[1]/U3 ( .Y(n98), .D0(\value[1] ), .D1(\value53[1] ),
    .S0(\n54[0] ) );
  OR2 U33 (.Y(n99), .A0(\value[1] ), .A1(\value[0] ) );
  OR2 U34 (.Y(n100), .A0(n99), .A1(\value[2] ) );
  DSEL2 U35 (.Y(\value53[0] ), .D0(n95), .D1(in[0]), .S0(latch) );
  OR2 U36 (.Y(n101), .A0(\value[3] ), .A1(n100) );
  NAND2 U37 (.Y(n102), .A0(\value[3] ), .A1(n100) );
  NAND2 U38 (.Y(n103), .A0(n101), .A1(n102) );
  DSEL2 U39 (.Y(\value53[3] ), .D0(n103), .D1(in[3]), .S0(latch) );
  NAND2 U40 (.Y(n104), .A0(\value[2] ), .A1(n99) );
  NAND2 U41 (.Y(n105), .A0(n100), .A1(n104) );
  DSEL2 U42 (.Y(\value53[2] ), .D0(n105), .D1(in[2]), .S0(latch) );
  NAND2 U43 (.Y(n106), .A0(\value[0] ), .A1(\value[1] ) );
  NAND2 U44 (.Y(n107), .A0(n99), .A1(n106) );
  DSEL2 U45 (.Y(\value53[1] ), .D0(n107), .D1(in[1]), .S0(latch) );
  AND2 U46 (.Y(n108), .A0(dec), .A1(n101) );
  OR2 U47 (.Y(\n54[0] ), .A0(n108), .A1(latch) );
  INV U48 (.Y(zero), .A(n101) );
  EDFF \value_reg[3] ( .Q(\value[3] ), .CP(clock), .D(\value53[3] ),
    .E(\n54[0] ) );
  EDFF \value_reg[2] ( .Q(\value[2] ), .CP(clock), .D(\value53[2] ),
    .E(\n54[0] ) );
endmodule
```

Note that the netlist is purely structural. It simply specifies which standard cells are used (such as "OR2"), what each instance is called (such as "U33") and, through the port list, implicitly how they are wired together.

13.3 Conclusion

Synthesis tools generally require a script in order to function correctly. Constructing these scripts can be an important and complex task. In this chapter, a simple sample script was provided focused on synthesizing a design to a standard cell library and achieve the correct timing results. The script is mainly aimed at preventing setup and hold violations from appearing in the final design. The details of the scripting language are beyond the scope of this book. Please refer to the documentation that comes with each synthesis tool for more details.

Exercises

13.1. Specify a clock to Synopsys that has a frequency of 200 MHz, a 50 percent duty cycle and a skew of 0.2 ns.

13.2. What is the difference between a compile and a compile incremental?

13.3. Sketch what logic is specified in the following netlist:

```
OR2 u36 (.Y(n101), .A0(\value[3]), .A1(n100));
NAND2 U38 (.Y(n103), .A0(n101), .A1(n102));
```

13.4. Take an example from the body or exercises of Chapter 6 and synthesize the fastest possible design by a strategy of reducing the clock period and doing incremental compiles. For example:

```
/* see if the design works with a faster clock */
Create_clock -period 9 -waveform {0 4.5} clock
compile -incremental
report_timing
/* if this design works, save it in case next one did not */
write -f db -o tmp9.db

/* see if the design works with a still faster clock */
Create_clock -period 8 -waveform {0 4} clock
compile -incremental
report_timing
/* if this design works, save it in case the next one did not */
write -f db -o tmp8.db
/* etc. */
```

You will need to iterate on this loop after your first compile but before the */*Fix hold times*/* comment. It is best if you break the current script into two files—one up to the first *report_timing* command and one after that. Enter the above commands by hand into design_analyzer or dc_shell. When you find a clock speed that does not work, then read back in the .db file for the fastest working clock speed (*read -f db tmp?.db*) and perform the rest of the original script.

This is a common technique to produce the fastest possible synthesized result. The alternative, that of setting impossibly slow clock periods, tends to be far less successful.

References

[1] CMOSX standard cell library, www.aue.com. Advanced Microelectronics is a division of the Institute for Technology Development, Jackson, MS, Figures reproduced with permission.

Chapter Fourteen

Synthesis to FPGA

14.1   Field Programmable Gate Arrays (FPGA) As a Target Technology

Synchronous digital circuitry can be thought of as composed of stages of combinational logic separated by register storage as shown in Figure 14.1.

The registers temporarily store the results of one section of combinational circuitry before it is passed on as arguments to the next. In the popular style of the two phase non-overlapping clock (as used in the MIPS example of Chapter 10), these registers would be clocked by the two phases alternately. Alternatively, the registers might be serving the function of temporary pipeline storage as also in the MIPS example. In this case the synthesizer can actually move logic across register boundaries in an attempt to equalize the electrical path delays in the stages.

Field programmable gate arrays have also been created with this model in mind. Each logical element contains basically a single output combinational function and a flipflop to temporarily store this output. These chips basically consist of a two-dimensional array of logical elements that may be personalized by control points set by the user. These control points are set at configuration time by various means such as fusible links, electrically programmable ROM, or RAM. There are also local- and long-distance interconnect lines running between the rows and columns, the access to which must be personalized in a similar way. Figure 14.2 gives a generic logic diagram that illustrates the most important features available in the logic elements provided by these manufacturers. In the figure, the combinational function is realized by a 16×1 *look-up table* (LUT) stored in a small RAM. Provision is made to bypass either the combinational logic or the flipflop storage in case the synthesizer is doing the kind of path balancing described in the preceding paragraph.

Because of the need for fast-carry propagation in adders, incrementers, or decrementers, there is usually a special provision for this, which runs down through a block of contiguous logic elements. In Figure 14.2, the LUT can be split for this purpose to make effectively two 8×1 LUTs, one of which is used to develop the carry. Provided the carry elements are

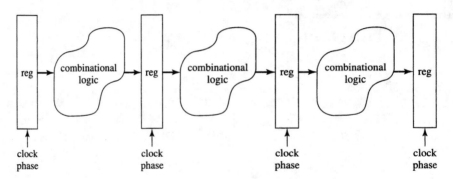

Figure 14.1 *General Synchronous Design Paradigm.*

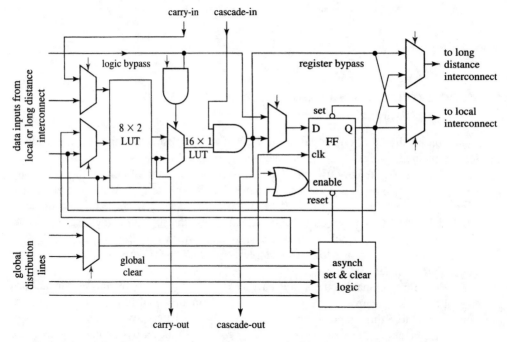

Figure 14.2 *Generic FPGA Logical Element (Simplified).*

contiguous on the chip, such a local carry is sometimes fast enough to obviate the need for the carry-with-less-delay type of organization discussed in Chapter 3.[1] A second fast chained connection is provided for cascading the LUT outputs down through an AND or OR structure. (The AND is shown in Figure 14.2 although an OR can also usually be accommodated via programmed inversions and DeMorgan's theorem.) This feature is particularly useful for realizing wide decoders for memory addressing. Such logic array blocks may be composed of eight or sixteen logical elements according to the manufacturers.

As labelled in Figure 14.2, there is provision to steer the output of one logical element to the inputs of another, either through local interconnect or via long-distance interconnects running in groups between rows and columns of logical array blocks. These connections are

---

[1]Turn this off if library modules with carry-look-ahead are called, such as set manual carry.

programmable and although not shown in Figure 14.2, are logically similar to the multiplexers shown inside the logical element. In the figure, grey arrows have been used to indicate programmable control. At the ends of the row and column long-distance interconnects where they reach the edges of the chip there are special I/O logic elements to communicate with the outside world. Also around the edges of the chip are located RAM cells (flipflops) which serve to personalize the programmable control points (the grey arrows) and are loaded up at chip initialization time. Finally, FPGA chips usually provide a small number of special, global low-skew lines, which are intended for such critical purposes as clock distribution and global reset. For a smooth synthesis flow the originating HDL source specifications and writing style might be made consistent with the available number of these global lines.

Synthesis vendors typically will provide interfacing instructions for each major FPGA vendor and vice versa. For a particular vendor combination the user must study the relevant manual sections and application notes. To illustrate, the *Verilog—Synopsys— Altera/Xilinx* flow of Chapter 12 is continued here. The chip families targeted here are the flex10k and XC4000 series from Altera and Xilinx. *RAM-based FPGAs* are ideal for an educational environment since they can be reused indefinitely, and there is little penalty if a nonfunctioning design reaches silicon. While the families used here are no longer cutting edge (being upstaged by the current flagships Apex and Virtex), they are the ones installed on the design laboratory packaged boards available through the university programs, and so are convenient to use to demonstrate the principles involved.

14.2   Using the Altera Tools

Before invoking the Altera *maxplus2* compiler, the user should be in the appropriate directory. If you want to keep all the FPGA reports separate, then create another subdirectory ". . . /synthwork/mapped*" and move to it the *<your_design_name>.edf* and *<your_design_name>.acf* files generated by the script from Chapter 12.

The first time through on a project the graphical user interface version of the tools will need to be invoked in order to set the project preferences.[2] For this, give the command *max2win* without arguments. When the window appears the following sequence of clicks in the user interface should be executed:

```
file menu > Project > current file or project > aclock
```

Then in *MAX+PLUS II* menu:

```
select compiler
```

Then in *Interfaces* menu:

```
> EDIF Netlist Reader Settings > Vendor > Synopsys ; OK
> Verilog Netlist Writer
> Verilog Netlist Writer Settings > Write Delay Constructs To
                                  > Verilog Output File OK
```

In *Assign* menu:

```
> Global Project Logic Synthesis > Define Synthesis Style > NORMAL : OK
> Device > Flex10k > Device family > EPF10k20 > OK
> Connected pins (any fixed pin assignments, such as
                    the already wired IO on the design laboratory package)
```

---

[2]It is possible to proceed entirely in command mode and avoid all the clicking by editing the project preferences in the *<your_design_name>.acf* file generated by the synthesis script.

Finally when all is ready, press the *START* button.

The *EPF10k20* chip has been selected since this is the one on the UP-1 board. More generally, if AUTO is selected instead, the tool will select the smallest chip of the family having sufficient capacity. This procedure is only really necessary the first time through on each new project. After such an initial run the project settings are recorded and thereafter reruns can be invoked by the command:

```
maxplus2 -c <your_design_name>.edf
```

The reports and the Verilog output files (*<your_design_name>.vo* and *alt_max2.vo*) are generated in the working directory. These .vo files may be moved to the hdl working directory where the vcs simulator can be invoked:

```
vcs test_<your_design_name>.v, <your_design_name>.vo, alt_max2.vo
```

14.3   Using the Xilinx Tools

If preferred, go to a separate mapped directory (as previously shown), to which the *<your_design_name>.sxnf* file produced by the script of Chapter 12 has been copied. Then invoke the command *xilinx*, which brings up the design manager tool window.

Select *File > New Project*, and *Browse* to select the *<your_design_name>.sxnf* file.

Select *Design > Implement* to bring up the implement dialog box. You will need to click on *Options* in order to set the simulation to Verilog. *VERILOG-XL* is a good choice.

Returning to the implement dialog box, select the *part*. For the XS40 design laboratory board, the XC4005xl-P84 is the appropriate choice.

Finally, click on *RUN* to bring up the flow engine window, which runs the appropriate script for you.

Unless you specified other file names in the Options window above, the output will be placed in files *time_sim.v* and *time_sim.sdf*. To run the gate-level simulation move these to the *hdl* directory and invoke the **vcs** simulator as follows:

```
vcs test_<your_design_name>.v, time_sim.v -P sdf.tab
```

The *sdf.tab* is a short file of magical incantations which will cause the wiring delay information in *time_sim.sdf* to be picked up by **vcs** in the form of a Verilog PLI table:

```
$sdf_annotate call=sdf_annotate_call
acc+=mip, prx:%CELL+
```

sdf.tab File.

For examples of university projects done with Xilinx chips see [Mencer98].

We end this section with the *aclock* example of Chapter 12 modified to target Xilinx. For this example the minutes are output to two seven-segment displays (supplementing the XS40 board) via BCD counters and combinational converters (see following) implemented as submodules within the FPGA, followed by the top-level *aclock* Specification #1 correspondingly modified from Chapter 12.

```
module count2d (clk, reset, enb_in, state, carry_out); // counts two digits
  input clk, enb_in, reset;
  output carry_out;
  output [7:0] state;
  wire    [7:0] state;
  wire    [3:0] d0, d1;
  wire    c0;
  assign state = {d1,d0};
  assign c0 = (d0 == 9);                    // carry out of lsd
  assign carry_out = (d1==5);               // carry out of msd
  cntd  LSD(clk, enb_in, reset, d0);        // least sig digit counter
  cntd  MSD(clk, c0, reset, d1);            // most sig digit counter
endmodule

module cntd(clk, enb, reset, q); // decade counter with clock enable and reset
  input clk, enb, reset;
  output [3:0] q;
  reg [3:0] q;

  always @(posedge clk or posedge reset)
    if (reset) q<=0;
    else if (enb) q <= (q==9) ? 0 : (q + 1);
endmodule
```

Replacement Counter for Minutes.

```
module enc7seg(num, seg);
// 7 segment display encoder, active low outputs:
  input [3:0] num;
  output [6:0] seg;              //       ---A---
  reg [6:0] seg;                 //      |       |
  parameter A = 7´b0000001; //      F       B
  parameter B = 7´b0000010; //      |       |
  parameter C = 7´b0000100; //       ---G---
  parameter D = 7´b0001000; //      |       |
  parameter E = 7´b0010000; //      E       C
  parameter F = 7´b0100000; //      |       |
  parameter G = 7´b1000000; //       ---D---
  always @(num)
    case (num)
      0 : seg = ~(A+B+C+D+E+F);
      1 : seg = ~(B+C);
      2 : seg = ~(A+B+G+E+D);
      3 : seg = ~(A+B+G+C+D);
      4 : seg = ~(F+G+B+C);
      5 : seg = ~(A+F+G+C+D);
      6 : seg = ~(A+F+C+D+E+G);
      7 : seg = ~(A+B+C);
      8 : seg = ~(A+B+C+D+E+F+G);
      9 : seg = ~(A+B+C+F+G);
      default: seg = 7´b1111111; // blank
    endcase
endmodule
```

Replacement Converter for Minutes.

```
`include ``countertc.v``
`include ``comparator.v``
`include ``mux.v``
`include ``enc7seg.v``
`include ``count2d.v``

module aclock(bell, clk, clr, hrs_mins, hz,
        led_ampm, led_hrs0, led_hrs1, led_hrs2, led_hrs3,
        segm0a,segm0b,segm0c,segm0d,segm0e,segm0f,segm0g,
        segm1a,segm1b,segm1c,segm1d,segm1e,segm1f,segm1g,
        set_A, set_T, toggle_sw);
   input clk, clr, hrs_mins, set_A, set_T, toggle_sw;
   output bell, led_ampm, led_hrs3, led_hrs2, led_hrs1, led_hrs0, hz;
   output segm1a,segm1b,segm1c,segm1d,segm1e,segm1f,segm1g;
   output segm0a,segm0b,segm0c,segm0d,segm0e,segm0f,segm0g;
   wire [7:0] A_MINS_state, T_MINS_state; // counter states
   wire [3:0] A_HRS_state, T_HRS_state;
   wire [12:0] outbus; // drives lights and 7 seg encoders
   wire [6:0] mseg1, mseg0; // converted output drives 7 seg displays
   wire equal, bell, hz;
   assign {segm0g,segm0f,segm0e,segm0d,segm0c,segm0b,segm0a} = mseg0;
   assign {segm1g,segm1f,segm1e,segm1d,segm1c,segm1b,segm1a} = mseg1;
   assign {led_ampm,led_hrs3,led_hrs2,led_hrs1,led_hrs0}=outbus[12:8];
   assign bell = equal && toggle_sw;
   countertc #(2,3) TRI(clk,clr,1`b1,,clk3);// divides by 3
   countertc #(3,4) CD(clk3,clr,1`b1,,hz);//countdown by 12 to 1Hz
   countertc #(6,60) T_SECS(hz,clr,1`b1,,TScarry);
   count2d       T_MINS(mtm,clr,etm,T_MINS_state,TMcarry);
   countertc #(4,12)T_HRS (mth,clr,eth,T_HRS_state,THcarry);
   countertc #(1,2) T_AMPM(THcarry,clr,1`b1,T_AMPM_state,);
   count2d       A_MINS(hz,clr,eam,A_MINS_state,);
   countertc #(4,12)A_HRS (hz,clr,eah,A_HRS_state,AHcarry);
   countertc #(1,2) A_AMPM(AHcarry,clr,1`b1,A_AMPM_state,);
   mux       #(13)   MX(set_A,{T_AMPM_state,T_HRS_state,T_MINS_state},
             {A_AMPM_state,A_HRS_state,A_MINS_state},outbus);
   comparator #(13)CMP({T_AMPM_state,T_HRS_state,T_MINS_state},
             {A_AMPM_state,A_HRS_state,A_MINS_state}, equal);
   mux    #(1) ETM(set_T,1`b1, ~hrs_mins, etm);   // muxes
   mux    #(1) ETH(set_T,1`b1, hrs_mins, eth);   // for
   mux    #(1) EAM(set_A,1`b0, ~hrs_mins, eam);   // counter
   mux    #(1) EAH(set_A,1`b0, hrs_mins, eah); // enables
   mux    #(1) MTM(set_T, TScarry, hz, mtm); // muxes for
   mux    #(1) MTH(set_T, TMcarry, hz, mth); // counter inputs
   enc7seg LED0(outbus[3:0], mseg0);
   enc7seg LED1(outbus[7:4], mseg1);
endmodule
```

Specification #1: *Aclock* Modified to Target Xilinx.

Note on argument lists: These have been given in simple list form in most of these examples to reduce the quantity of text. However it should be noted that the order of arguments in the gate-level netlists produced by the FPGA vendors differ. For example, Altera generates arguments lexigraphically with all the inputs first and then all the outputs, whereas Xilinx generates a unified lexigraphic ordering. Therefore the argument lists of the invocations inside the testbenches given here may need to be reordered depending on the target.

```
module TPRX(clk, Din, raddr, waddr, we, Dout); //wrapper for synthesis to Xilinx LUT's
  input clk, we;
  input [3:0] raddr, waddr;
  input [7:0] Din;
  output [7:0] Dout;
  wire  [7:0] Dout, Din;
  // invoke 8 of the two port ram primitives from table 14 -1:
  RAM16X1D u0(.WCLK(clk),   .SPO(Din[0]), .WE(we),  .DPO(Dout[0],
        .A0(waddr[0]),     .A1(waddr[1]),    .A2(waddr[2]),   .A3(waddr[3]),
      .DPRA0(raddr[0]), .DPRA1(raddr[1]), .DPRA2(raddr[2]), .DPRA3(raddr[3]) );
  RAM16X1D u1(.WCLK(clk),   .SPO(Din[1]), .WE(we),  .DPO(Dout[1],
        .A0(waddr[0]),     .A1(waddr[1]),    .A2(waddr[2]),  .A3(waddr[3]),
      .DPRA0(raddr[0]), .DPRA1(raddr[1]), .DPRA2(raddr[2]), .DPRA3(raddr[3])  );
  RAM16X1D u2(.WCLK(clk),   .SPO(Din[2]), .WE(we),  .DPO(Dout[2],
        .A0(waddr[0]),     .A1(waddr[1]),    .A2(waddr[2]),  .A3(waddr[3]),
      .DPRA0(raddr[0]), .DPRA1(raddr[1]),.DPRA2(raddr[2]),  .DPRA3(raddr[3])  );
  RAM16X1D u3(.WCLK(clk),   .SPO(Din[3]), .WE(we),  .DPO(Dout[3],
        .A0(waddr[0]),     .A1(waddr[1]),    .A2(waddr[2]),  .A3(waddr[3]),
      .DPRA0(raddr[0]), .DPRA1(raddr[1]),.DPRA2(raddr[2]),  .DPRA3(raddr[3])  );
  RAM16X1D u4(.WCLK(clk),   .SPO(Din[4]), .WE(we),  .DPO(Dout[4],
        .A0(waddr[0]),     .A1(waddr[1]),    .A2(waddr[2]),  .A3(waddr[3]),
      .DPRA0(raddr[0]), .DPRA1(raddr[1]),.DPRA2(raddr[2]),  .DPRA3(raddr[3]) );
  RAM16X1D u5(.WCLK(clk),   .SPO(Din[5]), .WE(we),  .DPO(Dout[5],
        .A0(waddr[0]),     .A1(waddr[1]),    .A2(waddr[2]),  .A3(waddr[3]),
      .DPRA0(raddr[0]), .DPRA1(raddr[1]),.DPRA2(raddr[2]),  .DPRA3(raddr[3])  );
  RAM16X1D u6(.WCLK(clk),   .SPO(Din[6]), .WE(we),  .DPO(Dout[6],
        .A0(waddr[0]),     .A1(waddr[1]),    .A2(waddr[2]),  .A3(waddr[3]),
      .DPRA0(raddr[0]), .DPRA1(raddr[1]),.DPRA2(raddr[2]),  .DPRA3(raddr[3])  );
  RAM16X1D u7(.WCLK(clk),   .SPO(Din[7]), .WE(we),  .DPO(Dout[7],
        .A0(waddr[0]),     .A1(waddr[1]),    .A2(waddr[2]),  .A3(waddr[3]),
      .DPRA0(raddr[0]), .DPRA1(raddr[1]),.DPRA2(raddr[2]),  .DPRA3(raddr[3])  );
endmodule
```

Specification #2: RAM Wrapper for Xilinx.

The alternative is to use a paired argument list, as described in Section 2.2, as also used in Specification #2 of the RAM wrapper in Section 14.4.

14.4   Generating Memory Arrays

Most interesting designs contain sections of embedded memory of one kind or another. As far as FPGA chips are concerned, the different types of RAM on the chip may be summarized in the following *FPGA RAM-usage* list below:

1. The RAM used to program the interconnections which give the chip a particular user specified functionality. These are usually loaded at the outset and remain fixed as long as power is applied.
2. The RAM aggregated from the storage flipflops of each logical element.
3. The RAM composing the LUT of the regular logical element, usually 16×1, or 32×1.
4. The RAM in embedded logic arrays if present, usually 256×8 and configurable also as 512×4, 1024×2, 2048×1. These can either serve as RAM or ROM in a design.

Table 14.1   *Xilinx Memory Primitives.*

Name	Remarks	Augmented Ports
RAM16X1		WE
RAM16X1D	dual port, synch write, asynch read	DPRA3,2,1,0,WCLK,WE
RAM16X1S	dual port, synch write, asynch read	WCLK
RAM32X1		A4
RAM32X1S	dual port, synch write, asynch read	A4, WCLK
ROM16X1	read only	
ROM32X1	read only	A4

The only distinction of the ROM will be that it is preloaded with a bit pattern that stays constant through the functioning of the design.

Since there is no refresh, all of these implementations are static RAM. If there is no indication to the contrary, the RAM in the Verilog specifications will end up being synthesized as type number 2 in the above list. Since this is clearly wasteful, this should be strictly limited to small scratchpad applications. Otherwise vendor-supplied memory generation software is usually available which will allow synthesis to either types 3 or 4.

14.4.1   Using Look-up Tables (LUTs) As Memory (such as Xilinx)

For Xilinx chips, embedded memory is generated using method number 3 in the FPGA RAM-usage list. Using this method, we are limited to the sizes of the LUTs (look-up tables) inside the logical elements. This is either 16×1 or 32×1 similar to that shown in Figure 14.2. They are available in asynchronous and synchronous versions similar to the ones specified at the end of Chapter 5, shown in Table 14.1. The standard output port is O, and standard inputs are D, A3, A2, A1, A0, augmented as noted in Table 14.1.

If the user requires a larger memory, then multiple instantiations of the primitives can be accumulated inside a wrapper specification. For example, in the *fifosctpr* specification, the required two-port Ram, 16×8 TPRX is built from the available 1 bit components using the Specification #2 wrapper shown on page 235. Note the paired argument list method is being used here.

14.4.2   Using Embedded Array Blocks As Memory (such as Altera)

The following treatment uses as an example the *genmem* program[1] provided by the Altera corporation which synthesizes to type 4 in the FPGA RAM-usage list. This program generates two output files: A functional simulation model (*.v*)—used for functional simulation prior to synthesis or place-and-route.

- simulation model (*.v*)—for functional checking before synthesis or place-and-route
- library timing model (*.lib*)—containing the information that the synthesizer uses.

Invoking *genmem* without arguments produces a list of available alternatives (shown on the following page).

In the *hdl* directory for the project, the *genmem* program is invoked as in the following example command which would generate the necessary output files for the asynchronous RAM sixteen words deep and eight bits wide required in the *fifosctpr* example to follow.

```
genmem asyndpram 16x8 -Verilog
```

---

[1] Now merged into the Altera "Quartus" software.

```
genmem -- Generate Memory Simulation Model, Version 2.8
Copyright (c) 1996-1998 Altera Corporation

genmem COMMAND-LINE USAGE:
genmem <type> <size> [-vhdl] [-verilog] [-viewlogic] [-o]

OPTION:      DESCRIPTION:
<type>       One of the following memory types:
             asynram   Asynchronous RAM
             asynrom   Asynchronous ROM
             synram    Synchronous RAM
             synrom    Synchronous ROM
             csdpram   Cycle-shared dual-port RAM
             asyndpram Asynchronous dual-port RAM
             syndpram  Synchronous dual-port RAM
             csfifo    Cycle-shared FIFO
             scfifo    Single-clock FIFO
             dcfifo    Dual-clock FIFO


<size>       Expressed as two numbers separated by the letter `x`
             <word>x<width> where:
             <word>   must range between 2 and 32768v(32K)
             <width>  must range between 1 and 160


-vhdl        Generate Synopsys-compatible VHDL output (default)
-verilog     Generate Synopsys-compatible Verilog HDL output
-viewlogic   Generate VHDL model for Viewlogic
-o           Overwrite the output file
```

Alternatively, calling *genmem* for a *synram* and selecting option 1 (registered data out) will result in the two files:

syn_ram_32x8_iuor.v syn_ram_32x8_iuor.lib

To use the *genmem* program with Synopsys synthesis it is necessary to make two modifications to the project *.script* file format given in Chapter 12. First the corresponding RAM/ROM timing model should be added to the existing FPGA library. Using the 32×8 synram and the Flex10k library as an example, this may be done by adding the following two lines to the synthesis script:

read -f db flex10k.db update_lib flex10k_fpga -o syn_ram_32x8.lib

Second, and also in the script, a *set_dont_touch* attribute should be attached to the *syn_ram_32x8_iuor* module, for example by adding the line:

set_dont_touch syn_ram_32x8_iuor

The Synopsys compiler then passes this module instantiation as a *black box* directly to the *Altera MAX+PlusII* software via the *EDIF* file. Then when *MAX+PlusII* encounters the *syn_ram_32x8_iuor* instance in the *EDIF* file, it will map it to the appropriate macrofunction on the FPGA chip.

It is also necessary to make two modifications to the Verilog source. To instantiate the memory module, the original memory submodule invocation should be replaced with one using the file identifier and port names of the *.v* file generated by *genmem*. The signal names and instance name shown must match those in the source code of the design.

To let the synthesizer know about the port declarations and directions, a skeleton module declaration for the memory should be added in the same source file which contains the instantiation. This can be easily done by cutting and pasting the first few lines of the *.v* file generated by *genmem*.

The LPM file is unused because this is being used as a RAM. If the embedded memory is to be utilised as a ROM, then the *LPM_FILE* string will be used to point to a hexadecimal file for preloading. This will be demonstrated in the continuation of the *aclock* example in the subsequent section.

To illustrate we conclude this section by modifying the *fifosc* specification of Chapter 8 so as to replace the homebrew two-port RAM used there with either Xilinx LUT or Altera embedded array versions. The specification will serve for either one by including or commenting out the indicated lines in the *fifosctpr.v* Specification #3 following.

14.5   Using Embedded Arrays As ROM

The declaration part of the specification is augmented to incorporate a ROM which converts the output of the minutes counter to drive a seven-segment display. Unfortunately the UP-1 board has only two of these, so the *ampm* and *hours* counter outputs must be fed to separate light emitting diodes (see Figure 12.2). The declaration part of the specification is repeated and augmented in Specification #4 and follows the principles of embedded memory for the ROM as described in the previous section.

The *converter.hex* file is for loading the ROM and must be in the *Intelhex* format. This ROM then converts from a count of up to fifty-nine minutes in straight binary into two sets of seven-segments plus period (the periods are unused here).

```
:140000000303039f0325030d0399034903c1031f030103092e
:14000a009f039f9f9f259f0d9f999f499fc19f1f9f019f090c
:140014002503259f2525250d2599254925c1251f25012509c6
:14001e000d030d9f0d250d0d0d990d290dc10d1f0d010d09cc
:140028009903999f9925990d9999994999c1991f990199092a
:140032004903499f4925490d4999494949c1491f4801470943
:08003c000101010101010101b4
:00000001ff
```

Converter.hex File for Loading ROM. ·

The fields in each row of the Intelhex format are as follows (numbers in parenthes indicate length of field in bytes, with each byte represented by two hexadecimal characters):

```
colon/# of bytes of data(1)/load address(2)/record type(1)/data(variable)/checksum(1)
```

The record types used here are either 00 (indicating a data record) or 01 (indicating end-of-record). The checksum is supposed to be such that all the bytes in the row including the checksum itself sum to zero (a wrong checksum results in a warning). There should be no

```
`include ``atpr.v``              // from homebrew library
// `include ``asyn_dpram_16x8.v`` // from Altera genmem-for simulation only
// `include ``TPRX.v``            // for either simulation or synthesis for Xilinx
// `include ``/usr/local/pkg/cad/synopsys/dw/dw06/src_ver/DW_ram_r_w_s_dff.v``
           // from Synopsys DW library (with full path name)-for simulation only
// if Altera, substitute for synthesis:
//module asyn_dpram_16x8 (Data,RdAddress,WrAddress,RdEn,WrEn,Q);
//parameter LPM_FILE = ``UNUSED``;
//parameter Width = 8, WidthAd = 4, NumWords = 16;
//input [Width-1:0] Data;
//input [WidthAd-1:0] RdAddress;
//input [WidthAd-1:0] WrAddress;
//input RdEn;
//input WrEn;
//output [Width-1:0] Q;
//endmodule

module fifosctpr (clk, flush, insert, remove, // inputs-for xilinx reorder args as
                                              unified list
      Win_0,  Win_1,  Win_2,  Win_3,  Win_4,  Win_5,  Win_6,  Win_7, // inputs
      empty, full,                                         // outputs
      Wout_0,Wout_1,Wout_2,Wout_3,Wout_4,Wout_5,Wout_6,Wout_7);
 parameter nw=15, as=5, ws=8;              // capacity, addrsize, wordsize
 parameter k=1;                            // tap point for fsr
  input  clk, flush, insert, remove;
  input  Win_0,  Win_1  Win_2,  Win_3,  Win_4,  Win_5  Win_6,  Win_7;
  output Wout_0,Wout_1,Wout_2,Wout_3,Wout_4,Wout_5,Wout_6,Wout_7;
  output full, empty;
  reg full, empty;
  reg [as-1:0] wp, rp;   // pointers
  reg [as-1:0] wpo, rpo; // pipelined pointers
  reg [ws-1:0] Wout;
  wire [ws-1:0] Win;

// map ports to separate wires for low level simulation
  assign Win = {Win_7, Win_6, Win_5, Win_4, Win_3, Win_2, Win_1, Win_0};
  assign Wout_7=Wout[7], Wout_6=Wout[6], Wout_5=Wout[5], Wout_4=Wout[4];
  assign Wout_3=Wout[3], Wout_2=Wout[2], Wout_1=Wout[1], Wout_0=Wout[0];

// alternatives for memory array:
  atpr #(nw+1,as,ws) TPR (Win, rp, wp, insert&&~full&&clk, Wout,); // homebrew
                                                                   memory
// TPRX       TPR (clk, Win, rp, wp, insert&&~full, Wout);  // include if Xilinx
// asyn_dpram_16x8  TPR (.Q(Tout), .Data(Win), .WrEn(insert&&~full&&clk),
                 .RdEn(remove), .WrAddress(wp), .RdAddress(rp)); // for
                                                                 Altera
// DW_ram_r_w_s_dff #(ws,16,1) TPR (.data_in(Win), .rd_addr(rp),  .wr_addr(wp),
                 .wr_n(~(insert&&~full)), .clk(clk), .rst_n(1`b1),
                 .cs_n(1`b0), .data_out(Wout)); // if Synopsys DW
always @(posedge clk)
   // ... control same as for fifosc of chapter 8
endmodule
```

Specification #3: *fifo (fifosctpr)* Using FPGA Memory.

```
module syn_rom_64x16_iuor (Q, Address, Memenab, Outclock);
   parameter LPM_FILE = ``converter.hex´´;
   parameter Width = 16, WidthAd = 6, NumWords = 64;
   input   [WidthAd-1:0] Address;
   input   Memenab;
   output  [Width-1:0] Q;
   input   Outclock;
endmodule

module aclock(apwr_on, clk, hrs, mins, set_0, set_1, toggle_sw, bell,
                  led_ampm, led_hrs3, led_hrs2, led_hrs_1, led_hrs_0,
                  segm1a,segm1b,segm1c,segm1d,segm1e,segm1f,segm1g,
                  segm2a,segm2b,segm2c,segm2d,segm2e,segm2f,segm2g
              );
.. // submodule instantiations as before with:
   syn_rom_64x16_iuor
   // synopsys translate_off
   #(LPM_FILE)
   // synopsys translate_on
   ROM(.Q(mseg),.Address(outbus[5:0]),.Memenab(1`b1),.Outclock(cphB));
```

Specification #4: *Aclock* **augmented for embedded ROM.**

spaces between the fields. The contents of the hex file shown here correspond to the active low values required by the usual seven-segment display chips.

14.6   FPGA Reports

In a similar manner to that of the last chapter, the log file should be perused for error messages. If the compile is successful, the result can be viewed in the various report files that are generated.

For the case of Altera, excerpts from the *aclock.rpt* are given in the Excerpts #1 and #2. The first excerpt starts with a brief summary of the facilities used on the selected FPGA chip. It shows the project compiled successfully but with one warning about the output of the *clockgen* module being used to clock the others. This shouldn't matter in a low-performance project like an alarm clock. This excerpt also reports that the converter "ROM" has been fitted into two of the embedded RAMs of this chip. This excerpt concludes with summaries of the statistics of the current fit.

Excerpt #2 is taken from about the middle of the report and shows a pin diagram of the chip. In order to get it to fit in the space here, it has been necessary to slightly edit and abbreviate it. The pin assignments can be checked against the fixed pin requirements required on the project board.

In the case of Xilinx similar report files are produced in subdirectory xproj/ver1/rev1.

Of these the map.rpt has details of logic removed or added by the software as well as other information which can be used to improve the design. Note that the aclock.par file includes a fun "design score," which can be used to compare successive iterations of the design, as shown in Excerpt #3.

```
MAX+plus II Compiler Report File
Version 9.21 2/10/99
Compiled: 07/19/1999 15:09:10
Copyright (C) 1988-1999 Altera Corporation


** DEVICE SUMMARY **
Chip/       Input Output Bidir  Memory  Memory   LCs
POF       Device        Pins Pins  Pins  Bits % Utilized LCs % Utilized
aclock    EPF10K20RC240-3  6          21    0   896      7 %  69    5 %

** PROJECT TIMING MESSAGES **
Warning: Found ripple clock-warning messages and Report File information
on tco, tsu, and fmax may be inaccurate

** EMBEDDED ARRAYS **
|lpm_rom:converter|altrom:srom|content: MEMORY (
        width       =   16;
        depth       =   64;
        segmentsize =   64;
        mode        =
MEM_READONLY#MEM_INITIALIZED#MEM_REG_DATAOUT_CLK1;


Project Information

** RESOURCE USAGE **
Total dedicated input pins used:      2/6        ( 33%)
Total I/O pins used:                  25/183     ( 13%)
Total logic cells used:               7/1152     (  0%)
Total embedded cells used:            14/48      ( 29%)
Total EABs used:                      2/6        ( 33%)
Average fan-in:                       1.00/4     ( 25%)
Total fan-in:                         7/4608     (  0%)

** CLOCK SIGNALS **
Type  Fan-out Name
INPUT    4    CLK

** CLEAR SIGNALS **
Type  Fan-out Name
LCELL    3    init_reg
** TIMING ASSIGNMENTS **
            User Actual
Type Location  Assignment  Value Status Critical Path
fmax    CLK       100.0 ns  8.0    n     CLK to register CG0.Q to register
                                         |clockgen_n3:CLKGEN|mreg1.Q
```

Excerpt #1 from .rpt File.

```
     1 R R RRR R    R R RRR R R    R R RRR R R    R RR  R. ... R 1
     e E E E E E    E E E E E E    E E E E E E    E E E  a E ... E e
     s d S S S S S G S S S S S S V S S S S S S S G S S S G G  p S ... S d
     e _ E E E E E N E E E E E C E E E E E E N E E N N w E    ... E _
     g h R R RRR R D R R RRR R R C R R RRR R R D R R D D  r R    ... R h
     m r V V V V V I V V V V V V I V V V V V V  I V V V I I _ V ... V r
     2 s E E E E E N E E E E E E N E E E E E E N E E N N o E  ... E s
     g 2 D D D D D T D D D D D D T D D D D D D T D D T T n D  ... D 0
     ----------------------------------------------------------------
     /240 238 236 234 232 230 228 226 224 222 220 218 216 214 212 210 ... 182\
     /239 237 235 233 231 229 227 225 223 221 219 217 215 213 211 209 ...  181\
         #TCK | 1                                             180 | ^DATA
    ^CONF_DONE | 2                                            179 | ^DCLK
        ^nCEO | 3                                             178 | ^nCE
         #TDO | 4                                             177 | #TDI
       VCCINT | 5                                             176 | GNDINT
       segm2d | 6                                             175 | led_ampm
       segm2f | 7                                             174 | led_hrs3
       segm2e | 8                                             173 | RESERVED
     led_hrs_1 | 9                                            172 | RESERVED
       GNDINT | 10                                            171 | RESERVED
       segm2c | 11                                            170 | VCCINT
       segm2b | 12                                            169 | RESERVED
         bell | 13                                            168 | RESERVED
       segm1g | 14                                            167 | RESERVED
       segm1a | 15                                            166 | segm1f
       VCCINT | 16                                            165 | GNDINT
       segm1c | 17                                            164 | RESERVED
       segm1b | 18                                            163 | RESERVED
       segm1d | 19                                            162 | RESERVED
       segm1e | 20                                            161 | RESERVED
       segm2a | 21                                            160 | VCCINT
         ...              EPF10K20RC240-3
         mins | 38                                            143 | RESERVED
          hrs | 39                                            142 | RESERVED
        set_0 | 40                                            141 | RESERVED
        set_1 | 41                                            140 | VCCINT
         ...
       #nTRST | 59                                            122 | VCCINT
     ^nSTATUS | 60                                            121 | ^nCONFIG
         \ 62 64 66 68 70 72 74 76 78 80 82 84 86 88 90 92 ... 120/
         \61 63 65 67 69 71 73 75 77 79 81 83 85 87 89 91  ... 119/
     -------------------------------------------------------------
     R R RR R R RR R G RR R RR R R V R RRR R R R G R RR V G C G      ... R R
     E E EE E E E E N E E E E E E C E E E E E E N E E E C N L N      ... E E
     S S S S S S S S D S S S S S S C S S S S S S D S S S C D K D ... S S
     E E E E E E E E I E E E E E E I E E E E E E I E E E I I I      ... E E
     R R RR RRR R N RR R RR RR N R RR R R RR N R R R N N N          ... R R
     V V V V V V V T V V V V V V T V V V V V V T V V V T T T    ... V V
     E E E E E E E    E E E E E E  v E E E E  E    E E E        ... E E
     D D D D D D D    D D D D D D  D D D D D D    D D D          ... D D
```

Excerpt #2 from .rpt File.

```
PAR: Xilinx Place And Route M1.5.25.
Copyright (c) 1995v1998 Xilinx, Inc.  All rights reserved.
Mon Jul 19 16:21:00 1999
...
  ``aclock´´ is an NCD, version 2.27, device xc4010xl, package pc84, speed-3
....
Device utilization summary:
   Number of External IOBs        26 out of 61      42%
   Number of Global Buffer IOBs    1 out of 8       12%

   Number of CLBs                 62 out of 400     15%
    Total Latches:                 0 out of 800      0%
    Total CLB Flops:              37 out of 800      4%
    4 input LUTs:                116 out of 800     14%
    3 input LUTs:                  9 out of 400      2%
   Number of BUFGLSs               1 out of 8       12%


Constraints are met.
...
No errors found.
Completely routed.


This design was run without timing constraints.
It is likely that much better circuit performance can be obtained by
trying either or both of the following:
 -Enabling the Delay Based Cleanup router pass, if not already enabled
 -Supplying timing constraints in the input design
...
Generating PAR statistics.
  The Delay Summary Report
  **The Score for this design is: 524**

  The Average Connection Delay for this design is:          3.429 ns
  The Average Connection Delay on critical nets is:         0.000 ns
  The Average Clock Skew for this design is:                2.312 ns
  The Maximum Pin Delay is:                                14.723 ns
  The Average Connection Delay on the 10 Worst Nets is:     9.083 ns
...
PAR done.
```

Excerpt #3 from Xilinx Place-and-Route Report.

14.7   Gate-Level Simulation

As described in Sections 14.2 and 14.3, the FPGA software can be set to produce the gate level netlists in Verilog form which can then be resimulated using the original test-benches. If this uses simple argument lists, the beginning of the *.vo* or time_sim.v files can be checked for the argument order if in doubt. The original high-level simulation output should have been retained in a file, for example:

```
simv > aclock.outh
```

in order to facilitate comparison with that of the low (gate) level simulation output, such as:

```
simv > aclock.outl.
```

In Table 14.2 we illustrate side by side the simulated output from the design *fifosc.v* of Chapter 8. Notice how in the low-level simulation on the right, the output values sometimes need to settle, but otherwise the two versions exhibit similar behavior.

Table 14.2   *Comparison of High- and Low-Level Simulation Output for fifosc.v.*

Chronologic VCS simulator
 Contains Viewlogic proprietary information.   copyright 1991–1997
Compiler version 4.0.2;   Runtime version 4.0.2;

time	flsh	ins	rmve	E	F	Win	Wout
0	1	0	0	x	x	0	x
15	1	0	0	1	0	0	x
60	0	1	0	1	0	1	x
75	0	1	0	0	0	1	x
90	0	1	0	0	0	3	x
150	0	1	0	0	0	4	x
180	0	1	0	0	0	5	x
210	0	1	0	0	0	6	x
240	0	1	0	0	0	7	x
255	0	1	0	0	1	7	x
270	0	0	0	0	1	7	x
300	0	0	1	0	1	7	x
315	0	0	1	0	0	7	1
330	0	1	0	0	0	8	1
345	0	1	0	0	1	8	1
360	0	0	0	0	1	8	1
570	0	0	1	0	1	8	1
585	0	0	1	0	0	8	2
615	0	0	1	0	0	8	3
645	0	0	1	0	0	8	4
675	0	0	1	0	0	8	5
705	0	0	1	0	0	8	6
735	0	0	1	0	0	8	7
765	0	0	1	1	0	8	8
780	0	0	0	1	0	8	8
810	0	1	0	1	0	5	8
825	0	1	0	0	0	5	8
840	0	0	1	0	0	5	8
855	0	0	1	1	0	5	5
870	1	0	0	1	0	5	5

```
$finish at simulation time   9000000
 VCS   Simulation   Report
Time: 900000000 ps
CPU Time:   0.020 seconds;
Sun Aug  1 22:41:20 1999
```

time	flsh	ins	rmve	E	F	Win	Wout
0	1	0	0	x	x	0	x
15	1	0	0	1	0	0	x
60	0	1	0	1	0	1	x
75	0	1	0	0	0	1	x
90	0	1	0	0	0	2	x
120	0	1	0	0	0	3	x
150	0	1	0	0	0	4	x
180	0	1	0	0	0	5	x
210	0	1	0	0	0	6	x
240	0	1	0	0	0	7	x
255	0	1	0	0	1	7	x
270	0	0	0	0	1	7	x
300	0	0	1	0	1	7	x
315	0	0	1	0	0	7	X
315	0	0	1	0	0	7	1
330	0	1	0	0	0	8	1
345	0	1	0	0	1	8	1
360	0	0	0	0	1	8	1
570	0	0	1	0	1	8	1
585	0	0	1	0	0	8	2
615	0	0	1	0	0	8	3
645	0	0	1	0	0	8	4
675	0	0	1	0	0	8	5
705	0	0	1	0	0	8	6
735	0	0	1	0	0	8	7
765	0	0	1	1	0	8	0
765	0	0	1	1	0	8	8
780	0	0	0	1	0	8	8
810	0	1	0	1	0	5	8
825	0	1	0	0	0	5	8
840	0	0	1	0	0	5	8
855	0	0	1	1	0	5	d
855	0	0	1	1	0	5	5
870	1	0	0	1	0	5	5

```
$finish at simulation time   9000000
          VCS   Simulation   Report
Time: 900000000 ps
CPU Time:   0.050 seconds;
Sun Aug  1 22:39:57 1999
```

Ideally the synthesis process would be constructive, but there are a number of reasons why a successfully synthesized design may still not function as planned:

- The source may have been correct Verilog for the high-level simulation but still ambiguous for the synthesis policy, resulting in a guess by the synthesizer that differs from the intent of the designer.
- The actual routing delays may be different from the statistical estimates made by the synthesizer. This will be increasingly true for "sub-micron" technologies in which the interconnection delays are comparable to the propagation delays of the gates. Typically this results in there being not enough time remaining in the clock cycle for the set-up time of the destination flipflop.
- More usually, the specification is just not robust enough. The high-level simulation is idealized and the timing ambiguities simply do not reveal themselves until gate level is reached.

14.7.1   *Some Usual Suspects*

A frequent error message at gate level has to do with either the setup or hold times of the flipflops. The scenarios in the following Figures (14.3 and 14.4) illustrate how such error messages can easily arise, first for setup violation, and second for hold violations. In the first case, a lengthening of the clock period could be tried. In the second the source could be made more robust by separating the RAM reference and the pointer update by a *posedge clk*.

14.7.2   *Downloading the Implemented Design*

The easiest way to download the .bit files generated by the tools is from a PC via a cable that comes with the vendor's laboratory package and attaches to a serial port. For this a PC version of the corresponding software will be required which includes the tools for the downloading. In the case of Xilinx, there is also software that uses the cable to stimulate

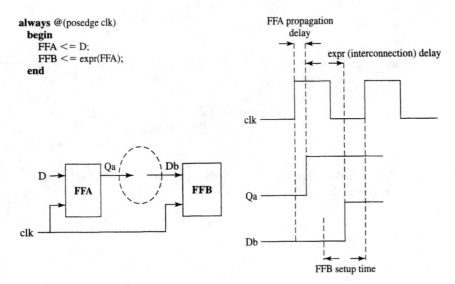

Figure 14.3   *A Common Example of a Setup Violation.*

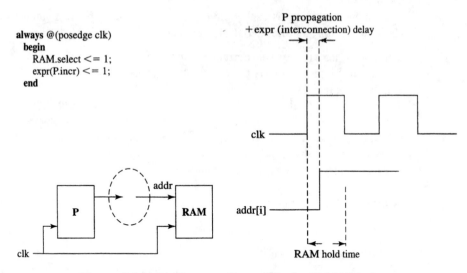

Figure 14.4   *A Common Example of a Hold Violation.*

and sense signals from the hardware in real time in order to check that the hardware behaves in the same way as the gate-level simulation.

An excellent tutorial on using the Altera University Program UP1 board, with a large number of example designs, has recently become available [Hamblen99].

14.8   Conclusion

Synthesizing to FPGA is much less painful than synthesizing to standard VLSI cells. However getting the design to work at gate level is still one of the most difficult tasks described in this book. Debugging the gate-level simulation is more difficult than for the original simulation at high level because:

- *There is less information available.* The only points which are viewable are the ports around the chip periphery, and the simulator may show these as all x's with only some cryptic remark such as *"hold violation on DFF 2357."* A clue might be obtained by scanning through the *.vo* file for the identifier and trying to recognize any user given identifiers in the neighborhood. A stop-gap measure to try is slowing the clock in the testbench. Otherwise in order to gather more information the whole synthesis may have to be rerun with some critical internal points brought out via augmented top-level arguments.
- *Debug runs are expensive.* Not as expensive as post-silicon, it is true, but still involving all the time necessary for reediting the source, rerunning the synthesis, place-and-route, and finally low-level simulation. We can try to minimize the number of reruns by choosing our tests well and adopting some of the measures described in the next chapter.

Exercises

The following make suitable projects at this stage for specification, synthesis, and fitting to a FPGA with embedded ROM:

14.1. Modify *aclock* to add stopwatch function. Another project in this style is the kitchen timer [Wolf98].

14.2. Computerized Tic-Tac-Toe game [Wakerly99].

14.3. High-speed square generator [Wey98].

14.4. Low-power divider [Nan99]. For more background on the SRT dividers see also [Lang94], [H&P90], and [Soderquist96].

14.5. Cordic sine-cosine generator [Phatak98].

14.6. If the Altera UP-1 board is available together with a PC having a spare parallel port and a spare monitor, then a visual output of the contents of important registers can be added to any of the processor projects of Chapter 10 using the method of [Hamblen99], p. 145.

References

[H&P90] Hennessy & Patterson, *Computer Architecture: A Qualitative Approach* (2nd ed.) Appendix A, Morgan-Kaufman, pp. A57–61

[Hamblen99] Hamblen, J., and Furman, M., "*Rapid prototyping of digital dystems: A tutorial approach,*" Kluwer, 1999

[Lang94] Lang, T., et al.,"Implementing division with FPGA," *J. VLSI Signal Proc.* 7 (1994), pp. 271–285

[Nan99] Nanarelli, A., and Lang, T., "Low power divider," *IEEETC*, Jan. 1999, pp. 2–14

[Mencer98] Mencer, O., see PAM-Blox Web site at http://umunhum. stanford. edu/PAM-Blox/

[Soderquist96] Soderquist, P., and Leeser, M., "Area and performance tradeoffs in floating-point and square root implementations," *ACM Computing Surveys,* 28:3 (Sept. 96) pp. 538–564

[Wolf98] Wolf, W., *Modern VLSI Design,* Prentice-Hall, 1998, pp. 418–437, pp. 525–535

[Wey98] Wey, C-L., and Shieh, M-D., "Design of a high speed square generator," *IEEETC* 47:9 (Sept. 98), pp. 1021–1026

[Phatek98] Phatak, D. S., "Double step branching CORDIC: A new algorithm for fast sine and cosine generation," *IEEETC* 47:5 (May 98) p. 587. See also *IEEETC* (Feb. 93) p. 920

[Wakerly99] Wakerly, John, *Digital design: principles and practices,* Prentice-Hall, 99, pp. 520–528

Chapter Fifteen

Gate-Level Simulation and Testing

15.1 Ad-hoc Test Techniques

As discussed in Section 14.7, even for modest designs, debugging runs at gate level will still be painful. In order to be able to obtain the maximum amount of information without resynthesizing and rerouting, there are some ad-hoc techniques that can be followed.

First as suggested in Section 6.4, it is a good plan to incorporate a reset operation into major submodules to ensure that everything gets off to a start from a known state. In a hierarchical design the same reset control can be brought down through all the argument lists. When the design is simulating then some of this extra functionality might be pruned back down.

Second, if there are internal signals, which may yield important debug information, then during initial development these should be brought out through the argument lists to the ports of the top-level module. Although pins are limited it is important to retain the maximum amount of flexibility in this matter, so that reruns can be done just by changing the testbench. Some designs have a natural bus structure in which some major bus sees signals from a number of important points in the design. In such a case we might try to bring out this bus to the pins during the initial development phase. For example, in the MIPS design of Chapter 10, the destination bus and the S1 and S2 busses carry important information.

Some designs have crucial buried registers. The *instruction register* and the *program counter* of standard processors are classic examples. In the simple FIFOs of Chapters 8 and 9 the pointer register(s) are examples. To retain the necessary flexibility in the case of several registers of this nature, a scheme such as that diagrammed in Figure 15.1 can be used. For the MIPS design, there is a group of important registers of thirty-two bits, and another group having five bits. Extra multiplexers to bring these out could be temporarily added.

Exhaustive testing ceased to be possible around the time that processor word lengths passed from sixteen to thirty-two (they are now sixty-four). In its absence, the selection of the actual cases to be tested is somewhat of a creative art. We try to divine and include the

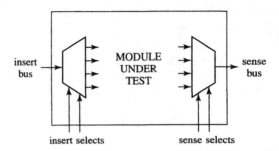

Figure 15.1   *Augmentation for Gate-Level Test.*

crucial so-called *corner* cases. These are cases that, if validated, will imply the correct behavior of other cases in between.

A simple initial strategy is to check that the test suite is sufficient to exercise every line in the HDL sources and every arc in the state diagram of each controller. Line coverage tools are available to assist in this. However these will not test for the coverage of *pair arcs*. These are the transitions in the producted state diagrams when there are interactions between multiple controllers, and these are much more vast in number. This is another reason to try to minimize the number of **always** blocks in the Verilog specifications.

The next section reviews the classical automatic test generation methodology.

15.2   Scan Insertion in Synthesis

The purpose of the above ad hoc methods is to verify that the result produced by synthesis and routing meets the original design intent. If this result is satisfactory, and a part is going into manufacture, a more systematic approach is required to test that the production copies are true.

The classical method of scan testing converts a sequential function testing problem into a combinational one which is more tractable. The principle was originally suggested in [Eichleberger77] and has become the most widely used method of *design-for-test*. Ideally all the register cells in the design are threaded together into a small number of long chains in order to shift in the test vectors and shift out the results. For this purpose the flipflops are augmented with input multiplexers whose select inputs differentiate the test mode from the normal functioning. Sometimes for various reasons all the flipflops in a design are not so convertible, leading to a *partial scan*. Such reasons may be that the design makes use of the asynchronous inputs to the flipflops in an essential way, or that there are tristate connections. In terms of the idealized view of a synthesized synchronous system originally presented in Figure 14.1 the full scan may be illustrated as shown in Figure 15.2.

Once converted to a combinational function, the method of path sensitization can be employed. This was originated in [Roth66] and improved in [Goel81]. Single *stuck-at* faults are systematically posited at each gate output and corresponding test vectors generated by sensitizing paths from primary chip inputs, and propagating paths to primary chip outputs. Finally a best sequence of test vectors is generated that can detect the maximum aggregated number of faults. The method is well covered in standard texts, such as [Weste93] or [Smith97].

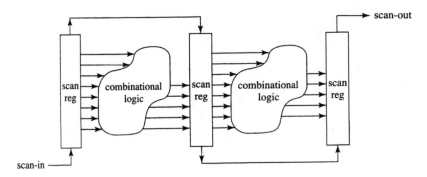

Figure 15.2   *Scan Chain Principle.*

Following this classical methodology, industry tools such as the Synopsys *test compiler* will survey the register cells for possible scan problems, generate a set of test vectors of specified size, and provide corresponding testbenches in either VHDL or Verilog together with the expected responses. They will also estimate the resulting fault coverage, defined as the number of detectable stuck faults as a fraction of the total possible number of such faults that could affect the outputs. This is the prime advantage of the method, since the known fault coverage gives some degree of confidence. Coverage in excess of 90 percent is often achieved using this method. The single stuck-at fault assumption also seems to work well for detecting many other kinds of faults and multiple faults.

The major disadvantage of the method is that the tests must be controlled and sequenced from off-chip, usually with the aid of very expensive automatic test equipment. The method is also not so suitable for memory intensive designs. With the continued increase of complexity of IC designs it has been necessary to try to speed this process up by employing many parallel scan paths, and sharing this I/O with the functional pins.

Automatic scan test generation tools have been used for project sizes up to approximately 200K gates. After this point the time needed to shift the large test vector sets in and out and the difficulty of reaching adequate test coverage levels reduces the effectiveness of the method.

15.3   Built-in Self Test

Instead of being dependent on expensive off-chip test equipment, the built-in self-test (BIST) approach seeks to place both the test circuitry and the test generation on-chip, to be run at on-chip speeds.

Some types of circuits have specialized testing sequences but a completely general method is to use pseudo-random test sequences generated by an appropriate maximal length feedback shift register. These are applied to the inputs of a combinational circuit under test and the outputs are merged into another FSR such as the multiple insertion signature register (MISR) shown in Figure 15.3.

When the test ends after some prescribed number of clock cycles, a characteristic *signature* number is left residing in the MISR, which can be compared with what would result from a circuit having no faults. The 2^m possible such signatures that might result divide the true and faulty circuits into as many equivalence classes, where m is the length of the MISR. Clearly some faulty circuits may fall into the same equivalence class as the

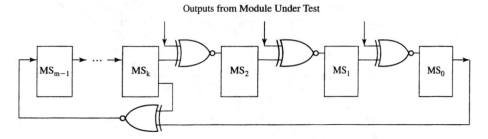

Figure 15.3   *Multiple Input Signature Register (MISR).*

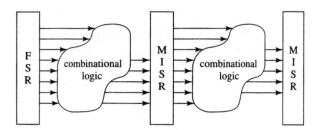

Figure 15.4   *Built-in Self-Test (BIST) with MISRs.*

fault-free one, and the probability of such *aliasing* would be 2^{-m} if all the faults were statistically independent. Such statistical independence is not likely, but with suitable m the performance of this method has been found fairly good. It has also been found that the *corrupted FSR* of the MISR itself can act as a reasonable input pseudo-random generator for testing the next circuit down the line [Kim88]. This gives rise to the general model illustrated in Figure 15.4. A comparator attached to the last stage could check for equality with an aggregated signature corresponding to all circuits good.

The advantage of the FSR BIST method is that it can operate at on-chip speeds. The disadvantage is that, unlike the method of the previous section, there is no way to know the resulting fault coverage other than the estimate furnished by the aliasing probability.

One problem is if m is large then we will have a statistical sampling which again falls far short of exhaustive test. In the case of circuits that are regular interconnections of identical cells, a possible solution is to partition the array into smaller slices, generate a complete test for such a slice, and then iterate this test across the array. The concept of *CI testability* [Hayes81] exploits the notion that the cascaded connections between slices can be identical on the input and output sides, and the parallel (noncascaded) outputs can also identical. Although it may be necessary to augment the slices to achieve this, if this condition is satisfied, then it is only necessary to check that the parallel outputs are identical slice to slice, and a constant number of tests is sufficient for an array of arbitrary size.

15.3.1   *Specialized Tests: An Example*

Important special classes of circuits such as ALUs, RAMs, and PLAs have been extensively studied and specially tailored test methods have been developed for them.

Most embedded RAMs now are encapsulated together with a corresponding built-in self-test. Many practitioners are of the opinion that no design should incorporate embedded RAM without BIST [Gupta97]. For RAMs, the class of *marching* tests has been

Table 15.1   *5N March Test Algorithm.*

Addr	Load P = 0	March1 fwd P = 1	March2 fwd P = 0	March3 bck P = 1	March4 bck P = 0
0	Wr(dbg)	Rd(dbg);Wr(!dbg)	Rd(!dbg);Wr(dbg)	Rd(dbg);Wr(!dbg)	Rd(!dbg);Wr(dbg)
1	Wr(dbg)	Rd(dbg);Wr(!dbg)	Rd(!dbg);Wr(dbg)	Rd(dbg);Wr(!dbg)	Rd(!dbg);Wr(dbg)
2	Wr(dbg)	Rd(dbg);Wr(!dbg)	Rd(!dbg);Wr(dbg)	Rd(dbg);Wr(!dbg)	Rd(!dbg);Wr(dbg)
...	\	\	\	/	/
N − 1	Wr(dbg)	Rd(dbg);Wr(!dbg)	Rd(!dbg);Wr(dbg)	Rd(dbg);Wr(!dbg)	Rd(!dbg);Wr(dbg)

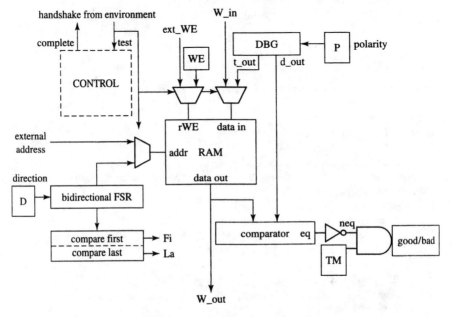

Figure 15.5   *On Chip BIST for RAM.*

proved to detect any stuck fault in the cell array, the decoder, address register, drivers, and
sense amplifiers. In addition, such tests are capable of detecting any cross effect from one
cell in the array to any other.

A built-in self test scheme of this type may be found in [BDT88]. In the example
that follows, this will be used to demonstrate how a synthesizable self-testing specification
may be written.

The basic form of a marching test is illustrated in Table 15.1. We call this the *5N
march test* because there are a total of five passes through the address space.[1] In the case of
a RAM with a word size greater than one, this 5N march is repeated for each data background. For this we use the DBG data background generator of Chapter 5. In the table,
(dbg) indicates that the output of the data background generator is being read or written
direcly, while (!dbg) indicates that the 1's complement of the output is being used instead.
In the headings of the table, the variable P indicates the polarity setting for the DBG module in the organization of Figure 15.5.

---

[1]It is also often called the 9N test because four of the marches invoke double references to the memory.

The specification is given in two parts. Specification #1a consists of the declarations, while Specification #1b is the control. It is essentially a synthesizable testbench for the instantiated RAM module. Since it is constructed using the principles of the control-

```verilog
`include ``comparator.v``
`include ``mux.v``
`include ``ramerr.v``
`include ``fsrb.v``
`include ``dbg.v``
//* indicates that this is included for development testing only
module rambist(clk, ext_WE, reset, test, Win,
        adbg_0, dbg_1, dbg_2, adbg_3, adbg_4, adbg_5, adbg_6, adbg_7,     //*
        addr_0,addr_1,addr_2,                                            //*
         bad, complete,
        D, L, P,                                                         //*
        Wout);
 parameter nw=8, as=3, ws=8; // capacity, address_size, word_size
  input clk, ext_WE, reset, test;
  input  [ws-1:0] Win
  input  [as-1:0] ext_addr;
  output [ws-1:0] Wout;
  output addr_2, addr_1, addr_0, D, L, P;                               //*
  output  adbg_7, adbg_6, adbg_5, adbg_4, adbg_3, adbg_2, adbg_1, adbg_0; //*
  output complete, bad;
  reg bad,      //1 = bad
     complete, //1 = test complete
     D,         // direction  0 = right (forward), 1 = left (backward),
     P,         // polarity,  1 = invert
     L;         // loading
  reg  WE, DBG_init, DBG_next, F_s, F_r;
  wire  [ws-1:0] ramDin, DBG_dout, DBG_tout; //interconnections
  wire [as-1:0] addr, f_addr;
  wire [as-1:0] first = -1;
  wire [as-1:0] last = -2;
  wire tst_eq;
  wire [ws-1:0] adbg = DBG_dout;                                        //*
assign addr_2=addr[2], addr_1=addr[1], addr_0=addr[0];                  //*
assign adbg_7=adbg[7], adbg_6=adbg[6], adbg_5=adbg[5], adbg_4=adbg[4];  //*
assign adbg_3=adbg[3], adbg_2=adbg[2], adbg_1=adbg[1], adbg_0=adbg[0];  //*
//instantiate submodules to size and identify
ram        #(nw,as,ws) RAM(~clk&&~oddeven, rWE, addr, ramDin, Wout);
dbg        #(ws)    DBG(~clk, DBG_init, DBG_next, P, DBG_dout, DBG_tout);
fsrb       #(as,2)  PTR(~clk, D, F_s, F_r, f_addr);
comparator #(ws)    CMP(DBG_dout, Wout, tst_eq);
mux        #(as)    MUXA(test, ext_addr, f_addr, addr);
mux        #(ws)    MUXD(test, Win, DBG_tout, ramDin);
mux        #(1)     MUXWE(test, ext_WE, WE, rWE);
comparator #(as)    CMP0(f_addr, first, Fi);
comparator #(as)    CMP1(f_addr, last, La);
```

Specification #1a: Rambist Declarations and Instantiations.

```
always @(negedge clk)
 if (reset) oddeven<=0; else oddeven<=~oddeven;
always
begin @(posedge clk)
  if(oddeven) // start onlt on odd clock
  begin
  if(~test) // functional (non-test) mode
   begin
    DBG_next<=0; DBG_init<=1; RAM_slct<=0; //get ready to start test
    L<=1; D<=0; P<=0; complete<=0; bad<=0; F_r<=1; F_s<=0; WE<=0;
   end
  if (test)
  begin  // test mode
  DBG_init<=0; F_r<=0; RAM_slct<=0;
  if (~tst_eq && WE && ~L && ~Fi && ~La) bad<=1;
  casez ({L,D,P,F0,F1,WE})
   6'b100?0?: begin WE<=1; F_s<=1; end           // start & contn load march
   6'b100011: begin WE<=0; P<=1; L<=0;F_s<=1; end // end of load march0
   6'b00???0: begin WE<=1; F_s<=0; end           // continue march fwd(read)
   6'b00??01: begin WE<=0; F_s<=1; end           // continue march fwd(write)
   6'b001011: begin WE<=0; P<=0; F_s<=1; end     // end of march1 fwd(write,P=1)
   6'b000011: begin WE<=0; P<=1; D<=1; F_s<=0; end // end of march2 fwd(write,P=0)
   6'b01???0: begin WE<=1; F_s<=0; end           // continue march bck(read)
   6'b01?0?1: begin WE<=0; F_s<=1; end           // continue march bck(write)
   6'b011101: begin WE<=0; P<=0; F_s<=1; end     // end march3 bck (write,P=1)
   6'b010101: begin WE<=1; D<=0; F_s<=1;         // end march4 bck (write,P=0)
             if (DBG_tout[ws-1]) begin F_s<=0; complete<=1; end
                                                 // this was final DB
             else begin L<=1; DBG_next<=1; end // go to next DB
            end
   default: begin $display(``error''); end
  endcase
    @(posedge clk) begin DBG_next<=0; F_s<=0; end
   end
  end
 end
endmodule
```

Specification #1b: Rambist Control.

point writing style of Chapter 9, the test controller is automatically synthesized. When not in test mode, the circuit functions as an ordinary RAM through the external address and data ports.

For checking the cell-to-cell dependencies it is only necessary for the return march to be in the exact opposite sequence to the forward one, so the *fsrb* bidirectional feedback shift register similar to the one from Chapter 5 has been employed as an address pointer instead of using a counter. This is to be prefered in the sense of exercising the decoder tree but does not test the lowest address. For simplicity in the following implementation this address has been left untested although it would be a comparatively simple matter to add a multiplexer and extra control so as to insert the missing address into the march sequences. Two comparators

have been used to detect the march terminations, although in a truly built-in version the first
and last outputs of the RAM decoder might be pushed into service for this purpose.

The specification has been written in the control-point style. In this specification, the
pointers are advanced and the RAM referenced on two different clock strikes. It would be
easy to modify it in the style of the *fifosc* of Chapter 8 so that the operation is sped up to a

```
`timescale 1 ns / 100 ps
module test_rambist;
 parameter as = 3, ws = 8; dt = 20;
 integer i;
 reg clk, reset, WE, RESET, TEST;
 reg [ws-1:0] W_in;
 reg [as-1:0] ext_addr;
 wire [as-1:0] addr;
 wire [ws-1:0] W_out, dbg;
 wire addr_2,addr_1,addr_0; //* = this is included for development test only
 wire dbg_7,dbg_6,dbg_5,dbg_4,dbg_3,dbg_2,dbg_1,dbg_0;                     //*
 assign addr[2]=addr_2,addr[1]=addr_1,addr[0]=addr_0;                     //*
 assign dbg[7]=dbg_7,dbg[6]=dbg_6,dbg[5]=dbg_5,dbg[4]=dbg_4;              //*
 assign dbg[3]=dbg_3,dbg[2]=dbg_2,dbg[1]=dbg_1,dbg[0]=dbg_0;              //*

 rambist RB(clk, WE, RESET, TEST, Win,
            dbg_0,dbg_1,dbg_2,dbg_3,dbg_4,dbg_5,dbg_6,dbg_7,             //*
            addr_0,addr_1,addr_2,                                        //*
            BAD, COMPLETE,
          D, L, P,
          Wout);

 always begin #dt clk=1; #dt clk=0; end // master clock

 initial
  begin
  $display(``time fsr dbg LDP, COMPL BAD``);
  $monitor(``%5g   %d  %h  %b%b%b   %b     %b``,
  $time, addr, dbg, L,D,P, COMPLETE, BAD);
  clk<=0; RESET<=1; TEST<=0; ext_WE<=0;
  @(negedge clk); @(negedge clk); @(negedge clk); @(negedge clk);
  RESET<=0;
  @(negedge clk); @(negedge clk); @(negedge clk); @(negedge clk);
  TEST<=1;
  for (i=0; i<255; i=i+1)
   begin @(negedge clk); @(negedge clk);
         if (COMPLETE) begin TEST<=0; $finish; end
   end
  $stop;
  end
endmodule
```

Testbench for Rambist.

single clock per cycle. But the two-phase version is illustrated here for simplicity. Note that as usual the submodules are activated one clock phase later than the control point settings in order to allow for set up time. A **casez** statement has been utilized to control the passage through the various stages of the *5N* march. This method of specification is compact and leads to a small control-state machine for this BIST. During the marches subsequent to the load, the RAM is being switched from read to write before enabling the next advance of the pointer (see the march diagram of Table 15.1). In this case the write enable WE is really being set up for the subsequent action. In the intended function, any discrepancy between a written and a read pattern in the memory during the marches is used to set a flag *good/bad*.

Now it is only necessary to stimulate the circuit to switch it from the regular functional mode into the test mode. For this a stimulating module *test_rambist* (#1) will still be required, which itself is unsynthesizable. Its function is merely to communicate with the *rambist* module by means of a handshake to start the test and then allow a sufficient time to complete the test.

As written, the simulation produces final BAD signal of zero, indicating a good memory. This is not surprising, seeing that we have correct specifications and we are operating in the realm of pure software! To validate our BIST we need to rerun it with a *ram* specification which deliberately includes a stuck error, such as the *ram_bad* Specification #2.

The rambist example of this section is actually not too different from the ones being used in current industrial practice [mptest98]. Some of the differences are a somewhat more complex march including data retention, and a signature register at the output that compresses the output result in such a way so as to reveal which row is bad by comparing against signatures generated in simulation. This is done because instead of just throwing away the whole chip, there now exists the option to bypass one or two bad rows by means of laser illumination of fusible links.

Current processor chips include at least level 1 cache. When the instruction and data caches are included, together with the tag arrays, translation lookaside buffers, and various buffering queues, plus the microinstruction ROM, this totals to eight or nine embedded memories or more, all equipped with BIST structures similar to the one shown in this section. The area penalty is usually quoted in the range 3–4 percent and the fault coverage close to 100 percent.

```
module ram_bad (ph, W_slct, addr, data_in, data_out);
 parameter n = 64, a = 6, w = 32;
  input ph, W_slct;
  input [a-1:0] addr;
  input [w-1:0] data_in;
  output [w-1:0] data_out;
  reg   [w-1:0] data_out;
  reg   [w-1:0] ram_data [n-1:0];

always @(posedge ph)
   if (W_slct) ram_data[addr] <= data_in;
   else if (addr==5) data_out<=0;
   else  data_out <= ram_data[addr];
endmodule
```

Specification #2: RAM with Stuck Error.

Exercises

15.1. A problem with design for test is that it assumes that the test circuitry itself is fault free. In the case of the scan insertion circuitry of Section 10.2, this is usually checked with an initial test sequence that shifts an alternating sequence of 0's and 1's in and out of the scan register. Devise an initial test sequence for the *rambist* that would test at least some of the augmented test circuitry.

15.2. Modify the rambist specification of this chapter so as to speed it up to one test every clock cycle (see suggestion in text).

15.3. Modify the rambist specification of this chapter so as to test the two-port RAM (three-port RAM) [Hamdioui94].

15.4. Specify and simulate some of the methods used in industrial FIFO BIST [Zorian94].

15.5. Adapt the BIST for ALU using CI testability illustrated in the design of [Czerny88] to instead target an FPGA.

15.6. Add a built-in self-test to the Booth multiplier of Chapters 8 or 9 based on the scheme of [Gizopoulos99] or [Gizopoulos98].

References

[BDT88] Beenker, F., Dekker, R., and Thijssen, L., "A realistic self-test machine for static random access memories." In *Proc. IEEE International Test Conference*, August 1988, pp. 353–361

[Czerny88] Czerny, E., et al., "Built-in self-test of a CMOS ALU," *IEEE Design and Test,* August 1988, pp. 38–48. See also *Proc. IEEE Intl. Test Conf.* 1994, pp. 378–387

[Eichleberger77] Eichleberger, E. B., and Williams T. W., "A logic design structure for LSI testing," *Proc. 14th Design Automation Conference*, June 1977, pp. 462–468

[Goel81] Goel, P., "An implicit enumeration algorithm to generate tests for combinational logic circuits." *IEEE. Trans. Comp.*, C-30:3, March 1981, pp. 215–222

[Gizopoulos98] Gizopoulos et al., "Built-in self test for Booth multiplier," *IEEE Design & Test,* 15:3 (July–Sept. 1998), pp. 105–111

[Gizopoulos99] Gizopoulos et al., "An effective BIST scheme for parallel multipliers," *IEEE Trans. C,* 48:9 (Sept. 1999), pp. 936–950

[Gupta97] Gupta, R. K., and Zorian, Y., "Introducing Core-based system design," *IEEE Design and Test*, Oct. 1997, pp. 15–25

[Hamdioui94] Hamdioui and Van de Goor, "Built-in self-test for two-port RAM," *IEEE Intl. Test Conf.* 1994, pp. 378–387

[Hayes81] Sridhar, T., and Hayes, J. P., "Design of easily testable bit slice systems," *IEEE Trans. Comp.* C-30, 1981, pp. 842–854

[Kim88] Kim, K., et al., "On using signature registers as pseudorandom pattern generators in BIST," *IEEE Trans. CAD*, 7:8, 1988, pp. 919–928

[mptest98] Special issue on microprocessor testing, *IEEE Design & Test,* July–Sept. 1998

[Roth66] Roth, J. P., "Diagnosis of automata failures: A calculus and a method," *IBM Journal of R&D*, 10:4, pp. 278–291

[Smith97] Smith Michael J. S., *Application specific integrated circuits*, Addison-Wesley, 1997

[Weste93] Weste, N., and Eshraghian, K., *Principles of VLSI Design*, 2nd ed., Addison-Wesley, 1993

[Zorian94] Zorian, Y., Van de Goor, A. J., and Schanstra, I., "An effective BIST scheme for ring-address type FIFO's," *Proc. IEEE Intl. Test Conf.* 1994, pp. 378–387

Chapter Sixteen

Alternative Writing Styles

16.1 Introduction

If the objective is to make it more likely that the specification corresponds to the designer's intentions, then a way to facilitate this is to make the specification language more high level and more functional. This process is analogous to the increase in power that is conferred in software engineering by using functional languages over imperative languages. Using industry standard languages and tools, some amount of this can be achieved by using appropriate writing styles. Using this method there is a progressive restriction in the number of allowable constructs, represented by the inclusion relation:

```
Verilog 1364 standard > synthesizable subset > writing styles
```

The control-point style of Chapter 9 is a case in point. It is effective for a certain types of designs and not for others. In certain cases the resulting circuits exhibit performance limitations. Clearly one style does not fit all. In this chapter some alternative writing styles are illustrated. These styles are again subsets of the Verilog language and are therefore accepted by industry simulators. But they require different synthesis tools, sometimes implemented as a preprocessor to the current dominant industry RTL synthesizer tools. In other cases (such as the self-timed style) a specialized target technology is necessary. This process may be thought of as a stopgap measure. Eventually, and when more is understood about this subject, the industry will have to bite the bullet and start over with a whole new design language, may be a single one this time. Section 16.6 contains some of the proposals to patch up Verilog in the meantime.

16.2 Behavioral Compiler Styles

The Synopsys *Behavioral Compiler* [KDTR95], [Knapp97], abbreviated as *BC* in what follows, is suited to modules whose operations are composed from a sequence of a large number of sub-operation assignments and in which a scheduler can have some freedom to move the suboperations in the time dimension during optimization.

Just like the control-point style, the BC styles are synchronous and are variations of the implicit state specification style introduced in Section 8.1—states are separated by clock-edge statements. As in all implicit styles, a controller is automatically synthesized from each **always** block without need of an explicit state transition specification. In the BC styles while the source is directly accessible to industry simulators, it needs to be passed through a scheduler before going to synthesis.

This compiler accepts a slightly different Verilog/VHDL subset from the designer compiler considered so far. The *sharp* delay operator is now permitted and can be used to obtain simple pipelined effects. Unlike the design compiler style, it is permitted to mix blocking and non-blocking assignment types within an **always** block. In the BC styles, the blocking assignment is interpreted as being movable in time by the scheduler while the non-blocking assignment is regarded as being tied to a particular clock cycle. All module outputs are registered.

There are three BC styles, called *IO modes*, differing in how much freedom is allowed to the scheduler:

cycle-fixed: I/O operations are tied to particular cycles and may not be moved across clock-edge boundaries. So only internal register reads/writes and combinational functions remain as possibilities for rescheduling. The same testbench can be used in pre- and post-synthesis simulations, and if only I/O is being monitored and the clock period leaves enough time for gate propagation and setup and hold times, then the results should be identical.

superstate-fixed: Same as above except that the scheduler can insert extra clock edges to expand a state into a *superstate*. Because of this possible expansion, the testbench must communicate via the four-phase bundled data convention [Sut89], [MC80]. Providing it does, and again that only I/O is being monitored, then the simulation results should be the same for pre- and post-synthesis except for the stretching. This mode is appropriate for designs with protocols which do not have a fixed timing bound.

free-floating: Allows unrelated writes (not on the same port) to be permuted in time. This mode is advocated as a good means of initial design exploration. However, the user must insert necessary ordering constraints by means of comments external to the language and this detracts somewhat from the simplicity.

To illustrate, the long suffering FIFO is now reprocessed by the BC in the cycle-fixed and superstate styles. Of course the FIFO is not really an ideal candidate for the BC treatment, but it is simple and will serve well to illustrate the differences from the Design Compiler used in Chapters 8 and 9. Although this is not well advertised, the same implicit writing style used in Chapter 8 is processed without complaint by the BC compiler. In the following this specification is refered to as *fifbccf* although it is the same as the *fifosl* of Chapter 8.

BC makes a distinction between *signals* and *variables* which stems from an equivalent distinction in VHDL. In Verilog as well as BC, the variables can be thought of as intermediate results of an extended dataflow computation. These are stored into internal memory or registers and are assigned with the blocking assignment (=). In the simple FIFO example specification from Chapter 8 the only occurences of this were in the

```
analyze -f verilog fifobccf.v
elaborate -schedule fifobccf
create_clock -period 100 clk
bc_check_design -io cycle_fixed -constraints
bc_time_design
report_resource_estimates
schedule -io cycle_fixed -eff medium
report_schedule -var -op -summ -a
write -hier -output fifobccf_rtl.db
verilogout_levelize = true
write -f verilog -hier -output fifobccf_rtl.v
quit
```

fifobccf.script #1 for BC Scheduling.

assign statements. The reset methodology normally associated with implicit styles (see Section 8.1) is not necessary for the particular design example here since the *flush* itself is essentially a reset behavior called explicitly by the outside environment.

To run this specification through the behavioral compiler, a script (#1) is given above. After scheduling, this produces an RTL version of the specification (*fifobccf_rtl.v*) and a database version ready for the Design Compiler or the FPGA compiler.

If the behavioral compiler is invoked with the command

```
bc_shell -f fifobccf.script > fifobccf.log
```

then all the comments and reports will be merged into a single log file in the same style as described for DC in Chapter 12. Excerpts (#1–4) from the log file generated for the *fifibccf* are reproduced for easy reference. In #1, after the **analyze** stage is completed, the **elaborate** stage issues a warning on the absence of a *reset*. Most designs need a reset to start things off in a known state and the BC documentation recommends in fairly specific terms how it should be done [KTDR95], [Knapp97].

After creating the clock and finding errors which would prevent scheduling, the **bc_time_design** command causes the computation of the time delays taken by the various sub-operations. This would need to be done anyway, before scheduling could get underway.

Next, the **schedule** command is given and first reports that a three-state controller with one-hot coding will be employed. After the scheduling is complete, the corresponding report is called for, from which excerpts are illustrated in #2, #3, and #4.

In Excerpt #2 of the scheduling report the ports of the FIFO are listed together with a table of the read and write actions on these ports and the cycle of the synthesized controller in which they occur.

An index of these read and write actions is given in the continuation of the scheduling report in Excerpt #3.

The scheduling report ends in Excerpt #4 with the Mealy machine state transition table of the synthesized controller. This is equivalent to what the user and the design compiler together implicitly achieved for the specifications of the FIFO in Chapters 8 and 9.

Perusing the RTL output by BC for enlightenment is on a level of futility comparable with examining the netlist or gate schematic produced by DC—or by examining the assembly code produced during the compile from a high-level programming language in

```
analyze -f verilog fifobccf.v...
elaborate -schedule fifobccf
Information: The clock transition at line 15 is not
followed by an if statement. No synchronous reset will be
inferred for the always block `block_13´ at line 13.
(HLS-137)
...
bc_check_design -io cycle_fixed -constraints
... No errors were found.
bc_time_design
... Cumulative delay starting at insert_30:
  insert_30 =  0.000000
   eql_30 =  0.000000
   wp_31 =  1.664100
   ram_data_31_2 =  1.664100
   wp_34_2 =  1.664100
   empty_31 =  1.664100
   rp_32 =  1.664100
   wp_34 =  1.664100
   wp_34_3 =  1.664100
   wp_32 =  1.664100
   ram_data_31 =  1.664100
   Win_31 =  1.664100
   wp_34_4 =  1.664100
   eql_32 =  6.408900
    full_32 =  23.379700
...
schedule -io cycle_fixed -eff medium
...
Control FSM has 3 states.
One-Hot coding style selected, state vector is 3 bits long.
State Code
s_0_0 1--
s_0_1 -1-
s_0_2 --1
```

Excerpt #1 from *fifobccf*.log File.

software engineering. The average person will not obtain much benefit from it. In the present example, the RTL output is 10177 characters of Verilog, versus the 973 characters that went in. So the moral drawn here is: Always work only from the highest level specification available. To illustrate this point, an excerpt from the *fifobccf_rtl*.v file is given (#5). Among the extra features inserted over that of the original *fifsl* specification are many extra compiler-assigned identifiers and three case statements.

To continue synthesis from the BC scheduled design, Script #2 could be used for either the DC_shell or the FPGA_shell. In these particular examples the resulting areas and path times then turn out slightly larger than for the DC compiler applied to the original specifications directly.

```
report_schedule -var -op -summ -a ...
Resource types
========================================================
   Win.....1-bit input port
   Wout....1-bit registered output port
   full....1-bit registered output port
   loop....loop boundaries
   p0......1-bit registered output port empty
   p1......28-bit registered output port ram_data
   p2......1-bit input port flush
   p3......1-bit input port insert
   p4......1-bit input port remove
   rp......3-bit registered output port
   wp......3-bit registered output port
```

			p o r t	p o r t	p o r t	p o r t	p o r t	p o r t	p o r t	p o r t	p o r t	p o r t	p o r t
cycle	loop	Win	p2	p3	p4	Wout	p0	full	p1	rp	wp
..0...	..L0..	.....	.....	.....	......	.....	......	....	....	......	....	......
..1...	......	.R31.	.R16.	.R30..	.R24..	.W25..	..W31..	..W32..	.R31a..	..R32..	.R32a.
......	......	.....	.....	......	......	......	..W26..	..W25a.	.R2...	..R26..	.R31b.
......	......	.....	.....	......	......	......	..W18..	..W18a.	.W31a.	..R25a.	.R26a.
...2..	..L2..	.....	.....	......	......	......	......	....	....	..R28b.	.R34b.
......	..L1..	.....	.....	......	......	......	......	....	....	..R28a.	.R34a.
......	......	.....	.....	......	......	......	......	....	....	..R28..	.R34..
......	......	.....	.....	......	......	......	......	....	....	.W28..	.W34.
......	......	.....	.....	......	......	......	......	....	....	.W20..	.W20a

Excerpt #2 from *fifobccf.log* File.

Very similar scripts serve for the superstate version next. The superstate version of the FIFO is given in *fifo* Specification #1. In this version the interactions between the FIFO and the outside world are governed by handshakes: *flush* rdy; *insert* rdy; *remove* rdy. However, since all BC styles are synchronous, the transitions of the component signals of each handshake are snapped to transitions of the clock. As a result, it might happen that some of the *superstate cycles* get stretched by an integral number of clock cycles. To contrast this with the cycle-fixed style, Figure 16.1 illustrates post-synthesis waveforms for the cycle-fixed and superstate styles with example signals in italics drawn from the BC *fifo*'s. The handshakes may also be compared with those of the self-timed style of Section 16.5 which are similar except that those are asynchronous and not constrained to the transitions times of a clock.

In the specification of this FIFO the superstate cycles are separated by @(*posedge clk*) statements. One starts off the **always** block. Then extra ones have been inserted in order to delay the sensing of the *rdy* handshake signal from the setting of it. Care has been taken to see that each branch of the principal extended **if** statement has been balanced with

```
Operation name abbreviations
==========================================
  L0.......loop boundaries block_13_design_loop_begin
  L1.......loop boundaries block_13_design_loop_end
  L2.......loop boundaries block_13_design_loop_cont
  R16......1-bit read flush_16
  R24......1-bit read remove_24
  R25......28-bit read ram_data_25
  R26......3-bit read rp_26
  R28......3-bit read rp_28
  R30......1-bit read insert_30
  R31......1-bit read Win_31
  R32......3-bit read rp_32
  R34......3-bit read wp_34
  R25a.....3-bit read rp_25
  R26a.....3-bit read wp_26
  R28a.....3-bit read rp_28_2
  R28b.....3-bit read rp_28_3
  R31a.....28-bit read ram_data_31
  R31b.....3-bit read wp_31
  R32a.....3-bit read wp_32
  R34a.....3-bit read wp_34_2
  R34b.....3-bit read wp_34_3
  W18......1-bit write empty_18
  W20......3-bit write rp_20
  W25......1-bit write Wout_25
  W26......1-bit write empty_26
  W28......3-bit write rp_28_4
  W31......1-bit write empty_31
  W32......1-bit write full_32
  W34......3-bit write wp_34_4
  W18a.....1-bit write full_18
  W20a.....3-bit write wp_20
  W25a.....1-bit write full_25
  W31a.....28-bit write ram_data_31_2
------------------------------------------
  Timing Summary
------------------------------------------
  Clock period 50.00
  Loop timing information: block_13...2 cycles (cycles 0-2)
------------------------------------------
  Area Summary
------------------------------------------
  Estimated combinational area    15
  Estimated sequential area        9
  TOTAL                           24
  3 control states
  3 basic transitions
  9 control inputs
  11 control outputs
```

Excerpt #3 from *fifobccf*.log File.

```
State graph style report for process block_13:
-----------------------------------------------
present       next
state  input  state  actions
-----------------------------------------------
s_0_0   c1    s_0_1  (no actions)
s_0_1   c2    s_0_2  a_0  Win_31 (read)          a_4  ram_data_31 (read)
                     a_11 rp_32 (read)           a_13 wp_31 (read)
                     a_14 wp_32 (read)           a_20 empty_31 (write)
                     a_32 ram_data_31_2 (write)
s_0_1   c4    s_0_2  a_21 empty_26 (write)
s_0_1   c6    s_0_2  a_22 empty_18 (write)       a_28 full_18 (write)
s_0_1   c8    s_0_2  a_26 full_32 (write)
s_0_1   c10   s_0_2  a_1  flush_16 (read)
s_0_1   c11   s_0_2  a_5  remove_24 (read)
s_0_1   c13   s_0_2  a_2  insert_30 (read)
s_0_1   c15   s_0_2  a_3  ram_data_25 (read)     a_6  rp_25 (read)
                     a_7  rp_26 (read)           a_12 wp_26 (read)
                     a_18 Wout_25 (write)        a_27 full_25 (write)
s_0_2   c17   s_0_1  a_8  rp_28 (read)           a_9  rp_28_2 (read)
                     a_10 rp_28_3 (read)         a_34 rp_28_4 (write)
s_0_2   c18   s_0_1  a_35 rp_20 (write)          a_39 wp_20 (write)
s_0_2   c19   _0_1   a_15 wp_34 (read)           a_16 wp_34_2 (read)
                     a_17 wp_34_3 (read)         a_38 wp_34_4 (write)
+++++   c20   s_0_0  (no actions)
-----------------------------------------------
**********    Branch Conditions    **********
-----------------------------------------------
state  condition source
-----------------------------------------------
c1     true
c2     (branch 0 of conditional SPLIT_L37)
...
c19    (branch 0 of conditional SPLIT_L37)
c20    true
```

Excerpt #4 from *fifobccf*.log File.

an equal number of @(*posedge clk*) statements. If this is not so, the **BC_check** command will issue errors.

The log file resulting from invoking the BC compiler and scheduling on *fifobcss* is very similar to that already shown for the cycle-fixed version except that the new *rdy* signal is inserted into the tables. Otherwise, the number of scheduling states and the estimated area is similar.

16.2.1 *Booth Multiplier*

As a simple example a little more suited to the BC style, the Booth multiplier of Chapters 8 and 9 is now redone in the cycle-fixed style. The Specification (#2) is given here.

```
n618 = (n616 | n617);
U67_z21[3] = (wp_reg_Q[2] & U62_z16[1]);
U67_z21[2] = (wp_reg_Q[2] & U62_z16[0]);
...
U65_z19[1] = (n141 & U64_z18[1]);
U65_z19[0] = (n141 & U64_z18[0]);
n120 = (n253 | n255);
case({n253, n255})
 2'b10:
   begin
     n148 = ~((n149 ^ rp_reg_Q[0]));
     U81_z27[1] = ~(rp_reg_Q[2]);
     U81_z27[0] = ~(rp_reg_Q[1]);
     U78_z24[2] = ~(n148);
     U78_z24[1] = ~(U81_z27[1]);
     U78_z24[0] = ~(U81_z27[0]);
     s_1_Z = U78_z24;
   end
 2'b01:
   s_1_Z = 3'b000;
 default:
   s_1_Z = 3'bxxx;
endcase
```

Excerpt #5 from the *rtl* Output.

```
read fifobccf_rtl.db
compile -map_effort low -verify -verify_effort low
report_area
report_timing
report_fpga
report_cell
write -f edif -hier -o mapped/fifobccf_rtl.edf
current_design = fifobccf_rtl
include/usr/local/pkg/cad/maxplus2/synopsys/bin/syn2acf.cmd
sh/usr/local/pkg/cad/maxplus2/synopsys/bin/syn2acf fifobccf_rtl
quit
```

Script #2: Completion of Synthesis with DC_shell.

The main difference from the implicit style specification of the same module in Chapter 8 is the extra (*posedge clk*) statements inserted to meet the BC scheduling condition that all loops must have the same number of clock edges.

16.2.2   *Behavioral Compiler – A Summary*

The effectiveness of the BC style depends heavily on the characteristics of the design project. For example, the fixed-point datapath of the MIPS example of Chapter 10 has absolutely rigid single- and double-cycle states to fit into the pipeline. This would not profit

```
module fifobcss(clk, flush, insert, remove, Win,empty, full, Wout, rdy);
 parameter nw=7, as=3, ws=4; k=2; // capacity, addrsize, wordsize, fsr tap
  input  clk, flush, insert, remove;
  input  Win;
  output Wout;
  output full, empty, rdy;
  reg  full, empty, rdy;
  reg    [ws-1:0] ram_data [nw-1:0];
  reg    [ws-1:0] Wout;
  wire [ws-1:0] Win;
  reg  [as-1:0] wp, rp;
 always
  begin @(posedge clk)
  if (flush)
       begin
          full<=0; empty<=1;
          @(posedge clk);
          rp<=0; wp<=0;
          while (flush) @(posedge clk);
          rdy<=1;
          @posedge clk);
       end
   else
    case(1´b1)
     remove: begin
             full<=0; Wout <= ram_data[rp];
             if (wp==rp) empty<=1;
             @(posedge clk);
             rp <= ~{(~rp[k]^~rp[0]), ~rp[as-1:1]};
             while (remove) @(posedge clk);
             rdy<=1;
             @posedge clk);
           end
     insert: begin
             empty<=0; ram_data[wp] <= Win;
             if (wp==rp) full<=1;
             @(posedge clk);
             rp <= ~{(~wp[k]^~wp[0]), ~wp[as-1:1]};
             while (insert) @(posedge clk);
             rdy<=1;
             @posedge clk);
           end
    default: @(posedge clk); // idle
   endcase
  end
endmodule
```

Specification #1 of *fifo*: BC Superstate Style.

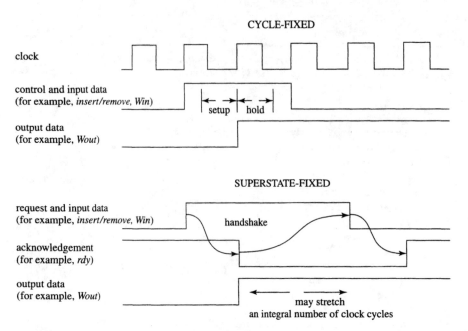

Figure 16.1   *BC Cycle-Fixed and Superstate Waveforms after Synthesis.*

from the BC style. On the other hand, a multiplier or other parts from the floating point datapath might benefit greatly since these have many internal states and are off the pipeline.

BC styles are subject to the same constraints as synchronous procedural styles generally. For example every loop must be broken with a clock edge. Added to this for the cycle-fixed and superstate styles is that I/O operations cannot cross clock-edge boundaries. This needs some amount of care where loops and conditionals are involved in order to ensure that there is no possible evaluation of the conditional that could result in one I/O operation merging into the state of a neighbor.

The fact that all outputs are registered means that a response to an external input cannot happen until the next clock edge. For a hierarchical structure this implies a clock period delay between the control point of a module and the resulting data I/O action. This is comparable with the clock phase delays introduced between hierarchical levels in the control-point style of Chapter 9. Similar remarks apply to the sensing of status from the synthesized module to the environment in time to affect the choice of the next operation.

Four years after its introduction the BC style still remains somewhat controversial, and the Synopsys *module compiler* is now seen by some as a prefered successor. However, many successful designs have been completed using it.

16.3   Self-Timed Style

Although there have been some experimental asynchronous computers, all commercial computers to date have been synchronous. However, the continued integrity of synchronous operation is being brought into question because of the increasing difficulty of managing clock skews across complex chips with submicron line widths. On the other hand, the issues involved to guarantee correct operation of asynchronous circuits are complex

```
module boothcf(clk, mult, mcand_in, mplier_in, product_out);
 parameter w=4; // small wordsize for test
  input clk, mult;
  input [w-1:0] mcand_in, mplier_in;
  output [2*w-1:0] product_out;
  reg [2*w:0] ppm, pps;
  reg [w-1:0] ccs, mcand;
  assign product_out = pps[2*w:1];
always
 begin
  if (mult) // set up for new multiplication
  begin
   ccs <= {w+1{1´b1}}; // initialize shift count
   mcand <= mcand_in;        // load multiplicand
   ppm <= {{w{1´b0}}, mplier_in[w-1:0], 1´b0}; // load multiplier
   @(posedge clk);
   pps <= ppm;
   @(posedge clk);
  end
  else if (ccs[0]) // internal cycles of multiplication
   begin
    case (pps[1:0])
     2´b01: ppm<= {pps[2*w:w+1]+mcand, pps[w:0]}; // add mcand
     2´b10: ppm<= {pps[2*w:w+1]+~mcand+1, pps[w:0]};//subtr mcand
     2´b00, 2´b11: ppm<=pps; // no operation
    endcase
    @(posedge clk);
    ccs <= ccs>>1; // shift count right
    pps <= {ppm[2*w],ppm[2*w:1]};//long arithmetic right shift
    @(posedge clk);
   end
  else
   begin @(posedge clk); @(posedge clk); end
 end
endmodule
```

Specification #2: *boothbccf*.

and subtle and inevitably lead to an area penalty that can be substantial. Nevertheless there is now somewhat of a resurgence of interest in asynchronous circuits because of the potential for:

- Freedom from clock trees and clock skew.
- Performance governed by the average of the path delays instead of the worst.
- Reduced noise because switching is more evenly distributed in time (less crosstalk between wires and RF applications).
- Automatic power-save when there is no switching (instead of sleep modes as in Chapter 11).
- Ability to freely substitute faster submodules as the circuit technology improves.

The so-called "fundamental mode" model of classical switching theory inherited from the 1950s depended on the assumption that after any change of a single input, any other change must wait for the circuit to settle. This is really not practical for current complex designs with hundreds of input pins and internal state variables. In its place the notions of *delay-insensitive* and *speed-insensitive* circuits have been introduced. The former is generally taken to mean that the circuit will operate correctly irrespective of variations in the propagation delays in either gates or wires, while the latter is only insensitive to delays on the gates assuming time skews produced in the interconnections are bounded by the delay of the fastest gate. A compromise is perhaps the *quasi-delay-insensitive* circuit [Martin89] in which some wires (*intra-module wires?*) obey the speed insensitive assumption while others (longer distance between modules?) are controlled by handshakes and are delay insensitive.

Early attempts to synthesize these classes of circuits, such as that of [Meng89], incurred a large area penalty because correct operation was guaranteed by means of extensive handshaking between modules and special complex (non-gate) circuits at the module outputs [Brzozowski92]. Work since then has concentrated on methods to reduce the area overhead and yet still avoid errors due to logic hazards and races, such as that of [Beerel98]. A promising recent variation is that of burst-mode circuits [Yun99] which operate correctly if the environment obeys the fundamental mode assumption with respect to bursts (a set of input changes unordered in time with respect to each other within the set). Even though this model seems at first sight unlikely, some amount of success has been achieved using ordinary gates with a number of practical controller type of applications for which the assumptions hold true.

The example developed here follows the handshaking philosophy. The principle is that each submodule signals when it completes its operation, and the handshake communication ensures that no required operation is either lost or multiply invoked. Unlike the handshakes of the BC superstate style which are snapped to clock edges, these handshakes occur as soon as possible on the time axis.

A self-timed specification style will be illustrated with a similar *fifo* as in previous chapters. To start, the standard *fifo* components used so far will need to be modified into self-timed forms *fsr_st.v* and *ram_st.v* to signal completion of their operations with a *rdy* flag. These are the similar modules as used in Sections 5.7 and 5.8 except now augmented for the self timed operation.

Ideally the completion signals coming from the lowest-level modules have a finite latency, and then the ready signal coming from a higher-level module is derivative from these, meaning that it comes true at the end of a sequence of microoperations invoked on the lower modules. In practice it is difficult to generate a delay for the ready signals of the bottom-level modules through the synthesizer, especially when targeting FPGA chips. For a custom target it is conceivable that such a delay could be generated by a hand-crafted gate chain that is set to "don't touch" during synthesis. The delay of this unit would need to be set so as to exceed the propagation delay of the corresponding operations. However, for the specifications that follow, a clock has been used solely to generate the necessary delay and ensure that the completion signal does not come true until after the operation is truly finished. If this seems to the reader like cheating, see the discussion at the end of this section.

The specifications of the bottom level modules *fsr_st* (#3) and *ram_st* (#4) are given on the following page.

```
module fsr_st(aapwr_on, ack, adelay, enb, flush, rdy, slave);
//feedback shift register
 parameter n = 3, k = 1;  // register length, tap point
 input aapwr_on, adelay, ack, enb, flush;
 output rdy;
 output [n-1:0] slave;
 reg    getrdy, rdy;   // completed previous operation
 reg    [n-1:0] master, slave;
 always @(aapwr_on or enb or ack)
  if (aapwr_on) getrdy <= 0;
   else if (enb)
     if (flush) begin master <= 0; getrdy <= 1; end
      else // if insert or remove
        begin master <= ~{(~slave[k]^~slave[0]),~slave[n-1:1]};
              getrdy <= 1;
          end
    else if (ack) getrdy <= 0;
    else ;
 always @(negedge adelay)
    begin rdy <= getrdy;
          if (~enb) slave <= master;
    end
endmodule
```

Specification #3: Self-Timed *fsr* Module.

```
module ram_st(aapwr_on,ack,addr,adelay,data_in,insert,select, rdy,slave);
 parameter n=7, a=3, w=4; // capacity, addrsize, wordsize
  input aapwr_on, adelay, select, insert, ack;
  input  [a-1:0] addr;
  input  [w-1:0] data_in;
  output [w-1:0] slave;
  output rdy;
  reg [w-1:0] master, slave;
  reg [w-1:0] ram_data [n-1:0];
  reg getrdy, rdy; // completion flag
 always @(aapwr_on or select or ack)
  if (aapwr_on) getrdy <= 0;
   else if (select)
    begin
     if (insert) ram_data[addr] <= data_in;
     else        master <= ram_data[addr];
     getrdy <= 1;
    end
   else if (ack) getrdy <= 0;
   else;

 always @(negedge adelay)
   begin rdy <= getrdy; if (~select) slave <= master; end
endmodule
```

Specification #4: Self-Timed *ram* Module.

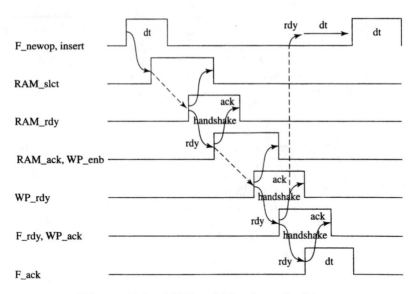

Figure 16.2   *Self-Timed Waveforms for fifo_st.*

With the bottom-level modules available, the *fifo* itself can now be specified. To help follow these specifications it may be helpful to refer to Figure 16.2. For each operation of the *fifo*, a sequence of operations on the submodules is invoked under the control of the handshakes. For example, Figure 16.3 illustrates with the *insert* operation. This operation first invokes the *RAM_slct* signal which initaties a write operation on the RAM. When this is complete, as indicated by the return of *RAM_rdy*, then the enable operation *WP_enb* initiates the advance of the *fsr* write pointer, WP. Finally when this in turn is complete, as indicated by WP_*rdy*, the ready signal of the *fifo* is generated, F_*rdy*.

The operation of the circuit can be alternatively specified in the form of a *state transition diagram* first introduced by [Chu86]. This is a variation of a Petri net showing graphically the sequence of transitions on the signals, with + for a positive going edge and – for a negative going one. Where two directed edges converge, then the indicated transition cannot occur until both the origin transitions have occured first. Such a transition diagram for the *insert* operation is shown in Figure 16.3. The dotted edges indicate the places where the submodules are doing their computations.

Self-timed modules will certainly not work unless all the handshakes get off to a start in the correct state. For this reason a "power-up" initializing sequence has been added to all the modules and initiated by the *apwr_on* control point. Also, correct asynchronous sequencing action depends on the signals in the sensitivity list of the **always** block being one-hot. See Specification #5 for illustration.

The highest-level specification is the "outside world" or, in this example, see Testbench #1, which interacts with the *fifo_st* module via the handshake:

        new operation, F_newop : fifo ready signal, F_rdy.

This design was synthesized to FPGA as an illustration of a self-timed writing style. However, although synthesis tools ostensibly cater to asynchronous operations, the fact is that both these and the FPGA tools are almost exclusively targeted at synchronous operation.

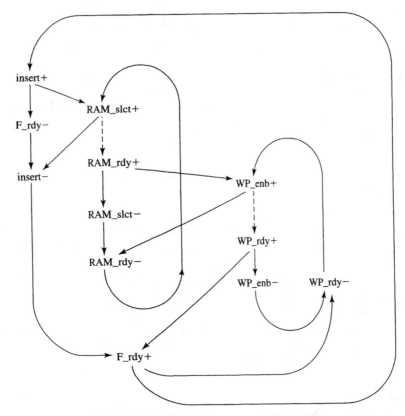

Figure 16.3   *Signal Transition Graph.*

When "breaking the rules" as we have done here, the user will find the log files replete with warnings that the FPGA logical elements are not ideal for this purpose and the synthesizer is doing the best it can! Also, with present tools, the "combinational feedback loops" formed by the ready and acknowledge handshakes (see Figures 16.2 and 16.3) must be broken by a clock edge. In fact as successive tool versions have been released, the vendors have been tightening the noose in this respect and narrowing the constructs that will be accepted. At high-level simulation almost anything goes, but at gate level, asynchronous operation is very tricky. Nevertheless the fact that the design here operates correctly at gate level for both Altera and Xilinx says something about their consistency at least. The synthesized areas are about twice those of the equivalent synchronous designs synthesized earlier.

More important, the synthesized nets must be free of hazards. For this to work correctly at gate level in general, the following conditions would need to be satisfied: The completion (ready) signals need to be delayed more than the computation in their corresponding module and must change state not more than once per activation (otherwise the purpose of the handshake would be defeated). One way of doing this is to realize each ready signal with an atomic complex gate [Meng89]. Such gates can not be easily realized with current device and synthesis technology. As an alternative, progress is recently being made in synthesis methods that produce hazard-free covers [Beerel98], [Pastor98]. Unfortunately the look-up tables used in current FPGA logical elements do not meet any of these criteria. Until FPGAs with features to support asynchronism become available

```
module fifo_st(apwr_on, delay, f_ack, flush, f_newop, insert, remove,
               Win_0, Win_1, Win_2, Win_3,
               empty, full, rdy, Wout_0, Wout_1, Wout_2, Wout_3);
 parameter nw=7, as=3, ws=4; // capacity, address_size, word_size
 input apwr_on,delay,f_ack,f_newop,flush,insert,remove,Win_3,Win_2,Win_1,Win_0;
 output Wout_3, Wout_2, Wout_1, Wout_0, empty, full, rdy;
 reg    WP_enb,RP_enb,RAM_slct,RAM_ack,WP_ack,RP_ack, empty, full, getrdy, rdy;
 wire [as-1:0] wp, rp;
 reg  [as-1:0] addr;
 wire [ws-1:0] Win, Wout;
 assign Win = {Win_3, Win_2, Win_1, Win_0};
 assign Wout_3=Wout[3],Wout_2=Wout[2],Wout_1=Wout[1],Wout_0=Wout[0];
 wire equal = (wp==rp)? 1:0;
 ram_st #(nw,as,ws
                 RAM(apwr_on,RAM_ack,addr,delay,Win,insert,RAM_slct,RAM_rdy,Wout);
 fsr_st #(as,1) WP(apwr_on, WP_ack, delay, WP_enb, flush, WP_rdy, wp);
 fsr_st #(as,1) RP(apwr_on, RP_ack, delay, RP_enb, flush, RP_rdy, rp);

always @ (apwr_on or f_newop or RAM_rdy or WP_rdy or RP_rdy or f_ack)
 if (apwr_on)
    begin RAM_slct<=0; WP_ack<=0; RP_ack<=0; RAM_ack<=0; getrdy<=0; end
 else if (f_newop)
    if      (flush) begin  empty<=1; full<=0; addr<=rp; WP_enb<=1; end
    else if (insert) begin RAM_slct<=1; addr<=wp; empty<=0; end
    else if (remove) begin RAM_slct<=1; addr<=rp; full<=0; end
    else ;
 else if (RAM_rdy)
   begin
    if      (insert) begin RAM_slct<=0; WP_enb<=1; RAM_ack<=1; end
    else if (remove) begin RAM_slct<=0; RP_enb<=1; RAM_ack<=1; end
    else ;
   end
  else if (WP_rdy)
    if      (flush) begin WP_enb<=0; RP_enb<=1; WP_ack<=1; end
    else if (insert) begin WP_enb<=0; WP_ack<=1; RAM_ack<=0;  getrdy<=1; end
    else ;
  else if (RP_rdy)
    if      (flush) begin RP_enb<=0; RP_ack<=1; WP_ack<=0; getrdy<=1; end
    else if (remove) begin RP_enb<=0; RP_ack<=1; RAM_ack<=0;  getrdy<=1; end
    else ;
  else if (f_ack)
    begin
     if  (insert)   if (equal) full<=1; else full<=0;
     else if (remove)if (equal) empty<=1; else empty<=0;
     RP_ack<=0; WP_ack<=0; getrdy<=0;
    end
  else;

 always @(posedge delay) rdy <= getrdy; // for fpga implementation: delay rdy signal
endmodule
```

Specification #5: Self-timed FIFO, *fifo_st*.

```
module test_fifo_st;
 parameter wbits = 4, dt = 10;
 reg dclk, PWRon, newop, FI_ack, flush, insert, remove;
 reg  [wbits-1:0] Win;
 wire [wbits-1:0] Wout;
 wire [2:0] wp, rp;
 wire Win_3, Win_2, Win_1, Win_0, Wout_3, Wout_2, Wout_1, Wout_0;
 integer i;
 assign Win_3=Win[3],Win_2=Win[2],Win_1=Win[1],Win_0=Win[0];
 assign Wout = {Wout_3, Wout_2, Wout_1, Wout_0};
 fifo_st FI(PWRon, dclk, FI_ack, flush, newop, insert, remove,
            Win_0, Win_1, Win_2, Win_3,
            Empty, Full, rdy, Wout_0, Wout_1, Wout_2, Wout_3);
 always begin #dt dclk=1; #dt dclk=0; end
 initial begin
  $display(`` t newop fir  wp rp Win Wout E F rdy´´);
  $monitor(``%4g   %b   %b%b%b  %d %d  %d  %d   %b %b   %b´´,
  $time, newop, flush, insert, remove, wp, rp, Win, Wout, mpty,Full, rdy);
  PWRon<=1; newop<=0; flush<=0; insert<=0; remove<=0; Win<=0; dclk<=0;
   @(negedge dclk); @(negedge dclk) PWRon<=0;
   @(negedge dclk); @(negedge dclk) flush<=1; newop<=1;
   @(negedge dclk) newop<=0;

 for (i=0; i<7; i=i+1)
  begin @(posedge rdy); flush<=0; insert<=0; Win<=Win+1;
   @(negedge dclk) FI_ack<=1;
   @(negedge dclk) FI_ack<=0; insert<=1; newop<=1;
  @(negedge dclk) newop<=0; end

 for (i=0; i<7; i=i+1)
  begin @(posedge rdy); insert<=0; remove<=0;
   @(negedge dclk) FI_ack<=1;
   @(negedge dclk) FI_ack<=0; remove<=1; newop<=1;
   @(negedge dclk) newop<=0; end

 @(posedge rdy); remove<=0; insert<=0; Win<=4´h5;
   @(negedge dclk) FI_ack<=1;
   @(negedge dclk) FI_ack<=0; insert<=1; newop<=1;
   @(negedge dclk) newop<=0;

 @(posedge rdy); insert<=0;
   @(negedge dclk) FI_ack<=1;
   @(negedge dclk) FI_ack<=0; remove<=1; newop<=1;
   @(negedge dclk) newop<=0;

 @(posedge rdy); remove<=0;
   @(negedge dclk) FI_ack<=1;
   @(negedge dclk) FI_ack<=0; flush<=1; newop<=1;
   @(negedge dclk) newop<=0;
 @(posedge rdy)  $finish;
end endmodule
```

Testbench #1 for *fifo_st*.

[Hauck94], this style is only really usable for an appropriate custom VLSI target technology with atomic complex gates.

Notwithstanding all these difficulties, some practical asynchronous designs have been achieved. A good summary is in [Brunvand99]. This would seem to show that it ought to be possible for a family of synthesis tools and FPGA products to support this style eventually.

16.4   Encapsulated Style

Along with the recent emphasis on design reusability, a number of styles have been advocated with an object-oriented flavor, for example SBL [Gopal85], *OO VHDL* [Swamy95]. Software languages 'C,' C++, and Java have also been advocated for hardware systems modelling; see for example the discussion in the next chapter. As another example of such a style, here we introduce our encapsulated style called *Vpp* [Smith96]. Unlike OO VHDL it is directly accessible to present industry simulators without the necessity of a translator. Unlike the BC styles, it permits operator inference over arbitrary user-defined modules instead of just the combinational operators of Table 3.1. Like the BC "free-floating" style it is useful for design exploration at the stage where the designer wants to explore functionality quickly without the burden of associating it with strict timing. A fact that readers will find out for themselves is that most of the errors encountered while trying to get HDL models to work have to do with timing. So a style that abstracts the timing away provides a useful, quick, confidence check on feasibility.

The essence of an encapsulated module is summarized in Figure 16.4. Such a module may be exercised only by a fixed repertoire of legal operations. In the case of sequential modules, the data operated upon is encapsulated in internal registers.

In such a module each operation uses arguments selected from the dataports, and they are activated by some combination of signals on selected control port(s).

As an obvious example the ALU module comes readily to mind with its repertoire of operations, but in fact most commonly-used modules can fit this mold as illustrated in the following specification (#6) for a RAM. For the encapsulated operations Verilog *tasks* rather than functions have been utilized in order to allow for multiple outputs and the possibility of internal delays. Verilog tasks can neatly characterize the functionality of the modelled operations, together with the datapath input and output arguments with which they are instantiated. The RAM specification has two operations, *read* and *write*, realized with one task each.

One reason that the Vpp style is a useful exploratory tool is that the details of timing are abstracted away. The semantics of the operations as realized by Verilog tasks are conceptually self-timed—the next operation (task) does not start until the previous operation (task) has completed, whatever time that takes.

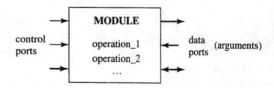

Figure 16.4   *Encapsulated Style Module.*

```
task read;
    input  [a-1:0] addr;
    output [w-1:0] data_out;
       data_out = ram_data[addr];
endtask

task write;
   input [a-1:0] addr;
   input [w-1:0] data_in;
      ram_data[addr] = data_in;
endtask
```

Specification #6: Encapsulated RAM.

```
`include ``ram.v´´
`include ``fsr.v´´
`include ``mux.v´´
`include ``comparator.v´´
module fifo_vpp (w_in, w_out, full, empty);
 parameter nw = 7, as = 3, ws = 4;//capacity,address size,word size
 input  [ws-1:0] w_in;
 output [ws-1:0] w_out output full, empty;
 reg WE, equal, Full, Empty;
 reg [as-1:0] wp,rp,addr; // initially model interconnects as regs
 reg [ws-1:0] w_out;
  //instantiate submodules to size and indentify (using dummy args)
  wire [as-1:0] wp_d, rp_d, addr_d;   //dummy arguments
  wire [ws-1:0] w_in_d, w_out_d;      // ,,
  wire we_d;                                         // ,,
  ram          #(nw,as,ws) RAM(addr_d, w_in_d, w_out_d);
  fsr          #(as)       RP(rp_d);
  fsr          #(as)       WP(wp_d);
  mux          #(--`       MUX(we_d, rp_d, wp_d, addr_d);
                          CMP(rp_d,wp_d,equal_d);
```

tion #7a: *fifo* in Vpp Style.

trol inputs are completely implicit and do not appear in
modules at all.
sary submodule operations are accessed directly by

.operation(arguments)

+ uses the dot operator for *instance.function.* It works
rpret the dot as getting a task from another file.
a hierarchy is needed. For this purpose we use again
cification is shown in #7a.
difference from the earlier specifications is that now
mmy arguments whose purpose is just to impart the

```
task flush;
  output full, empty;
  begin
    WE=0;WP.reset(wp);  RP.reset(rp);
    CMP.compare(rp,wp,equal);
    full=WE&&equal;  empty=~WE&&equal;
  end
endtask

task insert;
  input [ws-1:0] w_in;
  output full, empty;
  begin
    WE=1;MUX.select(WE,rp,wp,addr);
    RAM.write(addr,w_in);
    WP.shift(wp);
    CMP.compare(rp,wp,equal);
    full=WE&&equal; empty=~WE&&equal;
  end
endtask

task remove;
  output [ws-1:0] w_out;
  output full, empty;
  begin
    WE=0; MUX.select(WE,rp,wp,addr);
    RAM.read(addr,w_out);
    RP.shift(rp);
    CMP.compare(rp,wp,equal);
    full=WE&&equal; empty=~WE&&equal;
  end
 endtask
endmodule
```

Specification #7b of *fifo* in Vpp Style.

argument dimensions. Then the actual operations follow in task form with the real arguments in Specification #7b.

The abbreviation *Vpp* has been used for this writing style because roughly speaking, it bears a similar relationship to Verilog as C++ does to 'C.' Each module type is equivalent to a class in C++ or Java, and the tasks are its methods. An inheritance mechanism for submodules could also be useful, although that has not been incorporated here.

In this style, modules are parameterized to size in all levels of the hierarchy. The dummy arguments with the module identifiers in the fragment given in Specification #7a serve only to indicate this dimensionality to the interpreters or compilers of standard industry simulators. Inside an upper level task body the operations invoked on lower-level modules are consistently themselves further task calls. The semantics of these operation calls between a **begin** and an **end** statement are sequential: Each task must complete before the next commences. If it is known that several operation calls could be effected concurrently then the **begin . . . end** might be replaced with a **fork . . . join** pair. Of course

```
module test_fifo_vpp;
 parameter as = 3, ws = 4; // address size, wordsize
 reg [ws-1:0] Win;
 reg [ws-1:0] Wout;
 reg f, e;
 reg [3:0] i;
 wire fulld, emptyd;        // dummy arguments
 wire [ws-1:0] Wind, Woutd;  // dummy arguments
  fifo_vpp FIFO(Wind, Woutd, fulld, emptyd);
  initial
  begin
  $display(``time wp rp Win Wout full empty´´);
  $monitor(``%2g    %h %h    %h    %h    %b      %b´´,
  $time, FIFO.wp, FIFO.rp, Win, Wout, f, e);
  FIFO.flush(f,e);
  Win = 0;
  for (i=0; i<7; i=i+1) begin Win=Win+1; if (~f)FIFO.insert(Win,f,e); end
  for (i=0; i<7; i=i+1) if (~e) FIFO.remove(Wout,f,e);
  Win = 4´h5;
  if (~f) FIFO.insert(Win,f,e);
  if (~e) FIFO.remove(Wout,f,e);
 end
endmodule
```

Testbench #2 for *fifo* in Vpp style.

this is unsynthesizable with current tools, but the Vpp style needs a *scheduler* to group the partial orderings into concurrent sets, as was demonstrated earlier with the SBL compiler in a similar situation [Awad91]. Again, in order that the Vpp style be directly accessible to industry simulators, each variable used to communicate between the submodules, such as an *interconnection*, must (temporarily) be declared as a Verilog **reg**. This is because Verilog demands that task outputs be registered. Each such **reg** will revert to a **wire** during the transformation to the synthesizable form. An essential feature of the encapsulated style is that as the hierarchy is expanded upward, the invocations will be in the same style. Even the testbenches can be written in the same style as a natural extension of the design hierarchy. This implies that the testbenches themselves could be translatable and synthesizable by the same method. By this means modules of a design could be easily converted to the corresponding built-in self-test (BIST) versions. For example, a testbench for the *fifo* module is shown above for reference.

In its raw form, although the Vpp style is directly simulatable, it requires a translation in order to be accepted by industry synthesizers. In a similar way that a scheduler is used to transform the Synopsys BC styles into RTL style, we could use a scheduler to transform the Vpp style into the control-point style of Chapter 9 which as also organized around module operations. A similar transformation was implemented with the SBL hardware description language [Awad91]. For direct accessibility to industry Verilog simulators, the bottom-level submodule specifications must include delay operators. Otherwise the simulator attempts to place all the transitions in the same time slot. These delay statements would be ignored by the scheduling process employed to transform the Vpp style into synthesizable forms.

16.5   Future HDL Development

A committee of Open Verilog International (OVI) (www.OVI.org) has been charged with
the development of an architectural HDL with the goal of three orders of magnitude speed
improvement over existing Verilog simulators (it is notable that no members of the committee are from academia). At this time this has not advanced very far beyond a wish list,
but the broad idea is that it should support higher-level data structures and operators, and
have a translator to the existing Verilog or VHDL, somewhat similar to the ideas of Section 16.4. One proposed methodology is to take the model of the Hennessy & Patterson
DLX (very similar to the MIPS200 of Chapter 10) and use it to compare the specifications
in the various candidate versions of the language.

Another committee, this one from IEEE, is looking into extensions of Verilog at a
more immediate level. Among the proposals being considered are:

- A *generate* statement for an array of modules similar to that existing in VHDL. This
  has already found its way into the proposed Verilog AMS standard (discussed in
  Chapter 17).
- Multidimensional arrays.
- Sensitivity list separated by commas instead of "or".
- Allow assignment to wire in a procedural block.
- Mutable bit select.
- Initial assignments to register.
- ifndef conditional compilation.
- Struct/record types.

Some of the proposals on this list are oriented to making Verilog more like commonly
used software languages. Also some of these same items have found their way into a similar commercial effort called *superlog* (see www.Co-Design.com). For an equivalant pro-
posal for a "super VHDL," see www.inmet.com/SLDL/.

Exercises

16.1. We can make a good project for the BC superstate and self-timed styles from the
floating point adder/subtractor.[1] Except that instead of the combinational version
of Problems 3.17 and 9.6, we employ shift register modules for the operator align-
ment and result normalization stages, together with a carry-completion adder
[Blaauw76], [Gilchrist55]. Each of these three submodules provides a completion
signal when its (variable duration) operation is complete.

a. Write a BC superstate specification and testbench, and simulate and schedule
   using the BC compiler. Then continue to synthesize using the FPGA compiler
   and maxplus2 or Xilinx, and verify the operation at gate level.

b. Draw a signal transition graph for the submodule activations of this floating
   point adder in the style of Figure 16.3. Hence write a self-timed specification and
   test module in the style of *fifo_st*. Simulate at high level, synthesize using the
   FPGA compiler and maxplus2 or Xilinx, and verify the operation at gate level.

c. Respecify in the encapsulated style of Section 16.4. Note that this will simulate
   without the handshake on the completion signals because the tasks will automatically hand over as soon as they are done.

---

[1]Good flowcharts of such a floating point add-subtract may be found in [Stallings97].

16.2. Recast selected examples and exercises from Chapters 6, 7, 8, and 9 into behavioral cycle fixed or superstate style and run through the BC and FPGA compilers.

References

[Beerel98] Beerel, P. A., Myers, C. J., and Meng, T. H., "Covering conditions and algorithms for the synthesis of speed-independent circuits," *IEEE Trans. CAD*, 17:3 (March98), pp. 205–219

[Blaauw76] Blaauw, G. A., *Digital System Implementation*, Prentice-Hall, 1976

[Gilchrist55] Gilchrist, B. J. H., et al., "Fast carry logic for digital computers," *IEEE Trans.*, EC:4 (December 1955), pp. 133–136

[Brunvand99] Brunvand, E., Nowick, S. M., and Yun, K., "Practical advances in asynchronous design and asynchronous/synchronous interfaces," TAU99 (*Proc. Intl. Workshop on Timing Issues in the Specification and Synthesis of Digital Systems, March 1999*)

[Brzozowski92] Brzozowski, J. A., and Ebergen, J. C., "On the delay-sensitivity of gate networks," *IEEE. Trans.* C41:11 (Nov. 1992), pp. 1349–1360

[Chu86] Chu, T. A., "Synthesis of self-timed control circuits from graphs: An example," *Proc. Intl. Conf. Computer Design*, Oct. 1986, pp. 565–571

[Gopal85] Gopalakrishnan, G., Smith, D. R., and Srivas, M. K., "An Algebraic Approach to the Specification and Synthesis of Digital Designs," *7th Intl. Symp. on Computer Hardware Description Languages and Their Applications*, Tokyo, Japan, Aug. 29–31, 1985

[Hauck94] Hauck, S., et al., "An FPGA for implementing asynchronous circuits," in *IEEE Design and Test*, 11:3, 1994, pp. 60–69

[KTDR95] Knapp, D. W., Ly, D. T., MacMillen, D., and Miller, R., "Behavioral synthesis methodology for HDL-based specification and validation," *Proc. ACM/IEEE Design Automation Conference*, 1995

[Knapp97] Knapp, D. W., *Behavioral Synthesis: Digital System Design Using the Synopsys Behavioral Compiler*, Prentice-Hall, 1997

[Meng89] Meng, T. H.-Y., Brodersen, R. W., and Messerschmitt, D. G., "Automatic synthesis of asynchronous circuits from high-level specifications," *IEEE Trans. CAD*, 8:11 (November 1989), pp. 1185–1205

[Pastor98] Pastor, E., et al., "Structural methods for the synthesis of speed-independent circuits," *IEEE Trans. CAD* 17:11 (November 1988), pp. 1108–1129

[Smith96] Smith, D. R., "Hardware synthesis from Encapsulated Verilog Modules," *Intl. Conf. on Application-Specific Systems, Achitectures, and Processors*, Chicago, Aug. 1996

[Stallings97] Stallings, W., *Computer Organization and Architecture*, 5th edition, Prentice-Hall, 1999, p. 307

[Yun99] Yun, K. L., and Dill, D. L., "Automatic Synthesis of extended burst-mode circuits (part 1 and part 2)," *IEEE Trans. CAD*, 18:2 (Februrary 1999)

Chapter Seventeen

Mixed Technology Design

17.1   Introduction

The tools used so far pertain to designs of purely digital logic targeted at a single circuit technology. Yet a large proportion of applications either need or are best implemented by designs in mixed technology. Now that device fabrication has reached the point where it is possible to place a whole system on a single chip, it is becoming common for macro-modules based on different technologies to be embedded in the same chip.

One example of this already encountered in Chapter 14 were the embedded RAMs inside FPGAs. Although these are in the same CMOS circuit technology as the rest of the chip they were not designed with the same toolset. One of the most common embedded components is a processor. This is used to execute the parts of the design algorithm which are not time critical and can be implemented more cheaply and flexibly in software than in pure hardware.

Many current applications, such as set-top boxes, wireless hand-sets, and palm tops, are at least part analog. So analog components must coexist on the same chip coupled through connection components such as analog-digital converters. In terms of layout on the surface of the chip, analog and digital circuitry are quite distinct, with much larger transistors and capacitors used in the analog parts. And the tools for analog design are also quite different and in general more CPU intensive. Finally, many chip projects interact through sensors and actuators with other system parts which may be characterized in another discipline entirely such as mechanical or chemical.

Clearly some tools or methods are needed to coordinate the design of these disparate parts and verify that the system as a whole functions correctly. These topics have been gathered together in this chapter.

17.2   Digital/Analog

Versions of analog HDLs such as VHDL-A and Verilog-A have now been approved as IEEE standards. Using available simulation software for Verilog-A [Fitz98] it is possible to simulate a variety of analog behaviors using a *signal-flow* style similar to that described in Chapters 3 and 5 for digital Verilog. With this software it is also possible to simulate some parts of a design in the signal-flow style and other parts/submodules using the Spice electrical simulator. The Spice methodology is an example of a *conservative* style. It involves both voltage and current using the Kirchoff flow and potential laws to converge on a solution. Spice is also purely structural whereas the signal-flow style is largely behavioral. Finally Spice is more computationally intensive compared with the signal-flow style. So, using Verilog-A and signal-flow style, it is possible to obtain a rapid early evaluation check on the behavior of a pure analog system and follow up later with more detailed verification of critical sections using the more accurate Spice tool. But the real payoff will come with the advent of the analog and mixed system HDLs, such as *Verilog-AMS*. In the run-up towards IEEE standardization, working documents are sometimes available on Web sites such as that of Open Verilog International (www.OVI.org). Using Verilog-AMS it would be possible to explore the functioning of a true mixed digital-analog design or even designs with sections in nonelectrical disciplines.

At the moment simulators are available for Verilog-A, and EDA developers await the outcome of the AMS standardization. With the digital HDLs, of course, the original language design was conducted with a view to documentation and simulation only, resulting in the language constructs being fairly well set in concrete before their adaptation to synthesis was well understood. This situation is not resolved even now.

One such issue is that of a connect statement between one discipline and another, for example, digital to analog. Should a *connection module* be automatically inserted, giving an effect analogous to coertion from an integer type to a real type in software languages? In that case what kind of conversion module should be chosen? (There are many.) Or should modules with mixed-port types be a specific responsibility of the designer, with suitable internal conversion constructs inserted explicitly? Actuators and sensor modules, which usually convert between the mechanical and electrical disciplines, raise similar questions.

A design example is given here that follows the second philosophy. Besides demonstrating structural design on a hierarchy of submodules with mixed ports, it will also serve to illustrate many of the official behavioral constructs of Verilog-A. This design is the well-known successive approximation analog-to-digital converter. Although its overall function is of course just this conversion, it is in fact composed from a number of mixed-port submodules. In the block diagram organization illustrated in Figure 17.1 a definite boundary (dashed line) between the analog and digital disciplines runs through the overall organization as well as some of the submodules themselves.

The operation of the successive approximation analog-to-digital converter was introduced in Problem 8.3, Chapter 8. The single "1" in the index register is clocked through all the bit positions starting with the most significant position. At each successive position the current bit is added through the exclusive-OR gates to the current approximation in the accumulation register. If the sampled input analog voltage from pin A_in compares small, a second exclusive-OR operation is used to wipe out the trial bit. After the index reaches the least significant bit the conversion is available at the output. Then a new sample is started and the whole process repeats. This is another example of a logarithmic search.

First the submodules are discussed. The *ringcount* is a pure digital module which is a version of the parameterized ring counter of Chapter 5. It is used here for the one-hot position indicator, denoted *index* in Figure 17.1. The sample-and-hold module is essentially a switch followed by storage on a capacitor and buffered with an operational amplifier. The operational amplifier has resistors in the feedback and input paths and these constrain the overall amplification to their ratio, in this case unity. The signal flow is from

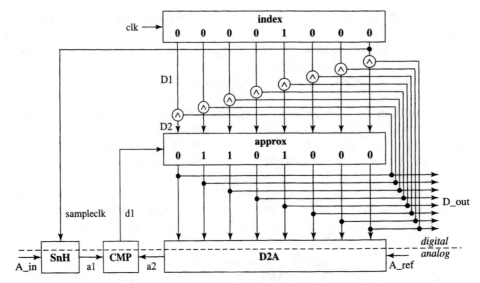

Figure 17.1   *Successive Approximation Block Diagram.*

```
module samplehold(clock, S_in, S_out);
 input clock, S_in;
 output S_out;
 real sample;
 electrical S_in, S_out;
 analog
  begin
   sample = ((clock==1)? V(S_in) : sample);
   V(S_out) <+ transition(sample,1u,1u,1u);
  end
endmodule
```

Figure 17.2   *Sample-and-Hold.*

left to right only. The switch is digitally controlled but passes analog signals, usually by means of a CMOS transmission gate.

The following three specifications follow the spirit of a connection module in the proposed Verilog-AMS language.

In the specification for the sample-and-hold module (Figure 17.2) there is a distinction between electrical, real, and digital signals. A **real** datatype in Verilog is continuously valued and also conveys the notion of storage, like a **reg** in the digital domain. The **analog** statement is a replacement for the **always** statement of Verilog-D, and used when the enclosed block contains analog or mixed analog and digital signals and operations. The *transition* operator was invented to filter an expression like the *sample* signal in the diagram, which jumps from one value to another, into a piecewise continuous form suitable for the analog domain. The remaining arguments represent propagation delay, rise, and fall times. If they are not present in the specification they default to the current time unit in use. The *contribution* operator <+ makes an assignment to an electrical node with a similar intention to what the non-blocking assignment <= does for a node in the digital domain.

The choice of symbol indicates that contributions are added together in a temporary until the end of a simulation cycle when the actual assignment is made. The contributions could be current or voltage, as represented by V(node) as here. In a signal-flow type of analysis they must be one or the other, not both.

Unlike the one in Chapter 5, this comparator is an analog one (Figure 17.3). It is essentially an amplifier with a differential input and a saturating output. The specification utilizes the *cross* event operator. When the analog expression of the first argument crosses zero, a simulation event is generated and the associated action is carried out. The +1 or −1 in the second argument allows the direction of the zero crossing to be taken into account. The cross operator allows two optional extra arguments for time and value tolerance as did the transition operator (not used in this example). Again the signal flow is in only one direction, from left to right.

The digital-to-analog converter module (Figure 17.4) can be built from a resistive ladder network and operational amplifier. In the specification below a **for** expression is used inside the transition operator to model the progressive weighting by one-half that is produced by the ladder network.

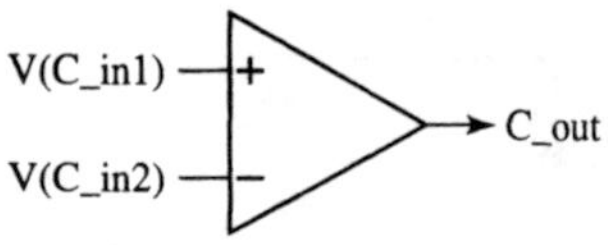

```
module comparator(C_in1, C_in2, C_out);
input C_in1, C_in2;
output C_out;
wire    C_out;
electrical C_in1, C_in2;
analog
  begin
  @(cross(V(C_in1) -V(C_in2),+1) assign C_out=1;
  @(cross(V(C_in1) -V(C_in2),-1) assign C_out=0;
  end
endmodule
```

Figure 17.3   *Analog Comparator.*

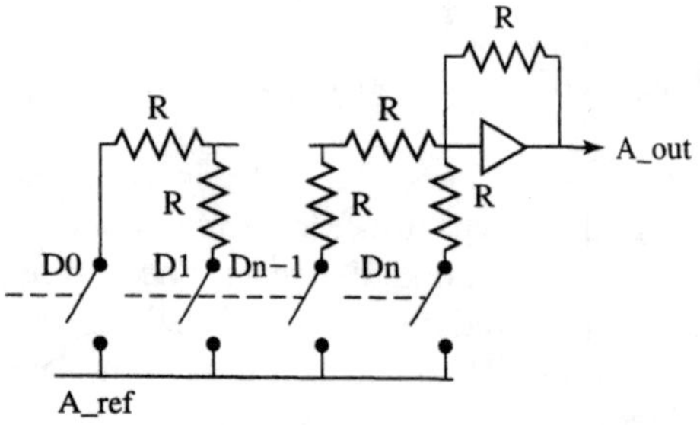

```
module d2a(D, A_ref, A_out);
parameter n=8;
 input [n-1:0] D;
 input A_ref;
 output A_out;
 integer i;
 electrical A_ref, A_out;
 analog
   V(A_out ) <+
 transition (begin sample = 0;
                 for (i=0; i<n; i=i+1)
                   begin
                   sample = sample +
                                  V(A_ref)*D[i];
                   sample = sample/2;
                   end
               end
             );
endmodule
```

Figure 17.4   *Digital-to-Analog Converter.*

It should be emphasized again that the point of the signal-flow analysis of Verilog-A and Verilog-AMS is not to replace the accuracy of the conservative analysis, but to unify the treatment of the analog and digital parts and be able to check their joint operation at an early stage of design.

The benefits start to come when the parts of the system are all put together, in this case for Specification #1 of the complete *a2d* converter module. This is mostly structural, with the *a1*, *a2*, *d1* analog and digital variables serving as the interconnections between the submodules. In the behavioral part, the same odd/even clock methodology, as in the cache and MIPS examples of Chapter 10, has been used to effect the two successive exclusive-OR operations of Figure 17.1. It would have been possible, using a similar technique to that of the *fifosc* example of Chapter 8, to specify this with a single clock per approximation cycle at the cost of some extra area.

```
`include ``samplehold.v´´
`include ``comparator.v´´
`include ``d2a.v´´
`include ``ringcount.v´´

module a2d(apwron, clk, A_in, ref, approx);
input apwron, clk, A_in, ref;
output [7:0] approx;
reg [7:0] approx;
reg oddeven;
wire [7:0] index;
wire apwron, clk, d1;
wire a1, a2, A_in, ref; // reals not allowed on input ports
wire ph2d = clk && ~oddeven;
wire sampleclk = index[0] & ph2d;
  samplehold   SnH(sampleclk, A_in, a1);
  comparator   CMP(a1, a2, d1);
  d2a          D2A(clk, approx, ref, a2);
  ringcount    RC(apwron, ph2d, index);
always @(negedge clk)
  if (apwron) oddeven <= 0;
  else oddeven <= ~oddeven;

always
  begin @(posedge clk)
  if (apwron) approx  <= 0;
  else if (oddeven) // start only on odd clock
    begin
     if (index[0]) approx  <= 0;
     else approx <= approx ^ index; // new trial bit inserted
     @(posedge clk);
     if (~d1) approx <= approx ^ index; // if small, reset last trial bit
    end
  end
endmodule
```

Specification #1: Successive Approximation Analog-to-Digital Converter.

The type of specification described in this section can be effective for overall design exploration and synthesis. Of course it must be supplemented with more accurate verification in a conservative simulation discipline, particularly for critical subsections. Usually it will not be possible to simulate the whole design using a conservative discipline.

This section and example is only intended to introduce the notions of analog and analog-mixed-signal design languages and methods. The reader interested in going further is refered to the existing text on Verilog-A [Fitz98] and the forthcoming Verilog-AMS standard.

17.3   Hardware/Software

17.3.1   *Simulation of Large Hardware Designs*

Even a pure hardware design, if of any size, will inevitably involve software engineering. This is because unlike the small-to-medium designs in this book, the testing of a large project cannot be done by manual observation of the tabular or graphical waveform output of a simulator alone. Recourse must be had to custom debugging environment programs which will control the tests and sift through and analyze the simulator output, possibly supplemented by formal verification tools of the types discussed in Section 7.3.

In the case of Verilog, control of simulation tests can be assisted by the *Program Language Interface* (PLI) feature of the language standard. This provides a means for a user to access and modify data inside a compiled Verilog data structure, or be called when some signal inside that structure changes. The standard contains an accumulated list of some 190 of access routines written as 'C' functions that can be called from user-written programs. One way of using these within Verilog source descriptions is to create new user defined system task calls (distinguished by identifiers starting with the $ symbol). The existing system calls used in the standard simulators described in Chapter 4 ($monitor, $stop, etc.) are implemented in just this way. Going the other way, a compiled simulator like VCS actually produces the simulation models in 'C' code. There is an option to halt compilation at that point and view the 'C' versions of the modules of the Verilog source, in which the correspondence to the original source can be fairly easily recognized.

The complexity of current designs is such that it would take tens of machine-years to complete some of the test suites using a pure event simulator. So a mixed approach has often been used in the past, using a general purpose language such as 'C' or C++ to control the tests and communicate with hardware submodules described in Verilog and VHDL via equivalent *bus-functional module* interfaces [Dearth98], [Rincon97]. In such a scheme the communications can be fully peer-to-peer, enabling more flexible testing in which either the test or the Verilog model can initiate the actions.

17.3.2   *Hardware/Software Co-Design*

The embedded processor cores being employed in many current applications now impose a software component in the design itself. In these schemes most of the design functionality resides in software in the embedded processors and only time critical or essential I/O or analog functions remain in synthesized hardware.

In the hardware organization diagrammed in Figure 17.5, the architecture could alternately serve for:

1. A software simulation environment to test synthesized hardware (see previous section).
2. A synthesized PC peripheral being tested in its intended environment.

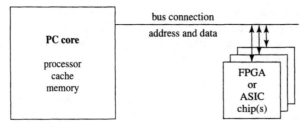

Figure 17.5   *Hardware/Software Architecture.*

3. A hardware/software design with an embeddded processor and synthesized hardware.

The interface shown might be a direct connection to processor-cache bus [Olukotun94], or a connection through a peripheral bus such as the peripheral component interface (PCI) standard. This is more likely in current technology, since the system bus is more likely separated from the cache bus. To assist in this there are "PCI megafunction cores" which can be dropped into the same FPGA or ASIC in which the designer's other functionality is synthesized.[1]

There is one difference in #3 above from #1 and #2: Some decision has to be made for each sub-task whether it is best implemented in software or hardware from the cost, power, and timing/performance points of view. This decision is hardly trivial since:

- The embedded processor option must factor in the extra costs of memory (RAM, ROM, flash).
- Low power is often achieved by selective clock inhibit or power down (see Chapter 11). How much of the time would the ASIC or embedded processor be in those modes?
- The performance of routines on the embedded processor is complicated by factors such as we are now dealing with compiled[2] code not assembly code, and these software processes are often under the control of a real-time operating system.
- The increasing cache complexity of current processors makes the number of wait states hard to assess [Malik97], as well as the cache flushing caused by process preemptions in real time.

For example, if some component task must be speeded up, this might be done either by substituting a faster processor core, increasing the cache size, or using special purpose synthesized hardware [Li99]. As a first step the whole application is coded in some general purpose software language and partitioned into tasks along convenient code boundaries. Then using some kind of instruction trace package an estimate is made of how fast each sub-task would run if in pure software or in pure hardware. Using these estimates the final allocation decisions for the tasks are made according to some heuristic algorithm and the parts destined for hardware translated into HDL and synthesized. For this purpose there are now available commercial packages for automatic translation from general purpose software languages to the Verilog or VHDL necessary for current synthesis tools.

---

[1]Available for example from all three of the vendors illustrated in this book.

[2]Apparently many embedded processor applications have been programmed in assembly code by hand [Marwedal97] for the stated reason that compilers do not produce efficient code. This was exactly what was said about the applications of the first generation of microprocessors—a point of view that was soon abandoned.

The naïve method of test with an embedded processor core would be to compile and load the machine code into the processor model inside the simulator. This is much like what was done on a small scale in Chapter 10 for testing the MIPS200. Such an approach would have a number of problems:

- The simulation would be impossibly slow.
- Any bug would have to be traced by relating the assembly or machine code statements back to the location of the corresponding position in the source code.
- Core providers are reluctant to supply the embedded processor source models.

Accordingly, it is much better to test from the source code directly, where the debugging environments are superior. Issues involved in the choice of a general purpose source language are discussed after the next section.

17.3.3   Embedded Core Design

With design complexities increasing the only practical way for designers to meet decreasing chip deadlines is to utilize components that have been used and well-tested in previous projects. Of course, processors are not the only embedded components which are now available from an increasing variety of intellectual property (IP) providers. A recent survey [Gupta97] listed the following *embedded cores*: Memories (RAM, ROM), processors (RISC, CISC, DSP), BIST (RAM, PLA, ADC), encriptors, bus controllers and network interfaces, and multimedia data compressors. These ranged in size from 1,000 gates for the ADC to 96,000 gates for the 68030 CISC processor core. Such cores may be marketed in three forms:

1. *Soft cores*: These consist of a synthesizable HDL specification that can be parameterized and aimed at different technology targets. In this book they are exemplified by the home brew submodules introduced in Chapters 5 and 8. Such cores would be fully retargetable to different technologies. The disadvantages are that the performance is not defined, and most core providers would not be happy with their designs being in a publicly readable form.

2. *Firm cores*: These are already synthesized into gate-list form in internal database format, and perhaps taking advantage of special features of the target technology such as carry chains and cascade chains. In this book these are exemplified by the Synopsys DesignWare modules and the Altera LPM library. They are still malleable regarding placement and routing but the intellectual property of the core designer is protected.

3. *Hard cores*: These have been committed to fixed layout and timing and are all ready to be dropped into a chip. The disadvantage is that they are technology dependent and the rigid format may make placement and routing of the remainder of the project design more difficult or even impossible.

Among the difficulties faced by the system integrator are [Zorian99]:

- The cores range over at least three design methodologies: digital logic, memory, and analog, not to mention different transistor types (CMOS, biCMOS, SOS), and often, different power supply requirements.
- Since the cores will not have been fabbed in the integrator's target technology, one cannot assume they will be free of fab errors at least, and which DFT (design-for-test) method might be appropriate (functional test, scan, BIST, IDDQ—see Chapter 15).

- Since the core may be embedded far from the pins, which are a scarce resource anyway, the issue of a test access method is critical. Should existing functional busses be reused? Or extra busses routed around or through the other cores?
- The core may need to be enclosed in a wrapper, which might include such things as interface standardization, BIST, or clock skew equalization.

The industry is at the present time struggling with ways to make sense of all these complications and has organized the *Virtual Socket Interface Alliance* (www.vsi.org). It is not surprising that this is divided into as many as seven working groups and their work is yet to be finished.

17.3.4   *Design Languages for SOC (system-on-a-chip)*

For large-scale chips featuring hardware/software and embedded cores, clearly some interaction is needed between the HDL of the synthesized hardware and the source language of the software parts. For this purpose the Verilog PLI is not well suited. This is because the PLI is set up primarily for events in the hardware to initiate actions in the software. It would seem more natural for the software to "be the boss" and initiate the actions in the hardware.

Those in industry who must deal with large designs often prefer to create at least the initial models in general purpose object oriented languages such as C++ or Java directly, both for the testbenches and the hardware under test.

Advantages of this approach are:

- These languages are more mature than Verilog and VHDL and have superior development, debugging, and maintenance environments.
- If the overhead of the event management of HDL simulators can be dispensed with, the simulation can potentially be speeded up by two or so orders of magnitude.
- The lines between hardware and software are blurred, enabling decisions to be deferred as to which parts of the design are to be implemented in pure hardware and which in routines running on an embedded processor (previous subsection).

The disadvantages of this approach are:

- These general purpose languages were not designed to express such hardware essentials as concurrency and clocking; they need to be extended with library packages to handle parallelism and event timing [Dave97].
- Since the software languages were not designed for hardware description, the user may be forced to spend inordinate amounts of nonproductive time trying to bend the features of the language for the hardware parts.
- An automatic translation to HDL puts distance between the designer and the HDL description which is the reference point for debug and optimization of synthesized hardware.

For the EDA industry much hangs on the choice of language for this purpose, how augmented, and whether a single language can indeed fit all. So a battle royale is now taking place. Many believe that a suitably augmented version of C++ should be the choice since the 'C' language family was created for systems programming and has intimate access to device hardware [Liao97]. The SystemC initative is sponsored by an industry group led by Synopsys, Co-Ware, and Frontier Design (see www.SystemC.org). On the other hand other elements of industry as well as academia [Olukotun97], [Young98] are advocating Java, because it is simpler, it is highly portable via JVM, and it is being widely adopted in education and the upcoming driving applications. At the moment Java has definite disadvantages: Its run time performance is unpredicatable (due to automatic garbage collection), there are no mechanisms for time-outs or asynchronous events, and there is no direct access to hardware. Two competing industry groupings, the Jconsortium (HP, Microsoft) and the Real Time Java Experts Group (Sun, Lucent, IBM) have set out to modify it for real-time applications.

The fact that these efforts are being made reminds us that current HDLs are still far from ideal for their purpose. Estimates of the speed-up in simulation using general purpose HLLs should be tempered with the realization that this will depend on the nature of the design being modelled and the writing style of HLL being employed. In this book we have seen variations of an order of magnitude between different specifications of identical functional modules in various RTL writing styles. So ideally it would be better if there were available more advanced object-oriented HDLs (see Section 16.5). However such change is difficult in an industrial environment in which huge amounts of money have been invested in tools based on existing languages

17.4   A Small Example

To bring all the topics of this chapter together, a case study will be presented in which we will trace the history of electronics in cameras. Electronics was first introduced into cameras in the form of pure analog design. The original objective was to semiautomate the exposure control in a manner that would be satisfactory for advanced photogaphers. A somewhat simplified illustration of the central function from an early system [Muenster89] is given in Figure 17.6. Among the parts not shown is the initiation of power-on and clocking which is controlled from partial depression of the shutter release button.

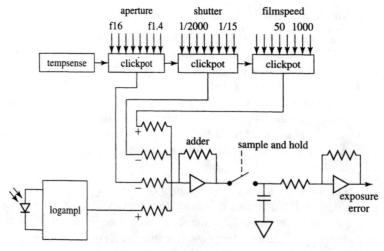

Figure 17.6 *Exposure Control: Analog.*

The current from the light sensitive diode is fed through a logarithmic amplifer. The aperture, shutter and filmspeed settings are input via potentiometers with click stops. Each successive clickstop position corresponds to a doubling (halving) of the light, but since the potentiometers are linear, and are refered from a voltage having the same temperature sensitivity as the photodiode, they are directly summable with the output of the logarithmic amplifier. When the sum is zero (counting the aperture and shutter time inputs negatively), the exposure settings are correct and the temperature dependence is eliminated.

It is interesting that in the original analog version [Muenster89] the complete analog system including the amplifers was too complex to simulate at the circuit level, and so was verified using an operator and functional level simulator, the then-equivalent of Verilog-A rather than Spice.

The next step was to replace the analog exposure control with a mixed analog-digital ASIC. This is illustrated in Figure 17.7. In our example, the aperture, shutter, and filmspeed settings could be input in a purely digital fashion via a scan arrangment similar to the manner in which keyboard input is usually implemented. In such an arrangement the vertical lines of the matrix are pulled weakly high and then one is pulled low corresponding to the conjunction of an active switch position and an active horizontal can control line.

This time the temperature sense output is fed to the reference input of the A2D converter so that the input entering the digital part can be directly added to the values of the settings that are stored in the ROM. (In the ASIC version the combination of encoder and

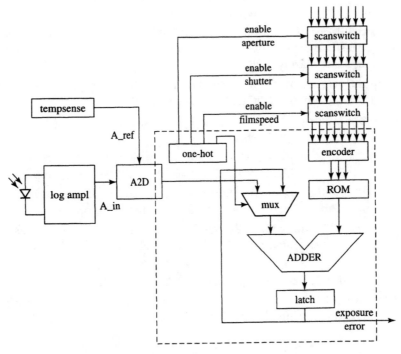

Figure 17.7   *Exposure Control: AMS.*

ROM might better be replaced by a PLA.) Again the clocking and initiation is not shown. The resulting implementation might be prefered for robustness and the extra opportunity for fine tuning via the values stored in the ROM.

The next step was to replace the digital part (enclosed by a dashed rectangle in the figure) by an embedded processor. This processor could encompass the digital part of the A2D module as well as the data ROM as part of its memory space. It provides more flexibility and an upward path to incorporate other features of fully automatic cameras such as automatic aperture and focus control, as well as the light flash control modes and automatic zoom.

Of course camera technology has come a long way in a short time. Now there are available "digital"[3] cameras based on semiconductor "CCD" arrays in the film plane and containing embedded processors and memory, removable flash memory cards for storing the images, or even a hard disk drive. The single processor is now replaced by several. A fast pipelined 32-bit general purpose core running a real time OS monitors the camera controls, initiates imaging operations, and manages file storage. A frame processor analyzes images for exposure and focus. Finally a special purpose digital signal processor (DSP) does image transforms such as edge enhancement, color saturation, and image compression [Taylor98]. All of the processor cores as well as many of the major modules in the special purpose chips are drawn from the intellectual property of third-party vendors. The digital camera thus became one of the first examples of a system on a chip.

References

[Dave97] Dave, B. P., et al., "Hardware-software co-synthesis of embedded systems," *Proc. Design Automation Conf.*, June 1997

[Dearth98] Dearth, G., Meeth, S., and Whittemore, P., (Sun Microsystems) "Networked object oriented verification with C++ and Verilog," *IVC/VIUF Conf.*, San Jose, March 1998

[Gupta97] Gupta, R. K., and Zorian, Y., "Introducing core-based system design," *IEEE Design and Test*, Oct. 1997, pp. 15–25

[Fitz98] Fitspatrick, D., and Miller, I., *Analog behavioral modelling with the Verilog-A language*, Kluwer, 1998

[Li99] Li, Y., and Wolfe, W. H., "Hardware/Software Co-synthesis with memory Hierarchies," *IEEE Trans. CAD* 18:10 (Oct. 1999), pp. 1405–1417

[Malik97] Malik, S., et al., "Static timing analysis of embedded software" (tutorial), *Proc. Design Automation Conf.*, June 1997, pp. 232–237

[Marwedal97] Marwedel, P., "Code generation for core processors" (tutorial), *Proc. Design Automation Conf.*, June 1997, pp. 232–237

[Muenster89] Muenster, I., et al., "A CMOS Camera Control IC," *IEEE Custom Integrated Circuits Conference*, San Diego, May 1989

[Olukotun94] Olukotun, K., et al., "A software-hardware Co-synthesis Approach to digital system simulation", *IEEE Micro*, Aug. 1994, pp. 48–58

---

[3]Not *all* are digital; since the CCD and other sensors are still analog, analog-to-digital converters are required.

[Olukotun97] Olukotun, K., and Helaihel, R., "Java as a specification language for hardware-software systems," *IEEE/ACM Intl. Conf. on Computer Aided Design,* Nov. 1997

[Rincon97] Rincon, A. M., et al., "Core design and system-on-a-chip integration," *IEEE Design and Test,* Oct. 1997, pp. 26–35

[Smith89] Smith, D. R., and Lin, J. C., "Specification driven design and simulation of hybrid analog/digital integrated circuits," *4th Intl. Workshop on Higher Level Synthesis,* Kennebunkport, Maine, 1989

[Taylor98] Taylor, R., "Developing Photo Opportunities of the Digital Sort," *Integrated System Design,* January 1998, p. 30

[Young98] Young, J. S., et al., "Design and specification of embedded systems in Java using successive formal refinement," *Proc. DAC98,* pp. 70–75

[Zorian99] Zorian, Y., Marinissen, E. J., and Dey, S., "Testing embedded-core-based system chips," *IEEE Computer,* 32:6 (June 1999), pp. 52–60

Appendix A

Verilog Examples

A.1 Combinational Logic Structures

Continuous assignment statements are a very useful and compact language structure for specifying small collections of gates. The following examples are intended to go beyond those provided in the text and illustrate concepts that sometimes are found to be difficult.

Multi-Bit Gates

Arrays can be used to concisely specify multi-bit variables. Sets of gates can be specified to operate on all the bits in a bus, or just a subset. For example:

```
module multi1 (in1, in2; out1, out2);

input [3:0] in1, in2;
output [3:0] out1, out2;

wire [3:0] out1;
wire [1:0] out2;

assign out1 = in1 & in2;
assign out2[1:0] = in1[3:2] ^ in2[1:0];
assign out2[3:2] = in1[1:0] | in2[3:2];
endmodule
```

Note the following points:

- Sub-fields of arrays of bits can be specified on either side of the assignment.
- The operators "&" and "|" are used rather than "&&" and "||," as the former are intended to model gates while the latter are intended to construct Boolean algebra on single-bit true-false variables.
- Technically the 'wire' declarations are not needed here as *out1* and *out2* are outputs and all outputs are assumed to be of a 'wire' type unless otherwise declared.

The following example specifies some more complicated multi-bit operators:

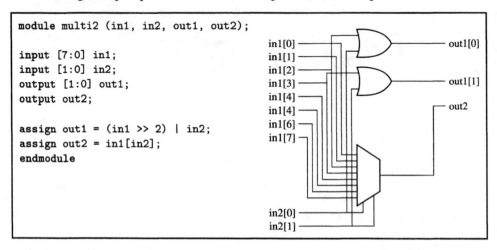

```
module multi2 (in1, in2, out1, out2);

input [7:0] in1;
input [1:0] in2;
output [1:0] out1;
output out2;

assign out1 = (in1 >> 2) | in2;
assign out2 = in1[in2];
endmodule
```

Note the following with respect to this example:
- The right shift operator ">>" simply rearranges the wires so that bit 2 of *in1* becomes bit 0, bit 3 becomes bit 1, etc. Then, since *out1* is only two bits wide, only the lower two bits of *out1* are used. The following statement would produce an identical result:

    ```
    assign out1 = in1[3:2] | in2;
    ```

- In the second statement, a single bit of an 8-bit variable, *in1*, is selected by the value of the 3-bit variable, *in2*, thus specifying an 8:1 multiplexor. This is a simple way to specify larger muxes than can be produced using the "?:" statement.

Unary Reduction Operators

Unary reduction operators always produce one-bit outputs from multi-bit inputs. Consider the following example:

```
module (in1, in2, out1, out2);

input [2:0] in1;
input       in2;
output      out1, out2;

wire out1, out2;

assign out1 = |{in1, in2};
assign out2 = ^in1;
endmodule
```

Note the following:

- The use of concatenation { } to produce a 4-input gate.
- That a multi-input XOR gate is built out of a tree of 2-input gates.

Multiple-input Multiplexors

Multiplexors requiring more than two inputs can also be specified using procedural code, usually by using a **case** or **casez** statement. The 8:1 multiplexor described in the example above can be specified procedurally as follows:

```
module (in1, in2, out2);

input [7:0] in1;
input [2:0] in2;
output out2;

always@(in1 or in2)
  case (in2)
    2'b000 : out2 = in1[0];
    2'b001 : out2 = in1[1];
    2'b010 : out2 = in1[2];
    2'b011 : out2 = in1[3];
    2'b100 : out2 = in1[4];
    2'b101 : out2 = in1[5];
    2'b110 : out2 = in1[6];
    2'b111 : out2 = in1[7];
  endcase
endmodule
```

Demultiplexor

A demultiplexor is the converse of a multiplexor. It takes one input and directs it to any of N inputs, based on the number specified in the select lines. It could be captured either using procedural code or continuous assignment. Both of the statements, given on the next page, describe identical behavior.

Note the following in this example:

- It is assumed that we want a demux output to be 00 unless selected. The default at the start of the procedural block in the first example provides for this *and* prevents specifying unintended latches.
- The use of the for loop in the first version to iterate across the output bits.
- Verilog does not permit ports containing two-dimensional arrays. Thus *out2* is declared as 16 bits wide rather than 8×2 bits, as the designer would prefer to think of it. A bit is a bit, so this does not matter.
- The second version has more structure. It specifies an explicit 3:8 decoder that takes a 3-bit input and sets one of eight lines, as per the number specified in the input. It uses AND gates for the actual demux. This design is likely to be smaller and faster than the first design. It could also be described using a for loop. That exercise is left to the reader.

```verilog
module (in1, sel, out2);

input  [1:0] in1;
input  [2:0] sel;
output [13:0] out2;

reg [15:0] out2;

integer   I;

always@(in1 or sel)
  begin
    out2 = 14´h0;   /* default = 00 */
    for (I=0; I<=7; I=I+1)
     if (I == sel)
        begin
          out2[I] = in1[0];
          out2[I+1] = in1[1];
        end
  end
endmodule

/*----------------------------*/
module (in1, sel, out2);

input  [1:0] in1;
input  [2:0] sel;
output [15:0] out2;

reg [7:0] select;

/* address decoder */
always@(sel)
   case (sel)
     3´b000 : select = 8´b00000001;
     3´b001 : select = 8´b00000010;
     3´b010 : select = 8´b00000100;
     3´b011 : select = 8´b00001000;
     3´b100 : select = 8´b00010000;
     3´b101 : select = 8´b00100000;
     3´b110 : select = 8´b01000000;
     3´b111 : select = 8´b10000000;
   endcase

   assign out2[1:0] = in1 & select[0];
   assign out2[3:2] = in1 & select[1];
   assign out2[5:4] = in1 & select[2];
   assign out2[7:6] = in1 & select[3];
   assign out2[9:8] = in1 & select[4];
   assign out2[11:10] = in1 & select[5];
   assign out2[13:12] = in1 & select[6];
   assign out2[15:14] = in1 & select[7];
endmodule
```

Decoder

A decoder takes a narrow input and decodes it to a wider range of bits. Typically it is part of the control logic. The commands to individual units are encoded so as to save wires and then a decoder is used to determine the individual control bits.

The previous example included a non-priority 3:8 decoder. Three inputs were decoded to choose one of eight control lines. It is non-priority as none of the input combinations has priority over any of the others. This decoder implemented the following truth table:

Inputs	Outputs
sel	select
000	00000001
001	00000010
010	00000100
011	00001000
100	00010000
101	00100000
110	01000000
111	10000000

In contrast, in a priority decoder, certain combinations of inputs are given priority over others. For example, consider the following truth table:

Inputs		Outputs	
Op[1:0]	Funct[4:0]	Sel[1:0]	B
01	xxxxx	11	1
11	00011	01	1
11	00001	10	1
otherwise	otherwise	xx	x

This truth table specifies that if $Op = 01$, then the outputs are set independently of the value of *Funct*. *Op* has priority over *Funct*. The last line of the table merely indicates that for values of *Op* and *Funct* not specified, we don't care what the outputs are. This permits the logic optimization routines in the synthesis tools to do a better job than if we gave the outputs 0 or 1 values in this line. (You may recall that '*x*'s in the Karnaugh map permit greater optimization of the logic. That is all we are specifying here.)

The following Verilog module captures the above truth table:

```
module pri_encoder (Op, Funct, Sel, B);
input   [1:0] Op;
input   [4:0] Funct;
output  [1:0] Sel;
output        B;

always@(Op or Funct)
  casez ({Op, Funct})
    {2´b01, 5´b?}      : begin
                          Sel = 2´b11;
                          B = 1´b1;
                        end
    {2´b11, 5´b00011} : begin
                          Sel = 2´b01;
                          B = 1´b1;
                        end
    {2´b11, 5´b00001} : begin
                          Sel = 2´b10;
                          B = 1´b1;
                        end
    default           : begin
                          Sel = 2´bxx;
                          B = 1´bx;
                        end
  endcase
endmodule
```

Note the use of casez when ?-valued inputs are specified.

Encoder

An encoder takes a multi-bit input and encodes it as a different, often shorter, bit stream. As such it is implementing a truth table with fewer outputs than inputs and it is coded much the same way as a decoder. An example is a gray-code encoder. In a gray code encoder the position of the '1' bit in a N-bit data stream is captured with a code in which only one bit changes between adjacent values in the sequence. The following truth table uses a gray code in the output:

Input	Output
00000001	000
00000010	001
00000100	011
00001000	010
00010000	110
00100000	111
01000000	101
10000000	100

A Verilog module to capture this truth table can be specified as follows:

```
module encoder (value, gray_code);

input [7:0] value;
output [3:0] gray_code;

always@(value)
  case (value)
     8'b00000001 : gray_code = 3'b000;
     8'b00000010 : gray_code = 3'b001;
     8'b00000100 : gray_code = 3'b011;
     8'b00001000 : gray_code = 3'b010;
     8'b00010000 : gray_code = 3'b110;
     8'b00100000 : gray_code = 3'b111;
     8'b01000000 : gray_code = 3'b101;
     8'b10000000 : gray_code = 3'b100;
  endcase
endmodule
```

Priority encoders, when required, can be captured using a casez statement.

Proper Initialization

Modeling hardware initialization in Verilog can sometimes be a little tricky. You might recall that in hardware design, one purpose of the reset is to initialize the hardware to a known state. Showing that the reset is working correctly in pre-synthesis, Verilog can be a little tricky due to subtle bugs. The Verilog simulator initializes all variables to unknown or 'x'. Thus, one would think that if the simulation is showing an 'x' where 0 or 1 is expected after the reset has been asserted, then there is a bug in the reset design that needs to be fixed. Unfortunately, an incorrect 'x' can be turned into a 0 or 1 and look correct, even when it is not.

Consider the following code fragment (for a decoder):

```
always@(a or b)
  case (a)
     2'b00    : b = 4'b0001;
     2'b01    : b = 4'b0010;
     2'b10    : b = 4'b0100;
     default : b = 4'b1000;
  endcase
```

At first sight, this looks fine. Let's assume that a is meant to be initialized to 11 by the reset, and is thus propagated through this logic block to initialize b to 1000. However, what if there is a hardware bug that results in 'a' not being assigned to any 1-0 combination on reset. The Verilog simulator will leave a = xx after reset. However, when 'a' is propagated through the logic above, a = xx will catch the default and b will be set to 1000. The signal b will look fine and the fact that a is incorrect will not be caught. (If this is not caught before the hardware is made then *a* and *b* will actually take on some random combination of 0's and 1's, depending on the gate details—'*x*'s don't occur in the actual hardware.) A coding style that will catch this particular bug is as follows:

```
always@(a or b)
   casez   (a)
      2'b00   : b = 4'b0001;
      2'b01   : b = 4'b0010;
      2'b10   : b = 4'b0100;
      2'b11   : b = 4'b1000;
      default : b = 4'bxxxx;
   endcase
```

Here, if *a* contains unknowns (*x*), then *b* will appear as *x* and the incorrect reset design is more likely to be caught. The case statement becomes a casez to ensure that an '*x*' input is recognized.

Tristate Buffers and Buses

In order to reduce the amount of overall wiring required, often multiple units share a common bus in order to communicate amongst themselves. On such a bus it is important that during any particular clock cycle only one unit can drive the bus, the others must disconnect any drivers during that cycle. Tristate buffers are used to enable this. A tristate buffer is a non-inverting driver that can adopt one of three output states:

- Logic-0 if its input is 0 and the enable is on.
- Logic-1 if its input is 1 and the enable is on.
- A high impedance, or disconnected state, if the enable is off, irrespective of the input logic value. In this state the driver is disconnected from the bus by opening the joining transistor switches. In Verilog, the high impedance state is represented by the symbol '*z*'.

The following Verilog fragment describes three units A, B and C, that we wish to drive a common bus:

```
tri      [7:0]    bus;
wire     [7:0]    Aout,
Bout, Cout;
wire
EnableA, EnableB,
EnableC;

assign bus = EnableA ? Aout : 8'hzz;
assign bus = EnableB ? Bout : 8'hzz;
assign bus = EnableC ? Cout : 8'hzz;
```

Note that it is important that only one of *EnableA*, *EnableB*, or *EnableC* be active during any clock cycle. Sometimes, a specialized bus arbiter must be designed to make sure that each unit gets its proper share of the bus.

In general, buses should only be used when the savings in wiring are significant since they are more difficult to verify and debug that the equivalent set of point to point wirings.

A.2 Sequential Logic Structures

Bus Arbiter

As described in the section above discussing tristate buffers, a control unit is necessary to decide which driver is going to be active during any particular bus cycle. Such a unit is referred to as a bus arbiter. The following Verilog module describes a parameterized bus arbiter that can implement either of two common schemes:

- *Round Robin Arbitration.* The driving units take turns owning the bus. If the unit does not have an active request in when its turn comes around, it misses its slot and the next requesting unit is enabled to drive the bus.
- *Priority Arbitration.* Different driving units are assigned priorities. During any cycle, the requesting unit with the highest priority is granted permission to drive the bus.

```verilog
module arbiter(clock, reset, roundORpriority, request, priority, grant);

    integer i,j,k,p,q,r,s,t,u,v; //index for ``for´´ loops

    // parameters
    //-----------------------------------------------------------------
    parameter NUMUNITS = 8;
    parameter ADDRESSWIDTH = 3; //number of bits needed to address
                                // NUMUNITS
    //-----------------------------------------------------------------
    // input and output declarations
    //-----------------------------------------------------------------
    input clock;
    input reset;
    input roundORpriority;
    input [NUMUNITS-1 : 0] request;
    input [ADDRESSWIDTH*NUMUNITS-1 : 0] priority;

    output [NUMUNITS-1 : 0] grant;

    //hack for 2-D input
    reg [ADDRESSWIDTH-1 : 0] prio [NUMUNITS-1 : 0];
    reg [ADDRESSWIDTH-1 : 0] tmp_prio;
    always@(priority)
    begin
        for (i=0; i<NUMUNITS; i=i+1)
        begin
            for (j=0; j<ADDRESSWIDTH; j=j+1)
                tmp_prio[j] = priority[i*ADDRESSWIDTH + j];
            prio[i] = tmp_prio;
        end
    end
```

(Continued)

(continued)

```verilog
reg [NUMUNITS-1 : 0] grant;    //registered output
reg [NUMUNITS-1 : 0] grantD;   //input to ``grant´´ flipflop

reg [ADDRESSWIDTH-1 : 0] next;     //index of next unit in round-robin
reg [ADDRESSWIDTH-1 : 0] nextNext;   //input to ``next´´ flipflop

reg [ADDRESSWIDTH-1 : 0] scan [NUMUNITS-1 : 0];
//stores info on the order in which to scan units for round-robin

reg [NUMUNITS-2 : 0] found;
//in round-robin search, stores info on where assignment is made

reg [ADDRESSWIDTH-1 : 0] selectPrio[NUMUNITS-1 : 0];
//holds the priorities of only those units requesting the bus

reg [ADDRESSWIDTH-1 : 0] min;
//holds the minimum priority of all units currently requesting the bus

reg [NUMUNITS-1 : 0] minPrio;
//units that have the minimum priority

wire [NUMUNITS-1 : 0] prioRequest;
//request signals for only those units with minimum priority

reg [NUMUNITS-1 : 0] finalRequest;
//requests actually examined depending on ``roundORpriority´´

// flipflop for ``grant´´ signals
always@(posedge clock)
begin
    if(!reset) grant <= 0;
    else grant <= grantD;
end

// flipflop for ``next´´ register
always@(posedge clock)
begin
    if(!reset) next <= 0;
    else next <= nextNext;
end

//selects the priorities of units sending requests
always@(request or prio[7] or prio[6] or prio[5] or prio[4] or
        prio[3] or prio[2] or prio[1] or prio[0])
begin
    for(k=0; k<NUMUNITS; k=k+1)
        selectPrio[k] = request[k] ? prio[k] : NUMUNITS-1;
end
```

```
//selects priority or round robin operation
always@(prioRequest or request or roundORpriority)
begin
    for(r=0; r<NUMUNITS; r=r+1)
        finalRequest[r] = roundORpriority ? prioRequest[r] : request[r];
end
//this logic finds the minimum priority out of all units sending a
//request
always@(selectPrio[7] or selectPrio[6] or selectPrio[5] or
        selectPrio[4] or selectPrio[3] or selectPrio[2] or
        selectPrio[1] or selectPrio[0])
begin
    min = selectPrio[0];
    for (p=1; p<NUMUNITS; p=p+1)
        if (selectPrio[p] < min) min = selectPrio[p];
end

//this logic decides if the units have minimum priority
always@(min or minPrio or prio[7] or prio[6] or prio[5] or prio[4]
        or prio[3] or prio[2] or prio[1] or prio[0])
begin
    for (q=0; q<NUMUNITS; q=q+1)
        minPrio[q] = (prio[q]==min) ? 1:0;
end

//produces request signals for units that have minimum priority
assign prioRequest = minPrio & request;

//produces the ``scan´´ array
always@(next)
begin
    for(s=0; s<NUMUNITS; s=s+1)
        scan[s] = (next+s < NUMUNITS) ? next+s : next+s-NUMUNITS;
end

//produces the found array
always@(finalRequest or scan[7] or scan[6] or scan[5] or scan[4] or
        scan[3] or scan[2] or scan[1] or scan[0])
begin
    found[0] = finalRequest[scan[0]];
    for(t=1; t<NUMUNITS-1; t=t+1)
        found[t] = found[t-1] || finalRequest[scan[t]];
end
//produces inputs to ``grant´´ flipflops
always@(finalRequest or found or scan[7] or scan[6] or scan[5] or
        scan[4] or scan[3] or scan[2] or scan[1] or scan[0])
```

(*continued*)

(concluded)

```
begin
    grantD[scan[0]] = finalRequest[scan[0]];
    for(u=1; u<NUMUNITS; u=u+1)
        grantD[scan[u]] = finalRequest[scan[u]] && ~found[u-1];
  end
  always@(grantD)
  begin
    nextNext = 0;
    for(v=0; v<NUMUNITS-1; v=v+1)
        if(grantD[v]) nextNext = v+1;
  end

endmodule //arbiter
```

Index